ENCOUNTERING JESUS IN THE NEW TESTAMENT

Finn West

MICHAEL **PENNOCK**

ENCOUNTERING
JESUS
IN THE **NEW** TESTAMENT

ave maria press   notre dame, indiana

The Subcommittee on the Catechism, United States Conference of Catholic Bishops, has found this catechetical text, copyright 2009, to be in conformity with the *Catechism of the Catholic Church*.

Nihil Obstat:	The Reverend Michael Heintz Censor Liborum
Imprimatur:	Most Reverend John M. D'Arcy Bishop of Fort Wayne-South Bend
Given at:	Fort Wayne, Indiana, on 23 June 2008

The *Nihil Obstat* and *Imprimatur* are official declarations that a book or pamphlet is free of doctrinal or moral error. No implication is contained therein that those who have granted the *Nihil Obstat* or *Imprimatur* agree with its contents, opinions, or statements expressed.

Scripture texts in this work are taken from the *New American Bible with Revised New Testament and Revised Psalms* © 1991, 1986, 1970, Confraternity of Christian Doctrine, Washington, D.C., and are used by permission of the copyright owner. All rights reserved. No part of the *New American Bible* may be reproduced without permission in writing from the copyright owner.

English translation of the *Catechism of the Catholic Church* for the United States of America copyright © 1994, United States Catholic Conference, Inc.— Libreria Editrice Vaticana. Used with permission.

Other references cited as Notes on page 284.

Founded in 1865, Ave Maria Press is a ministry of the United States Province of Holy Cross.

www.avemariapress.com

ISBN-10: 1-59471-165-8   ISBN-13: 978-1-59471-165-7

Project Editor: Michael Amodei.

Cover and text design by Brian C. Conley.

Photography acknowledgments on page 333.

Cover photo: *Word of Life* courtesy of Notre Dame Archives,
    Group of Female Saints by Toscani, Giovanni © Scala / Art Resource, NY

Printed and bound in the United States of America

To the members of

the Theology Department of St. Ignatius High School (Cleveland, Ohio)

in gratitude for their support, love, and prayers over the years.

Engaging **Minds**, **Hearts**, and **Hands**

"An education that is complete is one in which the hands and heart are engaged as much as the mind. We want to let our students try their learning in the world and so make prayers of their education."

—Bl. Basile Moreau,
Founder of the Congregation of Holy Cross

In this text, you will find:

an in-depth look at the New Testament, helping to explore the political, cultural, and geographical world of Jesus in order to know him better.

connections made between your life and the Paschal Mystery so that you are able to recognize and appreciate the "little deaths" and "little resurrections" in your daily life.

practical activities to help you to understand Jesus' mission to establish God's Kingdom to the ends of the earth with ways you can participate in this charge.

contents

"Who Do You **Say That I Am?**"

When Jesus went into the region of Caesarea Philippi he asked his disciples, "Who do people say that the Son of Man is?" They replied, "Some say John the Baptist, others Elijah, still others Jeremiah or one of the prophets." He said to them, "But who do you say that I am?" Simon Peter said in reply, "You are the Messiah, the Son of the living God."

–Matthew 16:13–16

CHAPTER **OVERVIEW**

OFFERING **A SON**

God's love for humanity is so great that he sent his Son, Jesus Christ, to live in our midst and to die for our sins.

COMING TO KNOW **GOD AND JESUS**

God implanted in all of us a desire to know him.

THE FUNDAMENTAL DOCTRINE: **THE INCARNATION** (*CCC*, 456–463)

God the Father has revealed Jesus to us so that we can know the way to eternal life.

LEARNING ABOUT **JESUS**

Setting Jesus in his historical context can help us to understand more of what the Church believes about Christ and how this knowledge can improve our faith.

NAMES AND TITLES **FOR JESUS**

There are many titles for Jesus that, when analyzed, can help us to know and love him more deeply.

Offering **a Son**

"But Zion said, 'The Lord has forsaken me, my Lord has forgotten me'" (Is 49:14).

In the second of the Suffering Servant Songs from the Book of Isaiah, the prophet shares perhaps the most dramatic example of divine love in the entire Bible. Speaking to a Chosen People held captive about liberation and restoration, the prophet reminds the people of God's ever-faithful love:

> Can a mother forget her infant,
>   be without tenderness for the child of her womb?
> Even should she forget,
>   I will never forget you. (Is 49:14–15)

It is true that human parents, for many reasons, are sometimes not able to offer care for their children. But the message of this passage is that divine love is so beyond human love that it constitutes one of the greatest mysteries of faith. Even still, the love of our parents only hints at the depth of God the Father's love for all humans when he sacrificed his only Son, Jesus Christ, to bridge the gap between us and the eternal life of Salvation.

The Father sent us his Son, Jesus Christ, to save us from sin and death. So precious are we in God's eyes that Jesus Christ came into human history, lived in our midst, and gave up his life for us.

What God has accomplished for us through his only begotten Son, Jesus Christ, is truly Good News. Jesus is salvation. A verse in the Gospel of John describes this love so well:

> For God so loved the world that he gave his only Son, so that everyone who believes in him might not perish but might have eternal life. (Jn 3:16)

John's Gospel connects belief in Jesus as God's Son to our achieving eternal life. This is the big reward for us—eternal life. The question of Jesus' identity, then, is an important one. Certainly Jesus thought so when he asked the Apostles what people were saying about him (see Matthew 16:13–16, quoted in the chapter opener). Note the various views his contemporaries had of him. Some saw Jesus as John the Baptist reincarnated. Others saw him as the famous Old Testament prophets Elijah or Jeremiah. Still others thought Jesus was a contemporary prophet who shared his origins with the other Old Testament prophets.

All of these were positive views about Jesus, but elsewhere the Gospels reveal that not everyone thought so highly of him. For example, some of the Jewish officials of his day thought of Jesus as a misguided rabbi who led the people astray. Some of the leaders even perceived him as a threat to the peace,

Who is Jesus of Nazareth, the person people of faith call "the Christ, the Son of God"? This important question is the subject of this book. Answering the question will require a perusal of the Gospels and their portrayal of Jesus. Also, the text will examine what the Catholic Church believes about this compelling person and discuss how we can meet Jesus today. More specifically:

- This Introduction stresses the importance of the Incarnation, discusses the historical context of Jesus' life and the Church's understanding of Jesus as Christ, lists where we can find Jesus today, and briefly touches on the meaning of the proper name *Jesus* and the titles *Christ, Son of God,* and *Lord.*
- Chapter 1 looks at the evidence for Jesus' existence and introduces the formation of the Gospels.
- Chapter 2 examines the world in which Jesus lived and other important information that will help us understand Jesus and his teaching.
- Chapter 3 offers a profile of Jesus, especially focusing on him as teacher, miracle-worker, and God-with-us (Emmanuel).
- Chapters 4 to 7 examine the four portraits of Jesus as presented in the Gospels of Mark (The Suffering Servant), Matthew (The Teacher), Luke–Acts (The Savior and Universal Messiah), and John (The Word of God).
- Chapter 8 focuses on what the writings of St. Paul reveal about Jesus.
- Chapter 9 investigates what the other New Testament writings reveal about Jesus and the meaning of the doctrines taught about Jesus by the early Church.
- Chapter 10 discusses how we can find and meet the living Jesus in our world today.

a fake king who raised false hopes for an oppressed people. They considered Jesus a danger and collaborated with the Romans to put him to death.

However, it was left to Peter to profess Jesus' true identity: "You are the Messiah, the Son of the living God." This remarkable claim—"You are the Christ, the Son of God"—is an identity Peter did not discover on his own. Jesus told Peter,

> Blessed are you, Simon son of Jonah. For flesh and blood has not revealed this to you, but my heavenly Father. (Mt 16:17)

Before examining where you are right now in your belief about Jesus, here are some thoughts about him from some people through the ages:

Jesus whom I know as my Redeemer cannot be less than God.

—St. Athanasius (ca. 293–373)

As a child I received instruction both in the Bible and in the Talmud. I am a Jew, but I am enthralled by the luminous figure of the Nazarene. . . . No one can read the Gospels without feeling the actual presence of Jesus. His personality pulsates in every word. No myth is filled with such life.

—Albert Einstein (1879–1955, physicist and atheist)

If Jesus Christ were to come today, people would not even crucify him. They would ask him to dinner, and hear what he has to say, and make fun of it.

—Thomas Carlyle
(1795–1881, Scottish essayist and historian)

He changed sunset into sunrise.

—St. Clement of Alexandria (150?–215?, a Father of the Church)

A man who was merely a man and said the sort of things Jesus said would not be a great moral teacher. He would either be a lunatic—on a level with the man who says he is a poached egg—or else he would be the Devil of Hell. You must make your choice. Either this man was, and is, the Son of God; or else a madman or something worse. You can shut him up for a fool, you can spit at him and kill him as a demon; or you can fall at his feet and call him Lord and God. But let us not come with any patronizing nonsense about his being a great human teacher. He has not left that open to us. He did not intend to.

—C.S. Lewis, (1893–1963, British author)

Not only do we not know God except through Jesus Christ; we do not even know ourselves except through Jesus Christ.

—Blaise Pascal, (1623–1662, French mathematician and philosopher)

Life passes, riches fly away, popularity is fickle, the senses decay, the world changes. One alone is true to us; One alone can be all things to us; One alone can supply our need.

—Cardinal John Henry Newman
(1801–1890, famous convert, writer, and defender of the faith)

EXAMINING YOUR BELIEF ABOUT JESUS

As you begin your study of Jesus, evaluate your own personal beliefs about him. Write a journal entry detailing why you strongly hold one of the following beliefs or why you disagree strongly with any of the statements.

1. Jesus is my Lord and my Savior.
2. Jesus was the greatest person who ever lived, but not God.
3. Jesus is the Christ, Son of the living God.
4. Jesus never claimed to be what Christians now believe about him.
5. Jesus is my best friend.
6. Jesus was a good philosopher and moral teacher, but not much different from other good philosophers and teachers.
7. Jesus died for the sins of humankind and is risen from the dead.
8. Jesus never existed.
9. Jesus is the "Alpha and Omega," the beginning and end of all humanity.
10. I simply don't know what to believe about Jesus. Tell me more.

FOR REVIEW

1. Name some of the different views that Jesus' disciples offered about his identity.
2. How did Peter identify Jesus?
3. List three interesting facts about the Apostle Peter.

FOR REFLECTION

Tell about an occasion from the news or your experience when someone gave up his or her life for another.

LEARNING MORE ABOUT PETER

Peter was the Apostle who acknowledged Jesus to be the Messiah and the Son of God. But Peter was not always the steadfast and dependable friend of Jesus. At times, he was weak and all-too-human. To learn more about St. Peter, read the following passages. Write answers to the questions that follow.

Matthew 4:18–22
What was Peter's profession?
Who was his brother?
Who else were among Jesus' first Apostles?

Matthew 8:5, 14
Where was Peter's home?

Luke 9:28–36
Which other Apostles were at Jesus' Transfiguration?
Who did the Apostles see with Jesus?
What did Peter propose to do?

Mark 14:27–31, 66–72
What did Peter say he would do rather than deny Christ?
Why did the woman think Peter was Jesus' companion?
What did Peter do when he realized he had betrayed Christ?

John 21:1–19
What did Peter do once he saw Jesus?
How many times did Jesus ask Peter to profess his love?
How will Peter die?

- *For your journal:* Answer the question Jesus posed to Peter: "Do you love me?" Offer evidence for your personal response.

Coming to Know **God and Jesus** (CCC, 27–142)

The Psalmist wrote, "As the deer longs for streams of water, so my soul longs for you, O God. My being thirsts for God, the living God" (Psalm 42:2–3).

The great theologian St. Augustine also penned these famous words: "You are great, O Lord, and greatly to be praised. . . . You have made us for yourself and our heart is restless until it rests in you."

Both of these quotations reveal an important truth: God, who created us out of love to share his life with him in eternity, made us in his own image and implanted in us a great desire to see him and to be united with him. "The desire for God is written in the human heart because man is created by God and for God" (CCC, 27).

It almost seems like God implanted a homing device deep within each of us to attract us to himself. For example, we all have a profound desire to be happy, yet no possession, award, amount of money can satisfy what for each of us is an unquenchable thirst for happiness. All true seekers find that only God can fulfill our deep cravings for happiness, for beauty and truth, for goodness and justice, and especially for love.

Human reason can discover with certainty God's existence. St. Paul understood this when he wrote:

> For what can be known about God is evident. . . . because God made it evident. . . . Ever since the creation of the world, his invisible attributes of eternal power and divinity have been able to be understood and perceived in what he has made. (Rom 1:19–20)

For example, humans using their intellect alone have come to the logical and correct conclusion that there must be an almighty, all-good, Creator God who brought everything into existence out of nothing, a First Cause who was not caused by any other. He is the Supreme Being who brought into existence other beings. He is a Grand Designer who created all the beauty, symmetry, and power that can be found in the universe.

Divine Revelation

As the existence of many varied and diverse religions throughout human history attests, human reason cannot plumb the depths of God's great mystery. God's ways are not our ways; his thoughts are not our thoughts (Is 55:8). We need God to come to us, to enlighten us about things that we cannot understand. We also need God to give us certitude about those religious and moral truths our minds can grasp (like the precepts of the Ten Commandments, for example, "You shall not kill"), but which are prone to error.

Thankfully, out of his infinite love, goodness, and wisdom, God has indeed revealed himself to human beings. Revelation means "unveiling." Through deeds and words, God freely chose to step into human history to reveal his plan of salvation in Jesus Christ. Through the story of Salvation History, passed on through the **Sacred Tradition** and the Sacred Scripture of the

Sacred Tradition—The living transmission of the message of the Gospel in the Church.

Church, we learn an awesome truth of God's communication with humanity: Through the grace of the Holy Spirit, all humans are adopted into the divine family as sons and daughters of our loving Father and brothers and sisters to his only begotten Son, Jesus Christ.

Divine Revelation is the free gift of God's self-communication by which he makes known the mystery of his divine plan. From the creation of Adam and Eve, God has revealed himself as a God of tremendous love, inviting our first parents into intimate union with him. However, their pride prevented them from accepting God's invitation. After the Original Sin, God did not cut off relations with them, but promised salvation for future generations. The subsequent story of God's saving activity in human history is known as **Salvation History**.

Salvation History reveals how God, out of his infinite love, established a series of covenants with humankind. A covenant is a sacred agreement between God and humans. God promised to be faithful to us forever while humans were to remain faithful to him. He promised to save and redeem us and give us eternal life. One important covenant was with Abraham, to whom God promised many descendents. Another was with Israel, whom God chose as his special people, freeing them from slavery and giving them the Law on Mount Sinai. When Israel fell into sin, the prophets told how God would redeem the people and save all the nations through a promised Messiah who would be from the family of King David.

The climax of Salvation History was, in fact, the coming of the Messiah, Jesus Christ, the fullness of God's Revelation. He is God's total Word-made-flesh who lived among us. He taught us in word and deed about God and completed the Father's work of salvation. Since the coming of Jesus Christ, God's final Word, and the sending of the Holy Spirit, Revelation is complete. There will be no further revelation after him.

Divine Revelation—God's self-communication whereby he makes known the mystery of his divine plan. God most fully revealed himself when he sent us his own divine Son, Jesus Christ.

Salvation History—The story of God's saving activity in human history.

LEARNING MORE ABOUT JESUS

"Who then is this whom even wind and sea obey?" (Mk 4:41)

—The Apostles after Jesus calmed the storm

Interview at least ten Christians to find out how Jesus has been revealed to them. Ask them to name a specific experience that helped them to know and believe in Christ.

Sacred Scripture and Sacred Tradition

The Church teaches that there is a single sacred "deposit" of the Word of God. Christ entrusted this deposit to the Apostles. Inspired by the Holy Spirit, they handed it on through their preaching and writing until Christ will come again. Today, this deposit is found in the Sacred or Apostolic Tradition of the Church and in Sacred Scripture (the Bible). Together they are like two streams that flow from the same fountain of Divine Revelation.

Sacred Tradition is the living transmission of the Church's Gospel message of Jesus Christ, which started from the first days of Christianity through the Apostles' preaching, witness, institutions, worship, and sacred writings inspired by the Holy Spirit. Today, we find this Tradition in the Church's teaching, life, and worship. Our blessed Lord and the Holy Spirit handed on (*tradition* comes from a word that means "handed on") the Word of God to the Apostles. The Deposit of faith is given to the whole Church, but it is the special task of the Apostles' successors—the pope and bishops—to "faithfully preserve, expound, and spread it abroad by their preaching" (*Dogmatic Constitution on Divine Revelation*, No. 9, quoted in *CCC*, 81).

Sacred Scripture (the Bible) is a library of divinely inspired writings, consisting of the Old and New Testaments. It is the written record of salvation that teaches without error what is necessary for salvation.

When we say that Scripture is inspired, we mean that the Holy Spirit inspired the human authors to use their unique talents to put into writing what God wanted written and nothing more. "The books of Scripture firmly, faithfully, and without error teach that truth which God, for the sake of our salvation, wished to see confided to the Sacred Scriptures" (*Dogmatic Constitution on Divine Revelation*, No. 11, quoted in *CCC*, 107).

Christ entrusted to the Church leaders the important task of interpreting God's Word—both Scripture and Tradition—authentically. This Christ-appointed teaching authority, which resides in the pope and the bishops in communion with him, is known as the **Magisterium** (from the Latin word for "teacher"). With the help of the Holy Spirit, the Magisterium serves the Word of God by listening to, guarding, and explaining it faithfully. The criteria for reading and interpreting Sacred Scripture involves (1) reading it with attention to the content and unity of the entire Bible; (2) reading it within the living Tradition of the Church; and (3) reading it by paying attention to the analogy of faith, that is, by attention to the inner harmony that exists among the various truths of the faith.

More information about the Old Testament and how it prepared us for the coming of Jesus Christ will be presented in the next chapter.

Magisterium—The official teaching authority of the Church that resides in the pope (the successor of Peter) and the bishops in communion with him.

◄◄ FOR REVIEW

1. Name some ways that human reason can reveal with certainty the existence of God.
2. What is the necessity of Divine Revelation?
3. Define *covenant*.
4. What is the sacred "deposit" of the Word of God, or faith?
5. What is the function of the Magisterium?

FOR REFLECTION

What is an experience you have had that has helped to reveal God to you?

The Fundamental Doctrine:
The Incarnation (CCC, 456–463)

> The Word of God, Jesus Christ, on account of his great love for mankind, became what we are in order to make us what he is himself.
>
> **—St. Irenaeus**

The fullness of Divine Revelation took place when God became man, when the Father sent his Son, Jesus Christ, to live with us, to teach us, and to die and rise to new life for us and for our salvation. This is the mystery of the **Incarnation**. Belief in this mystery is a distinctive sign of Christian faith.

The essential Catholic **dogma** of the Incarnation holds that Jesus Christ, the Son of God, "assumed a human nature in order to accomplish our salvation in it" (*CCC*, 461). The Word of God took on human flesh from his Mother Mary by power of the Holy Spirit. Thus, Catholics believe that Jesus Christ is both fully God and fully man.

The prologue to John's Gospel provides the strong scriptural basis for the doctrine of the Incarnation:

> In the beginning was the Word, and the Word was with God, and the Word was God. He was in the beginning with God. All things came to be through him, and without him nothing came to be. What came to be through him was life, and this life was the light of the human race; the light shines in the darkness, and the darkness has not overcome it. And the Word became flesh and made his dwelling among us, and we saw his glory, the glory as of the Father's only Son, full of grace and truth. (Jn 1:1–4; 14)

You might find the expression "the Word became *flesh*" a bit strange to state that Jesus became a man. Scholars believe the Gospel writer selected the word "flesh" to counteract a first-century heresy—*Docetism*—that taught that Jesus only *seemed* to be a man. (Docetism comes from a Greek word meaning "to seem.") Adherents of this heresy simply could not accept that God would so demean himself by becoming like us in all our weakness and humanity. To Docetists, Jesus was a ghostly figure who only *appeared* to instruct us about the divine.

A prime danger of Docetism is that if Jesus only *seemed* to be a man, then he only *seemed* to die and resurrect from the dead. These key events—Jesus' Death and Resurrection—are the basis of our salvation. If they were only phantasms and appearances, then we have not really been saved. Additionally, there would be no hope for our own resurrection from the dead.

By using the Greek word *sarks*, which the Latin translates with the root *carne* (meaning "flesh" or "meat"), the author of John's Gospel was insisting that Jesus was one of us. A human person cannot be a *human* being without a body. Thus, Incarnation literally means that God became flesh.

Incarnation—A core Catholic teaching that the Son of God took on human flesh in the person of Jesus Christ.

dogma—A central truth of Revelation that Catholics are obliged to believe.

The Purpose of the Incarnation

According to Church teaching, the Incarnation resulted in many benefits for all human beings:

- *First*, the Word became flesh to save us by reconciling us with God. Because of the Original Sin of Adam and Eve, humans inherited a fallen nature and were prone to sin, sickness, and death. Jesus' great sacrifice of love heals our human nature, overcomes sin, of has won for us everlasting life.
- *Second*, as God's Son, Jesus reveals God's love to us.
- *Third*, as God-made-man, Jesus serves as the perfect model of holiness. He is "the way and the truth and the life" (Jn 14:6) who teaches that the path to holiness is for us to give ourselves to others in imitation of him. "Love one another as I love you" (Jn 15:12).
- *Fourth*, by becoming man, the Word of God makes it possible for us to share in God's nature. "For the Son of God became man so that we might become God" (St. Athanasius, quoted in *CCC*, 460).

These statements emphasize the need for us to learn all we can about Jesus. Moreover, it is vitally important *to know Jesus himself*, the Living Lord who calls each of us by name. A primary intention of this text and course is that those who read it and participate in it will learn more about Jesus and get to know him more personally.

BECOMING ONE OF US

Many years ago, in a land far away lived a wise and good king who loved his people. He wanted to understand his people and learn how they lived. He wanted to endure their same hardships. Many times he would dress in the clothes of a beggar or a lowly worker and visit the home of his poor subjects. Little did they know that their visitor was their king.

One time he called on a desperately poor man who lived with his family in a run-down shack. He ate the meager dinner the poor man offered him. He spoke kindly to the man's family and treated them with profound respect and dignity. Then he returned to his palace.

Some time later the king stopped by to see the poor man again and revealed his true identity. "I am your king!" he said. The king was surprised that the poor man did not request some gift or money. Instead the man said, "You left your glorious dwelling to visit me and my family in this dank hovel. You ate the barely edible food we ate. You have made me very happy. To others in the kingdom you have given your rich gifts. But to me, you have given yourself!"

—Anonymous

The king in this story is a symbol for Jesus Christ. Through an incredible act of humility and love, God's Son took on human nature so that we might have eternal life. In the words of St. Athanasius, the "Word was not degraded by receiving a body. . . . He deified what he put on; and, more than that, he bestowed this gift upon the race of man."

EXTENDING EMPATHY

By means of the Incarnation, God displayed tremendous *empathy* for human beings. Empathy implies understanding and entering into another's feelings. You mirror God's act of entering into human life—the Incarnation—every time you empathize with another. Empathy can often be a profound act of love. In the following days, practice one of the following exercises in empathy:

- Seek out a lonely classmate and invite him or her to eat lunch with you; listen carefully and attentively to what the person says to you.

- Spend time helping a younger sibling with homework or offer to play with him or her.

- Call a grandparent and ask how things are going and offer to help with a chore.

- Encourage a teammate who has been having a rough time lately.

FOR REVIEW

1. Discuss one view from outside of Christianity that people have had about Jesus through the ages.

2. Why does the human heart long for God?

3. Explain how human reason can discover the existence of God.

4. What is Divine Revelation?

5. Where can we find the Deposit of faith?

6. What is Salvation History?

7. How must the Magisterium interpret Scripture?

8. What are the meanings of the terms Incarnation and dogma?

9. What scriptural passage highlights Catholic belief in the dogma of the Incarnation?

10. Who were the Docetists? What follows from their false concept about Jesus?

11. Discuss one benefit of the Incarnation for mankind.

FOR REFLECTION

Write a reflection on what for you is the most convincing proof of (1) God's existence and (2) God's love for you.

Learning about **Jesus**
(CCC, 422–429)

Who is the real Jesus?
How do you learn about him?
Where do you find him?

Examine your knowledge about Jesus. You probably learned what you know about Jesus from your parents, your teachers, talks given at retreats, priests who spoke about Jesus in homilies, television shows that dealt with Jesus, movies that depicted his life, and books and articles that you have read.

And where did these people and sources get their information? From similar people who came before them, especially the bishops and the popes who made sure through the ages that what was passed on was accurate knowledge.

But where did the original knowledge about Jesus come from? If you press it all the way back to Jesus' time, we conclude that it came from Sacred or Apostolic Tradition. This living transmission of the Gospel message is based on the Apostles, who had direct and personal contact with Jesus. They knew him when he was a teacher and healer walking in their midst. They witnessed his fate as a condemned criminal. Moreover, they claimed to have seen him *after* his Death, risen in power and glory. They experienced the power of the Risen Lord in their lives that transformed them from frightened cowards into bold proclaimers of the Good News (**Gospel**) of Jesus Christ, our Lord and Savior. They were so convinced of the truth of their message that they surrendered their own lives in preaching the simple message "Jesus is Lord!"

Their testimony is preserved in Sacred Scripture, most specifically in the four Gospels and the Epistles of the New Testament, written within a generation of Jesus' ministry. They are an accurate source of knowledge about Jesus Christ. Preserved and interpreted through the ages by the Magisterium of the Church, Sacred Scripture preserves the authentic message about the Jesus of history and the Christ of faith. Knowledge of Scripture is essential for anyone who wants to know Jesus Christ.

Tracing Jesus Christ in History
(CCC, 422–423)

History shows that there was a real man named Jesus (see Chapter 1). In his lifetime, he would have borne the name *Jesus bar Joseph* (Jesus, son of Joseph), *Jesus the Carpenter* (people were known by their professions), or *Jesus of Nazareth* (one's surname was often based on place of residence). He was born a Palestinian Jew in Bethlehem

Gospel—Literally, "Good News." Gospel refers to (1) the Good News preached by Jesus; (2) the Good News of salvation won for us in the person of Jesus Christ (he is the Good News proclaimed by the Church); (3) the four written records of the Good News—the Gospels of Matthew, Mark, Luke, and John.

of a woman named Mary. His birth year was probably between 4 and 6 BC, while King Herod the Great ruled in Palestine under the Roman Emperor Caesar Augustus.

Jesus lived a hidden life in Nazareth in Galilee. He learned the trade of carpentry from his foster father, Joseph. He practiced his Jewish religion faithfully by worshiping on the Sabbath, reciting daily prayers, celebrating the great religious feasts, and observing the precepts of the Jewish Law.

After being baptized by the prophet John the Baptist, perhaps sometime in AD 28, he began his own public ministry. He wandered the countryside teaching a message of repentance, the coming of God's Kingdom, and the need for all people to believe in him and his teachings:

> This is the time of fulfillment. The Kingdom of God is at hand. Repent, and believe in the Gospel. (Mk 1:15)

He performed works at which the people marveled. He cured lepers, restored sight to those who were blind and hearing to those who were deaf, fed the crowds with a few loaves of bread, and exorcised demons from the possessed. He gathered and formed disciples who were eyewitnesses to his life, teachings, and miracles.

Jesus was provocative. He asked for people to make a clear choice to turn from sin, accept God's love, and believe in him. His manner of preaching and his actions led some of the people to think of Jesus as a great prophet. But not everyone thought this way. Even some of his relatives thought he was crazy (Mk 3:20–21).

Also, a few of Jesus' words and actions threatened and angered the authorities. For example, he spoke with unique authority in his teachings, quoting no one. He gave novel interpretations of the Law. He claimed to speak for God. He performed marvelous deeds (miracles) that some attributed to the devil. And he associated with prostitutes and tax collectors.

Eventually the authorities colluded to arrest Jesus. One of his own Apostles betrayed him. The rest abandoned him. Some Jewish officials brought Jesus to trial and found him guilty of blasphemy, because he claimed to be God's Son. They turned him over to Pontius Pilate, the Roman prefect, who sentenced him to the cruelest form of capital punishment—crucifixion. This death penalty took place either in AD 30 or 33. It was alleged that Jesus claimed to be "King of the Jews," a crime interpreted under Roman law as sedition against the Roman Emperor, Tiberius.

These bare-bones facts highlight the life on earth of Jesus, a man that most open-minded persons would agree lived and taught approximately 2000 years ago. This Jesus is the most compelling person to walk the face of the earth. Some of the quotes given earlier in this chapter testify to this fact, as does this one:

> I find the name of Jesus Christ written on the top of every page of modern history.
>
> **–George Bancroft**
> (1800–1891, famous American historian)

WHEN WAS JESUS BORN?

In the sixth century, a Roman monk and mathematician, Dionysius Exiguus, or Dennis the Short, attempted to calculate a chronology of the Christian faith for Pope John I.

Dennis began the new Christian calendar in the year AD 1, or *Anno Domini* ("in the year of the Lord"). He set Jesus' birth in the year 754 on the Roman calendar. This date was problematic since the year 754 was at least four years after King Herod died. Since the Gospels mention Jesus' persecution at the hands of Herod, it is safe to assume that Jesus was actually born at least four years earlier than calculated, that is, approximately 4 to 6 BC ("Before Christ") on the Christian calendar.

Belief in Jesus Christ

Jesus is much more than simply a famous, influential person from the past. Catholics believe that God raised this man Jesus from the dead. The belief in Jesus' Resurrection claims that after his Death and burial, Jesus entered into God's powerful life and that he now shares that life, by the power of the Holy Spirit, with those who are willing to receive it through faith and Baptism.

Catholic faith also holds that Jesus Christ is Lord, that he is himself God. His Resurrection and Glorification reveal his true identity as God's only Son who fully shares the Father's superabundant life and glory. Moreover, with his Father, the Risen Christ sends the Holy Spirit to live in the hearts of believers, empowering them to live Christlike lives of love and service for others.

The real Jesus of faith is the resurrected Jesus, a living person, whom God has revealed as both Lord and Christ (Acts 2:36).

This is the Jesus you have been hearing about ever since you learned his name. He is the same Jesus who lived on this earth over two thousand years ago. But if it were not for the earth-shattering event of Jesus' Resurrection to a superabundant life with God, it is highly unlikely anyone would take note of his existence. Jesus of Nazareth would be a mere footnote in history.

Faith is a gift of God. It is primarily a response to a living God who is powerfully at work among all people through the resurrected Jesus Christ. Before we can exercise our faith, we must have the grace of God and the interior helps of the Holy Spirit.

Meeting Jesus Today

Because the Jesus who once lived on earth is alive as the resurrected Lord, it is possible, through the help of the Holy Spirit, for us to meet, know, and believe in him. Such faith in Jesus Christ is necessary for our salvation. Several ways to know Jesus are listed below.

Sacred Scripture. One way to meet Jesus is in the Bible. As noted above, Sacred Scripture is the written record of Revelation, that is, God's self-communication to humanity. Jesus is most present in the New Testament writings, most notably in the four Gospels. They record many of the miracles that Jesus performed for our sake and contain many of his teachings. The Gospels and other New Testament writings would never have been written had Jesus not been raised from the dead and the Spirit come to enflame the hearts of Jesus' disciples. The Gospels came into being to set down a written record of the Good News about Jesus Christ, Son of God. The author of John's Gospel wrote it this way:

> But these are written that you may (come to) believe that Jesus is the Messiah, the Son of God, and that through this belief you may have life in his name. (Jn 20:31)

Sacraments. The Risen Lord comes to us in the very special moments of our life:

- when we are initiated into the Catholic Church (Baptism);
- at a time when we need the special strength of the Holy Spirit to live the Christian life (Confirmation);
- when we are sick and in need of spiritual and physical healing (Anointing of the Sick);

- when we have sinned and need to hear the Divine Physician forgive us and welcome us back into the community of the faithful (Penance);
- when we are called to serve God as special ministers (Holy Orders);
- when we commit ourselves to a lifetime of sharing life and love with a spouse (Matrimony);
- and, most remarkably, on a daily basis, if we partake in the sign of love we call the holy Eucharist.

These Seven Sacraments are efficacious signs of grace, instituted by Christ and given to the Church. Through the sacraments, divine life is dispensed to us through the Holy Spirit.

Prayer. We can meet the living Lord in prayer by the grace and help of the Holy Spirit. We can talk to him any time as in a conversation with a friend. We can meet him when we come together with other believers, because, as he said,

> Where two or three are gathered together in my name, there am I in the midst of them. (Mt 18:20)

In others. Jesus lives in each of us. This remarkable truth gives us tremendous dignity. Yet, it also imposes on us the tremendous responsibility to be Christ for others.

In a special way, Jesus identified himself with the lowly, the outcast, the marginalized. He taught that we will be judged on how we welcome the stranger, feed the hungry, give drink to the thirsty, and visit the sick and imprisoned:

> He will answer them, "Amen, I say to you, what you did not do for one of these least ones, you did not do for me." And these will go off to eternal punishment, but the righteous to eternal life. (Mt 25:45–46)

WHAT THEY THOUGHT ABOUT JESUS

Read the following Gospel passages. Write what certain contemporaries of Jesus thought about him.

John the Baptist (Jn 1:29)

Jesus' relatives (Mk 3:21)

The people (Mt 21:10–11)

Herod Antipas (Mk 6:14–16)

 ## FOR REVIEW

1. List five significant historical facts about Jesus.

2. What might Jesus' surname have been?

3. What are the probable birth and death dates for Jesus?

4. Identify Dionysius Exiguus.

5. Why is Jesus more than just a famous person from the past?

6. Who is the "real Jesus"?

7. Name five different ways you can meet Jesus Christ today.

FOR REFLECTION

- Tell about a person who taught you about Jesus. How did he or she teach you?

- List five statements you know are absolutely true about Jesus.

- Which person most reminds you of Jesus? Why?

- If Jesus were your age and attending your school, what would he be like?

- What would you most like to learn about Jesus?

Names and Titles **for Jesus**

Theologians tell us that people pray as they believe. But people also believe as they pray. A famous prayer, called the "Jesus Prayer," is a wonderful example of both the believer and pray-er expressing his or her faith.

Each word of this prayer conveys profound meaning: "Lord Jesus Christ, Son of God, have mercy on me, a sinner." The following text sections analyze the important words of the prayer more deeply.

Jesus (CCC, 430–435; 452)

Jesus was a relatively common proper name in the first century, a late form of the Hebrew name *Joshua* (Yehoshua). Several New Testament persons bore this name, including a "Jesus the Just" (Col 4:11) and a prophet with the surname "Bar-Jesus" (Acts 13:6). An ancient manuscript even gives the first name of the criminal Barabbas as Jesus, a name probably dropped from most Gospel manuscripts because the Church did not want this known insurrectionist associated with Jesus the Savior.

It is not accidental that the Lord was named Jesus because, like all Hebrew names, it had profound significance. Jesus means "God saves" or "Yahweh is salvation." The author of Matthew's Gospel caught this meaning when he quoted the angel who appeared in Joseph's dream:

> [Mary] will bear a son and you are to name him Jesus, because he will save his people from their sins. (Mt 1:21)

The Old Testament revealed a God of salvation. Yahweh delivered Israel out of slavery in Egypt and forgave sin. In God's plan, it was most appropriate that the Son of God made man should bear the name Jesus. This special name shows that the very name of God is present in the person who would redeem and save humanity from its sins and ultimately from death.

By the end of the first century, the name Jesus fell out of favor for both Jews and Christians. Jews stopped naming their boys Jesus because of the conflict with Jewish Christians who they thought were misled by the prophet Jesus from Nazareth. Various New Testament letters and even the Gospels themselves point to some of the tensions between Jews and Christians of the first century, tensions that led to a definitive break between the two groups sometime after the First Jewish Revolt in AD 66–70.

Out of reverence for the holy name, most Christians stopped naming their boys after our Lord. Today, you will sometimes meet believers, most often of Spanish heritage, who will give the name Jesus to their boys. This practice has an interesting history. In the thirteenth century there was a heretical group known as the Albigensians who ritually mocked the Lord's name. To counteract this blasphemous practice, the Council of Lyons in 1274 prescribed a devotion to the Holy Name. The preaching of a certain Spanish Dominican, Didacus of Victoria, two centuries later led to the founding of a religious order that

NEW TESTAMENT NAMES

Use a dictionary or book of names to match the meaning of these New Testament names with the description that fits from the box at the right.

1. Joseph	6. Matthew
2. Mary	7. Martha
3. John	8. Andrew
4. Elizabeth	9. Susanna
5. James	10. Philip

a. "let God protect"	f. "may God add"
b. "virile one, manly"	g. "friend of horses"
c. "bitter" or "grieved"	h. "lady or mistress of the house"
d. "lily"	i. "God has shown favor"
e. "God is fullness"	j. "gift of God"

Complete the following assignments:

- Check a book of names and find the meaning of your baptismal or confirmation name. How does it convey special meaning to you?

- Look up a biography of a saint whose name you bear (or a favorite saint) and prepare a short report on his or her life. Sample biographies are given at http://saints.catholic.org/index.shtml.

we know today as the Society of the Holy Name of Jesus. Early Spanish members of this Society began the practice of using the holy name Jesus at the baptism of children. Their reasoning was that if we call on the saints to protect the newly baptized Christian by naming a child after them, why not call on the Lord himself in the same way?

In his Letter to the Philippians, St. Paul cites an early Christian teaching about how we should revere the name Jesus:

> God greatly exalted him and bestowed on him the name that is above every name, that at the name of Jesus every knee should bend, of those in heaven and on earth and under the earth, and every tongue confess that Jesus Christ is Lord, to the glory of God the Father. (Phil 2:9–11)

Christ (CCC, 436–440; 453)

Christians get their name from one of Jesus' most important titles—**Christ**. The word "Christ" derives from the Greek *Christos*, which, in turn, translates the Hebrew word Messiah. Christ means "anointed."

The Messiah was God's anointed one, the promised one born into the lineage of King David who would fulfill all the divine promises made to the Chosen People. Many contemporaries of Jesus thought the Messiah would be a political ruler. But the Father anointed Jesus with the Spirit to inaugurate God's Kingdom as a reign of peace, love, and service. Jesus accomplished his mission of suffering service through the threefold office of prophet, priest, and king:

- As *prophet*, Jesus was the Word of God who spoke for his Father and taught through his words and deeds the full message of salvation.

Christ—A title given for Jesus that means "anointed one." It translates the Hebrew word for Messiah.

- As *high priest*, Jesus was the mediator between God and humanity. He offered his life for all on the altar of the cross. Today, Jesus the Christ continues his priestly role at each celebration of the Eucharist.

- As *king*, Jesus, the rightful ruler of the universe, does not lord it over others. He did not come to be served, but to serve through suffering and dying for us and thus accomplish our salvation. Jesus rules with gentleness, compassion, and love. Along with the gift of the Holy Spirit, Christ's example inspires us to love and serve others in imitation of him.

Son of God (CCC, 441–445; 454)

The Old Testament sometimes referred to angels, the Chosen People, and the children and kings of Israel as "sons of God." It did so to show that God had special love for these creatures whom he adopted into a unique relationship.

Catholics believe that Jesus Christ is the one and only Son of God, that Jesus shares the same divine nature as God the Father. As John's Gospel teaches:

> In the beginning was the Word, and the Word was with God, and the Word was God. (Jn 1:1)

The divinity associated with the title is what Simon Peter meant when he professed Jesus to be the Son of God. It is what St. Paul meant when he proclaimed in the synagogues that Jesus is the "Son of God." And this is the truth that the Father revealed at Jesus' baptism and Transfiguration, when the heavenly voice was heard saying that Jesus is "my beloved son" (see Matthew 3:17; 17:5).

A hallmark of faith is the profound truth that Jesus is the unique Son of God. Jesus' miracles and his words reveal him to be such. He alone knows the Father. And although he teaches his followers to call God "our Father," Jesus also reveals a distinction between "my Father and your Father."

After his Resurrection, it became clear to the Apostles what Jesus meant when he said, "The Father and I are one" (Jn 10:30). Catholics hold that Jesus Christ is God's only Son. There is no one like him.

Lord (CCC, 446–451; 455)

In New Testament times, the title **Lord** could refer to a ruler or some powerful person. It was also used as a form of address similar to our salutation *sir*. Some people may have used it this way when they were talking with Jesus, especially when they were asking him for a favor.

However, when believers apply this title to Jesus, it means something entirely different. Lord translates the Greek word *Kurios*, which, in turn, renders the Hebrew word *Adonai*. This was the word the Chosen People used whenever the most holy name for God—Yahweh—would appear in the Hebrew Scriptures.

Therefore, to give Jesus the title Lord is to state quite boldly that *he is God*. Catholics believe that Jesus has the same sovereignty as God and that his Death and Resurrection have won

Lord—A title for Jesus which translates the Greek word *Kurios*, which rendered the Hebrew word for God. To call Jesus "Lord" is to call him God.

for us eternal life, a gift that only God can bestow. Jesus is the Lord of life, the One who deserves their total devotion and obedience. The power, honor, and glory that are owed God the Father are also due Jesus. It would be hard to find a more lofty and important title than Lord to affirm Jesus' divinity.

MORE NEW TESTAMENT TITLES FOR JESUS

Complete each of the following assignments:

1. Read the Scripture reference and briefly state what each title means.

   - Good Shepherd (Jn 10:11)

   - Living Water (Jn 4:14)

   - Bread of Life (Jn 6:35)

   - Light of the World (Jn 1:4–5, 9)

   - Divine Physician (Mt 9:12–13)

   - Judge (Acts 17:31)

2. Name a contemporary title for Jesus that might appeal to people today.

3. Which titles do you feel most comfortable using to address Jesus?

 FOR REVIEW

1. Write out the "Jesus Prayer."

2. What is the meaning of the name *Jesus*? Why is it appropriate for him to have this name?

3. What is the meaning of the term *Christ*? What kind of Messiah was Jesus?

4. What does it mean to call Jesus the Son of God? the Lord?

FOR REFLECTION

- How do you revere the name of Jesus at home? at church? in a public setting?

- What are ways you show special reverence for the Lord's name?

- Compose your own version of the "Jesus Prayer." Use at least two of your favorite titles for Jesus.

CHAPTER SUMMARY POINTS

- It was Simon Peter who identified Jesus as the Messiah, Son of God, when asked by Jesus about his identity.
- The human heart craves union with God, who implanted in each of us a desire to know and to love him.
- The human intellect can discover God's existence. However, out of his infinite love, goodness, and wisdom, God revealed himself in human history by making known the mystery of his divine plan.
- Jesus Christ is the fullness of God's Revelation, God's Word-made-flesh who completed the Father's work of salvation.
- We can find the single sacred deposit of Divine Revelation in Sacred Tradition and Sacred Scripture, the two streams that flow from the same fountain of Divine Revelation.
- The doctrine of the Incarnation holds that the Son of God became man in the person of Jesus Christ.
- The heresy of Docetism denied the essential humanity of Jesus, claiming that he only seemed to be a human being.
- From the very first moment of the Incarnation to his redemptive Passion and Death, Jesus Christ reconciles us with God, reveals the Father's love to us, demonstrates a perfect model of holiness to us in his person, and makes it possible for us to share in God's nature.
- Jesus of Nazareth was born in 4–6 BC and died in either AD 30 or 33 at the hands of Pontius Pilate.
- Catholics believe in the resurrected Jesus Christ, whom they hold to be the Lord and Savior.
- Catholics believe that the resurrected Lord is the "real" Jesus who shares God's life with us right now through the power of the Holy Spirit.
- Catholics believe that we can meet the living Jesus Christ in his Word (the Sacred Scriptures), the Seven Sacraments, prayer, other people, and, in a special way, through the poor and outcast.
- The "Jesus Prayer"—"Lord Jesus Christ, Son of God, have mercy on me, a sinner"—reflects many profound truths Catholics hold about Jesus.
- The proper name *Jesus* means "God saves" or "God is salvation." This appropriate name reveals the mission Jesus accomplished for us.
- The title *Christ*, or *Messiah* in the Hebrew, means "anointed one." Anointed by the Holy Spirit, Jesus serves as the High Priest, God's perfect prophet, and as a king who leads through compassionate service.
- The title *Son of God* reveals Jesus' unique relationship with God the Father, sharing his very nature from the beginning of time.
- By proclaiming Jesus *Lord*, Catholics hold that Jesus is God himself.

LEARN BY DOING

kerygma—The core teaching about Jesus Christ as Savior and Lord.

1. **Hearing St. Peter.** Acts 2 records an important "kerygmatic" sermon preached by Peter to those in Jerusalem after the descent of the Holy Spirit on Pentecost Sunday. The term **kerygma** refers to the essential preaching of salvation through the life, Death, and Resurrection of Jesus Christ. Read this sermon and then outline its basic points in your journal.

2. **God's Love**. Create a PowerPoint® presentation of pictures that you download from the Internet, scan, or take yourself that powerfully illustrate for you that God exists. For example, you might select pictures that highlight the awesomeness, beauty, and organization found in creation. Or you might select pictures that depict God's love shown in his most magnificent creation: the human being. Select an appropriate piece of background music for your presentation and words of praise from an appropriate creation Psalm like Psalms 8, 104, 139, or 148.

3. **Read and report** on the classic book *Black Like Me* by John Howard Griffin. It recounts how the author, a white man, darkened his skin by medication and dye and "incarnated" himself in the Deep South of mid-twentieth-century America to experience personally the discrimination suffered by blacks at the hand of racial prejudice and Jim Crow laws. A riveting story even today, Griffin's book is a classic in empathy and race relations.

PRAYER LESSON

Thanksgiving and humility are two attitudes every believer can take from meditating on the doctrine of the Incarnation. First, we should *thank* God for all his great gifts—life, health, family, friends, and the eternal life won for us by his Son, who became one with us. A Christian who forgets the language of gratitude cannot be on speaking terms with God. At the least, God's giving of his Son deserves our thanksgiving for his great gift.

Second, we should imitate Christ's *humility*. He bent low to raise us high. Our task as Christians is to bend down and help raise up others who are too weak, powerless, or lonely to help themselves. Let us learn from Christ's humility, celebrated so beautifully in this ancient hymn quoted in Philippians:

> Who, though he was in the form of God, did not regard equality with God something to be grasped. Rather, he emptied himself, taking the form of a slave, coming in human likeness; and found human in appearance, he humbled himself, becoming obedient to death, even death on a cross. Because of this, God greatly exalted him and bestowed on him the name that is above every name, that at the name of Jesus every knee should bend, of those in heaven and on earth and under the earth, and every tongue confess that Jesus Christ is Lord, to the glory of God the Father.
>
> —Philippians 2:6–11

Lord, it is beyond our power of imagination to realize
fully what you have done for us by taking on human flesh.
All we know is that you can feel what we feel,
not only our joys and simple pleasures,
but especially our sufferings in both body and spirit.
We turn these over to you as a gift and as an offering.
May our good feelings be a sign of our gratitude for all you have given us.
May our sufferings be an offering of atonement for the times we have
failed to be your friend.
Thank you, Lord Jesus Christ. Amen.

The **Historical Jesus**

CHAPTER ONE

In the fifteenth year of the reign of Tiberius Caesar, when Pontius Pilate was governor of Judea, and Herod was tetrarch of Galilee, and his brother Philip tetrarch of the region of Ituraea and Trachonitis, and Lysanias was tetrarch of Abilene, during the high priesthood of Annas and Caiaphas, the word of God came to John the son of Zechariah in the desert.

–Luke 3:1–2

CHAPTER **OVERVIEW**

ONE OF **A KIND**

A famous soliloquy points to the uniqueness of Jesus.

HISTORICAL EVIDENCE FOR **THE EXISTENCE OF JESUS**

There is evidence from outside the Bible—particularly from Jewish and Roman sources—that support the existence of the life and ministry of Jesus.

THE SCRIPTURES **AND JESUS**

Three main criteria were used by the early Church to determine which books of Scripture were the inspired Word of God and worthy for inclusion in the New Testament canon.

THE FORMATION OF **THE GOSPELS**

The Gospels were formed through three stages: that of the historical Jesus (6 BC–AD 30), the oral tradition (AD 30–50), and finally the actual writing of the Gospels and other New Testament books (AD 50–ca. 120).

HOW THE CHURCH **INTERPRETS THE NEW TESTAMENT**

Catholics understand that the Bible should be read prayerfully and critically and viewed through several "lenses" through which the Church believes Scripture can be studied profitably.

One of **a Kind**

Many would hold that Jesus is the most interesting person who ever lived. More books are written about him than any other human being. People either love him or hold him as a flash point for hate. Some in Judaism and Islam hold him as a prophet; atheists scoff at claims to his divinity; skeptics do not know what to make of him.

Christians, however, marvel at him. Consider anew this famous soliloquy:

ONE SOLITARY LIFE

Here is a young man who was born in an obscure village, the child of a peasant woman.

He worked in a carpenter shop until he was thirty.

He never wrote a book. He never held an office. He never owned a home. He never had a family. He never went to college.

He never did one of the things that usually accompany greatness. He had no credentials but himself.

While he was still a young man the tide of public opinion turned against him. His friends ran away. He was turned over to his enemies. . . . He was nailed to a cross between two thieves.

While he was dying, his executioners gambled for the only piece of property he had on earth, and that was his coat.

When he was dead, he was laid in a borrowed grave through the pity of a friend.

To this point you might think that this "solitary life" was anything but remarkable. Jesus was a condemned criminal and a "loser" by human standards. However, the anonymous author of this passage reminds us of an undeniable truth about Jesus in his concluding passage:

[Twenty] centuries have come and gone, and today he is . . . the leader of the column of progress. I am far within the mark when I say that all the armies that ever marched, and all the kings that ever reigned, have not affected the life of man upon this earth as has this One Solitary Life.

FOR REFLECTION

If Jesus were to appear physically to you, name one question you would like to ask him. List several of the questions you and your classmates would like to ask Jesus. Write answers for how you think he might answer them.

RELATING WITH JESUS

- Rate your relationship with Jesus. Write a paragraph that uses as many of the following adjectives that you feel are appropriate: active, passive, exciting, dull, close, distant, friendly, estranged, personal, shallow.

- St. Francis of Assisi wrote about Jesus, "You are wisdom. You are peace. You are beauty. You are eternal life." Compose your own version of St. Francis's address to Jesus.

Historical Evidence for **the Existence of Jesus**

Jesus was a great teacher, but he left no writings behind. Nor are there any written records of him that date from his lifetime. However, no credible historian today denies the existence of Jesus of Nazareth. The New Testament writings, especially the Gospels, which are first-century documents, shout the news that Jesus existed and do so while citing many verifiable historical persons and events.

There are numerous other references outside the canon of Sacred Scripture referring to Jesus and his message dating from the second century and later, but most of these are Christian in nature, and thus may not be considered objective sources by neutral observers. This poses a good question: Do we find any historical record for the existence of Jesus in early Roman or Jewish sources, that is, from non-believers? The answer is yes. There is historical evidence of Jesus' existence from both Roman and Jewish independent sources. Some of these are detailed in the sections that follow.

Tacitus (55–117?)

Writing in his *Annals* approximately AD 115, the Roman historian Tacitus reports the famous fire that broke out in Rome under the reign of the corrupt and notorious Emperor Nero:

To suppress this rumor [that he had started the fire], Nero fabricated scapegoats and punished with every refinement the notoriously depraved Christians (as they were popularly called). Their originator, Christ, had been executed in Tiberias's reign by the governor of Judaea, Pontius Pilate. But in spite of this temporary setback the deadly superstition had broken out afresh, not only in Judaea (where the mischief had started) but even in Rome. All degraded and shameful practices collect and flourish in the capital.[1]

This quote indicates that Tacitus likely checked official Roman records to compile his history. He is the only Roman historian to mention Pontius Pilate, though two Jewish writers—Josephus and Philo—tell of Pilate's harsh rule in Judea. Tacitus verified that Jesus' public life took place during Emperor Tiberius's reign, an important fact also mentioned by the Evangelist Luke (see Luke 3:1–2).

Suetonius (70?–130?)

The Roman biographer Suetonius, in *The Twelve Caesars*, wrote about an incident that took place in Rome during the reign of Emperor Claudius (AD 41–54):

He expelled the Jews from Rome on account of the riots in which they were constantly indulging, at the instigation of Chrestus.[2]

The Acts of the Apostles (18:2) more accurately reports what really took place at the time of this Jewish expulsion from Rome in AD 48. When early Christian preachers went to the Roman synagogues to announce that Jesus of Nazareth was the awaited Messiah, they met with vigorous resistance, sometimes resulting in street riots. The emperor did not appreciate the fine distinctions between Jewish Christians, Christians, and Jews. To him they were all troublemakers, and this "Chrestus"—his term for Jesus Christ—was ultimately to blame. To preserve the peace, he thought it best to kick them all out of town.

Pliny the Younger (62–113)

Pliny the Younger was a masterful and prolific letter writer in ancient Rome. He served as legate to Bithynia (in modern Turkey) from AD 111 to 113. During his time in Bithynia, he met Christians who did not submit themselves to Roman law and beliefs. In a long letter to the Emperor Trajan, Pliny asked for advice on how to deal with the "superstition" practiced by Christians. His letter covered these points:

- Pliny reported that Christianity had spread so rapidly that the pagan temples had fallen into disuse. The merchants who sold sacrificial animals were in serious economic trouble.
- He supported Christians who openly rejected Christ and then promised to worship the pagan gods and the emperor.
- Pliny condemned Christians to death who persisted in their beliefs about Jesus Christ.
- He also informed Trajan of the Christian custom of celebrating the Eucharist on "a fixed day of the week."

Trajan's reply reassured Pliny that he had acted well in relation to the Bithynian Christians. He confirmed that Pliny should punish any believing Christians who came to his attention, but also said that Pliny should not go looking for them. Trajan saw the Christians as potentially dangerous, but not so much a threat that they had to be hunted down like criminals.

The ancient Roman and Greek writers (e.g., Lucian of Samosata, AD 120–180) admittedly do not tell us much about Jesus, but they do at least write under the assumption that he existed.

Josephus: Jewish Historian
(37–101?)

An important reference to Jesus comes from the colorful Jewish historian Flavius Josephus. Born Joseph ben Matthias in AD 37, Josephus commanded the Jewish forces in Galilee during the First Jewish Revolt against the Romans (AD 66–70). The Romans captured him, but because he predicted that the commander-in-chief of the Romans in Palestine, Vespasian, would one day be emperor, his life was spared. Vespasian did become emperor in AD 69, and Josephus became his friend and a citizen of Rome.

Josephus wrote *The Jewish Wars* and a twenty-volume history of the Jews, the *Jewish Antiquities*. These two works are a major source of historical information on life in the Holy Land under Roman rule.

In the *Jewish Antiquities*, Josephus tried to prove to the Romans and to the Jew-hating emperor Domitian (AD 81–96) that the Jews were a noble people. In the eighteenth book of the series, he mentioned John the Baptist, calling him a good man. In the final book, he noted that Annas the Younger—the son of the high priest mentioned in the Gospels—put to death James the Just (in AD 62), the leader of the local church in Jerusalem. He refers to this James as "the brother of Jesus who is called the Christ."

Of most interest, however, is Josephus' account of the Palestinian rule of Pontius Pilate (AD 26–36). Note the references to Jesus Christ. Remember these were written by a non-believer:

> Now about this time lived Jesus, a wise man, if indeed he should be called a man. He was a doer of wonderful works, a teacher of men who receive the truth with pleasure, and won over many Jews and Greeks. He was the Christ. And when Pilate, at the information of the leading men among us, sentenced him to the cross,

those who loved him at the start did not cease to do so, for he appeared to them alive again on the third day as had been foretold—both this and ten thousand other wonderful things concerning him—by the divine prophets. Nor is the tribe of Christians, so named after him, extinct to this day.[3]

There is a problem with this passage. Can you suggest a theory about what might have happened as it was handed down through the ages?

Scholars do not believe that this passage comes entirely from Josephus because parts of it sound as though a believer wrote it. They theorize that certain passages that support Church belief were added later by a Christian copyist. Examples of this are the phrase, "if indeed he should be called a man," and references to Jesus as the Christ (Messiah) and his Resurrection. The Church Father Origen maintained that Josephus never accepted Christianity.

Regardless of what Josephus either wrote or believed, the significant point for our purposes is that he did not question the actual historical existence of Jesus or that Jesus was put to death at Pilate's order sometime between AD 26 and 36. Further, he attests that Jesus' followers were very much on the scene at the end of the first century.

Another reference to Jesus occurs in the Babylonian Talmud, a commentary on Jewish law written in the third century after Christ. This passage mentions a certain Yeshu (Jesus) who practiced magic and led Israel away from true Jewish worship. It also reports that this man had

disciples and was "hanged on the eve of Passover."

 FOR REVIEW

1. List some reasons why it is important for Catholics that non-Christian sources validate that Jesus really existed.

2. Identify Tacitus, Suetonius, and Pliny the Younger.

3. What opinion did Tacitus have of Jesus' followers?

4. What did Tacitus call Christianity?

5. Why is Josephus important for proving that Jesus actually existed?

FOR REFLECTION

- Emperor worship was expected by some of the Roman rulers—under pain of death. Is there anyone or anything you would be willing to die for? Why or why not?
- What are some of the false gods people worship today? How are they enticed to do so?

The Scriptures **and Jesus**
(*CCC*, 102; 124–125; 128–130; 134; 140)

Our primary source material about the historical Jesus and his earliest followers is the New Testament. A library of different types of writings, the New Testament contains twenty-seven books, the most important of which are the four Gospels (Matthew, Mark, Luke, and John). Composed over a period of around seventy years, beginning in AD 50, the New Testament announces how God has dealt with human beings through his Son, Jesus Christ.

Testament was the word Jewish scholars from the third century

Testament—A word meaning "covenant," the open-ended contract of love between God and human beings. Jesus' Death and Resurrection sealed God's New Covenant of love for all time.

Septuagint—A second-century BC Greek translation of the Hebrew Bible made at Alexandria, Egypt.

BC used to mean "covenant" in their translation of the Hebrew Scriptures into Greek, known as the **Septuagint** (from a Latin word meaning "seventy" for the legendary seventy scholars who translated it). By calling their Sacred Scriptures the New Testament, Christians are proclaiming that God has established a *New Covenant* with his people in Jesus Christ.

The Old Testament as a Preparation for Jesus
(CCC, 54–64; 70–72; 128–130; 134; 138; 140)

> Through all the words of Sacred Scripture, God speaks only one single Word, his one Utterance in whom he expresses himself completely. (CCC, 102)

The Old Testament is truly the Word of God. Divinely inspired, it has permanent value because it gives witness to God's saving love in human history. It was written to prepare for the coming of Jesus Christ, the Savior of the world. The Old Testament prepares for the New Testament, and the New Testament fulfills the Old Testament. Both shed light on each other.

The central focus of the Old Testament's forty-six inspired books, written between 1200 and 100 BC, is the covenant theme of God's love for the Jewish people. All of its pages reveal a loving God who was preparing humanity for the coming of the Savior. Before tracing God's covenant in Salvation History, what follows is a brief overview of the books of the Old Testament. A short explanation of what each category of books contains is included.

Pentateuch
(*5 books:* Genesis, Exodus, Leviticus, Numbers, and Deuteronomy)

These sacred books, also known as the Torah, contain the Jewish Law and important instruction on beliefs and practice. They also report the origins of the world, of humans, and of God's selection of the Israelites. They include many memorable stories of our faith: Creation, Adam and Eve,

Noah, Abraham, the patriarchs and matriarchs of us all. They recount the stories of Jewish slavery in Egypt, Yahweh's covenant with the Chosen People, the Exodus, and Moses. They give us the Ten Commandments, a code for righteous living followed by Jews, Christians, and Muslims alike.

Historical Books

(*18 books:* Joshua, Judges, 1 & 2 Samuel, 1 & 2 Kings, 1 and 2 Chronicles, Ezra, Nehemiah, Ruth, Esther, Lamentations, Judith, Tobit, Baruch, 1 and 2 Maccabees)

The historical books of the Old Testament narrate how the Chosen People lived out the covenant in the Promised Land. The first six books have the same style as the book of Deuteronomy and describe how the Holy Land, Canaan or Palestine, was conquered and settled. They also describe the desire for monarchy, kings like Saul and David, and the declining monarchy up to the time of the Babylonian Captivity in 587 BC.

The next four books are written from the vantage point of a priestly writer. They relate the history of Israel from David through the Babylonian Captivity and the return under Ezra and Nehemiah.

The period after the Exile also produced some short moralistic tales to uplift and inspire the Jews. First and Second Maccabees record a shining moment in Jewish history: the successful revolt of the Jews against the Greek government in Syria (168–164 BC).

Wisdom Books

(*7 books:* Job, Psalms, Proverbs, Ecclesiastes, Song of Songs, Sirach (also called Ecclesiasticus), and Wisdom)

These works contain some of the most beautiful and practical religious literature in the world. Job wrestles with the ever-current problem of suffering and good versus evil. The Psalms contain many exquisite hymns and prayers for both public and private use. The Song of Songs is an allegorical love song that describes God's love for his people. The

IMPORTANT DATES IN OLD TESTAMENT HISTORY

ca. 1900 BC: God calls Abraham

ca. 1300 BC: Moses, Exodus

1000 BC: David anointed king

922 BC: Kingdom divided

721 BC: Fall of Northern Kingdom to the Assyrians

587–538 BC: Babylonian Captivity

164 BC: Maccabees cleanse the Temple

63 BC: Pompey captures Jerusalem

4–6 BC: Birth of the Messiah, Jesus Christ

other books offer much proverbial wisdom, timeless in its meaning and application.

Prophetic Books

(*16 books:* Isaiah, Jeremiah, Ezekiel, Daniel, Hosea, Joel, Amos, Obadiah, Jonah, Micah, Nahum, Habakkuk, Zephaniah, Haggai, Zechariah, and Malachi)

The *major prophets* are Isaiah, Jeremiah, and Ezekiel. They derive their name from the length of their books. (Daniel is in a class by itself. It is an *apocalyptic* writing containing highly symbolic language.)

The *minor prophets* are all the others listed. The Jewish canon calls them "The Twelve."

The prophets were powerful figures who spoke for Yahweh, often warning the people to remain faithful to the covenant or face dire consequences. Their words remain as forceful reminders of a just and faithful God who loves justice and requires believers to live faithfully and compassionately.

Catholics accept forty-six Old Testament books as inspired, while the Protestant Bible contains only thirty-nine inspired writings. The discrepancy between Catholic and Protestant Bibles has to do with the ancient versions of the Jewish Scriptures accepted by each group.

When the earliest Greek-speaking Christians took up the Hebrew Scriptures, they turned to the famous Greek translation, the Septuagint, the most common and popular version of the Old Testament used in the early Church. Because it was written in Greek, it was widely used by both Jews and Christians throughout the Roman Empire. The early Church, important Church Fathers, and finally the Council of Trent (1547) accepted this translation as the standard. It is the version that contains forty-six inspired books.

At the time of the Protestant Reformation, the Reformers adopted the official list of inspired works created by Jewish scholars around AD 90. In that year, Jewish scholars who had survived the Roman destruction of the Temple in AD 70 assembled at Jamnia, a city in northern Palestine, to consolidate their sacred books. It was then that they accepted into their official list only thirty-nine books, all of which were written in Hebrew. They dropped seven books that appeared in the Septuagint, books that were written in Greek sometime in the two hundred years before Christ. These seven works, which Catholics recognize as inspired, are 1 and 2 Maccabees, Judith, Tobit, Baruch, Sirach, and the Wisdom of Solomon.

Many Protestant Bibles print the disputed books in a separate section at the back of the Bible. They refer to these books (as well as some passages in Daniel and Esther) as *apocrypha*, that is, "hidden" or withdrawn from common use. Catholics refer to these books as *deuterocanonical*, meaning "a second canon" to indicate that the Jews do not accept them into their official canon.

Tracing God's Covenant

The very first book of the Bible reveals a loving God. This God created humans (Adam and Eve) and kept them alive even though they turned their backs on him. Original Sin disfigured the perfect world God created as humans divided into different nations and languages, causing confusion and suspicion, which led to more sin. But God did not abandon his creatures and renewed his promise to keep humanity alive with Noah at the time of the Flood.

In God's good time, he chose for himself a people—the Israelites—and formed them into his chosen ones. God's covenant with the Israelites began with the call of Abraham (ca. 1900 BC), through whom Yahweh would bless all nations. The covenant with the Chosen People was a special kind of contract marked by loving kindness (*hesed* in the Hebrew). God would always bless and be faithful to his people. In return, Abraham and his descendants were to obey and worship the one true God before all the nations.

The Old Testament books reveal many examples of God's loving kindness. Most notably, Yahweh rescued the Jews from slavery in Egypt (the Exodus) and renewed his covenant with Moses on Mount Sinai (ca. 1300 BC). At Mount Sinai, Yahweh promised the Hebrews a land; in return the people were to live the Law as a concrete demonstration of love for him.

For forty years God's People wandered the desert as a preparation to inheriting the Promised Land. Eventually, they entered Palestine and formed into a strong nation under God's anointed king, King David. David (ca. 1000–961 BC) was an ideal ruler who symbolized for the Jews the hope that one day Yahweh would send a Messiah who would rule with true justice and firmly establish God's peace throughout the world.

The Old Testament reveals how unfaithful the Chosen People were to the covenant. They continually sinned and fell into worship of false gods. Their dissolute living led to the disintegration of a united kingdom. The northern half of the kingdom fell to Assyria in 722 BC, and the southern kingdom of Judah was overrun by Babylonia in 587 BC. The prophet Jeremiah warned against infidelity to the covenant. Jeremiah also promised a New Covenant:

> "The days are coming," says the Lord, "when I will make a New Covenant with the house of Israel and the house of Judah. It will not be like the covenant I made with their fathers. . . . But this is the covenant which I will make with the house of Israel after those days," says the Lord. "I will place my law within them, and write it upon their hearts; I will be their God, and they shall be my people." (Jer 31:31–33)

Other prophets like Amos railed against oppression of the poor, but their words fell on deaf ears.

Captivity in Babylon (587–538 BC) was a low point in Jewish history, but even in exile Yahweh did not abandon his people. Although Israel would never again be politically unified, prophets like the author of Second Isaiah kept alive the hope of an eventual return to the Promised Land. He also promised that God would send a Servant-Messiah who would save the people. When Persia captured Babylonia, the Jews were allowed to return to Israel. There they could once again worship Yahweh in the Temple of the Holy City. Prophets like Ezra and Nehemiah reorganized the Jewish religion and continually reminded the people of God's covenant.

And the Jews needed reminders of God's fidelity because foreign powers—Persians, Greeks, Seleucids, and finally the Romans—in turn ruled them in their homeland. It was during the rule of the Romans that Jesus was born. Through Jesus and in Jesus, Yahweh showed once and for all that he was faithful to his word. Yahweh's covenant was to be a New Testament sealed in the blood of his Son.

KEY OLD TESTAMENT READINGS

Read at least one Scripture passage from each category. Summarize each passage in your journal.

Covenant with Abraham
Genesis 12; 15; 19; 21–22

Moses and the Exodus
Exodus 1–6:13; 7–11; 12:21–41; 13:17–22; 14; 15:19–27; 19–20; 24; 32–34:9

Into the Promised Land
Joshua 3–4

David
1 Samuel 16–19; 2 Samuel 11–13

Prophets Remind Jews to be Faithful to the Covenant
Hosea 2:4–3:5; Amos 2:6–16; Jeremiah 52:4–16

Hope Kept Alive in Captivity
Isaiah 52:13–53:12

It is correct to say that "Jesus is the New Testament," God's covenant with all humanity. Jesus initiates a law of love that requires a change of heart. He is the perfect prophet who fulfilled all prophecies. As God's Son, he is God's perfect spokesperson. The New Testament writings show how his words and his actions reveal God's active presence in the world: saving, redeeming, and healing people.

Jesus' life and ministry fulfilled all the Old Testament prophecies concerning the Messiah's birth, his teaching and healing, his rejection by the leaders, and his Passion, Death, and Resurrection.

As Jeremiah foretold, Jesus was the covenant, signed and sealed in the blood he shed on the cross. His Resurrection ratified, that is, proved, the truth of this covenant. When the Son of God freely gave up his life for our salvation, he initiated a new relationship with all of humanity, not just with Israel. This new relationship requires faith in Jesus as God's Son, our Savior, Lord, and Messiah.

New Covenant—The climax of Salvation History, the coming of Jesus Christ, the fullness of God's Revelation.

inspiration—The guidance given to the human authors of Sacred Scripture so they wrote what God wanted written for our benefit.

Evangelist—A person who proclaims the Good News of Jesus Christ. "The four Evangelists" refers to the authors of the four Gospels: Matthew, Mark, Luke, and John.

The New Testament is about Jesus. It is written for everyone. It continues and fulfills the Old Testament; it does not contradict it. The Old Testament tells us about God's covenant with his Chosen People. The New Testament reveals that our loving God has extended his loving kindness, his salvation, to all people. Jesus is the **New Covenant**. In one way or another, all the New Testament books tell Jesus' story and what our relationship to him should be like.

The Scriptures as Inspired Writings (CCC, 105–108; 135–136)

Catholics believe that God is the true author of the Sacred Scriptures, both the Old and New Testaments. In other words, Catholics believe that the Holy Spirit inspired the human authors of the Bible. **Inspiration**, therefore, refers to the Holy Spirit teaching truth through the Bible without destroying the free and personal activity of the human writer. We must read and interpret the Bible inspired by the same Spirit who wrote it. The Second Vatican Council teaches:

> In composing the sacred books, God chose men and while employed by Him they made use of their powers and abilities, so that with Him acting in them and through them, they, as true authors, consigned to writing everything and only those things which He wanted. (*Constitution on Divine Revelation*, No. 11, see also *CCC,* 106)

The Spirit used the individual talents and insights of the various writers to compose the sacred text. Take, for example, the fact that we have four Gospels. The word *Gospel* means "Good News."

- Jesus is the Good News of God's love and salvation for all of humanity.
- But preaching about Jesus is also good news. To tell others about the Gospel of Jesus and what he accomplished for us is good news.
- Finally, there are four written versions of the Good News, what we call the four Gospels.

Why are there *four* written versions of the one Gospel, the Good News of Jesus? Apparently because God wanted four different perspectives or portraits of Jesus. Each *Evangelist*, or Gospel writer, was a uniquely talented author whom the Holy Spirit inspired to write his version of the Gospel of Jesus. The Evangelists wrote about Jesus for a particular first-century local church. For example, Matthew wrote for a local church of Jewish Christians.

Guided by the Holy Spirit, each Evangelist tailored his materials to speak to the needs and experiences of his audience. In addition, the Evangelist creatively organized the written and oral sources available to him to underscore certain theological themes the Spirit wanted him to stress in his Gospel. Throughout this process of adapting, editing, and organizing, the Holy Spirit was at work to make sure that what the Evangelist wrote was true about Jesus.

Canon of the New Testament (CCC, 120; 138)

The **canon** of the Bible refers to the official list of books the Church considers its inspired writings. The Greek word *kanon* literally means "measuring rod"; later it came to mean "rule" or "norm." There are forty-six Old Testament books and twenty-seven New Testament books on the official list Catholics hold to be inspired by God. The Church considers these the rule or norm for its teaching on faith and morals. Today, Catholic, Orthodox, and Protestant churches all accept the same canon of New Testament books.

The history of the development of the canon is complex. But through the first few hundred years of Church history, it was the Apostolic Tradition of the Church that determined which books were to be included in the canon and which were not under the inspiration of the Holy Spirit. Suffice it to say that by AD 200, the four Gospels, the Pauline Epistles, Acts, and some other Epistles were generally accepted as inspired. By the year 367, Church Father St. Athanasius fixed the New Testament canon at the present twenty-seven books. The Council of Trent (1545–1563) taught as a matter of Church doctrine that this canon was the inspired word God left with the Church.

The Church included in the canon those writings that met the following criteria:

- *Apostolic origin.* The canonical books had their origins with the Apostles, that is, they were inspired by apostolic witnesses. There were other written Gospels circulating in the second century. But only Matthew, Mark, Luke, and John were written in the first century. This lets us know that the Evangelists of these Gospels would have been in contact with Jesus' Apostles and preserved their true testimony about Jesus.

- *Widespread acceptance.* To be included in the canon of the Bible, the Church determined the writings must be widely circulated and accepted. For example, letters written to the Corinthians attributed to Paul had to be accepted throughout the entire Mediterranean world, that is, the Church of that time.

- *Conformity to the rule of faith.* The canonical writings needed to reflect the traditional faith of the early Church about Jesus and his teachings. They could not stray from the truth by offering something that was inconsistent to the other inspired writings. Heretical writings, that is, books that contradicted essential aspects of Christian faith about Jesus, were left out of the canon. In addition, they were usually condemned as dangerous to Christian faith.

canon—The official list of the inspired books of the Bible. Catholics list forty-six Old Testament books and twenty-seven New Testament books in the canon.

St. **Paul**

NON-CANONICAL GOSPELS

Gospel of Thomas

One example of a non-canonical Gospel is the Gospel of Thomas, discovered in 1945 at Nag Hammadi in Egypt. This pseudo-Gospel was probably written late—sometime in the second century—and contains the false teaching of a heresy known as Gnosticism. Unlike the inspired four Gospels, the Gospel of Thomas has no narratives about Jesus' birth, life, miracles, or Passion and Death. It merely contains 114 sayings or "secret teachings" that Jesus supposedly gave to his Apostle Thomas.

Some of these sayings parallel what we have in the canonical Gospels. But others claim to give secret *gnosis* (Greek for "knowledge") that guarantees immortality. These heretical views take a dim view of material reality, including the human body, and clearly contradict Jesus' teaching about the nature of God's Kingdom. Furthermore, the Gospel of Thomas demeans the female gender, even going so far as to teach that a woman cannot enter Heaven without becoming a male. For its failure to conform to the rule of faith, the Gospel of Thomas is considered heretical.

Gospel of Judas

In 2006 the National Geographic Society was behind the effort to release an ancient Coptic text titled the Gospel of Judas, which surfaced in the 1970s after its discovery in an Egyptian desert. The papyrus has been dated to the third and fourth centuries and is in poor shape, with many missing lines and being fragmented in over a thousand pieces. Scholars believe it was a translation of a Greek text, perhaps originally written sometime between AD 130 and 180.

Church Father Irenaeus of Lyons mentioned the Gospel of Judas in his *Against the Heresies* (180), calling it a "fictitious history." Its novelty lies in portraying Judas Iscariot, Christ's betrayer, in a highly favorable light, as the only disciple of Jesus who truly understood him. According to this account, it was to Judas alone that Jesus revealed "true" knowledge about the Kingdom, namely the Gnostic (and rather strange and bizarre) secrets about creation and humanity. For example, one of its teachings was that the God of the Old Testament, Yahweh, was evil. Another states that Jesus' father was Barbelo, the first emanation from a divine essence. The Gospel of Judas also held that an Old Testament figure like Cain, who killed his brother Abel, was really the good brother. Holding such beliefs, it was not much of a stretch for the Gnostics to portray Judas not as a villain who betrayed Christ, but as a hero who collaborated with Christ to have him turned over to the Jewish authorities, so he could escape his earthly form. Gnosticism hated the human body and saw it as evil and unreal.

Reputable scholars see little of accuracy concerning either the historical Jesus or Judas as portrayed in this text. However, it serves its purpose in revealing some of the beliefs of the heretical Gnostic sects that were on the scene in the second to fourth centuries.

 FOR REVIEW

1. What is our primary source of knowledge about Jesus?

2. What is the meaning of the word *testament*? How is Jesus himself the "new" testament?

3. What are the four major divisions of the Old Testament?

4. Why do Protestants only recognize thirty-nine Old Testament books as inspired?

5. List three examples that show how God was faithful to the Chosen People during the Old Testament.

6. What is biblical *inspiration*?

7. Define the term *Evangelist*.

8. Define canon of the Bible. What three criteria did the early Church use before including a particular book in the New Testament canon?

9. Identify the Gospel of Thomas and the Gospel of Judas.

FOR REFLECTION

Read Psalm 23, one of the Old Testament's greatest Psalms. Rewrite this beloved Psalm using a contemporary image of the Lord that appeals to your heart. Include verses of specific times when the Lord carried you.

NEW TESTAMENT BOOKS AND QUICK FACTS (*CCC,* 120; 130; 139)

Language

All twenty-seven books of the New Testament were written in *Koine* (common) Greek, the language spoken by the ordinary people. This Greek dialect was the international language of the Roman Empire. The New Testament also was influenced by the Greek translation of the Old Testament known as the Septuagint.

Dates

Scholars disagree over the exact dates of the various New Testament books. The approximate dates range from the AD 50s (some of Paul's letters) to the early second century (including the Gospel of John). The dates given below were suggested by Catholic Scripture scholar Fr. Raymond Brown in *An Introduction to the New Testament.*[4]

Mark 60–75 (most likely 68–73)

Matthew 80–90 (within a decade on either end)

Luke 85 (within five years on either end)

John 80–110 (probably in the 90s)

Types of Writing

Gospels (4). Narratives about Jesus' public ministry of teaching and healing and his Passion, Death, and Resurrection. "The Gospels are the heart of all the Scriptures 'because they are our principal source for the life and teaching of the Incarnate Word, our Savior'" (*CCC,* 125).

Acts of the Apostles (1). A continuation of the Gospel of Luke, which narrates the spread of the Gospel from the period immediately after Jesus' Resurrection to the imprisonment of St. Paul in the late 50s. It was written within five years of 85, like the Gospel.

Pauline Epistles (13). These were Epistles (letters) written by Paul or circulated in his name by his disciples. They are addressed to communities or to individuals and are arranged in order from longest to shortest.

Early Letters
1 Thessalonians (P) 50–51
2 Thessalonians (D) 51* or 90s

"Great" Letters
Galatians (P) 54–55
Philippians (P) 56
1 Corinthians (P) 56–57
2 Corinthians (P) 57
Romans (P) 57–58

"Prison" Letters
Philemon (P) 55
Colossians (D) 61–63* or 80s
Ephesians (D) 61–63* or 90s

Pastoral Letters
Titus (D) 65* or 95–100
1 Timothy (D) 65* or 95–100
2 Timothy (D) 64–67* or 95–100

P—most scholars agree Paul probably wrote these
D—probably written by a disciple of Paul
* earlier date likely correct if Paul wrote

Hebrews (1). Though called a letter, Hebrews is more likely a sermon or homily and probably not written by St. Paul. It was likely written in the 80s and is usually connected to Paul's circle of assistants.

Catholic Epistles (7). Seven letters written for the entire Church. They are called *catholic* because catholic means "universal" or "for all."

James 62 or 80s or 90s

1 Peter 60–63 or 70–90

Jude 90s

1 John ca. 100

2 John ca. 100

3 John ca. 100

2 Peter ca. 130

Revelation (Apocalypse of John) (1). A highly symbolic work written in the apocalyptic style which tells of visions of God, the risen Lord, and the future. It was written approximately 92–96.

From your own copy of the Bible, transcribe the name of each book of the New Testament with its abbreviation into your journal.

The Formation of **the Gospels**
(CCC, 124–127)

The Gospels are the heart of the Bible, containing the principal teachings about and of Jesus. The Church teaches, and biblical scholars agree, that there were three stages involved in the formation of the Gospels: (1) the period of the public life and teaching of Jesus; (2) a period of oral tradition and preaching by the Apostles and early disciples of Jesus; and (3) the written Gospels themselves. A further explanation follows.

Stage 1: The Public Life and Teaching of Jesus (6–4 BC–AD 30–33)

As noted in the Introduction, Jesus was born around 4–6 BC, lived a normal Jewish life in his youth, learned the carpenter trade, and came onto the public scene probably in AD 28. During his public life, he traveled the countryside and into the small towns, teaching, healing, and proclaiming the coming of God's Kingdom. He made it to Jerusalem for the great feasts. With the cooperation of some religious leaders who saw Jesus as a threat, the Roman prefect—Pontius Pilate—crucified him there, probably in the year AD 30.

Jesus' early disciples, at first frightened and confused, claimed to have seen him after his death and burial. They were convinced that Jesus was alive and glorified as God's Son and present to them by the power of the Holy Spirit. Their hearts burned with love and joy and excitement. It was the fact that the Apostles were eyewitnesses to Jesus' life and ministry that helped to form and preserve the Gospel in this first stage.

Stage 2: Oral Tradition (AD 30–50)

The disciples' lives changed. They began to live in light of the Resurrection. With the help of the Holy Spirit, they now knew that Jesus was the Messiah, the Promised One, the Son of God, and the Lord. The Apostles remembered Jesus' command to "Go out to the whole world; proclaim the Gospel to all creation" (Mk 16:16). They first preached in and around Palestine, announcing the marvelous things God had accomplished in Jesus. The early Christians believed that Jesus was the very fulfillment of God's Old Testament promises. They fully expected to remain pious Jews who believed that Jesus was the New Testament—the New Covenant between God and humanity. However, when their message met with resistance from some in the Jewish community, the Jewish Christians began to preach to Gentiles throughout the Roman Empire. This oral preaching took three key forms:

- *The* kerygma, *or preaching to unbelievers.* The Acts of the Apostles includes several sermons that Peter and Paul preached about Jesus. To help them in this preaching, they and the other Apostles and disciples would have followed a basic outline of Jesus' works, his Death, Resurrection, and Ascension. (Think of it like an outline you might work from in giving an oral report in class.) They would also have used many passages from the Old Testament to show how the prophecies made about the Messiah were fulfilled in Jesus. During this period, the disciples began to assemble collections of material about Jesus—for example, miracle stories, parables, the Passion narrative.

Later Evangelists would have drawn on these sources to help compose their Gospels.

- *The* didache, *or teaching.* This teaching was really further catechetical instruction for those who accepted Jesus. **Catechesis** literally means to "sound down," that is, to repeat the message and explain it in more depth. Early converts needed further knowledge about how to live a more Christ-filled life. Lists of sayings of Jesus, for example, and the Sermon on the Mount were probably assembled to help in this instruction.

- *The* liturgy, *or worship of the Christians.* The way people pray reflects their beliefs. The celebration of the Eucharist helped shape many of the Jesus stories that the Church preserved. Certain key events, teachings, and prayers of Jesus were recalled in the early Eucharistic celebrations. Some examples include Jesus' words at the Last Supper, the Lord's Prayer, and the story of Jesus' Passion. In some cases, different communities slightly varied the wording of what was remembered. However, they all faithfully recounted what Jesus did and said.

The material that was proclaimed, taught, and celebrated during this period of oral tradition was shaped by the different local churches of the day. The early preachers' and teachers' primary interest was to interpret the meaning of the key events, deeds, and sayings of Jesus that God wanted revealed. They wanted to enliven the faith of Christians. As a result, they did not set out to give a detailed biography of Jesus. However, what they remembered, saved, and proclaimed was the heart of Jesus' message—related to the Old Testament and adapted to the audiences who heard it.

It is important to note that although the four canonical Gospels were composed between AD 65 and 100, preaching about Jesus based on oral traditions carried on well into the second century.

Stage 3: The New Testament Writings (AD 50–ca.120)

> Since many have undertaken to compile a narrative of the events that have been fulfilled among us just as those who were eyewitnesses from the beginning and ministers of the word have handed them down to us, I too have decided, after investigating everything accurately anew, to write it down in an orderly sequence for you, most excellent Theophilus, so that you may realize the certainty of the teachings you have received. (Lk 1:1–4)

The final stage in the process was the actual writing of the Gospels and other books of the New Testament. The earliest New Testament writings are the letters of St. Paul. Next came the four Gospels and various other writings like the Acts of the Apostles and the book of Revelation. The passage above from Luke gives a good account of how these compositions were done. Luke examined the sources, including those from eyewitnesses,

catechesis—The process of religious instruction and formation in the major elements of the Catholic faith.

LECTIO DIVINA—THE CHURCH PRAYS WITH SACRED SCRIPTURE (CCC, 2708)

Besides Scripture *study* (as you are doing as part of this course), devotional reading of the Bible is a time-honored way to meet the living God. For centuries Catholics have practiced a method of prayer known as *Lectio Divina*, that is, "sacred reading." The purpose of the sacred reading of God's Word is not necessarily to cover a lot of territory or to use study aids or take notes. Its purpose is simply to *meet* God through his written word and allow the Holy Spirit to lead us into an even deeper union with him. Therefore, it is best to take a short passage, read it slowly and attentively, and let your imagination, emotions, memory, desires, and thoughts engage the written text.

Select Scripture readings from the Mass readings for the day (see www.usccb.org/nab/index.shtml) or choose your own favorite Scripture passage to practice *Lectio Divina*. Use the following steps developed from the Benedictine tradition:

1. *Reading (lectio)*. Select a short Bible passage. Read it slowly, paying attention to each word. If a word or phrase catches your attention, read it to yourself several times.

2. *Thinking (meditatio)*. Savor the passage by reading it again and reflecting on it. This time feel any emotions that may surface or picture the images that arise from your imagination. Pay attention to any thoughts or memories the passage might call forth from you.

3. *Pray (oratio)*. Reflect on what the Lord might be saying to you in this passage. Talk to him as you would to a friend. Ask him to show you how to respond to his Word. How can you connect this passage to your daily life, to the people you encounter everyday? Might there be a special message in this Scripture selection just *for you?* Pay attention to any insights he might send you.

4. *Contemplation (contemplatio)*. Sit in the presence of the Lord. Imagine him looking on you with great love in his heart. Rest quietly in his presence. There is no need to think here—just enjoy your time with him as two friends would.

5. *Resolution*. Take an insight that you gained from your "sacred reading" and resolve to apply it to your life. Perhaps it is simply a matter of saying a simple prayer of thanks. Perhaps it is to be more patient with someone in your life. Let the word the Holy Spirit spoke to you come alive in your life.

For Further Study

Learn more about *Lectio Divina* at the Order of Saint Benedict's website: www.osb.org/lectio

and then organized the material into that beautiful literary form known as the Gospel.

You may ask, "Why did the early Christians wait so long before writing anything down?" In the first century, the ordinary way of teaching and learning was through oral transmission. For his part, Jesus taught in easy-to-remember, vivid stories, short sayings, striking images, poetic language, and similar devices. For their part, his listeners had remarkable memories, especially compared to us today, who are used to the printed word, computers, and visual images. But eventually the oral preaching about Jesus and his teaching had to be committed to writing for three major reasons:

*   *The end of the world was not coming as quickly as the early Christians at first thought it would.* The first generation of Christians believed that Jesus would come back "to judge the living and the dead" sometime in their lifetimes. Why bother to write

anything down? There were more urgent things to do, like preaching the Gospel and preparing for the Lord's return. However, they were wrong about the exact hour of the Second Coming of Christ. Eyewitnesses began to die or, even worse, be put to death. It became increasingly necessary to preserve in a more accurate manner the apostolic testimony concerning Jesus.

- *Distortions were setting in.* This reason is related to the first. The New Testament itself gives evidence that after the Apostles preached in a certain local church, someone would come along and start to distort their message. For example, the Second Letter to the Thessalonians reported a problem that had crept up in a recent local church of converts (see 2 Thessalonians 3:11–15). To combat heretical teachings, the Church needed an objective written record of their beliefs—hence, the New Testament.

- *More instruction was needed.* A written record of the Apostles' preaching could serve as a handy teaching device for those who needed more instruction. Second, writings could also serve as helpful guides in worship services. The Church began rather quickly to include readings from their Sacred Scriptures into Eucharistic celebrations. Finally, the Church could circulate writings, for example, Paul's letters, to the growing Christian communities. They could provide a handy source for further instruction and, thus, help new converts maintain proper belief.

FOR REVIEW

1. What are the different types of writings in the New Testament?

2. What were the three stages in the formation of the Gospels?

3. Identify the terms *kerygma* and *didache*.

4. Why did the early Church finally decide to write the Scriptures?

FOR REFLECTION

What would it mean to call today's Church "Stage 4" of Gospel formation?

How the Church
Interprets the New Testament

(*CCC*, 109–119; 137)

The New Testament requires careful study simply because it is the most important collection of books ever written and assembled. These writings are a key fount of Divine Revelation and a meeting point with God. They tell the story of Jesus, God's Son, and his tremendous love for us. To read the New Testament seriously and prayerfully can help us grow closer to God and to each other.

But how should we read the New Testament? Two important questions arise that are important for all Catholics to consider:

- Do our Sacred Scriptures mean whatever we personally think they mean?

- Are we to take everything in the Scriptures as the absolute, literal truth?

These are good questions. Not all Christians agree on how to answer them. Some Christians do in fact limit the Bible's meaning to what they personally get out of it. Others take a more fundamentalist view, a view that everything in the Bible is absolutely, literally, and historically true, never to be understood symbolically. Catholics, however, believe that the Bible should be read both prayerfully and critically.

To interpret the Bible correctly means paying attention to what the human authors wanted to say and to what God wanted to reveal to us through their words (*CCC*, 109).

Today, many Protestant and Catholic scholars successfully use the historical-literary method of Bible criticism to study the New Testament. Criticism here is not a negative term; rather, it means looking at the biblical texts carefully in their historical and literary contexts. Historical research looks to the customs and ways of thinking at the time the events took place and were written. Literary criticism analyzes the writings themselves. Below we will briefly mention five subcategories of this historical-literary method: *source*, *historical*, *form*, *redaction*, and *textual criticism*. These methods look to the conditions of the time and culture when the authors wrote, "the modes of feeling, speaking and narrating then current" (*CCC*, 110). With the understanding that Scripture must always be read in light of the Holy Spirit who inspired it, answer questions like these:

- What is the larger context surrounding this passage?
- What religious, social, cultural, and historical realities influenced the Scripture writer?

- What was the writer trying to say? What did he actually say? How did he say it?
- How does what the writer wrote fit in with his larger work? with the rest of the New Testament? with the Old Testament?
- For whom was this text being written? What was this audience like? What were its needs? How might the writer have adapted his materials to help this particular audience understand the Gospel?
- What literary device, if any, appears here? How do we normally interpret this kind of literary device? What does this passage mean, taking this device into consideration?

These are the kinds of questions scholars bring to their study of the Scriptures. In addition, Catholic scholars believe that Scripture study is a sacred science, the pursuit of knowledge about God and his dealings with us. Thus, the scholarship takes place prayerfully with the scholars constantly seeking the guidance of the Holy Spirit who inspired the original texts: "Holy Scripture must be read and interpreted according to the same Spirit by whom it was written" (*Dogmatic Constitution on Divine Revelation*, No. 12).

Finally, Catholic scholars always approach their study in a spirit of humility, realizing that they are servants of God's Word. They will look to the Magisterium, the pope and bishops teaching with him, as a final authority for correctly understanding the meaning of Sacred Scripture. Jesus gave Peter and the Apostles, and their successors (the pope and the bishops), the power to teach in his name. He also promised that he would guide them when they were teaching on matters involving Christian faith and morals. The three general criteria the

Magisterium have given commentators to help them interpret Sacred Scripture according to the Spirit who inspired it are:

1. Pay attention to the content and unity of the whole Scripture. This means seeing how everything in the Bible relates to Jesus, who is the center and heart of Scripture.

2. Look at Scripture within "the living Tradition of the whole Church" (*CCC*, 113).

3. "Be attentive to the analogy of faith," that is, "the coherence of the truths of faith among themselves and within the whole plan of revelation" (*CCC*, 114).

The Church reminds us that there are two senses of Scripture: the literal and the spiritual (which has three divisions; see *CCC*, 117).

The *literal sense* is foundational. It refers to what the words of Scripture actually mean using sound rules for interpretation.

The *spiritual sense* refers to how the texts, realities, and events in the Bible can be signs. For example, the *allegorical sense* helps us understand how some event of the Old Testament prefigures Christ, for example, the crossing of the Red Sea symbolizes Christ's victory over death. The *moral sense* refers to how the events in Scripture can help us act justly. The *anagogical sense* (from the Greek word for "leading") helps us see how events lead us to our final destiny—Heaven. For example, the Church on earth is a sign of the heavenly Jerusalem. Given this background on how the Church interprets Scripture, we can turn to uncovering more about the subcategories of the historical-literary method.

Source Criticism

Source criticism tries to determine what source or sources the Gospel and other New Testament writers used to compose their works. For example, when Matthew wrote his Gospel, what did he have in front of him as he set out on his task? What did he take from the oral tradition? What written documents might he have used? Did he use another Gospel to help him in his general outline? One of the most fascinating results of scholarly research on the sources of the Gospels is the so-called "synoptic problem."

The Gospels of Matthew, Mark, and Luke are known as the **Synoptic Gospels**. The term Synoptic Gospel comes from the Greek *synoptikos*, which means "seen together." In studying these Gospels, scholars have noted that Mark contains 661 verses, Matthew has 1,068, while Luke includes 1,149. Matthew reproduces 80 percent of Mark's verses, while Luke replicates 65 percent of Mark's verses. These similarities permit scholars to set out these three Gospels in parallel columns so they can be closely compared. Here is an example:

Synoptic Gospels—The Gospels of Matthew, Mark, and Luke, which, because of their similarities, can be "seen together" in parallel columns and mutually compared.

Matthew 16:13–16	Mark 8:27–29	Luke 9:18–20
When Jesus went into the region of Caesarea Philippi he asked his disciples, "Who do people say that the Son of Man is?" They replied, "Some say John the Baptist, others Elijah, still others Jeremiah or one of the prophets." He said to them, "But who do you say that I am?" Simon Peter said in reply, "You are the Messiah, the Son of the living God."	Now Jesus and his disciples set out for the villages of Caesarea Philippi. Along the way he asked his disciples, "Who do people say that I am?" They said in reply, "John the Baptist, others Elijah, still others one of the prophets." And he asked them, "But who do you say that I am?" Peter said to him in reply, "You are the Messiah."	Once when Jesus was praying in solitude, and the disciples were with him, he asked them, "Who do the crowds say that I am?" They said in reply, "John the Baptist; others, Elijah; still others, 'One of the ancient prophets has arisen.'" Then he said to them, "But who do you say that I am?" Peter said in reply, "The Messiah of God."

Q—An abbreviation for *Quelle* (German for "source"), a common source of sayings of Jesus used by the Evangelists Matthew and Luke in the composition of their Gospels.

This observation has caused speculation concerning the relationship between and among these three Gospels. Perhaps the most widely accepted explanation is that Mark was the first Gospel written, perhaps sometime between AD 67 and 73. It was Mark who "invented" the Gospel form of literature. At a later date, most probably in the 80s, the authors of Luke and Matthew wrote their Gospels. One of their main sources was Mark, from whom they borrowed heavily, including Mark's basic narrative outline.

But scholars also observed that, besides taking large portions of material from Mark's Gospel, Matthew and Luke also have in common another 220–235 verses (in whole or part). Scholars theorize, therefore, that the authors of Matthew and Luke drew on a common source, known as "**Q**" (from the German *Quelle*, meaning "source"). This hypothetical document was not in the form of a Gospel, but was mostly a collection of sayings of Jesus that came down to the evangelists either in written or perhaps oral form.

In addition, scholars note that besides Mark and Q, Matthew and Luke use materials that were unique to each of them, termed "M" and "L," respectively.

Graphically, the relationship between and among the three Synoptic Gospels looks like this:

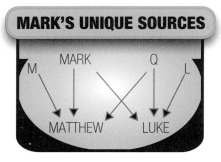

MARK'S UNIQUE SOURCES

Note how the sources Q, M, and L stand together. Remember that Q is a common source for Matthew and Luke; however, Mark did not use it. M has material unique to Matthew; L has material unique to Luke.

Q	M	L
Temptation of Jesus (Mt 4:1–11; Lk 4:1–13)	Coming of the Wise Man (Mt 2:1–12)	Story of the Shepherds (Lk 2:1–20)
The Beatitudes (Mt 5:3–6, 11–12; Lk 6:20–23)	Parable of the Weeds (Mt 14:24–30)	Jesus at Age Twelve (Lk 2:41–52)
Good Fruit (Mt 7:16–20; Lk 6:43–45)	Peter Walking on Water (Mt 14:28–33)	Parable of the Good Samaritan (Lk 10:29–37)
Parable of the Lost Sheep (Mt 18:12–14; Lk 15:3–8)	Parable of the Ten Virgins (Mt 25:1–13)	Zacchaeus Story (Lk 19:1–10)

Historical Criticism

Historical criticism tries to do a number of things. First, it attempts to discover what the evangelists really wanted to say when they wrote a particular text. This is called the *literal sense* of the text, that is, the determination of what the biblical authors intended and conveyed by what they wrote, drawing on knowledge of ancient languages, dating techniques, customs, traditions, archaeology, and the like. It asks questions related to the historical context.

Another major goal of historical research in recent decades is to determine the probability that what the Gospels report about Jesus and his teachings can be traced directly to him. Among the criteria historians have developed to study the historical Jesus are:

- *Linguistic analysis.* Jesus spoke Aramaic, a richly poetic language. It is highly likely that Gospel verses containing Aramaic words, or passages that are easily translated into Aramaic, are traceable to Jesus. Examples include *Abba* (Mk 14:36); *Talitha koum* (Mk 5:41); *Eloi, Eloi, lema sabachthani* (Mk 15:34).

- *Originality ("criterion of dissimilarity").* The argument goes that if a particular saying of Jesus was also common in the Judaism of his day, or resembles the beliefs of early Christians, then you cannot say with absolute certainty that it comes from Jesus. However, if Jesus says something unique and original—something that his contemporaries could not even dream of—then a strong

case can be made that it probably goes directly to him. Key examples would include Jesus' address of God as *Abba* ("papa"), his use of "Amen" to introduce his teachings, the original stories known as parables, and his teaching on how we must love our enemies. The problem with relying only on this criterion, however, is that Jesus may have had many teachings that paralleled Judaism, the religion he was raised in. Jesus is the "head of the body, the Church" (Col 1:18). There is a unity between Christ and the Church (the Church is called the "Bride of Christ"). Because of this unity the words of Jesus would have greatly influenced the beliefs and practices of the Church.

- *Convergence.* If texts do not rely on each other, or do not have the same source, you can make a strong argument that these sayings or events are likely to be authentic. For example, Matthew and Luke did not draw on each other when they wrote their Gospels. Both report (Matthew explicitly and Luke implicitly) that Jesus was born during the reign of Herod the Great in the Judean town of Bethlehem. It is likely that this is historically accurate.

- *Consistency.* If a saying or action "hangs together" with the whole body of Jesus' teaching or actions, then you can make a pretty good case that it is traceable to Jesus. Consider, for example, Jesus' saying that he was free to interpret the meaning of the Sabbath law. It was this unique claim to authority to teach on religious matters that so upset the authorities and led to his death. Harmless teachers of witty sayings do not anger authorities. Those who speak challenging words on their own authority do.

HISTORICAL AND SCIENTIFIC RESEARCH AND THE BIBLE

Believers have absolutely nothing to fear from open-minded, vigorous, honest historical research directed to the historical events depicted in Sacred Scripture. There is no conflict between the religious truths that Scripture reveals and the truths that science or history discover and report. The *Catechism of the Catholic Church* (159), quoting other sources, explains:

> Though faith is above reason, there can never be any real discrepancy between faith and reason. Since the same God who reveals mysteries and infuses faith has bestowed the light of reason on the human mind, God cannot deny himself, nor can truth ever contradict truth. (*Dei Filius* 4: DS 3017)

> Consequently, methodical research in all branches of knowledge, provided it is carried out in a truly scientific manner and does not override moral laws, can never conflict with the faith, because the things of the world and the things of faith derive from the same God. The humble and persevering investigator of the secrets of nature is being led, as it were, by the hand of God in spite of himself, for it is God, the conserver of all things, who made them what they are. (*GS* 36 § 1)

This is why popes have opened up the Vatican archives for researchers. Pope John Paul II even appointed a commission of historians, scientists, and theologians to reexamine the famous case against Galileo Galilei (1564–1642). Galileo and fellow scientist Copernicus both taught that the earth travels around the sun and therefore is not the center of the universe. In trying to protect the traditional view of God's creation of the world, the Church originally condemned Galileo's views as heretical. The result of the 1992 open search for truth was the commission report that said that the judges who condemned Galileo were in error.

Similarly, the Church appreciates the efforts of scientists who help explain the workings of the universe. Their research reveals the marvelous genius of our Creator God who brought everything into existence. Cardinal Baronius (1538–1607), quoted often by Galileo, put it well when he said, "The Bible teaches us how to go to Heaven, not how the heavens go."

Galileo **Galilei**

Simply put, scientific (and historical) research and Christian faith do not exclude each other. Take, for example, the theory of evolution and human life. Nothing in this theory denies or is opposed to the existence of a loving Divine Creator as depicted in Genesis who brought everything into existence out of nothingness. Good science does not, and cannot, say that humans were the result of chance in a random universe. Good science cannot exclude the existence of God who is the first cause of creation.

We must remember that the Bible is not a science book. The Bible is a written record of Revelation. It is inspired by God to reveal *religious* truths. It contains many literary forms, including poetry, parables, prayers, and, of course, historical narratives. One of the main responsibilities of the Magisterium is to help believers identify what are the truths of the faith revealed in the biblical texts and explain how they relate to scientific and historical research. These truths tell us who we are in relation to God and the world he created, who we are as material-spiritual beings made in God's image and likeness, and what our destiny is—eternal life of union with a loving Triune God.

Form Criticism

When we read the daily newspaper, we easily distinguish between various types and styles of writing. For example, it is not difficult to tell the difference between a news article and an editorial or a feature story and a cartoon. Like a newspaper, the New Testament also contains different types of writing. For example, an epistle (letter) is not the same as a Gospel. In addition, within each type of New Testament writing, there are also a variety of literary forms or genres. Form criticism focuses on these literary differences—both the type of New Testament book we are reading and the individual literary units each book contains. Form criticism also studies how these different literary units took on their particular shape during the period of oral tradition.

Form criticism particularly helps us read the Gospels intelligently. For example, two Gospel literary forms are *historical narrative* and *parable*. Each has its own rules for composition and ways of conveying truth. Parables, for example, are stories. Unlike historical narrative, they do not recount "real" events. Thus, we should read a parable like the Good Samaritan for its religious message, not its historical accuracy. As a unique story told by a master teacher, it drives home an important truth: love everyone, including your enemies.

Below is a list of some of the different forms you will meet while studying the Gospels.

FORM	DEFINITION	EXAMPLE
Miracle story: healing or exorcism	usually has these elements: introduction; request for help; Jesus' intervention; result; reaction	Jesus entered the house of Peter, and saw his mother-in-law lying in bed with a fever. He touched her hand, the fever left her, and she rose and waited on him. (Mt 8:14–15)
Miracle story: nature miracle	a powerful sign that shows Jesus' mastery over the elements	He awakened, rebuked the wind and the waves, and they subsided and there was a calm. Then he asked them, "Where is your faith?" (Lk 8:24–25)
Parable	a vivid short story told to convey religious truth, usually with a surprise ending	"The kingdom of heaven is like yeast that a woman took and mixed with three measures of wheat flour until the whole batch was leavened." (Mt 13:33)
Riddle	a question or statement that teases the mind; it requires thought and application	"Amen, I say to you, among those born of women there has been none greater than John the Baptist; yet the least in the kingdom of heaven is greater than he." (Mt 11:11)
Pronouncement story	a passage whose purpose is to set up an important saying of Jesus	cf. Mk 3:1–5, where Jesus heals on the sabbath to show that it is permissible to do so
Hyperbole	a deliberately exaggerated saying to highlight the topic under discussion	"If your hand or foot causes you to sin, cut it off and throw it away." (Mt 18:8)

Controversy	a passage wherein Jesus confronts his opponents	"Then repay to Caesar what belongs to Caesar and to God what belongs to God." (Lk 22:20–26)
Hymn/Prayer	used in early liturgies and incorporated into the Gospels	In the beginning was the Word, and the Word was with God, and the Word was God. (Jn 1:1f)
Revelation discourse	unique to John's Gospel, in which Jesus reveals his identity and demands a decision	"I am the gate. Whoever enters through me will be saved." (Jn 10:9)

Besides the forms listed here, the Gospels contain many others; for example, infancy narratives, genealogies, prophetic sayings, instructions to disciples, wisdom maxims, legal sayings, legends, predictions, proverbs, and the like. By recognizing and appreciating the forms, we are able to read the Gospels much more intelligently.

Redaction Criticism

Writers control their work by selecting material, arranging chapters, organizing their thoughts, editing the various drafts of their work in progress, and so forth. The four Gospel writers worked in the same way. They were both original authors and editors of their Gospels, compiling and adapting their various sources into single, unified works.

USING FORM CRITICISM

Read the following passages. Name the literary form from pages 45–46 that corresponds with each passage and explain why it meets the criteria for this literary form.

1. Mark 8:1–9
2. Matthew 17:19–20
3. Luke 1:46–55
4. John 6:51
5. Mark 1:23–26
6. Luke 12:49
7. Luke 10:29–37
8. Matthew 10:1–12
9. Mark 7:24–30

Redaction criticism focuses on the Evangelists as editors: how and why they arranged their sources the way they did (*redact* means "to edit for publication.") Redaction criticism tries to discover the particular theological slant or insight of the given writer and how this influenced his arrangement of the material.

Each of the four Evangelists paints a slightly different portrait of Jesus, highlighting certain aspects of his person and message. The Church preserved four Gospels because all are necessary to get the full picture of Jesus Christ that the Holy Spirit wished to leave with us. To help us understand the individual Gospels, we should keep in mind that each Evangelist wrote for a particular audience. Also, each Evangelist had a particular theological theme he wished to underscore in his own presentation of the Good News. The value of redaction criticism is that it helps us discover how the theology of each Evangelist, and the needs of his audience, helped shape and give form to his final work.

Briefly, redaction criticism has discovered that:

• Matthew wrote for a Jewish Christian audience. The author stressed how Jesus fulfilled prophecies made to the Chosen People and presented Jesus as the New Moses who gave humanity the new law of love.

- Mark wrote for a local church that experienced great suffering. The author presented Jesus as the Suffering Servant and said that Jesus' followers ought to follow him by accepting the challenges of their own crosses.
- Luke wrote for Gentile Christians. The author highlighted Jesus as the Universal Messiah who brings salvation to all, especially the oppressed, poor, and despised.
- John wrote for various churches around the Roman Empire. He presented a theologically rich view of Jesus as the Word of God, the Bread of Salvation, and the Way, the Truth, and the Life.

Textual Criticism

We do not possess any original manuscripts penned by the Evangelists or any other New Testament writer. However, we do have hundreds of handwritten Greek copies dating from AD 150 until the invention of the printing press. Textual criticism compares the minor changes and mistakes the copyists made down through the centuries so that the translations we have today are as accurate as possible.

Two points are interesting here. First, the differences between the vast majority of these copies are minor. The care with which monks and others transcribed the New Testament books is remarkable. Second, there are by far more copies of the Gospels and other New Testament writings written relatively close to the dates of their composition than of any other ancient writing.

At first, scribes wrote the New Testament on papyrus, a kind of paper made from a reed found in the delta of the Nile River and parts of Italy. Other writing was done on parchment made from the skins of animals. New Testament papyri and parchments reside in various libraries around the world. *Codex Vaticanus*

is the oldest (ca. AD 350) of all the important early collections of the New Testament. Two of the most famous papyri are the John Rylands Greek Papyrus and the Papyrus Bodmer.

There are many different translations of the Bible in hundreds of different languages. St. Jerome's translation of the entire Bible into Latin is known as the *Vulgate* (meaning "common"). His work took place in 383–384 at the request of Pope Damasus, who wanted the Sacred Scripture to be in Latin, the common language of the day. The Vulgate became the Church's official translation of the Bible from the original languages.

Today, we read the Bible in our own language. There are many translations of the New Testament into English, some under Protestant sponsorship, others under Catholic sponsorship. For centuries Protestants have been using the *King James Version* (1611). Contemporary Protestant translations include the following, all of which are available in editions approved for Catholic reading:

- The *New Revised Standard Version* (1990). Using a good sense of English and sound modern scholarship, this is the most important modern revision of the King James Bible.
- *Revised English Bible* (1989). This is the British equivalent of the *Revised Standard Version*.
- *New International Version* (1973–1978). A conservative translation by scholars from thirty-four different denominations. Many excellent study versions of this Bible are available.

Until the twentieth century, Catholics relied heavily on the *Douay-Rheims Version* (1582–1609) and its revision done by Bishop Challoner (1749–1763). The *Douay Bible* is a translation of the Latin Vulgate. In 1943, Pope Pius XII encouraged the translation of the Bible from the original languages. Two English translations by Catholic scholars include:

- *New American Bible* (1952–70; 1987). The Church uses this translation for the readings

Pope **Pius XII**

at liturgies in the United States. It is faithful to the original text, readable, and scholarly. It is the version quoted in this textbook. You can find it online at www.nccbuscc.org/nab/bible/index.htm.

- *The New Jerusalem Bible* (1985). An excellent translation of the French Bible, *La Sainte Bible*, which in turn is an important and scholarly translation from the original languages.

FOR REVIEW

1. What is *Lectio Divina*?

2. What is the historical-critical approach to studying the Bible?

3. What three rules of interpretation should Catholic biblical scholars follow when doing their work?

4. Discuss the difference between the literal and spiritual senses of Scripture.

5. What does source criticism address?

6. What is the so-called "synoptic problem"? Outline an acceptable approach to it.

7. Identify "documents" Q, L, and M.

8. What does historical criticism attempt to do?

9. Explain two methods scholars use to verify the historical reliability of sayings or events in the Gospels.

10. Explain the relationship between Biblical truth and scientific and historical research.

11. List, define, and give an example of five different literary forms found in the New Testament.

12. Define redaction criticism.

13. Identify the major theological concern of each Evangelist. Identify the audience for whom each Evangelist wrote.

14. What is textual criticism?

15. Name two important Catholic translations of the Bible into English.

FOR REFLECTION

Locate any three of the translations listed in the chapter. Copy into your journal their translation of the Golden Rule, Matthew 7:12. Answer: Which translation do you prefer? Why?

CHAPTER SUMMARY POINTS

- Three important Roman historians who allude to the existence of Jesus are Tacitus, Suetonius, and Pliny the Younger.
- The most important Jewish historian who verifies the existence of Jesus is Josephus, the author of *The Jewish Wars* and *Jewish Antiquities*.
- Our primary source of knowledge about Jesus' life is the Gospels.
- The word *testament* means "covenant." Jesus himself is the New Covenant God made with humanity.
- The biblical writings are inspired, that is, the Holy Spirit is the true author of Sacred Scripture. He taught truth without destroying the free and personal activity of the human authors.
- There are forty-six inspired Old Testament writings and twenty-seven inspired New Testament books. These seventy-three books form the canon, or official list, of Sacred Scripture.
- The central focus of the Old Testament is the covenant theme of God's love for the Jewish people. It serves as a preparation for the coming of the Savior.
- The Old Testament is divided into four main categories: the Pentateuch, Historical Books, Wisdom Books, and Prophetic Books.
- The Church included in the canon books that were traceable to the Apostles, gained widespread acceptance, and conformed to the rule of faith.
- There is no essential discrepancy between the truths revealed in the Bible and scientific and historical truth. "The Bible teaches us how to go to Heaven, not how the heavens go."
- The New Testament contains four Gospels, the Acts of the Apostles, thirteen Pauline Epistles, the book of Hebrews, seven "catholic" Epistles, and the book of Revelation.
- There were three stages to the formation of the Gospels: the period of Jesus' life (6 BC–AD 30), the period of oral tradition (AD 30–50), and the period of the New Testament writings themselves (AD 50–ca. 120). The Gospels were composed in the period between AD 65 and 100.
- The oral tradition consisted of the *kerygma*, or preaching to unbelievers; the *didache*, or further instruction in the faith; and *liturgy*, that is, worship.
- Gospels were finally written down because the world did not end as the early Christians expected, heresies were setting in and needed correction, and Christians needed an objective source for further instruction.
- Biblical interpretation must take into consideration what the human authors wanted to say and what God wanted to reveal through their words.
- Catholic biblical scholars must pay attention to the content and unity of the whole Scripture, look at Scripture through the living Tradition of the Church, and be attentive to the analogy of faith.
- The Church teaches that there are two senses of Scripture—the literal sense and the spiritual sense.
- Source criticism tries to determine what the Scripture writers drew on to compose their works.
- The Gospels of Matthew, Mark, and Luke are known as the Synoptic Gospels because they are similar and thus can be read (seen) together.
- When they wrote their Gospels, Matthew and Luke also had a common source—designated "Q" (German for "source"). It contained mostly sayings of Jesus. Matthew also used material known to him alone, designated "M," and Luke used material known to him alone, designated "L."
- Historical criticism attempts to ascertain the literal sense of the Scripture and also judge what is historically verifiable in the text.
- Linguistic analysis, originality, convergence, and consistency are some of the historical methods scholars use to verify the historical reliability of the Gospels.
- Form criticism focuses on the literary differences in each New Testament book and the individual literary units each contains.
- Literary forms in the Gospels are many, including miracle stories, parables, riddles, pronouncement stories, and genealogies.

- Redaction criticism highlights the Evangelists as editors. It studies how they shaped their sources and presented their Gospels in light of their theological points of view and the audiences for whom they were writing.
- Textual criticism compares the changes and mistakes in the various ancient biblical manuscripts that predate the invention of the printing press.
- St. Jerome's translation of the Bible into Latin is known as the Vulgate. Two important Catholic translations of the Bible into English are *The New American Bible* and *The New Jerusalem Bible*.

LEARN BY DOING

1. Read and outline the main features of Pliny the Younger's "Letter to the Emperor Trajan." Search the Internet for it under Pliny, Letters 10:96–97. (You can also find it at this website: http://ccat.sas.upenn.edu/jod/texts/pliny.html).

2. Read and report on the entry titled "Early Historical Documents on Jesus Christ" in the *Catholic Encyclopedia* online. You can find the encyclopedia at the New Advent website: http://home.newadvent.org.

3. Select a favorite verse from one of the Gospels. Find how it is translated in a foreign language you are studying, for example, Spanish. Copy the foreign-language translation, along with its English equivalent, into your journal. You can find many Bible translations at this website: www.biblegateway.com.

4. *Old Testament prophecies about Jesus.* Check out the following Old Testament prophecies concerning Jesus. Write in your journal the Old Testament passage and a corresponding New Testament passage that shows its fulfillment.

   a. **Born in Bethlehem:** Micah 5:1 (*Mt 2:1; Lk 2:4–7*)

   b. **To be born of a virgin:** Isaiah 7:14 (*Mt 1:18; Lk 1:26–35*)

   c. **Betrayed by a friend for thirty pieces of silver:** Zechariah 11:12; Psalm 41:9 (*Mk 14:10; Mt 26:14–15*)

   d. **Soldiers divided his garments and gambled for his clothing:** Psalm 22:19 (*Mt 27:35*)

   e. **Hands and feet would be pierced:** Psalm 22:17 (*Jn 19:18*)

   f. **Vicarious sacrifice:** Isaiah 53:4–6, 12 (*Mt 8:16–17; Rm 4:25; 5:6–8: 1 Corinthians 15:3*)

   g. **Resurrection of Jesus:** Hosea 6:2; Psalms 16:10; 49:16 (*Lk 24:6–7; Mk 16:6–7*)

5. Do an Internet search on either the Gospel of Thomas or Gospel of Judas. Identify one of the sayings in these Gnostic works that is clearly contrary to the canonical Gospels.

6. Read paragraph 11 and the entire paragraph 12 of the *Dogmatic Constitution on Divine Revelation*. Answer the following:
   - How did God use the writers of Scripture?
   - List three literary forms mentioned in the document.

7. Complete both of the following assignments:
   - Read Matthew 4:1–11 and Luke 4:1–13, the descriptions of Jesus' temptation in the desert. Compare and contrast the two versions.

- Read Matthew 5:3–6, 11–12 and Luke 6:20–23, the accounts of the Beatitudes. Explain the reason for the differences in the settings.

8. Read Matthew 4:12–17. Complete the following:

   - From a biblical dictionary read about and record four historical facts about Capernaum, an important city in Jesus' ministry.

   - From a Bible atlas, look at a map of Galilee in the time of Jesus. Note the location of Capernaum. Where is it in relationship to the Sea of Galilee? How far is it from Nazareth?

   - Look up these two Aramaic passages in the New Testament: *Talitha koum* (Mk 5:41) and *Eloi, Eloi, lema sabachthani* (Mk 15:34). Give their translation.

9. Complete this exercise in redaction criticism on the genealogy of Jesus. First, read Luke 3:23–28. Next, read Matthew 1:1–17. In your journal, list at least three major differences you find between the two. Based on your understanding of Luke and Matthew's audiences, answer these questions:

   - Why do you think Luke ends his genealogy this way: "Jesus . . . son of Adam, Son of God"? How does this differ from Matthew's version? From a redaction critic's point of view, why does this make sense?

   - How many names do the genealogies have in common? Consult a biblical commentary to explain these differences. Write your explanation.

   - Do the genealogies mean to suggest that Joseph is Jesus' natural father? Explain. (Check a commentary or an explanatory note in your Bible to help you answer this question.)

10. Do an Internet search on recent archaeological finds as they relate to the New Testament. Report on one of the discoveries and discuss its significance for New Testament studies.

PRAYER LESSON

Dear Jesus,

You lived "One Solitary Life," but today the nations of the world bow down before you. So do I.

But at times, Dear Lord, I feel like I am living one solitary life, too. No one notices me. My accomplishments often do not stand out, no matter how hard I try. I get lonely.

Help me realize that "If God is for us, who can be against us?" (Rm 8:31). If you stay at my side, I will never be lonely. With you as my friend, I have everything I need. Help me to know and to experience your love for me.

And, Jesus, I promise to take your love and share it with someone else. Amen.

- *Reflection:* Call on the Holy Spirit to help you to see with the eyes of Christ. Imagine the good Christ sees in you.
- *Resolution:* Be Christ to a lonely classmate or family member today by going out of your way to speak a kind word to them or do a good deed for them.

The New Testament
World of Jesus

He came to Nazareth, where he had grown up, and went according to his custom into the synagogue on the sabbath day. He stood up to read and was handed a scroll of the prophet Isaiah.

–Luke 4:16–17

CHAPTER **OVERVIEW**

JESUS **OF NAZARETH**

Truly knowing Jesus involves accepting him into our lives through the grace and interior help of the Holy Spirit.

PALESTINE: **THE HOLY LAND**

The Holy Land at the time of Jesus is described in its geography, major regions, and prominent cities.

LANGUAGE AND DIALECT **OF JESUS' TIME**

Jesus spoke Aramaic. This language, along with Hebrew, Greek, and Latin, helps us to appreciate certain aspects of the New Testament in a richer context.

RELIGIOUS FEASTS AND **PRACTICES OF JESUS' TIME**

The role of the Temple, the place of the synagogue, along with Passover and other Jewish religious feasts make up a key part of Jesus' life.

THE POLITICAL CLIMATE **IN FIRST-CENTURY PALESTINE**

Events like the Maccabean Revolt, rulers like Herod, and requirements under Roman law like paying taxes contributed to the life and ministry of Jesus.

JEWISH BELIEFS **AND PRACTICES**

The New Testament is deeply rooted in the Jewish people, their religious beliefs, practices, affiliations, and expectations for a Messiah.

RELIGIOUS SECTS **IN JESUS' TIME**

The Sadducees, Pharisees, Essenes, and Zealots were four important religious sects that were viable during New Testament times.

OTHER PEOPLE IN **THE NEW TESTAMENT**

Tax collectors, common people, Gentiles, and women were among special groups that had an impact on Jesus and the New Testament.

"To what shall I compare this generation? It is like children who sit in marketplaces and call to one another, 'We played the flute for you, but you did not dance, we sang a dirge but you did not mourn.'"

—Matthew 11:16–17

He spoke to them another parable. "The kingdom of heaven is like yeast that a woman took and mixed with three measures of wheat flour until the whole batch was leavened."

—Matthew 13:33

Jesus of **Nazareth**

Closely examine the two Gospel quotations above and the one on page 52. Though short, they reveal some important facts about Jesus' life. For example, we learn in the first two passages that Jesus was a keen observer of ordinary people. He watched the games of children and knew how a housewife made bread. Further, he used vivid images in his teaching. In the first passage, he compared those who refused to believe in him to whiny children at play. In the second, he compared the activity of God's Kingdom to the subtle effect of leaven (yeast) on bread.

Finally, the third passage reveals several other interesting things about Jesus:

1. He came from Nazareth.
2. He customarily prayed in the synagogue on the Jewish day of rest—the Sabbath.
3. Jesus could read.
4. Further, Jesus could read Hebrew, since the Sacred Scriptures of the Chosen People were written in this language.

From this very brief passage, we can conclude, therefore, that Jesus was an educated, literate, observant Jew.

It is amazing the gold you can mine about Jesus by carefully reading even the briefest of Gospel passages. But consider this dialogue between a recent convert to Christianity and a non-believing friend:

"So you have been converted to Christ?"

"Yes."

"Then you must know a great deal about him. Tell me: What country was he born in?"

"I don't know."

"What was his age when he died?"

"I don't know."

"How many sermons did he preach?"

"I don't know."

"You certainly know very little for a man who claims to be converted to Christ."

"You are right. I am ashamed at how little I know about him. But this much I do know: Three years ago I was a drunkard. I was in debt. My family was falling to pieces. My wife and children would dread my return home each evening. But now I have given up drink; we are out of debt; ours is now a happy home. All this Christ has done for me. This much I know of him."[5]

The new Christian in this story may not have known many facts about Jesus' life, but he really knew the Jesus who turned his life around. An important goal of reading the Gospels and learning background information on Jesus and his times is to get a clearer picture of this remarkable person who revolutionized human history. God desires that everyone come to knowledge of the truth, that is, Jesus Christ (see *CCC*, 74). This will require that we, like the new convert, accept—through the grace and interior helps of the Holy Spirit—Jesus into our lives.

FACTS ABOUT THE WORLD OF JESUS

Listed below are facts about Jesus and his times. Research and write about three other similar facts about Jesus. Plan to share them with your classmates.

- The population of Palestine in Jesus' day was about two million.

- We don't have a picture of Jesus dating from the first century because the second commandment forbade "graven images," which the Jews interpreted to mean portraits were forbidden.

- Jesus was not the only wonder worker of his day.

- The 33-foot long papyrus rolls used to record them determined the length of literary works in Jesus' day.

- The New Testament records that Jesus wrote only once.

- It was not considered unmanly for Jewish males of Jesus' day to outwardly show their emotions.

- In the Mediterranean-Judean background of Jesus, the achievements of the son were seen as a very direct reflection on the merits of his mother.

FOR REFLECTION

How would you explain the difference between "knowing of" Jesus and "really knowing" him?

Palestine: **The Holy Land**

Jesus' public ministry took place in the geographic area the Jews of New Testament times referred to as the Promised Land, the Holy Land, the Land of Israel, the Land of Judah, or simply the Land. The Greeks called this region *Palestine* after the Philistines, the seafaring pirates who once lived in the northern coastal areas. (Since the Philistines were great enemies of Israel, Jews hated this name.) Roughly the shape of a rectangle, Palestine stretches 145 miles north to south (from Dan to Beersheba) and from 25 miles wide in the north to its greatest width of 87 miles near the Dead Sea in the south.

Palestine has always held a strategic place in world history—the keystone of the "fertile crescent." It bridges two continents, playing a key international commercial, political, and cultural role. In the ancient world, it served as the crossroads for Egyptian, Syrian, and Persian expansions and later became an attractive target for the political conquests of Greece and Rome.

Geography

The geography of Palestine includes four major terrains. There is a coastal plain along the Mediterranean Sea from the Phoenician city of Sidon in the north to Gaza in the south. Jesus made only a brief visit to this region to Sidon and Tyre.

A second type of terrain is the dominant geographical feature in Palestine—a mountain range

The Road **to Bethlehem**

running north and south, paralleling the Mediterranean seacoast about fifty miles inland. On the crest of this chain the Jews built some of their principal cities, including Jerusalem and Bethlehem. West of

WHAT HAPPENED IN THE HOLY LAND?

Check the following New Testament references and the accompanying map. Write the correct location where each event took place.

- Where did the resurrected Jesus eat a meal with two disciples? (Lk 24:13)

- To which city was the traveler in the parable of the Good Samaritan going? (Lk 10:30)

- To what did Jesus compare Chorazin and Bethsaida? (Mt 11:20–22)

- Where was the birthplace of Peter, Andrew, and Phillip? (Jn 1:44)

- Where did the resurrected Jesus appear to the Apostles in John's Gospel? (Jn 21)

- Where did Jesus give sight to a blind man (Lk 18:35–43) and dine with Zacchaeus? (Lk 19:1-10)?

- Where did Jesus meet a woman at a well and reveal that he was the living water? (Jn 4:5)

Next, do an Internet search and download some pictures that illustrate different archaeological scenes from first-century Palestine. Create a PowerPoint® presentation that uses at least seven pictures you found in your research. Three sources to begin your research are:

- EIKON Image Database for Biblical Studies from Yale Divinity School: http://research.yale.edu:8084/divdl/eikon/index.jsp

- Holy Land Photos: www.holylandphotos.org

- BiblePlaces.com: www.bibleplaces.com

this mountain range were arable lands while to their east was a barren wilderness. The bulk of Jesus' activities took place in this region.

East of the mountains is the third type of terrain of Palestine—the great Rift Valley, through which flows the meandering Jordan River. Rising in the northern mountains, this river widens into the beautiful freshwater Sea of Galilee (also called Lake Gennesaret or Lake Tiberias in the New Testament) and then narrows into a fertile valley on its way to the saltiest of all bodies of water in the world—the Dead Sea. John the Baptist's ministry took place on both banks of the lower Jordan River where Jesus himself was baptized.

The fourth geographical terrain in Palestine is Transjordan—the hilly terrain east of the Jordan River and the Dead Sea. To the far north lies the famous Mount Hermon, which may have been the site of Jesus' Transfiguration. In the area of the Decapolis, the Scriptures report that Jesus drove an army of demons into a herd of pigs that threw itself off a cliff (see Mark 5:1–13).

Important Regions and Cities

The regions of Galilee, Samaria, and Judea figured prominently in Jesus' ministry.

Galilee in the north was the center of Jesus' earthly ministry. It was a relatively rich land of fertile, rolling hills, ruled in Jesus' lifetime by Herod

Antipas (4 BC–AD 37). The farmers and shepherds were somewhat prosperous because of the fertility of the land. The Sea of Galilee provided a livelihood for many fishermen. Peter and his father and brothers would have been among these. The population in Galilee was mainly Jewish, but many non-Jews also could be found in the area. This made Galileans more cosmopolitan in outlook. Judean Jews tended to look down on Galileans because of their more frequent relations with their non-Jewish neighbors to the north. Judean Jews also noticed that the Galileans spoke with a unique Aramaic dialect. Still, many Galilean Jews were very zealous about their religion.

Jesus and most of his Apostles were Galileans. Jesus grew up in Nazareth, a small town in Galilee of about 1,200 people. Nazareth lay two miles off the main road through southern Galilee. Many of the picturesque details that color Jesus' parables originated in his keen observation of Galilean life: birds of the air, flowers brilliantly arraying the fields, barns filled with grain, the sower planting his seeds in the fields, fishing nets straining under a heavy catch.

In recent decades, archaeologists have unearthed the Hellenistic city of Sepphoris, the former impressive capital of Galilee built by Herod Antipas. It was about an hour's walk from the small town of Nazareth and might have provided work for the carpenters Joseph and Jesus, although the Gospels do not say so one way or the other. During his public life, however, Jesus may have avoided this city since it was a power center for King Herod Antipas and others who opposed Jesus.

Other important cities in Galilee include Cana, Bethsaida, and Capernaum. Jesus performed his first miracle at Cana. He cured a blind man at Bethsaida and walked on water near this place. Capernaum served as the headquarters of Jesus' Galilean ministry. He most likely stayed at the house of the Apostle Peter. He frequently taught in Capernaum's synagogue. Jesus also performed many miracles in and around Capernaum and paid the Temple tax while residing there. A recent archaeological dig discovered a fourth-century synagogue in Capernaum. It most likely stood on the very location where Jesus once preached. Nearby, archaeologists have unearthed the fascinating ruins of a fifth-century church that may have been built on Peter's house.

Samaria was in the north-central region of the Holy Land, directly south of Galilee. The Samaritans descended from foreigners who intermarried with the old northern Israelite tribes at the time of Assyria's conquest of the northern Kingdom. Jews and Samaritans alike recognized Abraham as their common father. However, Jews viewed the Samaritans as foreigners, perhaps only a notch above the hated **Gentiles**.

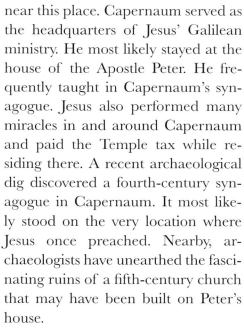

The Sea **of Galilee**

Gentiles—A term for non-Jews.

Like the Sadducees, the Samaritans accepted only the Law of Moses and thus considered sacred only the first five books of the Bible (the Pentateuch). Although monotheistic, they rejected the Temple at Jerusalem because they believed God chose Mount Gerizim as the proper place of worship. Jews looked on Samaritan worship as false. The Judeans destroyed the Mount Gerizim Temple in 128 BC, thus increasing the hate between the two ethnic groups. Galilean Jews usually avoided Samaria if they could on their pilgrimages south to Jerusalem, as Samaritans would often swoop down from the hills to attack them.

Although Jesus did not allow his Apostles to preach to the Samaritans (Mt 10:5), he himself was very loving toward them, even using one of them as the hero of his Good Samaritan parable (Lk 10:30–35). Jesus was also kind to a Samaritan woman (Jn 4:1–42) and praised a Samaritan leper for coming back to thank him for his cure (Lk 17:16). Some of Jesus' enemies tried to insult him by calling him a Samaritan (see John 8:48).

When the earliest Christians began their missionary work, they turned first to the Samaritans. Interestingly, today there still exists a Samaritan church of between five and six hunderd who meet on Mount Gerizim to offer sacrificial paschal lambs. Economically, Samaria was fairly prosperous. Its most important city was Samaria, a pagan city at the time of Jesus' ministry.

Judea in the south of Palestine was a dry, barren, craggy region. Its main inhabitants were the Jews who returned to the Holy Land after the captivity in Babylon. Many Jewish leaders settled in Judea, centering their life on the Temple. In the heart of Judea—lofted on two hills 2,255 to 2,400 feet above sea level—was Jerusalem, the political, economic, and religious center of Judaism. Most of the Judean population lived in this city or in Jericho.

As it is today in Israel, Jerusalem was the main city in Judea. The Jerusalem of Jesus' time featured many recently completed building projects. During his reign, Herod built a wall around the New City and constructed a theater, an amphitheater, a hippodrome, and a beautiful palace for himself in the Upper City. His greatest accomplishment, however, was the rebuilding of the Second Temple, one of the building wonders of the ancient world. Jerusalem's population at that time is hard to determine. Some scholars put it at 55,000 to 70,000 people, with as many as another 120,000 Jews from around Palestine and the Roman Empire flocking to the Temple area for the major Jewish festivals.

Jews who lived in Jerusalem worked at many different trades: wool merchants, leather workers, olive oil processors, bakers and butchers, manufacturers of ointments and resins, building tradesmen, traders of grain, and other occupations involving the production of food. Since the Temple was a major cultural and religious center, many Jews worked in various trades associated with it, for example, as scribes who interpreted the Law.

Other Judean cities of interest are Bethlehem, the birthplace of Jesus; Bethany, the home of his friend Lazarus, whom he raised from the dead; and Jericho, a town where Jesus healed a blind man and met a famous tax collector, Zacchaeus.

Southern Judea contained a barren wilderness where Jesus retreated to after his Baptism (Mt 4:1). There you can also find the 53-mile-long Dead Sea, which, at 1,300 feet below sea level, is the lowest point on earth. Its salt content is as high as 35 percent

The Dead **Sea**

(contrast this with Utah's Great Salt Lake at 18 percent and the ocean's at 3.5 percent). It is impossible for a person to sink in this body of water.

Finally, south of Judea was Idumea, which was brought under Jewish control by John Hyrcanus in 125 BC. This area was absorbed into Judea under Herod the Great's reign. It did not figure into Jesus' life.

FOR REVIEW

1. Where did Palestine get its name?
2. What are the four geographic areas of Palestine?
3. List two major cities that figure into Jesus' life that are located in Galilee and Judea.
4. Who were the Samaritans? Discuss two of their beliefs.

FOR REFLECTION

Why do you think God chose the particular time and place that he did to be incarnated?

Language and Dialect of Jesus' Time

Jesus spoke Aramaic, a Semitic language closely related to Hebrew and originally spoken by tribes from parts of ancient Syria and Mesopotamia. More precisely, the Gospels hint that Jesus spoke a Galilean version of western Aramaic, considered mainly as a regional dialect by Aramaic speakers in Judea. Note how Peter's tongue betrayed him when he denied knowing Jesus:

> A little later the bystanders came over and said to Peter, "Surely you too are one of them; even your speech gives you away." (Mt 26:73)

Aramaic became the official language of Assyria and later of the Persian Empire. It supplanted the native tongues of conquered peoples. When Jews returned to Palestine from Babylon in the sixth century BC, they adopted Aramaic in place of Hebrew as the common language of their land.

Although the Sacred Scriptures were read in Hebrew, in Jesus' day many people did not understand Hebrew. So the Scriptures were translated into Aramaic paraphrases (known as *Targums*) when the sacred Hebrew texts were read aloud in the synagogues. The Gospels (written in Greek) retain several Aramaic sayings of Jesus like *Ephphatha* ("be opened") and *Talitha koum* ("Little girl, get up!"). The Gospels also contain Aramaic place names like *Gethsemane* ("Oil Press") and *Golgotha* ("Place of the Skull"). They also use the Aramaic word *bar* for "son of," as in Bar-Jonah, Bartholomew, and Barabbas. Perhaps the most important example is the Aramaic word Jesus used when he addressed God as "Father"—***Abba***.

Abba—An Aramaic term of endearment meaning "daddy." Jesus used this word to teach that God is a loving Father.

Scholars believe some Hebrew might still have been spoken commonly during Jesus' lifetime, especially in the southern province of Judea. It may be that Jesus himself knew a little Hebrew, learned in the synagogue, and spoke it on his visits to Jerusalem or in his debates with the learned scribes and Pharisees.

The common language throughout the Roman Empire at this time was a colloquial Greek known as *Koine* ("common") Greek. It became the favored spoken language in the Near East because of Alexander the Great's conquests in the fourth century BC. Jesus may have had a limited knowledge of this language, finding it useful in his trade as a carpenter, especially if he did any work in a large city like Sepphoris. He may have spoken to Pilate in Greek.

Finally, some Latin was probably used in Palestine because of the presence of the Roman occupation forces. But Latin was more likely spoken only by and for the Roman officials. Almost certainly, Jesus did not speak Latin. Koine Greek was the common language of the Empire—the language of commerce and education. Jews who dealt with foreigners most often spoke Koine Greek with them.

Whether or not Jesus knew any Hebrew or Greek is an ongoing debate among biblical scholars. What most do not question is that his native tongue was Aramaic, the ordinary, everyday language of Jews in the first century AD. Interestingly, some scholars have taken the Gospel words of Jesus—written in Greek— and translated them back into his mother tongue, Aramaic. Their studies reveal much about Jesus' use of Semitic speech

forms which are very poetic and memorable—using techniques like alliteration, assonance, play on words, and parallelism. Some examples include:

1. *Parallel statements.* Aramaic, like most Semitic languages, often expresses an important thought a second time in a slightly different form. Both forms are complete, saying the same thing. An example:

> Give to the one who asks of you, and do not turn your back on one who wants to borrow. (Mt 5:42)

2. *Comparisons.* Except for Arabic, the Semitic languages do not have a special way to express the comparative and superlative degrees. For example, they do not have the equivalents of our words "better" or "best." Therefore, if you want to say that Jesus is the best or greatest of all kings, in Hebrew or Aramaic you would have to say "King of Kings." Here's another example from Jesus' teaching, where he is quoting an Old Testament law:

> You have heard that it was said, "You shall love your neighbor and hate your enemy." (Mt 5:43)

The Old Testament was not teaching that you must go out of your way to literally hate your enemies. What it was teaching was that the Jews should love their neighbor (defined as a fellow Jew) more than the enemy. Jesus took this teaching a step further:

> But I say to you, love your enemies, and pray for those who persecute you. (Mt 5:44)

INRI

Do you know what the INRI means on a crucifix? The meaning comes from the custom of Roman authorities of posting the crime of condemned criminals on their crosses. The idea was to advertise the crime to thwart others from even thinking about committing something similar. In Palestine, Romans would have affixed a sign in three languages: Greek, Hebrew, and Latin. At least one of these languages could be understood by visitors to Jerusalem during the religious festivals. INRI abbreviates the Latin words that would have been posted: *Iesus Nazarenus Rex Iudeorum,* which translates to "Jesus of Nazareth, King of the Jews."

Jesus calls on his followers to love everyone as a brother or sister.

3. *Exaggeration.* Use of hyperbole, or exaggeration, to drive home a point was common in Aramaic. English uses this technique, too, when we say things like "This test is going to kill me" or "I could eat a million of these." Exaggerated statements are to be taken figuratively. When Jesus said "Blind guides, who strain out the gnat and swallow the camel!" (Mt 23:24), he was saying that some of the teachers stressed others' small faults while ignoring their own sinfulness.

 FOR REVIEW

1. What was Jesus' native tongue? How do we know this?
2. What other languages might have been spoken in first-century Palestine?
3. What language did Jews speak when dealing with foreigners?

FOR REFLECTION

• Read Matthew 5:29. What form of speech does this represent? Why can we be fairly certain that Jesus did not mean it to be taken literally?

• Design your own *titulus* (small sign with a title) for a crucifix that announces to the world what you believe about Jesus of Nazareth. You can use abbreviations on the design. Separately, write out a short explanation of your titulus.

Religious Feasts and **Practices of Jesus' Time**

Jesus' practice of his Jewish faith revolved around the synagogue, Temple, and religious feasts.

Synagogue

Jesus learned his Jewish religion from his parents and from praying and studying in Nazareth's *synagogue*. Synagogue comes from the Greek word for "assembly." Many larger towns had more than one synagogue, and Jerusalem may have had hundreds. The synagogue served three main purposes:

1. It was a house of prayer where Scriptures were read and Yahweh was worshiped.
2. It was a place of discussion for legal settlements.
3. It was the local school.

Synagogues were typically built in towns once ten or more men could be assembled. First-century synagogues were similar from town to town, but none were *exactly* the same. (Over one hundred have been

discovered in Palestine, mainly in or near Galilee.) Typically found near rivers or springs so worshipers could purify themselves in running water, the rectangular insides of synagogues had stepped stone benches on three sides, with higher seats set aside for those of a more prestigious position. The scroll containing the Law (Torah) and the scroll containing the writings of the Prophets were kept in a cabinet called an *ark*.

Synagogues were opened three times a day for those who wished to pray. There were special services on market days, Mondays, and Thursdays. The most important day for regular worship was the sabbath (Saturday). Once ten men over the age of thirteen assembled, the simple service could begin. Sacrifices were not offered, nor did priests or Levites play any special role. Ordinary townsfolk conducted the service, though a "leader of the synagogue" (e.g., Jairus in Lk 8:41) was appointed to maintain the building and organize the meetings. His assistant was in charge of the sacred scrolls, which he handed to the readers for the day.

Typically, the congregation stood, facing Jerusalem, and recited various prayers, beginning with the confession of faith known as the *Shema* (Dt 6:4). Other prayers included the Eighteen Benedictions—prayers of praise and thanksgiving to God. The key part of the service was the careful reading of the Torah in Hebrew, followed by selected readings from the Prophets, again in Hebrew. These readings were translated simultaneously during the respective readings. All of this was done in a standing position. Then, the leader of the synagogue invited one of the guests—preferably someone well-educated or well-traveled—to explain the meaning of the readings in a homily. On one occasion, Jesus was invited to preach in Nazareth. Also, St. Paul frequently proclaimed God's Word in synagogues. The synagogue service ended with a brief prayer by the leader. It was also the custom for synagogue worshipers to leave alms for the poor—in money or in other gifts—as they left the place of worship.

Temple

For Jews, the one and only Temple was in Jerusalem. The Temple was where the Jews offered sacrifices to God. It was the holy place where Jews believed God dwelled in a special way. Only the priestly caste had a role in Temple worship. It was the priests who were able to sacrifice the unblemished lamb to Yahweh on a daily basis. Only the high priest could enter the most sacred space inside the Temple—the Holy of Holies—once a year, on Yom Kippur, the Day of Atonement.

The Temple standing during New Testament times was the third one constructed in Jerusalem. The first, Solomon's Temple, was destroyed by the Babylonians in 587 BC. The second Temple, that of Zerubbabel, was replaced by Herod the Great's magnificent Temple.

Depiction of the **Third Temple**

Construction of this third Temple began in 20–19 BC (see Jn 2:20). It took ten thousand workers supervised by one thousand priests to finish building the Temple in ten years. However, the work of decorating the Temple was still going on in Jesus' day. The Temple was completely finished in AD 64, only six short years before the Romans leveled it during the First Jewish Revolt (66–70).

The Temple was a marvelous structure, 2,350 feet in its perimeter, with eight main gates. Around the altar was a courtyard reserved for priests. Next were the courtyard of Israel (for males) and then the courtyard for women. Beyond that was the courtyard of the Gentiles. No Gentile could cross this courtyard under penalty of death.

The Law required Jews to pay a Temple tax and obligated Jewish men to make a pilgrimage to Jerusalem on the three major feasts of Passover, Pentecost, and Tabernacles. However, not all Jews could make it to the holy city for all the feasts.

Jewish Feasts

As mentioned, Passover, Pentecost and Tabernacles were the major Jewish feasts.

Passover (Pesah) was the most important Jewish feast because it celebrated the Chosen People's liberation from Egypt. The feast of Passover involved the ritual slaughter of the paschal lamb and the eating of a seder meal in the holy city of Jerusalem to commemorate the Exodus. Jesus' Last Supper was set around a Passover meal that he celebrated in Jerusalem. The Last Supper anticipated Jesus' sacrifice on the cross, the saving event that frees all people from sin and death.

Pentecost was a feast held fifty days after Passover. The word Pentecost means "fiftieth." Pentecost was originally a harvest festival. However, by New Testament times, it celebrated Yahweh's giving of the Law to Moses, the Sinai covenant.

Tabernacles (Booths) was a fall harvest celebration. Pilgrims to Jerusalem built huts out of branches to recall the time that Jews spent in the wilderness. They approached the Temple in procession waving branches while praising God. John's Gospel tells us that Jesus taught in the Temple during this feast (Jn 7:14–39).

The Gospel of John (10:22) also reports that Jesus traveled to Jerusalem for *Hanukkah* (Feast of Dedication), which was held in December to commemorate the Temple's rededication in 164 BC after it was profaned by the foreign ruler Antiochus IV.

FOR REVIEW

1. What took place in synagogues?
2. Describe a typical Sabbath service in Jesus' day.
3. List three facts about the Jerusalem Temple.
4. Which were the three great Jewish religious feasts? What did each celebrate?
5. What is Jesus criticizing in Matthew 23:2, 6?

FOR REFLECTION

Transcribe the Shema (Dt 6:4) and the verse that follows (Dt 6:5) into your journal. Write a short reflection on what it would mean concretely for you to love the Lord "with all your heart, and with all your soul, and with all your strength."

The Political Climate **in First-Century Palestine**

Recall that when Jesus was born, Palestine was part of the Roman Empire. Romans considered their empire to be the civilized world; outsiders were barbarians. The Roman Empire was large geographically. It extended as far north as Great Britain in northern Europe to Egypt in the southeastern part of the Mediterranean basin.

With the empire came a state of peace and security—the famous *Pax Romana* (Peace of Rome) and its other good effects: a common language, an intricate system of roads, a fair and just legal system, and a strong military force. Rome was intent on putting down piracy and banditry—a real problem in some parts of the empire, for example, in Samaria. Its aim was to guarantee workable trade and communication systems throughout the Empire. The relative stability brought by the Romans enabled Christian missionaries to evangelize peacefully throughout the empire, especially in the cities. This helps explain why Christianity spread so rapidly in the first few decades after Jesus' Resurrection.

Most Jews, however, hated Roman rule, seeing it as another in a long line of oppression. For almost six centuries, the Jews had been under the thumbs of foreign rulers: Babylonians, Persians, Greeks, and Seleucids. This last foreign dynasty, the Seleucids, especially under the hated rule of Antiochus IV (175–164 BC), was loathed because of its attempts to impose Greek culture (*Hellenism*) on all aspects of Jewish life. Devout Jews saw Greek pagan practices and culture as a direct threat to Jewish traditions and identity.

Antiochus committed many atrocities against the Jewish religion. He robbed the Temple of its gold, massacred protesters, and outlawed the Torah. Tragically, he ordered the deaths of anyone who refused to eat pork, observed the sabbath, or circumcised their sons. These last edicts, in effect, outlawed the Jewish faith and resulted in many deaths. A final outrage was his placing a statue of the pagan god Zeus in the sanctuary of the holy Jerusalem Temple.

Antiochus's notorious actions led to the famous Maccabean Revolt under Judas Maccabeus and his brothers. Their family name meant "hammer." The Maccabean rebels recaptured the Temple in 164 BC and rededicated it to Yahweh. This event is celebrated today in the Hanukkah festival. Eventually the Maccabean family established an independent Jewish state in 142 BC, led by the Hasmonean kings. This was the first independent Jewish nation for centuries. But the later rulers of the Hasmonean Dynasty, though fiercely proud of their Jewish nationalism, acted much like the spoiled and corrupt Hellenistic kings who preceded them. They, too, were subject to political intrigue and the adoption of Greek customs. Their weakness led to the collapse of the Hasmonean Dynasty when the Roman general Pompey intervened and conquered Palestine in 63 BC.

Herod

At first, Rome permitted the conquered Jews to have some semblance of self-rule under the Idumean Herod the Great. Herod was called a "half-Jew." He was a cunning, crafty, and bloodthirsty ruler. Matthew's story about Herod's killing of the male babies born within two years of Jesus' birth (Mt 2:16), though not documented in contemporary sources, certainly fits Herod's character. The Jewish historian Josephus tells us that Herod slaughtered several of his sons, one of his ten wives, and several other relatives for fear that they might usurp his throne.

Herod curried the favor of the emperor by building many wonderful edifices throughout Palestine and then dedicating them to the emperor. He even erected pagan temples and supported emperor worship. This was an abomination to the Jews. Though called "King of the Jews," Herod was no Jewish king. However, Herod redeemed himself somewhat in the eyes of his Jewish subjects by undertaking the construction of the magnificent Temple in Jerusalem. The Jews hated Herod the Great as a pagan, foreign ruler.

Herod died an agonizing death in 4 BC. Three of his sons, Phillip, Herod Antipas, and Archelaus divided the kingdom among them. Philip (4 BC–AD 34) controlled the lands to the north and east of the Sea of Galilee. The New Testament has little to say of him, though he is known as the fairest ruler of the three brothers. Herod Antipas (4 BC–AD 39) ruled Perea and Galilee, Jesus' home province throughout his life. Herod Antipas was the ruler who executed John the Baptist because John complained about Antipas's adulterous relationship with his half-brother Philip's wife, Herodias. Herod also spied on Jesus. Jesus revealed a lot about Herod Antipas's character when he called him "that fox" (Lk 13:32).

Archelaus (4 BC–AD 6) ruled most of Samaria, Idumea, and Judea. He was a bloodthirsty ruler, killing three thousand of his subjects within months of gaining power. Archelaus was extremely unpopular with his subjects, who badgered Rome to remove him. After nine years of hearing complaints, the emperor finally deposed him. In his place, Rome appointed a prefect (later changed to "procurator" under the reign of Claudius) who was directly answerable to the Roman governor in Syria. The New Testament mentions three Roman procurators: Pontius Pilate (AD 26–36), Felix (AD 52–60), and Festus (AD 60–62).

The Roman procurator's main tasks were tax collecting, approving or denying the death sentences imposed by the Jewish tribunal, keeping the peace by commanding auxiliary forces of non-Jewish residents of Palestine and Syria, and reporting to Rome about the general state of affairs. He also had the power to appoint and depose the Jewish High Priest. Jews greatly resented these powers. They especially hated Jewish tax collectors, the so-called *publicans* who collaborated with the Romans in exacting taxes.

Pontius Pilate figures prominently in the Gospel accounts because it was he who ordered Jesus' death by crucifixion. He was a cruel, heartless, and stern ruler who did nothing to endear himself to the Jews. Ruling from the seacoast town of Caesarea, he erected military standards in Jerusalem bearing the emperor's image. This act outraged pious Jews because Yahweh forbade graven images. Pilate also robbed the Temple treasury of funds to build an aqueduct. When the Jews protested, he disguised some of his men and had them infiltrate a crowd of protesting Jews. At a predetermined signal, they drew their swords and slaughtered many of the defenseless Jews. According to one of his political enemies, Pilate was guilty of "graft, insults, robberies, assaults, wanton abuse, constant executions without trial, unending grievous cruelty." He was eventually recalled to Rome and probably exiled to Gaul.

Rome's rule was harsh and hated by most Jews. However, Rome did allow the Jews considerable freedom in practicing their religion. Nevertheless, all Jews longed for the day when a Messiah would come to deliver them.

In 1961, Italian archaeologists discovered this broken limestone block at Caesarea on the Sea. The rock is engraved with these Latin words:

> . . . . . S TIBERIEVM
> . . [PO]NTIVS PILATVS
> [PRA]ECTVS IVDA[EA]E

The Pilate **Inscription**

The inscription is translated: "Tiberium, Pontius Pilate, Prefect of Judea," which indicates that Pilate built and dedicated a temple to Emperor Tiberius. This discovery provides physical evidence that Pilate was in Palestine during Christ's lifetime.

The Practice of Slavery

There were both Gentile and Jewish slaves in Palestine during the first century, but these slaves did not have to do the heavy work we associate with African slaves in the United States. Relatively few in number, the first-century Jewish slaves were mostly the servants of wealthy people and enjoyed many protections provided by Jewish law. For example, slaves working off a debt could not be made to work for more than ten hours a day nor on the Sabbath.

THE LETTER TO PHILEMON

Read Paul's Letter to Philemon, a very short 335-word letter. It was written during one of Paul's imprisonments, perhaps in Ephesus around AD 55 or from Rome in AD 61–63. It is a personal letter from Paul to Philemon. However, it contains many elements of the style Paul used in all his letters:

- Greeting (vv. 1–3)
- Thanksgiving (vv. 4–7)
- Body (vv. 8–20)
- Closing: Greetings and Blessing (vv. 21–25)

The subject of the letter involves Philemon's runaway slave, Onesimus. Paul baptized Onesimus and then sent him back to his master, the wealthy Philemon. Paul's advice to Philemon does not speak for the abolition of slavery, a firmly entrenched and widespread practice in the Roman world. But he did plant a seed that would, in future generations, blossom into a true Christ-like response to this major social issue.

Paul implicitly encourages Philemon not to punish his slave; he also hints that he should free him. For Paul, the key truth is that Onesimus is now the equal of Philemon. He is a brother transformed in Jesus Christ. Paul tells Philemon that he should welcome him as he would Paul himself.

Answer the following questions in your journal:

1. Who else is sending the Letter to Philemon?

2. What proof does the letter give that Philemon is a Christian?

3. What does Paul reveal about himself in this letter?

4. How does Paul want Philemon to receive Onesimus?

5. What does Paul promise to do concerning any possible harm Onesimus might have caused?

6. How does he try to convince Philemon that his offer is sincere?

7. What verse tells us that Paul hopes to see Philemon again?

8. What does Paul's Letter to Philemon tell us about Jesus and his Good News?

Teenagers face several forms of "slavery." For example, teens are often enslaved by drugs, alcohol, peer pressure, unrealistic expectations placed on them, or abusive relationships. Choose one form of slavery faced by teens. Explain it in a short essay. Include in the essay several practical steps teens can undertake to escape this form of slavery.

At the time St. Paul was making his missionary trips in the middle of the first century, slavery was widespread throughout the Roman Empire. A person could become a slave as a prisoner of war, by kidnapping, through debt, or by being born the child of a slave. Many slaves did do backbreaking work in mines or as rowers on ships. Others had it much better as servants to wealthy and understanding owners. Some slaves were well educated and even administered their masters' estate. Their faithful service often led to freedom.

The New Testament does not directly speak out against the *institution* of slavery, but rather attacks the principle of inequality on which one person owning another as property was based. Christian love, and unity in Christ, made believers realize that owning another human being was contrary to the Lord's message. Ultimately, this realization destroyed slavery, though it took many centuries for political entities to pass laws to ban it.

FOR REVIEW

1. Identify *Pax Romana*. List several of its benefits.
2. Identify: Antiochus IV, the Maccabean Revolt, the Hasmoneans, Pompey.
3. Describe Herod the Great. Who were his three sons who succeeded him, and what territories did they rule?
4. What functions did Roman prefects like Pontius Pilate have?
5. What was a debtor slave?
6. In the letter St. Paul sent to Philemon, what did Paul want Philemon to do?

FOR REFLECTION

The political climate was an important fact in Jesus' ministry. Recall that the Roman leader, Pontius Pilate, was the one who condemned him to death. How important do you think it is to elect people into office who share your religious convictions, for example, on life and justice issues? Can you be a follower of Christ and not be involved in politics?

Jewish Beliefs **and Practices**

The New Testament is deeply rooted in the Jewish people, and their religious beliefs, practices, affiliations, and expectations. Jesus was a pious Jew who held many beliefs in common with his fellow Jews. Jesus' Apostles and many of the later first-century Christians were also Jewish. Their acceptance of Jesus as the Messiah set them apart from other Jews. These Jewish Christians considered their first missionary task to preach the Gospel to other Jews. They believed that Yahweh had fulfilled his promises to the Jewish people in Jesus of Nazareth. The New Testament includes many references to Jewish beliefs and practices in the first century.

The Messiah

The New Testament period was high in messianic expectations. Most Jews strongly believed that Yahweh would send a Messiah very soon. The Hebrew word *masiah* translates to the Greek word *Christos* (Christ), which literally means, "anointed one." At first, the title

Chi-Rho: The first two letters of the Greek word for (*Christos*); a symbol for Jesus Christ.

apocalypse—A word meaning "revelation" or "unveiling." Apocalyptic writings, usually written in times of crisis, use highly symbolic language to bolster faith by reassuring believers that the current age, subject to the forces of evil, will end when God intervenes and establishes a divine rule of goodness and peace.

Pentateuch—The name for the first five books of the Old Testament: Genesis, Exodus, Leviticus, Numbers, and Deuteronomy. It contains the Law (Torah).

Torah—The Law or divine teaching revealed to Judaism. It is the foundation of the Jewish religion and is found in the Pentateuch.

Messiah applied to the king of Israel, God's anointed leader. Since King David's reign (ca. 1000 BC), the Jews understood their covenant relationship with Yahweh to include the promise to send a king who would represent Yahweh's love and care for his people. Unfortunately, David's successors were weak and corrupt. Punishment befell the nation with the successive destruction of both the northern and southern kingdoms.

But the belief in God's promise to provide a messiah never died among the Jews. Following the Babylonian Exile, the Jews increasingly believed that the messiah would usher in God's Kingdom or reign. Various groups in Jesus' day had different expectations of who or what kind of person the messiah would be. However, most Jews expected a political and military leader like David who would lead Israel to a great military victory, reestablish the prominence of Israel as an independent nation, and help establish God's Kingdom.

By the first century, many Jews (including John the Baptist) fully expected the coming of the messiah to be accompanied by an apocalyptic event. This **apocalypse** would be dramatic, pointing to the Messiah's identity and a glorious establishment of God's Kingdom.

The Covenant and the Torah

Primarily, the Jews were a covenant people. They believed Yahweh chose them as his special people, rescued and preserved them, and used them to lead others to the worship of the one true God. For their part, the Jews were to believe in and observe the Torah, or Law. The **Pentateuch**, the first five books of the Old Testament, contains the Torah, the heart of Jewish life. To the Jews, the **Torah** (derived from a word that means "instruction" or "guidance") is not a list of arbitrary rules. Rather, the Torah is God's Revelation of himself, what he expects as a response to his covenant love. He had created Israel as a special people, promising to bless, guide, and protect them forever. In return they were to recognize Yahweh as the one true God and keep the Law.

Studying the Torah was a form of worship and a lifelong task for Jews. More importantly, they were to live the Law because of its moral foundation. The Torah influenced every aspect of Jewish history, culture, morality, and worship. To live apart from the Law was to draw judgment on oneself and the nation. Sects like the Pharisees and the Essenes believed that God allowed foreign powers to dominate the Jews because so many Jews were not living the Law. Thus, they tried to live the Law perfectly—and taught others to do the same—in the belief that Yahweh would have to respond by sending a Messiah to rescue them.

Jesus had profound respect for the Law and instructed his followers to keep it. He said, "Do not think that I have come to abolish the law or the prophets. I have come not to abolish but to fulfill it" (Mt 5:17).

The Torah remains at the heart of the Jewish religion today. It, along with the Prophets (*Nebiim*) and Writings

(*Ketubim*—wisdom literature and the Psalms), makes up the sacred Hebrew Scriptures included in the Old Testament. The Jews abbreviate their holy writings as TANAK (T=Torah; N=Nebiim; K=Ketubim).

Judgment and Resurrection (CCC, 668–682; 1020–1060)

A common belief of Jews since the second century BC is that Yahweh will judge the dead by rewarding the good and punishing the evil. The prophet Daniel introduced the idea of the resurrection from the dead for those who merited it, though some Jews do not believe in a personal resurrection:

> Many of those who sleep in the dust of the earth shall awake; some shall live forever, others shall be an everlasting horror and disgrace. (Dn 12:2)

As the Son of God, Christ himself willed that the dead will be raised. He told a parable about the final judgment in Matthew 25:31–46, making it clear that he will be the judge of the living and the dead, separating between the sheep (righteous) and goats (evildoers). Catholics hold this as a core doctrine of faith, that, at death, each person will be judged whether or not they will go to Heaven, Hell, or Purgatory. Catholics believe that their resurrection will take place precisely because they are one with the Lord, who has conquered sin and death. See the *Catechism of the Catholic Church*, 668–682 and 1020–1060, for more information.

Spirit World

The New Testament records the accepted Jewish belief in the existence of **angels** and demons. From the earliest days, Jews believed in heavenly messengers (*angel* means "messenger"). In the centuries between the writing of the Old and New Testaments, belief among the faithful in angels expanded. Some important literature produced in this era—books like *Jubilees*, *Enoch*, and the Dead Sea Scrolls—divided the angels into groups, gave them names, and described some of their functions. For example, the book of *Tobias* tells how the angel Raphael appeared in human form.

The New Testament frequently mentions both angels and devils. Jews believed that various demons warred against God by being the sources of sickness, temptation, and sin. Jesus cast out many demons and saw his own suffering as a war against the evil one—Satan (Jn 12:31). Although Jews and Christians accepted the existence of demons, they believed that they were subject to God.

angels—God's messengers; angels are created beings that possess free will and intelligence but who are pure spirits, without bodies.

ANGELS

Read the following New Testament passages about angels and answer each question.

1. Who is the angel of the Annunciation? (Lk 1:11–22)
2. Which angel guards the people of Israel? (Dn 10:13, 21)
3. What did angels do after Jesus' temptation? (Mt 4:11)
4. What did an angel do after Jesus' agony? (Lk 22:43)
5. What function did the angels have at the Resurrection? (Jn 20:11–14)
6. What will they do at the Parousia? (Mk 13:27)

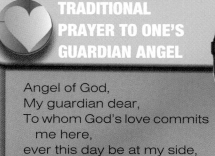

TRADITIONAL PRAYER TO ONE'S GUARDIAN ANGEL

Angel of God,
My guardian dear,
To whom God's love commits
   me here,
ever this day be at my side,
to light and guard, to rule and
   guide.
Amen.

Compose your own prayer to your guardian angel.

FOR REVIEW

1. What was the common first-century Jewish belief concerning the Messiah?

2. Identify the Torah and explain what role it played in the Jewish religion.

3. What is the meaning of the word "angel"?

FOR REFLECTION

Read the *Catechism of the Catholic Church*, 328–336. Write three interesting facts you learned about angels.

Ark of the Covenant—The portable shrine built to hold the tablets on which Moses wrote the Law. It was the sign of God's presence to the Israelites. King Solomon built the Temple in Jerusalem to house the Ark.

Sanhedrin—The seventy-one-member supreme legislative and judicial body of the Jewish people. Many of its members were Sadducees.

The Ark of **the Covenant**

Religious Sects **in Jesus' Time**

The historian Josephus describes four important religious sects that were viable during New Testament times. Josephus refers to these sects as "philosophies" within Judaism. They are the Sadducees, Pharisees, Essenes, and Zealots. More information on each follows.

Sadducees

The Sadducees' name derives from Sadok, the priest whom Solomon appointed to take charge of the **Ark of the Covenant** (1 Kgs 2:35). Because the Sadducees were mostly priests and aristocrats who cared for Temple practices and worship, they centered their activities in Jerusalem. They collaborated with the Romans to stay in power.

Theologically conservative, the Sadducees accepted only the Torah as inspired Scripture. The Sadducees also refused to accept the oral traditions and legal rulings of the scribes and influential Pharisee sect who attempted to apply the Torah to everyday life.

Josephus reported that the Sadducees stressed human free will and responsibility over trusting Divine Providence. Also, they did not believe in the resurrection of the dead, the immortality of the soul, or in angels. All these were important beliefs for Jesus and the Pharisees.

Many Sadducees, along with a few Pharisees, made up the seventy-one-member **Sanhedrin**, the major lawmaking body and supreme court of Judaism. It was this group that judged Jesus a threat and accused him of blasphemy.

We do not hear anything about the Sadducees after the destruction of the Temple in AD 70. Without a Temple in which to center their power and influence, the Sadducees lost both political and spiritual authority over their fellow Jews.

Pharisees

The term *Pharisee* means "separated one." Pharisees came into existence during the **Hasmonean Dynasty** (135–63 BC), when they separated themselves from the ordinary religious practices of that day. They believed in strict observance of the Law, which they thought kept them from sin, lukewarm religious practice, and Gentile influence. This group of laymen, many from the middle-class, actively pursued holiness.

Although numbering perhaps only six thousand adherents during the first century, the Pharisees had great influence over the people. Of all the Jewish sects, Jesus' beliefs and spiritual practice most closely paralleled the Pharisees. For example, the Pharisees believed in the resurrection of the body and divine judgment of the living and the dead. They held prayer, almsgiving, and fasting to be essential spiritual practices. The Pharisees also accepted as inspired the Prophets and the Writings as well as the Pentateuch (Torah).

Josephus himself may have been a Pharisee. He wrote this about them:

> The Pharisees live thriftily, giving in to no luxury. For they follow what the Word (of God) in its authority determines and transmits as good. They believe that to keep what (God) wished to counsel is worth fighting for. . . . [The Pharisees] are the most persuasive among the citizens.[6]

There was much to admire in the Pharisees. Their religious devotions were positive practices that inspired many of their fellow Jews. Some Pharisees, though, were perhaps too rigid in their application of the Torah to daily life. They developed an elaborate system of oral interpretation of the Law, which they held to be almost as sacred as the Law itself. These oral traditions sometimes missed the spirit of the Law. Jesus held the Law sacred, but he freed his followers from blind observance of man-made laws that superseded the needs of people. This is why some Pharisees did not like Jesus. He influenced people to do good without recourse to an elaborate system of minute observance of religious customs.

Although the Pharisees fulfilled the proper worship required for the Jerusalem Temple, their center of influence was the synagogue, where their scholarly study of the Law, and their pious attempts to live it, gained for them influence over the common people who looked up to and admired them. Many Pharisees were, in fact, scribes and experts in the Jewish Law.

Jesus criticized some Pharisees because they thought they could "earn" Heaven by keeping all their religious customs. Jesus taught that God's love and Kingdom are pure gifts, bestowed on saint and sinner alike. Conflict between these two approaches to God's goodness was inevitable. Nevertheless, Pharisees should not be viewed negatively because their intention was to be very thoughtful and good Jews. Two outstanding Pharisaic scholars of the first century were Rabbi Shammai (a conservative) and Rabbi Hillel (a liberal). Also, some Pharisees became disciples of Jesus, most notably St. Paul.

Hasmonean Dynasty—Descendants of the Maccabees who ruled in Judea after the ousting of the last of the Syrians in 141 BC until the establishment of the Roman authority in 63 BC. John Hyrcanus was the first ruler in this dynasty and ruled until 128 BC.

Scrolls of **The Torah**

JESUS DEBATES WITH THE PHARISEES AND SADDUCEES

Jesus engaged in debates with the Pharisees and Sadducees. Read about two of these debates. Answer the questions that follow each reference.

Read Mark 7:1–23.

- What did the disciples fail to do? (vv. 1–2)

- Why did the Pharisees think this was a problem? (vv. 3–6)

- What commandment does Jesus say they try to avoid? (vv. 8–10)

- How do the Pharisees excuse their obligation to keep this commandment? (vv. 11–18)

- From where does evil come? (vv. 14–20)

- List several actions that come from evil intentions. (v. 22)

Read Mark 12:18–27.

- What case do the Sadducees put before Jesus? (vv. 19–23)

- Who established the law quoted by the Sadducees? (v. 19)

- Was the question to Jesus sincere? Why or why not? (vv. 18–19)

- Jesus responds to the Sadducees by giving them a two-part answer. First, he answers their question on its own merits. How does he respond? (vv. 25–26) (Second, Jesus shows that he believes in the resurrection by quoting the same person as the Sadducees.)

- What is Jesus' argument in support of the resurrection? (vv. 26–27) [Hint: The Book of Moses = Torah = Pentateuch]

Finally, it was the Pharisees who helped to preserve Judaism after the destruction of the Temple by the Roman general Titus in the year AD 70. Under the famous rabbi Jonathan ben Zakkai, some Pharisees regrouped at Jamnia (present-day Jabneh near Tel Aviv). First, they formed a canon of sacred books, accepting only those written in Hebrew. They also established a liturgical calendar and unified synagogue worship.

However, significantly for Christians, the gathering at Jamnia ultimately separated Christians from the Jewish religion. Tension between Jews and Jewish Christians had been growing for decades. When Christians refused to fight the Romans in the First Revolt, the surviving Jews felt it was time to break with the Christian sect. They did this by introducing a petition in the synagogue prayer known as the Eighteen Benedictions. This addition cursed "heretics, apostates, and the proud," a direct reference to Christians. Matthew's Gospel, especially chapter 23, reflects some of the animosity Jewish Christians felt toward this move by the post-Revolt Pharisees.

Essenes

The Essenes were an apocalyptic group, that is, they believed God would usher in his Kingdom through a dramatic, even catastrophic event. The Essenes carefully read and produced commentaries on the Jewish Scriptures, hoping to find signs of the coming event. They lived strict, pure lives believing that they would be on Yahweh's side when the great day would come. Like the Sadducees, the Essenes disappeared from Jewish history after the destruction of the Temple. They probably hid their sacred writings in the caves in the Judean desert around the time the Romans came through the region in AD 67–68. Their writings—the **Dead Sea Scrolls**—were first discovered in 1947 by an Arab shepherd boy when he was tossing rocks into the caves and heard a jar smash.

The founder of the Essenes was a man known as "the Teacher of Righteousness," who taught that the Jerusalem priesthood and Temple worship were impure and that most Jews failed to live the Law. To better live a life of holiness, many Essenes withdrew to **Qumran** near the northwest shore of the Dead Sea. As celibates who did not marry, the Essenes at Qumran shared goods in common and tried to remain ritually pure by frequent washings throughout the day. Many of their ritual baths have been discovered in the archaeological remains of the Qumran monastery. Other Essenes resided in tight-knit religious groups in towns and villages, living disciplined lives of avoiding luxuries, sharing communal meals, doing pious works for the poor, and engaging in acts of ritual purification. The total number of this sect may have been about four thousand during Jesus' time.

When the day of crisis came, the Essenes expected three leaders to come on the scene: a prophet predicted by Moses (Dt 18:18–19); a kingly messiah in the line of King David; and, most important, a priestly messiah, who would establish pure worship and a reformed Temple.

Zealots

In his *Jewish Antiquities*, Josephus writes of a certain Judas the Galilean who led a revolt against the Romans for their taking a census (for the purpose of taxation) in the province of Judea (ca. AD 6–7). Judas believed that no foreign power had the right to collect taxes from the Jews who were given the Holy Land by God. To pay taxes would be equivalent to slavery. Acts of the Apostles tells us that he was killed and his followers scattered (5:37). Josephus credits Judas the Galilean, hailed as Messiah by his followers, as being the author of "the fourth branch of Jewish philosophy"—the Zealots.

Jesus had an Apostle known as Simon the Zealot. But the Apostle Simon did not belong to an *organized* revolutionary movement. There simply is no evidence to suggest that the Zealots were organized, active, and armed during the public ministry of Jesus.

However, an organized revolutionary faction known as the Zealots

Dead Sea Scrolls—Ancient scrolls containing the oldest known manuscripts of the books of the Old Testament in Hebrew. They were unearthed near Qumran on the Dead Sea between 1947 and 1953.

Qumran—An ancient Essene monastery on the northwestern shore of the Dead Sea. Near it were found the ancient Dead Sea Scrolls.

The Caves **at Qumran**

was in full swing by the time of the First Jewish War, 66–70. This revolutionary party despised Roman rule and fomented violence to overthrow it. A symbol of Jewish pride today is their famous stand at Masada, a fortress near the southeastern shore of the Dead Sea. Although the Romans defeated the Jews in AD 70, a pocket of Zealots resisted until 73 at this mountaintop fortress. Rather than surrender and be taken in chains to Rome, the Zealots at Masada took their own lives.

A second revolt spearheaded by the Zealots against Rome took place in AD 132–135 under a strong leader, Simon bar-Kokhba, whom many Jews thought was the Messiah. This Second Jewish Revolt ended in total disaster for the Jews; from that time on they were forbidden to set foot in the holy city of Jerusalem.

DEAD SEA SCROLLS ONLINE

Read more about the Dead Sea Scrolls and the Essenes at one of these Internet sites. Prepare a short report related topics you discover.

- Scrolls from the Dead Sea:
  www.ibiblio.org/expo/deadsea.scrolls.exhibit/intro.html

- The Essenes and the Dead Sea Scrolls:
  www.pbs.org/wgbh/pages/frontline/shows/religion/portrait/essenes.html

- Orion Center for the Study of the Dead Sea Scrolls:
  http://orion.mscc.huji.ac.il

- Dead Sea Scrolls at the West Semitic Research Center:
  www.usc.edu/dept/LAS/wsrp/educational_site/dead_sea_scrolls

- The Dead Sea Scrolls:
  http://virtualreligion.net/iho/dss_2.html

Researchers study **the Dead Sea Scrolls**

 FOR REVIEW

1. Identify these Jewish sects: Sadducees, Pharisees, Essenes, and Zealots. List several of the beliefs of each.

2. What was the Sanhedrin?

3. Identify Jonathan ben Zakkai.

FOR REFLECTION

Imagine you are a Jew of the first century who belongs to one of the sects described in this section. Write a short letter to your parents explaining how you have reconciled your particular Jewish faith with a newfound belief that Jesus is the Messiah.

Other People in **the New Testament**

The following groups mentioned in the New Testament are also of significance in a study of Jesus.

Tax Collectors

Most Jews hated any fellow Jew who would stoop so low as to work for the Romans. The tax collectors were often cheaters who tried to line their own pockets at the expense of their fellow Jews. Jesus associated with this despised group of people and even called one of them—Levi (Matthew)—to be an Apostle (Mk 2:14–15).

Common People

Most of Jesus' contemporaries were the common people who lived their daily lives removed from the intellectual disputes of the major sects. Some of them struggled to follow the Law, pray, and participate in the synagogue services. Others, including the Galileans, were often called "the people of the land," a scornful name Pharisees gave to those who were ignorant of the Law. The Pharisees thought the common people's ignorance kept them from holiness. Jesus had his greatest appeal among these simple people. They were open to hearing and responding to his message of conversion, repentance, and salvation. By extension, some Pharisees characterized Jesus and his disciples as "common people" because they did not strictly follow the oral law in regard to fasting (Lk 5:33) and washing (Mt 15:2).

Gentiles

Jews divided people into two classes: Jews and Gentiles (the nations of people who were not circumcised). Some Gentiles did convert to Judaism and were then known as *proselytes*. Other Gentiles, called "God-fearers," accepted many Jewish beliefs but did not undergo circumcision.

Pious Jews avoided contact with Gentiles. The Acts of the Apostles reports how the early Christian missionaries turned to the Gentiles only after most Jews rejected the Gospel. An early Church debate took place in Jerusalem around AD 49 and concerned whether Gentiles had to follow the whole Mosaic Law before becoming Christian. At first, a compromise resulted: Gentile Christians had to accept some Jewish dietary laws. Eventually, however, the Church became populated with more and more Gentiles and lost much of its Jewish influence.

Women

Women generally had a lowly position in first-century Palestine. In almost every way, Jews considered women inferior to men. Jewish men looked on women as property and too weak to follow the religious requirements of the Law. Jewish law allowed a man to divorce his wife for any reason as long as he gave his divorced wife a legal document saying she was free to remarry. It was much more difficult for a woman to divorce her husband.

Women were also segregated during synagogue and Temple worship and had few political rights. Their domain was the home, where they played a central role in child rearing. Motherhood was esteemed, while a childless woman was scorned and pitied. It was especially tough to be a widow, left alone in the world with no means of support. One protection widows had was that if a man died without children, his unmarried brother had to marry the widow and take care of her.

The Pharisees **question Jesus**

Jesus elevated the position of women, treated them as equals, and instructed husbands to love and cherish their wives. Many women were Jesus' disciples and were the most faithful to him at the end of his life. Jesus first appeared to a woman (Mary Magdalene) after being raised from the dead. Mary, the Mother of Jesus, is the first disciple and perfect Christian. Jesus' attitude toward women was, in many ways, revolutionary.

Mary **Magdalene** by Carlo **Dolci**

 **FOR REVIEW**

1. From the point of view of the Pharisees, who were "the people of the land"?

2. Who were the Gentiles?

3. Describe the situation of women in New Testament times and how Jesus revolutionized it.

FOR REFLECTION

Jesus went against the societal norms of his day and numbered women among his most important friends. Write a profile about the most important woman in your life. What makes her so special? What qualities do you most admire in her?

CHAPTER SUMMARY POINTS

- Palestine, the Holy Land, gets its name from the Philistines, a traditional enemy of the Jews. Palestine has always played a strategic role in world history.

- The three major regions of Palestine are Galilee, Samaria, and Judea.

- Galilee was the locale of most of Jesus' public life. He grew up in Nazareth, performed his first miracle at Cana, and used Capernaum as the base of his ministry.

- The Samaritans were descendants of foreigners who intermarried with northern Israelite tribes at the time of Assyria's conquest of the northern Kingdom. They accepted only the Pentateuch as inspired Scripture and worshiped God on Mount Gerazim.

- Jerusalem, Bethlehem, and the Dead Sea are located in Judea.

- Jesus spoke Aramaic, a Semitic language closely related to Hebrew. He may have known a little Greek and perhaps have been able to understand Hebrew, the language of the Sacred Scriptures.

- There were many synagogues in the Holy Land in Jesus' day. Synagogues were houses of prayer, places of meeting, centers for legal discussions, and often served as the local schools.

- The Temple was located in Jerusalem and was the center of Jewish sacrifice to Yahweh and the destination for the celebration of various religious festivals. The Temple Jesus worshiped in was built by Herod the Great.

- The three major Jewish feasts in Jesus' time were Passover, which celebrated the Exodus; Pentecost, which celebrated the Sinai covenant; and Tabernacles, a fall harvest festival.
- Politics dominated Jewish life. *Hellenism* (the love of Greek culture) was imposed by the Seleucid ruler Antiochus IV (175–164 BC).
- After Herod the Great's death, Palestine was ruled by his sons Archelaus (Samaria, Idumea, and Judea), Herod Antipas (Galilee and Perea), and Philip. Herod Antipas (4 BC–AD 39) was king during Jesus' lifetime.
- Slavery was a fact of the ancient world and the Roman Empire, though not that widespread in Palestine. Christ's teachings on the fundamental dignity of persons, after centuries, eventually led to the abolition of slavery throughout most of the world.
- Most Jews of the first century expected the Messiah to come very soon. They typically interpreted the coming Messiah as a Davidic figure, a military leader who would throw off Roman rule and establish God's Kingdom, restoring Israel's glory.
- The Chosen People responded to God's covenant by studying and trying to live the Torah (Law). The Torah is found in the first five books of the Old Testament known as the Pentateuch. Along with the Prophets and Writings, it makes up the Jewish Sacred Scriptures.
- Since about the second century BC, many Jews believed in the resurrection of the body and a judgment where God would reward the good and punish evildoers. The Jewish sect of the Sadducees, however, did not hold such a view.
- Most Jews believed in the existence of angels (divine messengers) and demons who warred against God.
- Four major sects (parties or philosophies) of New Testament times were the Sadducees, the Pharisees, the Essenes, and the Zealots.

LEARN BY DOING

1. Research and report on one of the following sets of Jewish feasts:

   - Passover, Pentecost, and Tabernacles
   - Yom Kippur and Hanukkah

2. Prepare a PowerPoint® presentation on Herod's Temple. You may wish to consult this website: www.bible-history.com/jewishtemple

3. Visit a synagogue and report on the Sabbath service held there. Interview the rabbi on the sacred objects used in the service. Take pictures of the synagogue and of the religious items to illustrate a talk you will prepare for your classmates.

4. Research the life of Pontius Pilate. Investigate the legend that he converted to Christianity and died a martyr.

5. Research several branches of modern Judaism, for example, Orthodox, Conservative, or Reformed Judaism. Note some major differences in their beliefs. Report on what each believes concerning the Messiah.

6. Do an Internet search to learn more about modern-day Samaritans. Prepare a brief illustrated report.

PRAYER LESSON

We began our chapter with the story of a man whose life was transformed by the love of Christ. St. Paul is another such person. Pray with devotion his beautiful reflection on the love of Christ:

What then shall we say to this? If God is for us, who can be against us? He who did not spare his own Son but handed him over for us all, how will he not also give us everything else along with him? Who will bring a charge against God's chosen ones? It is God who acquits us. Who will condemn? It is Christ (Jesus) who died, rather, was raised, who also is at the right hand of God, who indeed intercedes for us. What will separate us from the love of Christ? Will anguish, or distress, or persecution, or famine, or nakedness, or peril, or the sword? As it is written:

"For your sake we are being slain all the day;
we are looked upon as sheep to be slaughtered."

No, in all these things we conquer overwhelmingly through him who loved us. For I am convinced that neither death, nor life, nor angels, nor principalities, nor present things, nor future things, nor powers, nor height, nor depth, nor any other creature will be able to separate us from the love of God in Christ Jesus our Lord.

—Romans 8:31–39

- What in your life is troubling you right now? Who is against you? What is keeping you from the love of Christ?

- Pray for the Holy Spirit's guidance.

- *Resolution*: Re-read Romans 8:31–39. Resolve to pray with the confidence of St. Paul.

The
Essential Jesus

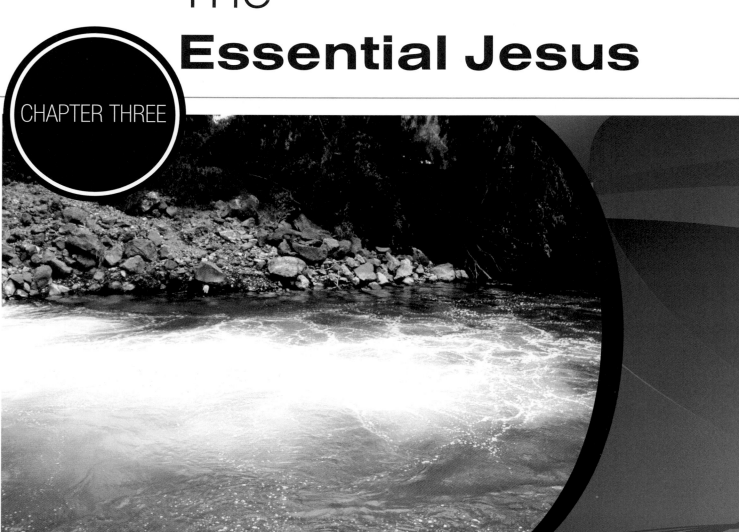

"This is the time of fulfillment. The Kingdom of God is at hand. Repent, and believe the Gospel."

—Mark 1:15

CHAPTER **OVERVIEW**

THE LIGHT OF **THE WORLD**

Jesus knocks on the door of our hearts and awaits our answer so that he may open the door to his Father's Kingdom and his love.

MYSTERIES OF **CHRIST'S LIFE**

Christ's whole life—including his infancy and hidden life in Nazareth—help us glimpse two meanings of an incomprehensible mystery: how the omnipotent God was able to be incarnate in order to bring our salvation.

JESUS **THE TEACHER**

Jesus was a teacher par excellence who was able to teach the mysteries of God's Kingdom through parables and proclamations.

JESUS THE **MIRACLE WORKER**

All of the Gospel accounts attest that Jesus was a miracle worker who performed works of wonder to reveal that God's Kingdom is at hand.

JESUS' OBEDIENCE **TO HIS FATHER'S WILL**

The Paschal Mystery, the summation of Jesus' mission and our road to salvation, is defined in the context of Jesus' obedience to his Father's will.

The Light **of the World**

The Light of **the World**

St. Gregory of Nazianzus (ca. 329–389), a famous Father of the Church, observed the following about Jesus:

He began his ministry by being hungry, yet he is the Bread of Life.

Jesus ended his earthly ministry by being thirsty, yet he is the Living Water.

Jesus was weary, yet he is our rest.

Jesus paid tribute, yet he is the King.

Jesus was accused of having a demon, yet he cast out demons.

Jesus wept, yet he wipes away our tears.

Jesus was sold for thirty pieces of silver, yet he redeemed the world.

Jesus was brought as a lamb to the slaughter, yet he is the Good Shepherd.

Jesus died, yet by His death He destroyed the power of death.[7]

If you accept all the above as true, then how attractive Jesus is indeed. Jesus invites all who hear his name to make a personal decision about him. Yet Christ never forces his love on anyone. Consider the famous painting titled "The Light of the World" by the nineteenth-century artist William Holman Hunt

THE CHALLENGES OF FOLLOWING JESUS

Here are some of Jesus' most challenging commands. Read through the list and determine which of these commands is most difficult for you to follow. Write a short explanation, citing examples of why you find this command so challenging. In addition, write about which practice would have the most positive impact on the world if lived out by many.

- Forgive those who mistreat you.
- Don't judge others.
- Get your priorities in order, then stop worrying.
- Be humble; put others first.

- Deny yourself some personal desires to follow Christ.
- Follow through on your commitments.
- Pray confidently for what you need.

The following New Testament passages correspond to Jesus' teachings above. Copy each passage into your journal. Below each, write a short paragraph discussing what it means to you or how you plan to live it out.

- Matthew 5:44
- Matthew 6:33–34
- Matthew 7:1
- Matthew 7:7

- Mark 10:31
- Luke 9:23
- Luke 11:28

(1827–1910).[8] Note how it depicts a patient, gentle Jesus standing before a closed, ivy-covered door. He is wearing a priestly breastplate and holds a lamp in one hand. He is standing at the door and knocking.

But no one answers. Yet Jesus still knocks. His eyes shine with compassionate love; his face beams welcoming.

Note carefully that there is no knob or latch on the outside of the door. It can only be opened from within.

So it is with us. Jesus stands waiting for us to answer, to open our hearts to him, his Father's Kingdom, and their love.

FOR REFLECTION

Describe your reactions to the Hunt painting. Tell about a recent opportunity that you have had to let Jesus into your life. What happened?

Mysteries of **Christ's Life**
(*CCC*, 512–518; 561–562)

The *Catechism of the Catholic Church* introduces the Gospel portrait of Jesus as a review of the "mysteries of Christ's life." This chapter will uncover in more detail the meaning of those mysteries. (The events associated with Jesus' last days, his Passion and Crucifixion, and his Resurrection and Ascension will be studied more thoroughly in chapters to follow.)

What is meant by the term *mystery*? First, theologically, mystery refers to God's infinite incomprehensibility. After all, God is essentially a mystery. God is so beyond us, so great, so omnipotent, so loving, so perfect—the human mind can never totally grasp his infinity.

Second, the New Testament uses the word "mystery" to refer to God's saving plan for human history. God's loving providence guides this plan, the mystery of our salvation and redemption, as he gradually reveals himself over time.

There is an interesting and intimate connection between these two understandings of mystery. The God who is a mystery is the same God who has chosen to reveal himself in human history. Christians believe, of course, that God revealed himself fully in the person of Jesus Christ.

It follows, therefore, that everything about Jesus—his actions, miracles, and teachings, as well as his Passion, Death, and Resurrection—all reveal a loving, infinite God of mercy. Pope John Paul II explained,

> The whole of Christ's life was a continual teaching: his silences, his miracles, his gestures, his prayer, his love for people, his special affection for the little and the poor, his acceptance of the total sacrifice on the Cross for the redemption of the world, and his Resurrection are the actualization of his word and the fulfillment of Revelation. (*Catechesi Tradendae* 9, quoted in *CCC*, 561)

One of the great values of studying the Gospels is to meditate on how Jesus' whole life, and especially his

Mystery—A term referring to God's infinite incomprehensibility, his plan of salvation and redemption, and the events of Jesus' life that show and accomplish this plan.

sacrifice on the cross, shows God's redeeming work in our midst. Jesus is our model. His life teaches us virtues like humility; his voluntary poverty shows us how to accept setbacks that come our way; his way of praying instructs us on how to pray.

Jesus' Infancy and Hidden Life (CCC, 522–534; 563–564)

Only the Gospels of Luke and Matthew tell us about Jesus' birth and years prior to the beginning of his ministry. Scripture scholar Fr. Raymond Brown concluded that Matthew and Luke used these vivid birth and infancy narratives to introduce *and* summarize the major theological themes of their Gospels.

Though Matthew and Luke's accounts differ from each other, each account represents an interest primarily in *theology* rather than history. Recall how the Gospel was first preached: The early disciples announced the Good News of Jesus' Resurrection and Glorification. They reviewed the deeds of his public life and the events of his Passion and Death. They proclaimed that Jesus' Death and Resurrection conquered sin and death, that he is the Savior of the world. Thus, the hearers of the Gospel should repent, believe the Good News of salvation, receive the Holy Spirit, and be baptized into Christ's body.

Only after many years of proclaiming this basic message—the *kerygma*—did the Church assemble the stories of Jesus' birth. These stories helped believers understand the full significance of Jesus' saving works and words. The symbolism of these stories reveals Jesus' identity and his purpose for coming into the world. By carefully studying what Matthew and Luke wrote about Jesus' birth, we can get an excellent overview of how their Gospels proceed.

Read the texts of Matthew 1–2 and Luke 1–2 before proceeding.

In comparing these two infancy narratives, you will be undertaking *redaction criticism*. Recall from Chapter 1 that redaction criticism studies the Evangelists as editors—how and why they arranged their sources the way they did. It attempts to discover the particular theological slant or insight of the given writer and how this influenced his arrangement of the material.

The chart below compares the outline of Matthew and Luke's infancy narratives.

MATTHEW	LUKE
• Genealogy of Jesus	• Jesus and John the Baptist's births foretold
• Conception of Jesus	• Annunciation to Mary
• Birth in Bethlehem	• Visitation
• Visit of the Magi	• Magnificat of Mary
• Flight into Egypt	• Birth and circumcision of John
• Slaughter of the Innocents	• Benediction of Zechariah
• Return to Nazareth in Galilee	• Hidden life of John the Baptist
	• Birth of Jesus
	• Visit of the Shepherds
	• Presentation in the Temple (Simeon and Anna)
	• Hidden life of Jesus
	• Jesus in the Temple

Adoration of **the Magi**

Matthew's Infancy Narrative

Scholars believe that the author of Matthew's Gospel was a Jewish Christian who was writing for Jews who became Christians. Therefore, his infancy narrative generously draws on themes from the Old Testament with which his audience would be very familiar. His purpose was to show that Jesus fulfilled Old Testament prophecies about the Messiah. Note how he accomplishes this:

- In the genealogy, Matthew traces Jesus' ancestry to Abraham, the father of the Jews. Jesus is the promised Messiah, greater than King David. He is the son of David, son of Abraham, the fulfillment of Jewish hopes.

- Jesus comes to us through the power of the Holy Spirit. He is divine and a man. Isaiah prophesied his origin:

  "Behold, the virgin shall be with child and bear a son, and they shall name him Emmanuel," which means "God is with us." (Mt 1:23)

- Matthew also reports that another ancestor of David, Joseph, accepts the angel's message about Jesus' divine origin. (It is interesting to note that Jesus' lineage is through his foster father, Joseph, and not his biological mother, Mary.)

- Jesus is born in Bethlehem, David's home and the town Micah (Mt 2:6) prophesied would be the home of the messiah. The *magi*—representing all Gentiles—are the first to recognize Jesus as a king when they present him the royal gifts of gold, frankincense, and myrrh. Here Matthew contrasts how many of the Chosen People would fail to recognize the adult Jesus as the Messiah. He also hints how the resurrected Lord would commission his Apostles to preach the Gospel to all nations, including the Gentiles (Mt 28:19). This mystery is known as the *Epiphany*, the time when Jesus is manifested as the Messiah, Son of God, and Savior of the world. Matthew's point is that the Gospel is meant for everyone, Jew and Gentile alike (*CCC*, 528).

- Matthew uses a specifically Jewish literary form known as *midrash* in his infancy narrative. Midrash relates past scriptural events to help explain and interpret the present event. The key intent is not necessarily historical accuracy of detail as much as it is to convey theological and religious truth. For example, the Slaughter of the Innocents by the wicked King Herod is not specifically documented in any contemporary historical record. However, it does remind the reader of the prophet Moses' own narrow brush with death as an infant (Ex 1–2). In Matthew's Gospel, Jesus is, in fact, the new Moses. Jesus' narrow escape from death as an infant at the hands of cruel leaders who were more interested in political intrigue than with the truth also portends his future.

- Joseph, the foster father of Jesus, brings to mind the Old Testament patriarch Joseph. You might recall that the Old Testament Joseph saved his starving kinsmen

Epiphany—The term to describe the mystery of Christ's manifestation as Savior of the world.

midrash—A literary form that relates past scriptural events to help explain and interpret present events.

The Flight **into Egypt**

by inviting them to come to Egypt. Jesus' foster father, Joseph, saves Jesus by taking the holy family to Egypt at the news of Herod's threat. Herod's slaughter and the flight into Egypt reveal that from the beginning the forces of darkness were opposed to the light. Jesus' "whole life was lived under the sign of persecution" (*CCC*, 530).

- Jesus is also the "new Israel" who leaves Egypt. As the prophet Hosea wrote: "I called my son out of Egypt." Joseph settles in Nazareth of Galilee, a part of the Holy Land pious Jews considered contaminated by Gentile influence. It is from this territory that Jesus would embark on his mission.

Luke's Infancy Narrative

Luke wrote for a Gentile Christian audience. He portrays Jesus as the Lord who came to save everyone, even the lowly. Among the other teaching points of Luke's infancy narrative are the following:

- Luke masterfully interweaves the announcements and the actual births of Jesus and his kinsman John the Baptist in the infancy narrative. Yet Luke clearly shows that it is Jesus, not John, who is the Messiah because it is Jesus who has divine origins. John is the immediate precursor and forerunner of Jesus. John is the one to "prepare the way," already recognizing from his mother's womb the coming of the Messiah. Jesus' mother, Mary, accepts in humble faith the mystery of God's work. Elizabeth recognizes the miracle that has taken place:

"Most blessed are you among women, and blessed is the fruit of your womb. And how does this happen to me, that the Mother of my Lord should come to me?" (Lk 1:42–43)

- John's father, Zechariah, blesses God's wondrous work in his benediction hymn. He addresses John at the time of his son's birth:

"And you, child, will be called Prophet of the Most High, for you will go before the Lord to prepare his ways." (Lk 1:76)

- Jesus' circumcision signifies his incorporation into the Jewish people. The circumcision prefigures Jesus' lifelong submission to the Law and his willingness to worship in the faith of his ancestors.
- Jesus' presentation in the Temple reveals him to be the firstborn son who belongs to God. The prophets Simeon and Anna recognize him as the long-expected Messiah, bless God for being allowed to see him, and predict the perfect sacrifice that the adult Jesus will endure for our salvation ("the sword of sorrow that will pierce Mary's heart").
- Jesus reveals himself first to the lowly. Jesus was born in poverty. He allows the shepherds to see him first. Pious Jews like the Pharisees derisively referred to shepherds as "people of the land." Their occupation would not allow them to faithfully keep the religious rituals demanded by the Law. Yet Jesus came to such as these. Jesus' poverty is also shown at the Presentation, when his parents offer "a pair of turtledoves or two young pigeons" as a sacrifice, the gift of poor people who could not afford the gift of a year-old lamb.
- Jerusalem plays a key role in Luke's Gospel; it is a key symbol in the Christian story. Luke covers in detail Jesus' journey to Jerusalem, the holy city, which "kills its prophets." It is in Jerusalem that Jesus' Passion, Death, and Resurrection accomplish our salvation. It is in this city that the Holy Spirit descends on the Apostles and sends them to the ends of the world to proclaim Jesus as Lord.

CRÈCHE DEVOTION

St. Francis of Assisi in 1223 is credited with the devotion of the Christmas crèche (Nativity scene with the crib). The devotion highlights our Savior's humility in coming to us as a helpless infant, lying in a manger between an ox and a donkey.

Research the origin of this devotion. Next, design your own Christmas crèche or download from the Internet pictures of two Nativity scenes that come from two different ethnic groups (for example, Polish and Mexican.) Finally, write a prayer or poem that expresses your personal devotion to the infant Jesus.

- The infancy narrative foretells Jerusalem's importance. As the Gospel opens, Zechariah is in Jerusalem. Mary and Joseph present Jesus in the Temple. And at age twelve Jesus travels to Jerusalem for the Passover feast. His time there as a youth points to a future day when he will again confound the learned, some of whom will plot his death.

- The infancy narrative ends with Jesus' returning in obedience to Nazareth to live with Joseph and Mary. His obedience contrasts with Adam's disobedience to God. It points to Jesus' obedience to his heavenly Father. Jesus' hidden life in Nazareth, where he learned a trade from Joseph and lived the ordinary life of a Jewish young man, reveals the mystery of how the God-made-man identifies with most humans, especially in our ordinariness.

Jesus' Baptism (CCC, 535–540; 565–566)

> It happened in those days that Jesus came from Nazareth of Galilee and was baptized in the Jordan by John. On coming up out of the water he saw the heavens being torn open and the Spirit, like a dove, descending upon him. And a voice came from the heavens, "You are my beloved Son; with you I am well pleased." (Mk 1:9–11)

Each of the four Gospels uses Jesus' baptism as the starting point of his ministry. The Gospels also all mention that Jesus was baptized by John the Baptist. Luke additionally adds that John the Baptist began preaching a baptism of repentance in the fifteenth year of the reign of Tiberius Caesar.

The Gospels report that John challenged his hearers to share their clothing and food with the poor. He told tax collectors to exact no more than what was owed. He instructed soldiers to be gentle with people and to be content with their salary. Eventually, he courageously condemned the behavior of King Herod Antipas, who had married Herodias, his brother's wife. This so incensed Herod that he arrested John and had him beheaded.

The Gospel writers compare John the Baptist to the Old Testament prophet, Elijah. Like Elijah, John wore a garment of camel's hair and a leather belt. His diet consisted of grasshoppers and wild honey. Some scholars have described John as the last of the Old Testament prophets. It was John's role to precede the Messiah and announce his coming.

Some first-century Jews believed John to be the Messiah. He clearly said this was not the case:

> John answered them all, saying, "I am baptizing you with water, but one mightier than I is coming. I am not worthy to loosen the thongs of his sandals. He will baptize you with the holy Spirit and fire." (Lk 3:16)

John baptized in the Jordan River, which was a symbol for Jewish freedom, the point of entry into the Promised Land after forty years of penance and suffering in the desert. Through baptism in the Jordan, John's followers showed their willingness to become like their ancient ancestors. They were willing to turn from self-centered sinfulness to be open

Baptism of **Christ**

again to God's Word. Thus, John's baptism was a public sign of repentance as they prepared for the coming of the Messiah.

After Jesus' years in Nazareth, the Holy Spirit led him to the Jordan, where John baptized him. Thus, the sinless Savior identified with all humans in their spiritual need. He took on the identity of his people as he was immersed in the waters of the Jordan. He allowed himself to be numbered among the sinners. Thus the mystery of Jesus' baptism displays the Lord's humility. From the beginning of his mission of preaching and healing, he accepted the role of God's Suffering Servant.

Each of the Gospel accounts of Jesus' baptism notes the role of the Holy Spirit descending on Jesus in the form of a dove and the heavenly voice that proclaims Jesus to be the Son of God. These three phenomena—the opening of the sky, the descent of the Spirit, and a voice—identify Jesus. Depending on which Gospel you read, the experience after Jesus' baptism can be seen as a private event, which Jesus later revealed to his Apostles, or a public event that was seen by all present at the time. Because of the inconsistencies, we cannot tell for sure who really witnessed these events. However, all the Gospel writers do emphasize the significance of Jesus' baptism in the following ways:

- The opening of the sky represents that God has come to his people in Jesus. His mission is about to begin.
- The dove is a symbol of joy, innocence, freedom, power, and peace all combined into one rich image. It suggests that we are at the dawn of a new age. This new era will erupt under the influence and direction of the Holy Spirit.
- The voice proclaiming "You are my beloved Son" (Mk 1:11) brings to mind the words of two Old Testament prophecies: Psalm 2:7, which promised the coming of the anointed king, the Messiah; and the prophet Isaiah, who talked about the Suffering Servant:

> Here is my servant whom I uphold,
> my chosen one with whom I am pleased,
> Upon whom I have put my spirit;
> he shall bring forth justice to the nations.
>   (Is 42:1)
> Yet it was our infirmities that he bore,
> our sufferings that he endured. (Is 53:4)

A technique of historical criticism is the *criterion of embarrassment*, which scholars use to determine what we can be sure really happened in Jesus' earthly life. This criterion would conclude convincingly that Jesus must have been baptized because it would have been embarrassing to the early Church to have to teach that the sinless one humbled himself in this way. Jesus' baptism is not something the Church would make up because it raises the potential question that Jesus might have had sins that needed cleansing.

Theologically, however, we know good reasons why Jesus did allow John to baptize him. For example,

- to show perfect submission to the Father's will,
- to foreshadow the baptism of his death for the remission of our sins, and
- to serve as the model for our own baptism.

Jesus' baptism reveals who he is and what his mission is to be. It shows that Jesus is about his Father's work of salvation. This work is accomplished by the power of the Holy Spirit. Thus, Jesus' baptism foreshadows baptism that is done in the name of the

Father, and the Son, and the Holy Spirit. Why? So the Lord's work can continue through his followers. At our own initiation into the Church, the baptismal waters take us sacramentally down into the waters with Christ so we may rise with him, be born anew in the Holy Spirit, and become adopted children of the Father.

The Temptations of Jesus

> For we do not have a high priest who is unable to sympathize with our weaknesses, but one who has similarly been tested in every way, yet without sin. So let us confidently approach the throne of grace to receive mercy and to find grace for timely help. (Heb 4:15–16)

Luke's Gospel reports that after Jesus' baptism, the Holy Spirit led Jesus into the desert to pray, fast, and prepare himself for his difficult mission ahead. During this forty-day retreat, Jesus was tempted by Satan. The passage from the Letter to the Hebrews reveals that Jesus' temptations help him identify with us. Like us, Jesus was tempted; unlike us, however, he never gave in to his temptations, that is, he never sinned.

Temptation to sin is not the same as sin itself. In the Old Testament, the Hebrew word for temptation meant "to try" or "to test." Temptation forces people to respond, showing what they will do or what they can do in a given situation. However, in his Letter to the Galatians, St. Paul warns us to be on guard and avoid all temptations. Jesus himself taught his Apostles to pray that they may not fall into temptation. Jesus knew us so well when he said, "The spirit is willing but the flesh is weak" (Mk 14:38).

FAST FOR CHRIST

The traditional spiritual practice of fasting can help a person focus on God. Added benefits of fasting include gaining a greater sensitivity to the needs of others and insights into things that have control over us. Fasting involves giving up something we usually need for a specific period of time. Usually, we fast from food since it is a great good that God gave us both to sustain and enjoy life. But we sometimes tend to gluttony, wanting more and more of a good thing. The object of our desires can become our god. This is true not only of food, but of any good thing—watching television, playing video games, shopping for consumer items, and so on.

Assignment: Attempt the spiritual discipline of fasting for seven days. Give up something you enjoy—snack foods, text messaging, the Internet, a ride to school—in order to remind yourself that only God has control of your life, not the various things people can become dependent on.

Jesus' forty days in the desert also recall Israel's forty years undergoing a test in the wilderness. The Chosen People were tempted often and gave in to sensuality, that is, to the fulfilling of their own appetites. They bowed down and worshiped false gods in the form of statues. They put the Lord to the test. Jesus, unlike the people in the desert, remained faithful to his Father. He is the New Israel.

Jesus' triumph over Satan also brings to mind the temptation of Adam and Eve in the

Garden. In Adam's case, Satan triumphed. Jesus, however, is the New Adam. He decisively conquers the devil and sends him away. Jesus' victory in the desert foreshadows his ultimate victory in his Passion, Death, and Resurrection.

Jesus' retreat in the desert helped him to clarify his identity as God's Son and what his mission was to be. As God-made-man, Jesus refused the easy way out. He would face temptation as any man would.

He would fight evil through a life of gentle, compassionate service of others. He would embrace the suffering that his mission of truth and service would eventually entail and invite others to believe in him. Satan's temptation is that he offers the easy way out; Jesus shows that though love is tough and demanding, it is the only way to proceed.

SCRIPTURE READING: JESUS IS TEMPTED

There was no eyewitness to Jesus' temptation in the desert. Mark simply records that Satan tempted him. Luke and Matthew report the nature of Jesus' three tests, though they disagree on their order. Jesus may have told his disciples of these temptations. Or, the Gospel writers may have summarized in this story the kinds of temptations Jesus experienced throughout his whole life.

Read the account of Jesus' temptations from Luke 4:1–13 while noting the following information for each temptation:

First Temptation: Turn stone into bread
Jesus' Response: "One does not live by bread alone" (Lk 4:4).
Meaning: Jesus refuses to work a miracle to satisfy his own human needs. He trusts that his Father will provide for him. Moreover, he does not envision his ministry as an economic Savior to a suffering people. His personal example would show that through suffering he would serve as Living Bread for all God's children.

Second Temptation: Do homage to Satan
Jesus' Response: "You shall worship the Lord, your God, and him alone shall you serve" (Lk 4:8).
Meaning: Jesus refuses to seek worldly power, especially by sharing power with Satan. His exclusive commitment is to his heavenly Father. Throughout his ministry, Christ resists the repeated appeal of the crowds to be a military, political leader. In contrast, he chooses to be a king for others, through suffering and humble service, not by mimicking the tyranny of worldly rulers.

Third Temptation: Prove you are God's Son
Jesus' Response: "You shall not put the Lord, your God, to the test" (Lk 4:12).
Meaning: Jesus refuses to test God, the loving Father, whom he knows intimately. Jesus will not perform a sensational deed to get people to believe in him. Rather, he realizes God's will is the way of service and suffering and wants his followers to respond to him in true freedom and in faith.

FOR REVIEW

1. Discuss two religious meanings of the word *mystery*.

2. List five ways Matthew and Luke's infancy narratives differ.

3. What major theological points were Matthew and Luke making in their infancy narratives?

4. Define *midrash*. Give an example of how Matthew used midrash in his infancy narrative.

5. What is the meaning of the Epiphany?

6. In Luke's infancy narrative, what was the significance of Jesus' circumcision and presentation in the Temple?

7. In Luke's Gospel, why does Jesus manifest himself first to the shepherds?

8. What role did John the Baptist play in Jesus' life?

9. What three significant events took place at Jesus' baptism?

10. Why did Jesus, the sinless one, get baptized by John?

11. Where are the accounts of Jesus' baptism placed in each of the Gospels?

12. Name the three temptations of Jesus. What did each mean?

FOR REFLECTION

- Imagine if Jesus Christ's birth were to take place today. To what group of people do you think he would appear first? Why? Write up your own Gospel account of what might take place at this modern-day Epiphany.

- Seven Christian *virtues*—chastity, agape love, humility, diligence, temperance, liberality, and gentleness—help us to avoid temptations and to offset each of the seven deadly vices listed on page 105. Transcribe the virtues into your journal, write a definition for each one, and provide an example of when you exercised the particular virtue in your own life.

Jesus **the Teacher**

In his day, Jesus was known as a rabbi (teacher), acknowledged as such by his disciples, the people, and even those who opposed him. He taught everywhere—in the Temple, in synagogues, in private homes, in fields, on hillsides, on the roadway. People flocked to hear him, seeking his views on the Law and other questions that concerned them: whether to pay taxes or not (Mk 12:13–17), matters concerning marriage and divorce (Mk 10:1–12), family quarrels over an inheritance (Lk 12:13–15), the mystery of suffering (Jn 9:2–3), the importance of the commandments (Mk 12:28–34), and so forth.

Yes, Jesus was a teacher, and a great one at that. Think of the best teachers you have had. Likely they were personable, easy to listen to, and taught important lessons in a relevant style. Jesus exhibited all of these qualities as a teacher and more. Even today his New Testament voice echoes down the centuries and touches our hearts. Jesus had several exceptional qualities, including the following:

Jesus was authentic. He instructed more by his deeds than by his words. Thus, he was genuine. The best example of this is Jesus' teaching on love. He said that the highest love we can show another is to lay down our lives for that person. Jesus did what he preached when he freely gave up his life for all of us.

Jesus pursued people. He was a wandering preacher and teacher who taught everywhere—on hillsides, on dusty roads, at the tables of the rich and poor, as well as in the synagogues and in the Temple.

Jesus loved life and related to people on their level. For example, Jesus went to a wedding feast and enjoyed himself. He performed his first miracle on this occasion. Jesus loved to eat and drink, so much that his enemies accused him of being a glutton and a drunk.

Jesus used colorful, down-to-earth language. For example, instead of giving a high-blown maxim like "Charity should not be ostentatious," Jesus said:

> But when you give alms, do not let your left hand know what your right is doing. (Mt 6:3)

Or notice the graphic image Jesus used to inform us of our vocation:

> You are the salt of the earth. But if salt loses its taste, with what can it be seasoned? It is no longer good for anything but to be thrown out and trampled underfoot. You are the light of the world. (Mt 5:13–14)

Notice, too, how the Aramaic-speaking Jesus used hyperbole (exaggeration) to tell us to avoid sin:

> If your right eye causes you to sin, tear it out and throw it away. . . . And if your right hand causes you to sin, cut it off and throw it away. It is better for you to lose one of your members than to have your whole body go into Gehenna. (Mt 5:29–30)

He does not want us to mutilate ourselves. Rather, Jesus stresses here the need to resist temptation rather than risk eternal separation from God.

Jesus spoke with authority. When rabbis of Jesus' day taught, they typically quoted prominent teachers to back up their positions. Jesus quoted no one. When he did cite Scripture, he gave novel, penetrating, and profound interpretations. He taught on his own authority, as proven by his use of the simple little word *Amen.* Amen is a Hebrew word that means "certainly." It was always used at the end of an oath, blessing, or curse. It showed agreement to what was said. However, Jesus used this simple word to *introduce* (not conclude) and to strengthen his own words: "Amen, amen, I say . . . " This way of speaking was

The Wedding **Feast at Cana**

so unusual that the Evangelists recorded it in their Gospel accounts. For example, John uses this structure twenty-five times in his Gospel.

Jesus was a brilliant debater. Jesus' opponents typically tried to trap him, to catch him in one of his teachings. Jesus was a clever teacher, though. He would have none of their games. One example involves the coin of tribute Jews were expected to give to the Roman emperor as a tax. Pious Jews hated paying it. One day the Pharisees approached Jesus with the question, "Is it lawful to pay the census tax to Caesar or not?" (Mt 22:17).

If Jesus said no, his opponents would then claim that he was preaching rebellion against Rome, a crime punishable by death. If he said yes, he would lose face with zealous Jews who hated the Roman tax. Jesus understood clearly the malice of the question. He asked his opponents to show him a coin. This was a clever move on his part because his opponents produced a Roman coin, something they should not have been carrying if they hated the Romans as much as they claimed. Their hypocrisy was immediately clear to everyone. Jesus' response:

> "Then repay to Caesar what belongs to Caesar and to God what belongs to God." When they heard this they were amazed, and leaving him they went away. (Mt 22:21–22)

Jesus saw through their ploy and made them look ridiculous.

Parables of Jesus (CCC, 546)

The English word **parable** transliterates the Greek word *parabole*, meaning "to throw" (*bollein*) "beside" (*para*). Parables compare something very familiar—like seeds, wheat, yeast, sheep, farmers, nets—to an unfamiliar idea about God's Kingdom. By using parables, Jesus challenges us to use our imaginations, emotions, and minds to grapple with the truth he is teaching. A story makes us think, to find hidden layers of meaning, to probe, and to reflect.

Jesus spoke in parables because such stories were able to convey truth in a more interesting, memorable way than simply teaching by reciting cold facts. Jesus' disciples did not take notes when he taught them; they had to commit his teachings to memory. The sign of a good teacher in Jesus' day was if a person could easily remember what the teacher taught. Jesus' stories were so vivid that his hearers could easily recall them. Although other rabbis of Jesus' day used poetic images to make comparisons in their teaching, none of their stories compare to Jesus' parables. His stand out and reveal the mind of a brilliant teacher.

parable—A typical teaching device Jesus used. It is a vivid picture story drawn from ordinary life that conveys religious truth, usually related to some aspect of God's Kingdom. It teases the listener to think and make a choice about accepting the Good News of God's reign.

PRINCIPAL PARABLES OF JESUS IN THE SYNOPTIC GOSPELS

"And he taught them at length in parables" (Mk 4:2). Listed below are Jesus' parables recorded in the Synoptic Gospels. Read one short parable from each of the Gospels. In your journal write your interpretation of its meaning.

Parable	Matthew	Mark	Luke
A Lamp Under a Bushel	5:15–17	4:21–22	8:16–18
New Cloth on Old Garments	9:16	2:21	5:36
New Wine in Old Wine Skins	9:17	2:22	5:37
The Sower	13:3–23	4:2–20	8:4–15
The Mustard Seed	13:31–32	4:30–32	13:18–19
Yeast	13:33		
Wicked Tenants of the Vineyard	21:33–45	12:1–12	20:9–19
The Budding Fig Tree	24:32–35	13:28–32	21:29–33
A House Built on a Rock	7:24–27		6:47–49
Wayward Children	11:16–19		7:31–35
Leaven	13:33		13:20–21
Lost Sheep	18:12–14		15:3–7
Weeds Among the Wheat	13:24–30		
A Treasure Hidden in a Field	13:44		
A Pearl of Great Value	13:45–46		
Dragnet	13:47–50		
The Unmerciful Servant	18:23–25		
Laborers in the Vineyard	20:1–16		

Parable	Matthew	Mark	Luke
A Father and Two Sons	21:28–32		
The Marriage Feast for the King's Son	22:1–14		
The Wise and Foolish Maidens	25:1–13		
The Servants and Their Talents	25:14–30		
Separating the Sheep from the Goats	25:31–46		
A Seed Growing Silently		4:26–29	
The Doorkeeper on Watch		13:34–37	
Two Debtors			7:41–43
The Good Samaritan			10:25–37
A Fiend at Midnight			11:5–10
The Rich Fool			12:16–21
Watchful Servants			12:35–38
The Wise Steward	24:45–51		12:42–48
The Barren Fig Tree			13:6–9
Dinner Guests			14:16–24
A Lost Coin			15:8–10
Prodigal Son			15:11–32
The Dishonest Steward			16:1–13
The Rich Man and Lazarus			16:19–31
Useless Servants			17:7–10
The Persistent Widow			18:1–8
The Pharisee and Tax Collector			18:9–14
Ten Pounds			19:11–27

A second reason for speaking in parables was to force the hearers to look at reality in a fresh way. The famous British scholar of parables C.H. Dodd captured this aspect well in his classic definition of parable as:

> a metaphor or simile drawn from nature or common life, arresting the hearer by its vividness or strangeness, and leaving the mind in sufficient doubt about its precise application to tease it into active thought.[9]

Parables "tease" the mind into active thought. Jesus wants us to change our perceptions about reality. If we do not, we will not see what he is talking about:

> They look but do not see and hear but do not listen or understand. (Mt 13:13)

Jesus' parables teach about the Kingdom of God. They are windows into the mystery of God's reign, helping us glimpse the marvelous work of God in our midst. They teach the nature of the Ruler in God's Kingdom—a compassionate, loving, incredibly generous King whom we can call Abba (Father). They teach what is required of those who wish to enter the Kingdom: repentance, humility, childlike trust, and responsible and decisive action. They teach how those living under God's rule must be forgiving, loving, and ready to serve. Finally, they speak of a future day when the Kingdom will be realized in all its glory, a day of judgment, and the need to always be ready for the coming of the King.

The teaching of the parables is usually surprising and clear, but to discover the meaning of each parable requires an open mind and an open heart. Chapters 4 through 6 will focus on several key parables in greater depth. At this point in your study, consider this very short parable of Jesus:

> To what shall we compare the Kingdom of God, or what parable can we use for it? It is like a mustard seed that, when it is sown in the ground, is the smallest of all the seeds on the earth. But once it is sown, it springs up and becomes the largest of plants and puts forth large branches, so that the birds of the sky can dwell in its shade. (Mk 4:29–32)

Note how Jesus compares the Kingdom of God to a mustard seed. This tiny seed starts incredibly small but blossoms into a large plant that brings life to many creatures of the air. So it is with God's Kingdom. It starts out small but will grow immeasurably, giving life to and providing shelter for countless people.

Jesus' Proclamations about God's Kingdom (CCC, 541–545; 551–553; 567)

> After John had been arrested, Jesus came to Galilee proclaiming the Gospel of God: "This is the time of fulfillment. The Kingdom of God is at hand. Repent, and believe in the Gospel." (Mk 1:14–15)

The central theme of Jesus' preaching was the coming of God's Kingdom. Jesus himself is the principal agent of this Kingdom. Jesus initiated the Kingdom through his words and deeds and by sending out his disciples to call people to himself. The Paschal Mystery of the Lord's Death and Resurrection accomplishes once and for all the coming of the **Kingdom of God**. The Kingdom of God has several special features, including those described in the following sections.

Field of **mustard**
inset: single mustard **seed**

The Kingdom is here now. The term Kingdom (or reign) of God refers to God's active participation in life, both in Heaven and on earth. God's presence can be detected in the actions of justice, peace, and love. Jesus ushered in God's reign. His healing of people's physical, emotional, and spiritual hurts were signs of the Kingdom. Although the reign of God starts small and often meets resistance, it will inevitably grow and powerfully transform all humanity.

The Kingdom is of a loving God, the Father. Jesus' address of God as "Abba" highlights God's love for everyone as

Kingdom of God—The proclamation by Jesus that inaugurated his life, Death, and Resurrection. It is the process of God's reconciling and renewing all things through his Son, to the point where his will is being done on earth as it is in Heaven. The process has begun with Jesus and will be perfectly completed at the end of time.

a parent tenderly loves a child. The proof of Abba's love is the sending of his only Son to live among us and gain eternal life for us.

> For God so loved the world that he gave his only Son, so that everyone who believes in him might not perish but might have eternal life. (Jn 3:16)

The Father is merciful beyond what we can imagine, like the loving father in the Parable of the Prodigal Son. Therefore, we should confidently approach him often in prayer, trusting that he will provide for us and answer our most pressing needs. Because God is so forgiving, Jesus taught that his disciples should be joyful people who imitate the Father by forgiving those who have hurt us and showing mercy to all.

The Kingdom is for everyone. God's reign embraces not only the Chosen People to whom it was first

The Return of **the Prodigal Son**

preached, but people of every nation as well. In a special way, the Kingdom belongs to the poor and lowly, those who accept it with humility. There is a special place at the table of the Kingdom for sinners: "I have not come to call the righteous to repentance but sinners" (Lk 5:32).

The Kingdom is a free gift from a merciful God; we cannot earn it. To enter the Kingdom we must accept the gift of Jesus' word, turn from our sins, and put on the mind of Jesus Christ. We must be light to the world,

allowing the Lord to shine through us by serving others. What we do to others, especially the "least of these," we do to the Lord. We must put into action his command:

> "You shall love the Lord, your God, with all your heart, with all your soul, and with all your mind." This is the greatest and the first commandment. The second is like it: "You shall love your neighbor as yourself." (Mt 22:37–39)

And who is our neighbor? Everyone, even our enemies.

The Church is the seed and beginning of God's Kingdom. Jesus promised that he would be with us until the end of time. One way he does this is through his Church, which he established through the Apostles. He entrusted special authority to Peter and his successors (the popes). The bishops and their helpers (priests) can forgive sins in Jesus' name, teach in matters of doctrine, and guide in matters of Church discipline. The Lord is also active in the communal life of the Church, participating in the lives of all its believers. The Church, the Body of Christ and Temple of the Holy Spirit, is the seed and beginning of God' Kingdom.

The Kingdom is united by the Holy Spirit. Until Jesus comes again in glory, he has sent the Holy Spirit—the Comforter—to unite his people in love with one another and with the Father and the Son. The Holy Spirit guides, strengthens, and sanctifies us as we try to follow in the Lord's footsteps and joyfully await the day of his arrival.

The Kingdom involves a life of service. Following Jesus means to do God's will, which involves living morally and serving others. Moral living and service will inevitably lead to suffering and to renouncing sin and the world's false enticements to happiness. Doing God's will requires self-denial and sacrifice, walking in the very footsteps of the Lord, even to the point of death, if necessary:

> Then Jesus said to his disciples, "Whoever wishes to come after me must deny himself, take up his cross, and follow me. For whoever wishes to save his life will lose it, but whoever loses his life for my sake will find it." (Mt 16:24–25)

However, Jesus promised that he will make the burden "light and easy" and that we will share in the peace and joy of the Resurrection. A life of service means dying to selfishness, but such sacrifice leads to an eternal life of happiness.

FOR REVIEW

1. Discuss at least two qualities that made Jesus an excellent teacher.

2. Name and define the characteristics of parables. Why did Jesus teach in parables?

3. List five key parables of Jesus.

4. What is the meaning of the term *Kingdom of God*?

5. List and discuss three important themes concerning the Kingdom of God in the teaching of Jesus.

FOR REFLECTION

• In your journal, write three paragraphs describing your idea of an outstanding teacher. Then, write another paragraph discussing how Jesus might fit this profile.

• Read and summarize Luke 18:9–14. What does this parable teach? What is its main point?

Jesus the **Miracle Worker** *(CCC, 547–550)*

> When it was evening, after sunset, they brought to him all who were ill or possessed by demons. The whole town was gathered at the door. He cured many who were sick with various diseases, and he drove out many demons. (Mk 1:32–34)

All of the Gospels attest that Jesus was a **miracle** worker. Miracles were a vital part of his ministry. They gave proof to the claim that God's Kingdom was at hand and that Jesus was the Kingdom's principal agent. They confirm that God the Father sent him. They invite faith in him and help reveal his true identity as God's only Son.

Scholars typically list four categories of Jesus' miracles.

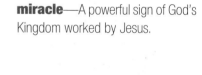
miracle—A powerful sign of God's Kingdom worked by Jesus.

1. Physical healings. Jesus was a healer *par excellence.* He caused blind people to see, deaf people to hear, and lame people to walk. He cured many dreaded skin diseases, healed a woman who had been bleeding for twelve years, and relieved the sufferings of many others.

2. Nature miracles. Jesus demonstrated mastery over the elements. He calmed a storm and walked on water. His cursing of a fig tree caused it to wither. He fed the five thousand when he multiplied the loaves and fish. He changed water into wine.

3. Exorcisms. An exorcism is the expulsion of an evil spirit. In Jesus' day, these spirits possessed and tormented people and sometimes drove them crazy. Among Jesus' exorcisms was his expulsion of a legion of spirits from a crazy man, sending the evil spirits into a herd of swine, which then ran off a cliff. On other occasions, Jesus healed epileptics, a possessed blind and mute man, and a demoniac who was in the local synagogue.

4. Raising from the dead. The Gospels report several examples of Jesus' bringing a dead person back to life: the widow's son at Nain; the daughter of Jairus; and his friend, Lazarus, whose corpse lay rotting in the grave.

Miracles and Faith

Not everyone in Jesus' day believed in miracles. Some people took offense at him because he would not work miracles to satisfy their curiosity or to prove himself to possess the powers of a magician. Some of his contemporaries refused to believe no matter what. For example, John's Gospel tells us about a man Jesus cured of his blindness (Jn 9:1–34). Jesus' opponents simply claimed that the man was never blind to begin with. On other occasions, people admitted Jesus could heal, but they gave credit to Satan, a charge that Jesus claimed was ridiculous. Jesus said, "Every Kingdom divided against itself will be laid waste and house will fall against house" (Lk 11:17), meaning, why would Satan do good to work against himself?

With an understanding of *miracle* as "a suspension of the laws of nature," many people today think that God simply does not get involved in the natural universe. They believe science will one day be able to explain everything that is unexplainable, the apparently miraculous. For example, contemporary unbelievers might say that Jesus was really like a modern-day psychiatrist. He knew what emotional disorders were afflicting people who came to him; he only said the right words to make them mentally well. Other skeptics interpret miracles like the multiplication of loaves and fish as merely symbolic. For example, they claim that the real "miracle" was that the little boy shared his food, thereby inspiring the rest of the crowd to share their food among themselves. Still others claim that Jesus' "raisings from the dead" were simply resuscitations of sick people in a deep coma. According to this explanation, Jesus may have known a form of artificial respiration that revived an apparently dead person.

In all these interpretations, note how skeptics limit God and his ability to work through an extraordinary person like Jesus. At root, many modern disbelievers are denying the divinity of Jesus or simply misapprehending the nature of a biblical concept of Jesus' miracles.

The New Testament Concept of Miracle

To understand the meaning of Jesus' miracles, we have to look at them from the biblical perspective. The Bible provides a religious understanding of miracles. It assumes that God continues to work in human history. God the Father proves his compassion through miraculous events performed by his Son.

The New Testament uses three different but related words to express the concept of miracle. The Synoptic Gospels use the word *dynamis,* which means "act of power." Note how the English words *dynamic* and *dynamite* are derived from this Greek word. On the other hand, John's Gospel uses the Greek words *ergon* ("work") and *semeion* ("sign") for miracle. In John's Gospel, Jesus' "works and signs" reveal Jesus' glory, purpose, identity, and relationship to his Father. Jesus' mighty works were both *power*ful and *sign*ificant.

These adjectives tell us something important about Jesus' miracles:

First, Jesus' miracles reveal God's power. This teaching has several corollaries:

- *In and through Jesus, God's power has broken into human history.* As the Creator of all, God is the ruler of nature. When Jesus calmed the storm, for example, he was demonstrating that he is closely identified with Yahweh, who is the master of the universe. The miracles help show who Jesus is and where he comes from.
- *Jesus has mastery over Satan and the forces of darkness.* When Jesus drove out demons, he was proclaiming that God has power over sickness and the evil it brings upon people. When he raised someone from the dead, Jesus showed that he has power over the worst evil of all—death. Jesus is crushing Satan's power.
- *Jesus has power to forgive sins.* Sin separates people from God and others. It makes us hate ourselves, other people, and God. It leads to death. When Jesus forgives sin, he is speaking as God. He helps free people from the alienation that causes spiritual suffering and death. His opponents criticize him for forgiving sin because they believe only God can forgive sin. Jesus performs miracles to show that he has the power to forgive sin and that he is God.
- *Thus, miracles reveal Jesus' identity.* Anyone who has the power demonstrated by Jesus' miracles—power over nature, sickness and death, Satan, and sin itself—must be God himself. The miracles help show that Jesus is God's Son.

Second, Jesus' miracles are signs of the coming of God's Kingdom. Again several related teachings follow:

- *Jesus dramatically witnesses to God's love and compassion through his miracles.* For example, when Jesus associated with the lepers—who were despised and avoided because of their dread disease—he communicates powerfully that God cares. When he cured them of this disease, he further shows that God has compassion for his people.

- *God's Kingdom is here; Satan's reign is ending.* Sin, sickness, and death entered the world when Adam sinned. Jesus is the New Adam who inaugurates God's reign over human hearts. The miracles are the signs of the advent of God's Kingdom and the end of Satan's power.
- *The miracles were a response to people's faith in Jesus.* Jesus taught that he is the Way, the Truth, and the Life. He performed miracles as a response to faith in him. For example, he raised Lazarus after his sister Martha proclaimed her faith in him:

"I am the resurrection and the life; whoever believes in me, even if he dies, will live, and everyone who lives and believes in me will never die. Do you believe this?"

She said to him, "Yes, Lord. I have come to believe that you are the Messiah, the Son of God, the one who is coming into the world." (Jn 11:25–27)

Jesus did raise Lazarus. This miracle was a powerful sign that Jesus has power to conquer even death. It symbolizes that through Jesus our own resurrection takes place. Our ultimate salvation—the conquering of our own death—comes through Jesus. He is the resurrection and the life.

John's Gospel reports that many Jews believed in Jesus after witnessing this miracle. But some went to the Pharisees, who along with the chief priests plotted Jesus' Death. Miracles force people to ask some basic questions: Is Jesus the sign we have been looking for? Is he the promised one? Is he the Messiah? In conclusion, it is accurate to say that Jesus' miracles help us to face and answer the question he posed for Peter and the other Apostles: "Who do you say that I am?"

THE MIRACLES OF JESUS

Listed below are some key miracles of Jesus. Follow the directions below to complete the exercise.

1. Read all of the versions of each miracle in **boldface** type.

2. Note what has taken place on the surface level; for example, Jesus cures a man's blindness.

3. Decide to which of the four categories of miracle described on page 98 this particular miracle belongs.

4. Next, interpret the deeper meaning of the miracle. How does it show God's power? What significance does it have?

5. Share your conclusions with your classmates.

Miracle	Matthew	Mark	Luke	John
Changing water into wine				2:1–11
Healing of the nobleman's son				4:46–54
Disciples' miraculous catch of fish			5:1–11	
Stilling of the Storm	**8:23–27**	**4:35–41**	**8:22–25**	
Demoniacs of Gerasenes	8:28–34	5:1–20	8:26–39	
Raising Jairus's daughter	9:18–26	5:21–43	8:40–56	
Healing the woman with a blood clot	9:20–22	5:24–34	8:43–48	
Healing of the two blind men	9:27–31			
Healing of possessed mute	9:32–34			
Healing of the Paralytic	**9:1–8**	**2:1–12**	**5:17–26**	
Cleansing of the leper	8:1–4	1:40–45	5:12–16	
Healing the centurion's servant	8:5–13		7:1–10	
The Demoniac at Capernaum		**1:23–27**	**4:33–36**	
Healing of Simon's mother-in-law	8:14–15	1:29–31	4:38–39	
Raising of the widow's son			7:11–17	

Miracle	Matthew	Mark	Luke	John
Healing at the pool of Bethesda				5:1–15
Healing the blind and deaf mute	12:22			
Feeding the five thousand	14:15–21	6:34–44	9:12–17	6:5–14
Walking on water	14:22–23	6:45–52	6:14–21	
Healing the man born blind				9:1–41
Healing the man with a withered hand	12:9–13	3:1–5	6:6–11	
Healing woman on the sabbath			13:10–17	
Healing the man with dropsy			14:1–6	
Cleansing the ten lepers			17:11–19	
Healing the Syrophoenician woman's daughter	15:21–28	7:24–30		
Healing the deaf and dumb man		7:31–37		
Healing of the suffering	15:29–31			
Feeding the four thousand	15:32–39	8:1–9		
Healing the blind man at Bethsaida		8:22–26		
Healing of the lunatic child	17:14–21	9:14–29	9:37–42	
Finding the coin in the fish's mouth	17:24–27			
Raising of Lazarus				**11:1–54**
Healing the two blind men	20:29–34	10:46–52	18:35–43	
Cursing the barren fig tree	21:18–22	11:12–24		
Healing of Malchus's ear			22:49–51	
Second miraculous catch of fish			21:1–14	

Jesus' Obedience to His Father's Will (CCC, 554–560; 568–570)

The historical Jesus was a remarkable person—an outstanding teacher and a wonder worker without peer. Yet both of these roles were a sign of contradiction. Though revered by the common people, Jesus threatened many of the religious and civil leaders of his day. Much in his demeanor and his message went contrary to their expectations. For example,

- Jesus claimed to fulfill the Law of Moses, yet he emphasized the spirit of this Law, a spirit that moved him to heal sick people on the Sabbath, contrary to what the authorities thought was necessary to keep the Lord's day holy.

- Jesus freely associated with people who were considered outcasts: common sinners, prostitutes, tax collectors, unclean people like lepers, and so forth. The conventional thinking was that if you were a companion of outcasts like these, you must be one of them.

- Jesus treated women with courtesy and profound respect. It was unheard of for a teacher like Jesus to have women travel with him, hear his teachings, and witness his miracles. It would have been scandalous for Jesus to speak to a woman in public like he did with the Samaritan woman at the well, or to let an unclean woman touch him, or to compare God to a woman as he did in one of his parables. It would have been outrageous for someone to tell men that they could not divorce their wives and remarry. After all, the men of his

Transfiguration—The mystery from Christ's life in which God's glory shone through and transformed Jesus' physical appearance while he was in the company of the Old Testament prophets Moses and Elijah. Peter, James, and John witnessed this event.

day saw women as inferior and the equivalent of property. And, finally, Jesus' appearance to women at his Resurrection would not have been taken seriously. Their testimony would not hold up in court; even the Apostles found this to be too much.

- Jesus' message contained so many one-of-a-kind teachings that he could only be considered controversial and dangerous: love your enemies, serve others, forgive others countless times, be first by being last, give up your life in order to find your life, turn the other cheek, watch your interior motivations, don't judge others, trust in God as a loving Father, and so forth.

- Jesus forgave sin. Only God could forgive sin. Was this man guilty of the capital crime of blasphemy?

Just what do you believe about Jesus? He requires you to make a decision. To a person of faith, like Peter, Jesus is the Christ, Son of the living God. Jesus even gave a glimpse of his true self when he revealed who he really was to some chosen Apostles (Peter, James, and John) by means of his **Transfiguration**. For a brief moment, Jesus showed his divine glory in the company of two Old Testament figures—Moses and Elijah—who the Old Testament had reported had seen God's glory on a mountain. Their presence brought to mind how the Law (given to the Chosen People through Moses) and the Prophets (of whom Elijah was the greatest prophet) had predicted the sufferings of the coming Messiah. In the Transfiguration, all three Persons of the Trinity appeared: the Father in the voice, the Son in Jesus, and the Holy Spirit in the shining cloud.

But Jesus instructed his Apostles not to spread word of this singular manifestation. This undoubtedly confused his disciples. For them, Jesus remained a sign of contradiction. Though revealed as the king of the universe and the Messiah of all people, Jesus' mission was not to be that of an earthly king who would use power to establish his Kingdom. Jesus showed that the way to glory was the way of suffering service—the way of the cross.

At the end of his ministry, Jesus freely decided to travel to Jerusalem, the city that was a place of death for several prophets. Though he entered Jerusalem to popular acclaim as David's son, Jesus did not seize power. Rather, he withdrew to pray, to teach in the Temple precincts, and to prepare for his own Passover from Death to Resurrection.

The **Transfiguration**

His popularity and his teachings were a threat to the establishment. Almost from the beginning of his ministry, leading figures plotted to remove Jesus from the scene. Jesus' coming to their center of power in Jerusalem played into their hands. They would arrest and try him and, with the collaboration of the Roman authority, would crucify him. This, they thought, would remove Jesus permanently and quell any enthusiasm for him and his message.

But as we know from viewing the rest of his story through the lenses of history and faith, Jesus' Passion and Death led to his Resurrection and Glorification. These events comprise the **Paschal Mystery**, the great mystery of God's love poured out to rescue all humanity from sin and death. This is the mystery the Evangelists wrote about in their unique Gospels. Jesus, the Christ, the Son of God has risen from the dead! We are called to believe, be baptized, and accept the Lord and his Holy Spirit into our lives.

Paschal Mystery—God's love and salvation revealed to us through the life, Passion, Death, and Resurrection and Glorification of his Son Jesus Christ. The sacraments, especially the Eucharist, celebrate the Paschal Mystery and enable us to live it in our own lives.

FOR REVIEW

1. Name one way that Jesus was a sign of contradiction to his contemporaries.

2. What is the meaning of the Transfiguration?

3. Why did Jesus go to Jerusalem toward the end of his ministry? What did it reveal about him?

FOR REFLECTION

Based on what you read in this section, write at least two paragraphs in your journal about what you find most attractive about Jesus.

CHAPTER SUMMARY POINTS

- God is a *mystery* in the sense that he is infinitely incomprehensible to humans. Yet mystery also refers to God's saving plan for our salvation, revealed most fully in the life, Death, and Resurrection of Jesus Christ.
- *Kerygma* refers to the core teaching about Jesus as Lord and Savior.
- Matthew's infancy narrative sets out to show how Jesus fulfills Old Testament prophecies about the Messiah.
- Matthew's birth narratives show Jesus as the New Moses and the New Israel.
- Luke's infancy narratives show his Gentile Christian audience that Jesus was the universal Savior.

- John the Baptist was the precursor to the Messiah, the forerunner of Jesus. He recognized the greatness of the Lord Jesus from his mother's womb. He preached repentance in preparation for the coming of the Messiah. He was compared to the Old Testament prophet Elijah.
- Jesus' circumcision signifies his incorporation into the Jewish people. His presentation in the Temple reveals that he is the firstborn Son who belongs to God.
- Simeon and Anna foresaw the Passion Jesus would endure for our salvation.
- By including the story of Jesus' manifesting himself first to the shepherds, Luke stresses a major theme of his Gospel: Jesus reveals himself to the lowly; the Gospel is open to everyone.

- Jerusalem plays a key role in Luke's account of Jesus. It is there that Jesus' Passion, Death, and Resurrection will accomplish our salvation.
- Jesus' obedience to his parents as he grew in wisdom, age, and grace in Nazareth contrasts with Adam's disobedience to God.
- Jesus accepted baptism from John the Baptist to take on the identity of his people. His humility prefigured his future role as God's Suffering Servant. The three events associated with his baptism—the opening of the sky, the descent of the Spirit, and the heavenly voice—reveal Jesus' true identity.
- Jesus' temptations in the desert show him as like us in everything but sin. Jesus rejected Satan and his wiles.
- Jesus was an outstanding teacher who was authentic and in touch with people. He spoke with authority (as attested by his novel use of the word *Amen*) and confounded his opponents in debate.
- Jesus typically taught in parables, that is, in vivid picture stories drawn from ordinary life to teach about God's Kingdom.
- The central message of Jesus revolved around the advent of God's Kingdom or reign.
- Jesus also taught that God is a loving Abba and that his love and forgiveness are for everyone.

- A principal way Jesus preached the Gospel was through working miracles. These involved physical healings, nature miracles, exorcisms, and bringing dead people back to life.
- Jesus' miracles reveal God's power. They show that he had mastery over Satan and the forces of darkness and that he could forgive sin. They reveal his identity as God's unique Son. His miracles are also signs of God's reign, forcefully proving God's love and compassion and increasing people's faith in him.
- Jesus was a sign of contradiction to his contemporaries. Though loved by many, certain religious authorities saw him as a dangerous threat and conspired to kill him.
- For a brief moment in his ministry, Jesus allowed God's glory to shine through in the event known as the Transfiguration.
- Jesus freely decided to walk the way of the cross by journeying to Jerusalem to embrace his vocation as the Suffering Servant who would redeem humanity.

LEARN BY DOING

1. After completing the Prayer Lesson on page 106, create a collage or PowerPoint® presentation illustrating the Lord's Prayer.

2. Note the similarities and differences of each Gospel account of the baptism of Jesus. For example, John's Gospel never clearly mentions that it was John the Baptist who baptized Jesus. Read each of the accounts and answer the questions that follow.

    Mark 1:9–11
    Matthew 3:13–17
    Luke 3:21–22
    John 1:29–34

- Who sees the sky opened?

- Who sees the dove descending?

- Who hears the voice of the Father?

3. After researching the Lord's Prayer, write a short report on the meaning of each of its petitions.

4. Listed below are some common temptations that people face during the course of a day. This list corresponds to the traditional seven deadly *vices*, that is, habits that destroy our relationship with God and others. Write a sentence for each vice, explaining how you combat the challenges described.

   - **Pride**: I think I am better than others.

   - **Covetousness**: I spend a lot of time dreaming about and getting material things, and I am stingy with my possessions.

   - **Lust**: I have a tendency to give in to my sexual desires, even sometimes seeking things like pornography to excite them. I am self-indulgent.

   - **Anger**: I have a short fuse. I let things bother me and take it out on others.

   - **Gluttony**: I have a tendency to indulge every whim I have. I do everything to excess. I can't say no to my appetites. I have a problem with alcohol.

   - **Envy**: The good fortune of others brings out the worst in me. I tear others down while I build myself up. I am sarcastic and super-critical.

   - **Sloth**: Laziness is my middle name. I slack off on homework and jobs around the house. I take the easy way out.

5. Using books or the Internet to research, report on at least three aspects of daily life in Palestine in the time of Jesus. Download images where appropriate.

6. After choosing a favorite parable, rewrite and illustrate it for a child preparing for his or her first Holy Communion.

7. Interview at least five people (three of them adults) to discover what they believe about Jesus' miracles and why they believe what they do. Prepare a report for the class.

PRAYER LESSON

Prayer played an important part in Jesus' life. The Gospels show that Jesus typically prayed before any major decision or action in his life. Jesus prayed at the beginning of his ministry; he also prayed near the end of his life in the Garden of Gethsemane before undergoing his Passion and Death. In both cases, Jesus sought to do his Father's will, not his own.

Jesus taught his followers how to pray. Investigate this by completing this example of redaction criticism. Study how Luke and Matthew adapted Jesus' teaching (*didache*) on prayer to their particular audiences. First, read Matthew 6:5–15 and Luke 11:1–14. Then study this outline:

MATTHEW

1. When you pray
2. Don't be phony
3. Don't babble on; keep your prayers short
4. Here's an example of a short prayer: Our Father
5. Pray with a forgiving heart

LUKE

1. Jesus himself prayed
2. Show us how to pray
3. Here's a formula: Our Father
4. Parable of the friend—Be persistent
5. Parable of the Father: Your prayer will be answered

Can you suggest why these might be different? In other words, how might Matthew and Luke have adapted Jesus' instruction on prayer to their particular audiences?

Matthew's Jewish Christian audience had a rich tradition of prayer. Thus, he assumes that they are already praying, but he wants them to keep their prayers short and to the point, as in the Lord's Prayer. They should also trust that God indeed will answer their prayers. Followers of Jesus should always be forgiving and not like some hypocrites of Jesus' day who would show off so others would think they were holy. This teaching on prayer would make a lot of sense to a Jewish convert who had accepted Jesus.

Luke, on the other hand, wrote for Gentile converts. His pagan converts did not necessarily have a heritage of prayer. Thus, Luke points to Jesus as one who often prayed (Jews would have known this). Luke also presents the Our Father as a formula of the perfect prayer, one in which we can call God "Abba." Luke assures his audience that Jesus' Father is loving and intimately concerned about his children. Pagans experienced something different: Their gods were often cruel and vindictive. Finally, Luke stresses the need to be persistent in prayer. He assures his audience that prayers will be answered. (Gentile Christians needed this reminder because Gentiles did not have the Jewish experience of Yahweh who indeed answered the prayers of his special people.)

- *Reflection:* Rate your own prayer life. For example, ask yourself, "How important is prayer in my life?"

- *Resolution:* The Lord's Prayer teaches us to forgive. Who most needs your forgiveness right now? What will you do to forgive this person? When will you do it?

The Gospel of Mark:
Jesus the Suffering Servant

CHAPTER FOUR

Whoever wishes to be first among you will be the slave of all. For the Son of Man did not come to be served but to serve and to give his life as a ransom for many.

–Mark 10:44–45

CHAPTER **OVERVIEW**

In order to recognize Jesus, we must view his actions and hear his words with the eyes and ears of faith.

Questions about key details of Mark's Gospel, including its date and purpose, are introduced.

Part One of Mark's Gospel (1:14–8:26) reveals Jesus to be an authoritative teacher, a healer, and a miracle worker who announces that the Kingdom of God is at hand while insisting that his identity remain a secret.

In the second part of Mark's Gospel, Jesus reveals himself to be a "Suffering Servant" who discloses that obedience to his loving Father leads to ultimate victory.

The first thirteen chapters of the Gospel introduce the Paschal Mystery of Christ's Passion, Death, and Resurrection.

Faith **Perspective**

An English teacher wrote the words "Woman without her man is a savage" on the overhead, and then she directed her students to punctuate them correctly. Note how the boys and girls came up with something different:

Boys: "Woman, without her man, is a savage!"

Girls: "Woman! Without her, man is a savage!"

As this exercise shows, everything is perception. Mother Teresa of Calcutta told of a young girl who joined her religious community, the Missionaries of Charity. On her first day, Mother Teresa sent the novice to a home for the dying. At the end of the day, she came home with a radiant smile on her face. Mother asked her why she was so happy. The girl replied, "Mother, I have held Christ in my hands for three hours."[10]

How is the story about perception? Think about how others, including yourself, might react to being with dying people all day. Would you see Christ in the faces of the poor, the lonely, the rejected, the dying?

In the same way, in Mark's Gospel Jesus is many times misperceived. For example, the people in his hometown of Nazareth did not, or simply refused to, see Jesus for who he really was. Some of his relatives even thought he had lost his mind. Many others experienced Jesus as a great teacher and miracle worker, but they saw in him a Messiah who would rule with force. They wanted to make him king. Opponents thought he got his power from the devil; they judged him a threat to the nation. Even his Apostles did not fully comprehend who Jesus really was. For example, at the Last Supper, they were arguing over who would be his chief lieutenants once he established his Kingdom. Even they would not come to realize fully who Jesus was until after the Resurrection.

Not until the blinders are taken off, and we cooperate with the gift of faith, can we see clearly and understand who Jesus is. He shows that the path to glory is the way of the cross. He asks his followers—all of us—"Are you willing to have faith and let me show the way? Will you follow me?"

LIFE-CHANGING SAYINGS

Read these short sayings of Jesus from the Gospel of Mark. Copy the sayings in your journal and write one sentence for each saying with your reflection on how you might apply its message to your life.

- "Those who are well do not need a physician, but the sick do. I did not come to call the righteous but sinners." (Mk 2:17)
- "Whoever wishes to come after me must deny himself, take up his cross, and follow me." (Mk 8:34)
- "[For] whoever does the will of God is my brother and sister and mother." (Mk 3:35)
- "If anyone wishes to be first, he shall be the last of all and the servant of all." (Mk 9:35)
- "Everything is possible to one who has faith." (Mk 9:23)
- "Watch and pray that you may not undergo the test. The spirit is willing, but the flesh is weak." (Mk 14:38)

FOR REFLECTION

Which of the sayings of Jesus listed on page 110 do you find most difficult to put into practice? Why?

Background on **Mark's Gospel**

We are not absolutely certain about the identity of the author of Mark's Gospel. Tradition holds that the author of this Gospel was John Mark, a traveling companion of Paul and Peter. Paul mentions him in his letters, as does the First Letter of Peter. An early bishop and writer, Papias, called Mark Peter's interpreter and claimed that his Gospel is based on Peter's stories about Jesus. Another early Church historian—Eusebius of Caesarea—noted that Mark himself did not know Jesus or witness his ministry.

Today, most scholars do not hold that Mark is based solely on Peter's testimonies, but on a number of oral and perhaps even written collections of Jesus' sayings and deeds. For them, the author of this Gospel is anonymous. However, it can be said with more certainty that the author of Mark's Gospel was most likely a Christian who came out of a Jewish background.

The Gospel was likely written sometime between AD 65 and 70. Since the audience for this Gospel was Gentile Christians who were suffering persecution for their belief in Jesus, it could be that the Gospel was written in Rome sometime shortly after Nero's persecution of the Christians there in AD 64–65. It was during this persecution that Peter was likely martyred.

Another theory holds that the author of Mark was writing for Christians in Syria or even Palestine to bolster suffering Christians during the First Jewish Revolt against Rome (AD 66–70). These Christians would have been hated by both Romans, who considered them Jews, and Jews, who considered the followers of Jesus to be outside of their faith. If this theory is correct, then the Gospel could have been written shortly before or after the destruction of Jerusalem in AD 70.

In writing the Gospel, the author of Mark drew on oral traditions (perhaps Peter's own testimony), written collections of the parables, miracle stories, and other sayings of Jesus, and an outline of Jesus' Passion story to masterfully weave his materials into the new literary form known as the Gospel. Mark gives a simple geographical framework for presenting the Gospel. This framework includes Jesus' baptism in the Jordan (1:1–13), his preaching and performing miracles in Galilee (1:14–9:50), his journey to Jerusalem (ch 10) and his preaching, rejection, and Crucifixion there (11:1–16:8). Matthew and Luke adopted this general outline in their own versions of the Good News.

Perhaps the most important question concerning the background of Mark's Gospel is, why was it written? A predominant theme in Mark's Gospel is for the readers to remain faithful to Jesus the Lord, who himself suffered and died for them. Jesus is presented as one who does mighty deeds and teaches with great authority. He is the Son of God and the Messiah. But he is also the Son of Man who suffers and walks the way of the cross. Mark links the suffering of Jesus with his Resurrection. His message to people of all ages is that Jesus walked the path of suffering to glory and eternal life. So must his followers undergo suffering before they gain their eternal reward.

The Winged **Lion is a symbol of Mark**

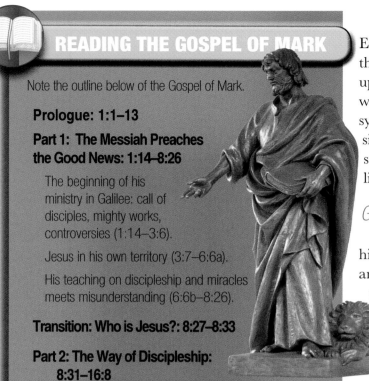

READING THE GOSPEL OF MARK

Note the outline below of the Gospel of Mark.

Prologue: 1:1–13

Part 1: The Messiah Preaches the Good News: 1:14–8:26

The beginning of his ministry in Galilee: call of disciples, mighty works, controversies (1:14–3:6).

Jesus in his own territory (3:7–6:6a).

His teaching on discipleship and miracles meets misunderstanding (6:6b–8:26).

Transition: Who is Jesus?: 8:27–8:33

Part 2: The Way of Discipleship: 8:31–16:8

The Son of Man is to suffer (8:31–10:52).

Jesus in Jerusalem (11:1–13:37).

Jesus' Passion, Death, and Resurrection (14:1–16:8).

Second Ending of Mark: 16:9–20

Read the entire Gospel in one sitting. It will take about an hour. If you want to break your reading into two segments, then first read to Mark 9:1. Read for the big picture. At this point, try not to get bogged down in details. It is okay not to understand everything. To make your reading more personal, try the following:

1. Begin by putting yourself in the presence of the Lord in prayer. Dedicate your reading session to him. Ask the Lord to allow you to see his love for you in it.

2. As you read, write down five verses that stand out and are meaningful for you, preferably something Jesus said.

3. As you read, make a note of any passages that may cause you some confusion. Write down the question you have about the passage.

The winged lion is the symbol of St. Mark the Evangelist, derived from Mark's description of John the Baptist's voice "crying out in the wilderness" upon hearing the Word of God (Mk 1:3). His voice was compared to that of a roaring lion. The lion symbolism also appears in the prophet Ezekiel's vision (Ez 1:10), where four winged creatures represent the four Evangelists: Matthew, a man; Mark, a lion; Luke, a bull; and John, an eagle.

Gospel Focus

Throughout the Gospel, Mark continually asks his readers two questions about Jesus. The hidden answers to these questions are sometimes known as the *messianic secret*: With the first question—"Who is this person?"—Mark shows how many of Jesus' contemporaries were not clear on Jesus' identity. Some saw Jesus as a threat or an enemy, an agent of the devil. Others saw him as God's agent who would throw off the Roman yoke. Still others, including the Apostles, continually misunderstood him. Jesus' interpretation of Messiahship either went over their heads or frightened them.

Second, Mark asks, "Will you follow Jesus?" Mark presents Jesus as the model of faith. All people are called to follow in his footsteps. The cost is high, but the payoff is great. The Quaker mystic William Penn summarizes well this aspect of Mark's Gospel:

> No pain, no palm; no thorns, no throne; no gall, no glory; no cross, no crown.

FOR REVIEW

1. Identify the author of the Gospel of Mark.

2. Where, when, and why was the Gospel of Mark written?

3. What is the basic narrative framework of Mark's Gospel?

4. What is the symbol for the Gospel of Mark?

FOR REFLECTION

In Mark 10:51, Jesus asks a blind man: "What do you want me to do for you?" Pretend Jesus is asking this of you. In your journal, write a one-paragraph response to Jesus' question.

Mark's Gospel **Reveals Jesus**

Part 1 of Mark's Gospel (1:14–8:26) takes place in Galilee. In these opening chapters Jesus reveals himself to be an authoritative teacher. His message centers on the Kingdom of God. Jesus announces that the Kingdom is at hand, that people should repent, and that he is God's agent in establishing the Kingdom. Jesus also reveals himself as a healer and worker of miracles. These roles reveal who he is and support his message about the Kingdom. However, most people, including even his closest disciples, misunderstand both who Jesus is and the meaning of his message.

This section examines some of these themes from Part 1 of Mark's Gospel about who Jesus is and the meaning of his message.

What the Prologue Reveals About Jesus (Mk 1:1–13)

> The beginning of the Gospel of Jesus Christ (the Son of God). (Mk 1:1)

This opening verse of Mark's Gospel underscores the main themes of the Gospel. Mark also states clearly in the prologue that Jesus himself is the Good News. It also directly answers the question hidden by the "messianic secret" of Jesus' identity. Mark tells us that the man Jesus (of Nazareth) is the Christ, the Messiah. This same person is, amazingly, the Son of God. From the opening verse there is no doubt about Jesus' identity. Readers of Mark have a distinct advantage over the Gospel characters, including the maddeningly dimwitted Apostles, who continually misinterpret and misunderstand Jesus, his teachings, and his way of the cross.

Jesus proclaimed the coming of the Gospel:

> This is the time of fulfillment. The Kingdom of God is at hand. Repent, and believe in the Gospel. (Mk 1:15)

The prologue declares what Catholics believe: God's Kingdom, which was announced and ushered in by Jesus, is intimately related to Jesus himself. The Kingdom is about God's salvation, peace, justice, and closeness to human beings. But this is exactly what Jesus is: He is God's salvation. He is God's peace and justice. He is the "man for others" who lives in our midst.

Later in the Gospel, Mark demonstrates exactly how Jesus' preaching, miracles, Passion, Death, and Resurrection prove Jesus' claims. At the beginning, however, Mark wants his readers to know that the Good News of the Kingdom is good news simply because of Jesus. God's justice and peace are entering human history because of one simple fact: Jesus is the Christ, the Son of God, and he lives.

Jesus' baptism by John the Baptist launches his public ministry. Clothed in camel-skin, John the Baptist brings to mind the prophet Elijah, who was to announce the coming of the Messiah. Jesus' baptism unveils his identity, as a dove, a symbol of the Holy Spirit, descends on him and a voice from Heaven reveals,

> You are my beloved Son; with you I am well pleased. (Mk 1:11)

The Synoptic Gospels are ambiguous about exactly who saw this vision. Perhaps only Jesus witnessed the dove, though bystanders may have heard the voice. In contrast, in John's Gospel, John the Baptist announces that he also saw the dove (Jn 1:32–34), convincing him that Jesus is the Son of God and enabling him to proclaim that Jesus is the "Lamb of God."

Mark ends his prologue with Jesus' symbolic forty-day retreat in the desert where he is tested by Satan. The forces of good and evil are present to Jesus. Jesus' obedience in the desert initiates a new Israel where Israel's sin in the original forty-year pilgrimage brought death and alienation. Jesus emerged triumphant, ready to preach faithfully his Father's Kingdom, even if it would lead to his Death.

Jesus the Authoritative Teacher

> The people were astonished at his teaching, for he taught them as one having authority and not as the scribes. (Mk 1:22)

Mark's Gospel makes it very clear that Jesus taught with authority. *Authority* is an interesting word with many nuances. Among its many meanings are these:

- the right to command;
- someone with official power;
- the source of reliable information;
- the ability to gain the respect of others and influence what they do; and
- knowledge, skill, or experience worthy of respect.

Authority comes from the word *author*, which means, among other things, "the creator or originator of something." In every case, all of these meanings apply to Jesus, the teacher with authority.

Take the first sense of authority, "the right to command." Every teacher needs students. So did Jesus. Note how he called his first disciples (Mk 1:16–20)—the brothers Simon and Andrew and also James and John, the sons of Zebedee. Jesus called; they followed. They dropped what they were doing to become "fishers of men." Soon after, he called the hated tax collector Levi, son of Alphaeus (2:14). He also immediately obeyed Jesus and left his former life behind. What is original here with Jesus the teacher is that *he* did the gathering of **disciples**. This was contrary to the custom of the day, when disciples sought out a learned and spiritual teacher. It was unheard of for teachers to be the ones to go out and solicit their students, but that is exactly what Jesus did.

Jesus' first major teaching is contained in Mark 2:1–3:6. This section involves five conflicts or controversies, all of which reveal Jesus to be an authoritative teacher by the way he handles them.

- In the first conflict (2:1–12), Jesus claims that he can forgive sin. From a Jewish perspective, this was an outrageous statement equal to **blasphemy**. Jewish beliefs held that only God could forgive sin. But Jesus showed that he had the power to forgive sin by backing up his teaching with action.

disciple—A follower of Jesus. The word means "learner."

blasphemy—Any thought, word, or act that expresses hatred or contempt for God, Christ, the Church, saints, or holy things.

- The second controversy (2:13–17) involved the call of hated Levi and Jesus' table fellowship with sinners. The conventional thinking was that if you associated with sinners then you, too, must be a sinner. Respectable and holy people would not think of socializing with outcasts. But Jesus forcefully defended his practice by teaching that God's Kingdom *includes*, not *excludes*. In challenging the complaining scribes and Pharisees, he said:

  > Those who are well do not need a physician, but the sick do. I did not come to call the righteous but sinners. (Mk 2:17)

- A third conflict involved Jesus' not fasting according to the strict obligations of Jewish law. But Mark presents Jesus as the author of a new age. He is the Bridegroom who is ushering in God's Kingdom. Fasting signifies penance. With Jesus here on earth, however, it is a time to rejoice and to celebrate:

  > No one pours new wine into old wineskins. Otherwise, the wine will burst the skins, and both the wine and the skins are ruined. Rather, new wine is poured into fresh wineskins. (Mk 2:22)

- The last two conflicts involve the Sabbath. Jesus is free to interpret the meaning of eating customs on the Sabbath. Why? Because Jesus, the Son of Man, is Lord of the Sabbath:

  > The sabbath was made for man, not man for the sabbath. (Mk 2:27)

- The final dispute involved the Pharisees who taught that it was unlawful to heal a chronic disease on the Sabbath. Since such a condition was not immediately life threatening, they considered working for such a cure on the Sabbath to be forbidden by the Third Commandment. Their hardness of heart that would forbid doing good and saving life on the Lord's Day was something that greatly angered Jesus. He was not deterred by their misguided interpretation of

God's law. He—the Savior, who was doing his Father's will—proceeded to cure a man with a withered hand in the synagogue on the Sabbath (Mk 3:1–5). This bold and singular action by Jesus evoked a harsh response from the so-called "religious authorities," who simply did not want *their* authority called into question. Who was this man who would so boldly challenge them? Mark tells us what they did to get even:

> The Pharisees went out and immediately took counsel with the Herodians against him to put him to death. (Mk 3:6)

Besides teaching with authority, Jesus was a creative, original, and influential teacher, one whose knowledge gained him the respect of the people. We see this in Mark's Gospel in the next section of Part 1—four parables about the Kingdom of God (4:1–34), the central focus of his message. In teaching about the coming of the Kingdom, Jesus made a point to say that the Kingdom of God is a mystery. We see this in The Parable of the Growing Seed (Mk 4:26–29). Something mysterious is happening to the seed; it grows without our knowledge of how. The parable teaches that God is in charge. In *his* good time, he will bring the Kingdom to fruition.

This same theme is apparent in the parable of the scattered seeds (traditionally called "The Parable of the Sower," in Mk 4:1–20, which we will analyze in greater depth in a later chapter). At first there will be apparent failure in the reception to Jesus' pronouncement about the Kingdom; however, do not despair, because this is to be expected when sowing seeds. The Good News is that the yield will be spectacular when it reaches people of faith. There is no stopping God's Kingdom. It will result in ultimate victory. As the parable of the lamp puts it (4:21–25), what remains hidden now will become crystal clear for all to see in the future.

Finally, like a mustard seed (4:30–32) Jesus' ministry might seem small now, but in his own providence, God will eventually bring it to fullness. The Kingdom that starts small will become so large that it will embrace the whole world.

These parables would have been a source of great encouragement to those in Mark's audience who were suffering for their faith. Jesus' message gave hope to his immediate hearers, to later Christians like Mark's audience, and to Christians down through the ages to our own day as we meet resistance in working for the establishment of Christ's Kingdom. There may be a struggle now, but in God's own mysterious and hidden way, his Kingdom will win out.

Jesus' parables forced his hearers—both the crowds and his disciples—to think and interpret. But anything that can be interpreted can be misinterpreted, which is exactly what those who refused to recognize or follow Jesus did. Everything seemed like a riddle to Jesus' opposition. But the disciples were given a glimpse of the depth of the mystery of God's Kingdom:

> The mystery of the Kingdom of God has been granted to you. (Mk 4:11)

TEACHING ABOUT JESUS

Be a "teacher of the faith." Create an engaging lesson for a group of teens or adults around The Parable of the Tenants (Mk 12:1–12). Use props, PowerPoint®, videos, and other elements to enhance the lesson. Research the meaning of the parable. Help your students explore some of these possible meanings of some of the symbols in this parable. For example,

- The vineyard represents Israel.
- The tenant farmers represent the religious leaders of Israel.
- The servants represent various Old Testament prophets.
- The owner of the vineyard represents God the Father.
- The son represents Jesus.
- Those who seize and kill the son represent Jewish authorities.
- Those to whom the vineyard is given represent Gentiles.

Explain, also, that this parable is likely an **allegory**. By definition an allegory is a sustained comparison, a story in which people, things, and events have symbolic meanings that represent something else. On the other hand, most parables have only one point of comparison.

Have your students apply the lesson you have taught them by writing an answer to the following: Why would this parable cause Jesus' enemies to be outraged?

Grade yourself on how well you did teaching the lesson. Write a complete evaluation of each element of the lesson and how well it worked.

allegory—A story involving a sustained comparison in which people, things, and events symbolically represent something else.

Jesus the Healer and Miracle Worker

Mark's Gospel records the various types of miracle stories described in Chapter 1. These include healing miracles, exorcisms, nature miracles, and a raising from the dead (Jairus's daughter).

Most of Jesus' miracles in all of these types fit the following pattern. Reread Mark 2:1–12 as a way to examine this pattern:

- An *introduction* presents the setting and situation. Jesus is teaching in a room so crowded that the friends of the paralyzed men lower him through the roof.
- Jesus is witness to the *display of faith* by the people who brought the man to him. He forgives the man's sins. Forgiving the man's sins raises the ire of some scribes who were thinking that Jesus was guilty of blasphemy, claiming to do what every Jew knew only God could do: forgive sins. Understanding their thoughts, Jesus said:

> "Why are you thinking such things in your hearts? Which is easier, to say to the paralytic, 'Your sins are forgiven,' or to say, 'Rise, pick up your mat and walk'? But that you may know that the Son of Man has authority to forgive sins on earth"— he said to the paralytic, "I say to you, rise, pick up your mat, and go home." (Mk 2:8–11)

- Jesus cures the man next—*his response* to the problem.
- The *result* of the miracle follows. In this case, the man got up, picked up his stretcher, and walked.
- Most miracle stories conclude with a *reaction* to the miracle. This miracle ended that way:

> They were all astonished and praised God saying, "We have never seen anything like this." (1:12)

Jesus' miracles in the Gospel of Mark are intimately related to his proclamation of the Kingdom. They depict Jesus as God's Son successfully battling the forces of evil. They prove that even in Jesus' public ministry, God's Kingdom is actively present. For example, Jesus conquers the unruly forces of nature, something the Old Testament tells us only God can do. He manifests his power over Satan, as in his unbinding the demon-possessed man from the territory of the Gerasenes (5:1–20). And he overpowers chronic sickness and even death, the worst sickness of all (as in the case of the woman with the blood flow and the raising of Jairus's daughter, 5:21–43).

Recall how the Synoptic Gospels use the Greek word *dynamis* (translated "power") to describe Jesus' miracles. The miracles in the Gospel of Mark do indeed demonstrate that the power of God has broken into human history in a unique way. They show that salvation is taking place *right now*—through God's agent, Jesus. Jesus' miracles also point to some important themes in his message. For example, as the cure of the paralytic proves, Jesus has the power to forgive sin. Forgiving sin by backing up his words with a healing is a powerful and convincing sign of Jesus' identity as God's Son.

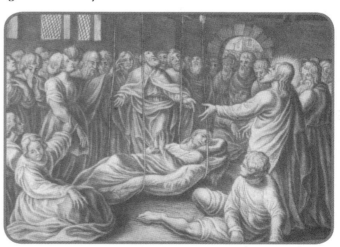

Jesus healing **the Paralytic**

Faith plays a major role in Jesus' miracles. On two occasions in Mark (5:34 and 10:52) and one in Luke (17:19), Jesus says, "Your faith has saved you." In some cases, the miracle increases faith to a remarkable degree, as in the case of exorcism of the Gerasene demoniac who begged Jesus to permit him to remain with him. But Mark also tells us what the lack of faith can do, even in Jesus' own hometown of Nazareth:

> So he was not able to perform any mighty deed there, apart from curing a few sick people by laying his hands on them. He was amazed at their lack of faith. (6:5-6)

Jesus' miracles call for faith in him and the Kingdom. "Repent, and believe the good news." Repentance, the turning away from sin, and faith in Jesus are intimately united.

Jesus the Compassionate Human Being

Of all the Gospels, Mark presents the most vivid portrait of the human Jesus. Note how Mark reports how Jesus "was not able" to perform many miracles at Nazareth, due to the people's lack of faith (6:5–6). So that readers would not misunderstand, Matthew explained what Mark really meant: "And he *did not* [emphasis added] work mighty deeds there because of their lack of faith" (Mt 13:58). (Luke dropped this reference altogether.)

In Mark's Gospel, Jesus is also occasionally angry, for instance when the disciples barred the children from approaching him (10:14). At other times, he shows his displeasure at the Apostles' slowness to grasp his message, like their inability to interpret the parable of the Sower (4:13).

Jesus is very human: He professes ignorance about the exact time of the world's end (13:32), and he curses a fig tree for its failure to bear fruit, even though it was not the season for figs (Mk 11:12–14). Luke drops this scene from his Gospel, maybe because it made Jesus appear silly. However, the perceptive reader knows that the fig tree is a symbol of Israel. What Jesus is really condemning is the lack of faith of his own people.

Mark holds nothing back in reporting reactions to Jesus. The most

remarkable case is the opinion of Jesus' relatives:

> When his relatives heard of this [that is, Jesus' preaching and healing ministry in Galilee] they set out to seize him, for they said, "He is out of his mind." (Mk 3:21)

Mark's Gospel is the only one to report this shocking, albeit typical, reaction of Jesus' family to his behavior.

The human side of Jesus presented by Mark can also be described as compassionate and loving. He embraces the children who come to him (9:36). He looks with love on the rich young man, even though the young man does not sell his goods to follow Jesus (10:21). Furthermore, Jesus' miracles prove his deep compassion for the suffering. Two heartwarming examples are when he responded to the plea of the father of the epileptic son by curing him (9:23–28) and when he heeded the cry for mercy from Bartimaeus, the blind beggar (10:46–52).

The Messianic Secret

While Mark's Gospel provides a look at the core of Jesus' humanity, there is an element of the Gospel that presents Jesus as wanting his divine identity to be kept a secret. Several passages—Mark 1:21–28, 32–34, 40–45; 3:7–12; 5:21–43; 7:31–37; and 8:22–23—indicate that Jesus directed even his own disciples to keep quiet about his identity.

Scholars term the problem identified in these verses the **messianic secret**. They explain it this way: Jesus is indeed the Messiah, the Christ,

Messianic Secret —A phrase that refers to certain passages in the Gospels where Jesus tells his disciples not to reveal his true identity.

THE SON OF MAN

The most frequently used title for Jesus in Mark's Gospel is **Son of Man**. It occurs fourteen times in Mark, thirty times in Matthew, twenty-five times in Luke, and thirteen times in John.

The Old Testament background to this title reveals two different things. First, Son of Man equates with a human being as distinct from God. It usually was used to contrast the poverty and weakness of humans versus God's might and power (see, for example, Isaiah 51:12 or Psalm 8:4). Thus, in using the title, Jesus was emphasizing his ordinary human nature, his identification with us. However, we get the idea that this title means more than that when we hear Jesus proclaim:

> And then they will see "the Son of Man coming in the clouds" with great power and glory. (Mk 13:26)

Daniel 7:14 and the Jewish books of Enoch and Esdras refer to the Son of Man as a supernatural figure, God's agent who will help usher in the fullness of God's Kingdom. He will also serve as the judge of all humanity. This is the second meaning of the term.

Jesus may have preferred Son of Man over other titles because he could shape it to his own meaning. Because people misunderstood the suffering aspect of Jesus' Messiahship, he may well have used "Son of Man" to emphasize his claim to be human like us, but also his supernatural identity as one sent by God.

Son of Man—A title Jesus used to refer to himself. It emphasizes both Jesus' humanity and divinity. Its origins are in Daniel 7:13: "I saw . . . one like a son of man coming on the clouds of heaven."

the Anointed One of God (Mark's Gospel makes this abundantly clear in the first verse of chapter 1). However, Jesus' contemporaries almost universally expected the Messiah to be a military ruler, a deliverer. Because of Roman oppression, many of Jesus' contemporaries interpreted the coming Messiah in purely political terms. Because Jesus' idea of the Messiah was radically different, and because he wanted people to approach him with true faith in him as one who serves, not as a military leader, he shunned publicity. Hence, the instructions to keep his identity secret.

This interpretation fits with Mark 8:27–33, the very heart of the Gospel. These verses hold the key to understanding both the messianic secret and the fundamental theme of the Gospel. Up to this point in his ministry, Jesus' actions and words met with both confusion and amazement. His disciples were slow to comprehend Jesus (Mk 8:21—"Do you still

not understand?"). Their slowness is symbolized in the cure of the blind man at Bethsaida (8:22–26), which took place in two stages. This is a symbolic way of saying that people's faith in Jesus was not total. People came to believe only gradually. They had a difficult time comprehending Jesus. In fact, only the demons recognized who Jesus truly is, no doubt because of their supernatural origins. However, Jesus would not allow them to speak (1:34).

Why this secret? Jesus did not want to be a sideshow, nor did he want people to think of him in false terms. He was the Messiah, yes, but in a way that even his closest disciples could not fathom. Now comes the famous scene on the road to Caesarea Philippi, where Jesus asked his Apostles the question concerning his identity. You will recall from our opening chapter how some mistakenly took him for a prophet, John the Baptist, or Elijah. It was Peter, speaking on behalf of the Apostles, who eventually correctly identified Jesus as the Christ. But Jesus ordered Peter not to spread the word about his true identity. Even Peter, the leader of the Apostles, did not grasp the true nature of Jesus' messiahship. Note Jesus' teaching:

> He began to teach them that the Son of Man must suffer greatly and be rejected by the elders, the chief priests, and the scribes, and be killed, and rise after three days. He spoke this openly. Then Peter took him aside and began to rebuke him. At this he turned around and, looking at his disciples, rebuked Peter and said, "Get behind me, Satan. You are thinking not as God does, but as human beings do." (Mk 8:31–33)

The secret of Mark's Gospel is revealed: Jesus is the Suffering Servant prophesied by Isaiah centuries before. He is the Messiah who takes up a cross, not a glittering throne.

When Jesus calls Peter "Satan," he makes it very clear that even his closest disciples are tempting him to walk the wrong path. Peter is like the devil, who tested Jesus in the desert. Peter judges by the wrong standards. Jesus will not perform deeds to serve himself, to test God, or to force people to believe. Unlike so many leaders, Jesus did not worship the god of power. He obeyed his Father by walking the rocky path to Calvary, not the marble floors of a Jerusalem palace. Glory comes after Jesus' suffering and Death. This is the way to salvation.

FOR REVIEW

1. What is Jesus' basic message about the Kingdom of God? What is his relationship to this message?

2. What does it mean to be a person who speaks with authority? Discuss several ways Jesus was an authoritative teacher.

3. How did Jesus differ from other teachers in relationship to his students?

4. Interpret the meaning of one of the parables in Mark 4:1–34.

5. Name and explain the basic elements of the typical miracle story in Mark's Gospel.

6. What do Jesus' miracles reveal about his identity?

7. What is the messianic secret?

8. Why does Jesus call Peter "Satan" in Mark 8:31–33?

9. What was Jesus' favorite title for himself? What does it mean?

10. Describe some qualities of the human Jesus as portrayed by the Evangelist Mark.

FOR REFLECTION

- If Jesus were a fellow student at your school, whom would he seek out for "table fellowship"? Explain your choice and how it would be consistent with what you read in Mark's Gospel.

- Read Isaiah 52:13–53:12, the Fourth Suffering Servant Song. The anonymous author of these verses, designated Second Isaiah, wrote these verses to encourage the exiled Israelites in Babylon. Its message is that redemption comes through suffering. In your journal, note five points from these verses that apply to Jesus. (Check marginal references or the footnotes in your Bible for help.) Also, write about a time when you suffered for your faith in Jesus.

- In your journal, write a short descriptive paragraph telling what you believe the human Jesus would have been like. Be sure to mention his most attractive qualities.

The Way **of Discipleship**

Part two of the Gospel turns to Jerusalem. On the journey to, and while teaching in this sacred city, Jesus reveals himself to be a "Suffering Servant" who discloses that obedience to his loving Father leads to ultimate victory. Jesus' Paschal sacrifice makes him the model of strength and hope for his followers, especially as we, too, undergo rejection for remaining faithful to him and his teachings. Mark challenges his readers to accept Jesus as the Messiah, but one who suffers crucifixion before he rises in glory.

Recall that Jesus predicted his Death and Resurrection soon after Peter identified him as the Messiah. Two more predictions of this fate occur in Mark 9:32 and 10:35. But just as Peter misunderstood Jesus, so, too, would the other Apostles. To counteract their misunderstanding, Jesus taught his followers that if they wished to be his disciples, then they would have to follow in his footsteps.

For example, after the first prediction, Jesus says:

> Whoever wishes to come after me must deny himself, take up his cross, and follow me. For whoever wishes to save his life will lose it, but whoever loses his life for my sake and that of the Gospel will save it. (Mk 8:34–35)

The message to Mark's readers is clear: Jesus' followers must be prepared to suffer as Jesus himself suffered. When Christians try to live their convictions in an unconvinced world, they must be ready to follow Jesus' way.

On the journey to Jerusalem (Mk 9:1–10:52), Jesus instructs his disciples on a number of topics (for example, the serious responsibility not to lead others to sin and on fidelity in marriage), but most especially on the true meaning of discipleship. His instructions also include his two other predictions about his Death and Resurrection (9:30–32). Unfortunately, the disciples still don't get it, as evidenced by their argument about who was the greatest among them (9:33–37). Jesus explains that:

> If anyone wishes to be first, he shall be the last of all and the servant of all. (Mk 9:35)

Even after the third prediction that he will be handed over to death, the Apostles still do not express a clear understanding of the meaning of discipleship. James and John ask for places of honor in Jesus' Kingdom. The only thing Jesus can promise them is suffering (10:35–40). However, the other Apostles are indignant at James and John for asking this, hinting that there is a growing understanding among them of what it means to be a disciple. In what many scholars identify as the climax of the Gospel, Jesus answers all questions about his identity and gives clear instructions on the meaning of discipleship:

> You know that those who are recognized as rulers over the Gentiles lord it over them, and their great ones make their authority over them felt. But it shall not be so among you. Rather, whoever wishes to be great among you will be your servant; whoever wishes to be first among you will be the slave of all. For the Son of Man did not come to be served but to serve and to give his life as a ransom for many. (Mk 10:42–45)

Mark masterfully follows up this revealing passage with Jesus' cure of the blind Bartimaeus (Mk 10:46–52). Unlike the healing of the blind man from Bethsaida that precedes this section (8:22–26) and required two attempts by Jesus to complete the miracle because of the surrounding lack of faith, Bartimaeus' healing by Jesus is instantaneous. The teaching is clear: If we have faith like Bartimaeus, listen to Jesus with open hearts, and depend on him as our Savior, then we will understand the secret of his Kingdom message:

> Amen, I say to you, whoever does not accept the Kingdom of God like a child will not enter it. (Mk 10:15)

This is a climatic teaching, yet to the end of the Gospel the Apostles remain confused about Jesus and his meaning. One of them—Judas—will betray Jesus.

Another—Peter, the very one who acknowledged Jesus' Messiahship—will deny knowing him.

The Apostles' inability to see represents both the local church for whom Mark wrote and us today. Betrayal and denial, especially when things got rough, were real temptations in the early Church. People were being killed for their faith in Jesus. Mark's Gospel continually encourages his audience to be faithful to Jesus. Being faithful means being willing to suffer for him, a message that is as true today as it was when Mark wrote his Gospel.

THE CHALLENGE OF DISCIPLESHIP: THE RICH YOUNG MAN (MK 10:17–31)

This famous story describes Jesus' encounter with a rich young man who wanted to know what he had to do to attain eternal life. He assured Jesus that he kept the commandments, but Jesus—who looked on him with great love—saw into his heart. Following the Law was not enough for this would-be disciple. He still lacked one thing.

What was missing with this young man was total, simple faith in Jesus, the faith of a child who trusts implicitly in his or her parents. For this young man to be really free, he needed to let go of what was holding him back from total commitment and a full loving response to Jesus—his possessions. Jesus tells him what he needs to do:

> You are lacking in one thing. Go, sell what you have, and give to the poor and you will have treasure in heaven; then come, follow me. (Mk 10:21)

But the young man could not let go of his wealth. He was sad at the thought of what true discipleship would mean: putting his total faith in Jesus, not in his possessions.

The test of his love for God and for neighbor simply meant to give what he had to the poor and attach himself to Jesus. But he was unwilling to do this, perhaps because of his enslavement to his possessions, his selfishness, or his lack of trust in the words of the one he had addressed as "good."

Jesus' teaching echoes down through the ages when he tells us how tough it is for rich people to enter Heaven. It would be easier for a camel to pass through the eye of a needle than for rich people—who think their wealth can buy them salvation—to gain God's Kingdom.

This teaching discouraged the Apostles. They, like their contemporaries, thought wealth in this life was a sign of God's special blessing. Jesus challenged this thinking because he, like the Old Testament prophet Amos, knew that inordinate wealth often caused a rift in society between the rich and the poor. He also knew Sirach's warning that riches can blind the wealthy from being honest and faithful to God (Sir 31:1–11).

"Then who can be saved?" they asked. Jesus' response is important for everyone to remember: Humans cannot save themselves. Only God can save us. God's saving grace helps us to repent from our self-centered ways. Salvation and entrance into the Kingdom are pure gifts of God's love and grace.

- Write a postscript for the rich young man. What do you think happened to him?
- Jesus said we should pick up our cross to follow him. What cross have you carried for our Lord? What cross might you be carrying now?
- Write a letter to Jesus telling him what you have to leave behind in your life to be a true disciple of his.

Arrival in Jerusalem (Mk 11:1–13:37)

The next major section of Mark's Gospel shows how Jesus ministers in the holy city of Jerusalem before his Passion and Death. He enters the city on a colt and is acknowledged as the Son of David. But, again, people do not really understand his true identity as a Suffering Servant, the paschal lamb who will offer his life for people.

During this time in Jerusalem, Jesus curses a fig tree, a symbol for Israel's leaders who were rejecting him. He also drives the moneychangers from the Temple precincts and wins verbal battles with his opponents over issues like his authority to teach (11:27–33), the payment of taxes to Caesar (12:13–17), the doctrine of bodily resurrection (11:18–27), the teaching about the greatest commandment (11:28–34), and the Messiah's relationship to David (11:35–37).

Jesus' telling the parable of the wicked tenants (12:1–12) directly threatens the religious leaders. The parable attacks them for misusing their authority and being like past leaders of Israel who had killed the prophets. Now they will use their power to kill the vineyard owner's son, Jesus. Then, according to the parable, the owner will destroy the wicked tenants and hand the vineyard over to others. This parable was a clear symbol of how God would one day welcome sinners and Gentiles into the Kingdom.

Near the end of his ministry in Jerusalem, Jesus takes his followers to the Mount of Olives for final instructions (13:1–37). Jesus warns them that all the earthly glory they see around them will one day be destroyed. He predicts the destruction of Jerusalem and the coming of the Son of Man. His warning to them—and to all readers of Mark's Gospel—is to always be on the watch, ready for the end.

FOR REVIEW

1. How did Peter misunderstand Jesus' prediction that he must suffer and die?

2. How are we to understand believing in a Messiah who suffered?

3. What lesson can a disciple of Christ glean from Bartimaeus?

4. Name two things Jesus did upon arriving in Jerusalem that angered Jewish leaders.

FOR REFLECTION

• What does it mean for you to have faith in Jesus and his Kingdom "like a child"?

• How are you "on the watch" for the coming of God's Kingdom?

The Paschal Mystery **in Mark's Gospel** (CCC, 571–573)

The Paschal Mystery of Jesus' Passion, Death, and Resurrection is the heart of the Gospel. Commemorated in today's Church during Holy Week, the Paschal Mystery encompasses God's love for his people. In Baptism we are initiated into this mystery. The Eucharist re-presents (makes present) the Paschal Mystery. This great mystery of God's love for his people, a mystery of suffering service that results in eternal life, is the climax of Mark's Gospel.

Scholars have said that the first thirteen chapters of Mark's Gospel serve as an apt introduction to the Passion narrative. Mark has shown that Jesus is indeed the Messiah; but time and again, he has indicated how Jesus is also the Son of Man who has come to suffer so we may have abundant life.

The Passion narratives were probably the oldest stories about Jesus circulating in the early Church. The four Gospels agree on the basic essentials of Jesus' Passion, but each Evangelist has his own way of telling the story. Mark's emphasis is to show starkly how everyone abandoned Jesus at the end. Judas betrays him; the three disciples fall asleep during Jesus' agony; Peter denies knowing him. When Jesus is arrested, everyone flees; even the young man lurking on the outskirts runs away, losing his clothing. The Jewish and Roman authorities harshly judge Jesus. The soldiers and later the people mock him. The only words Jesus cries from the cross—"My God, my God, why have you forsaken me?"—even seem to show that Jesus thought God the Father had abandoned him, too.

Mark's Passion narrative continues the theme of the rest of the Gospel: Jesus' path is a path of suffering and abandonment. To be a follower of Jesus means to follow in the Master's footsteps.

Historical Background (CCC, 574–594)

Before looking at the individual events of Mark's Passion narrative, let us briefly sketch some background leading up to Jesus' Death. Why did some of his opponents see Jesus as a sign of contradiction to their faith? After all, Jesus never abolished the Law; he fulfilled it. He also was respectful to the Temple when he celebrated the major Jewish feasts there.

Nevertheless, the following actions and teachings of Jesus led certain Pharisees, supporters of Herod Antipas, and some scribes and priests to see Jesus as a threat to Israel's institutions. These included his

- exorcisms;
- implicitly claiming to be the Savior God by forgiving sin;
- healing on the Sabbath, even claiming to be Lord of it;
- unique interpretations of the Law "as one who taught with authority";
- disregard for cleanliness and dietary laws;
- association with sinners and tax collectors;
- teaching that God is bounteously merciful toward all repentant sinners; and
- cleansing of the Temple and his prophecy that it would one day be destroyed.

To elaborate on just one of these factors, consider Jesus' attitude toward the Temple and how it must have alienated the leaders of his day. Jesus' actions at the Temple signaled to the religious authorities that he was claiming special authority over it, something

Judas and the thirty pieces of silver for betraying Christ

they claimed for themselves. Further, when Jesus said, "Destroy this temple and in three days I will raise it up" (Jn 2:19), he was pointing to himself as the new restored Temple. Jesus' preaching and actions revealed that he was the true agent of God's forgiveness and presence. Divine forgiveness was no longer limited to the animal sacrifices controlled by priests in the Jerusalem Temple. Nor could God's sure presence only be found in the Temple's Holy of Holies. Jesus himself was the Temple in whom God dwelled; he himself is the Father's only Son, the sacrificial victim who extends the Father's mercy to the whole world, not just to the Jews.

These claims would later come out at his trial when he was falsely accused of trying to destroy the Temple. Leading religious authorities thought Jesus was a false prophet who claimed to be God. Thus, out of ignorance and the hardness of their unbelief, many members of the Sanhedrin accused Jesus of blasphemy, a crime under Jewish law punishable by stoning to death. However, under Roman occupation, only Romans could exercise the death penalty. Thus, these Jewish authorities turned Jesus over to Pilate for execution as a political criminal, a threat to Caesar.

The Meaning of Jesus' Death (CCC, 595–598)

The discussion above leads to the important question as to who was responsible for Jesus' Death. Historically, Pontius Pilate, the Roman prefect of Judea, Samaria, and Idumea from AD 26–36, sentenced Jesus to death, possibly in April of AD 30. He knew Jesus was innocent, and hence violated his conscience in doing the politically expedient thing.

Jesus is brought before Pontius Pilate

A real tragedy of history has been the misguided and unjust assigning of the blame for Jesus' Death to the Jews as a people. As you read the various Passion narratives, you will see how it clearly shows that Jesus' trial was complex. For example, not all Jewish leaders were against him. Some Pharisees (like the leading figure of Nicodemus) and a prominent ally in the Sanhedrin (Joseph of Arimathea) were his supporters. There were other secret followers who may have voiced their support for Jesus during the various deliberations over what they should do with him.

To blame the Jews as a people for the Death of Jesus is anti-Christian. It is also wrong simply for the fact that all of Jesus' Apostles and the majority of his first disciples and early converts were Jews. In addition, we must never forget that the Gospel of Luke stresses how Jesus forgave his executioners on the cross, acknowledging that they did not know what they were doing. The real culprits for Jesus' Death are all of us—sinners. In fact, we who have the gift of faith and know who the Savior is crucify Christ in our hearts whenever we relapse into our sins and give way to our vices. The Second Vatican Council teaches:

> What happened in His passion cannot be blamed upon all the Jews then living, without distinction, nor upon the Jews of today. . . . Jews should not be presented as repudiated or cursed by God, as if such views followed from the holy Scriptures. (*Declaration on the Relationship of the Church to Non-Christian Religions*, No. 4)

In short, Jesus freely chose to be crucified to prove beyond doubt his immense love for us. In obedience to the Father, and according to God's definite

THE PASSION OF THE CHRIST

One of the most controversial (and highest-grossing) films in history is Mel Gibson's R-rated film *The Passion of the Christ* (2004), starring the Catholic actor Jim Caviezel as Jesus Christ. Supporters of the film praise it for making its viewers aware of the sufferings and Death that Jesus Christ underwent for our salvation. The film has been acclaimed for being the best film ever made about Jesus; for its attempt to be faithful to the historical setting, including using spoken Aramaic and Latin; and for artistic depictions of scenes not in the Gospel accounts, for example, the figure of Satan depicted as an androgynous figure milling around in the crowds. Millions of viewers have been deeply moved by the film and believe it has helped them appreciate anew God's great love for us manifested in the Death of his beloved Son, Jesus Christ, our Savior.

On the other hand, critics of the film fault Gibson for embellishing the Gospel accounts of the Crucifixion by drawing on the visions of the nineteenth-century mystic Blessed Anne Catherine Emmerich (1774–1824), reported in her *The Dolorous Passion of Our Lord Jesus Christ according to the Meditations of Anne Catherine Emmerich*. Harsher critics blame Gibson for inciting anti-Semitic passions in the viewers by his negative depiction of Jews and the comparably favorable treatment he assigned to the Roman authorities. Still others say that Gibson unnecessarily used unrelenting, brutal, and at times sadistic savagery to embellish Christ's sufferings. Further, because the film focuses on the Passion and Crucifixion, the film's detractors hold that it does not give the proper context to Jesus' life before his arrest, his teachings about love, and the various controversies that led to his death.

Regardless of how one judges the artistic or historical merits of Mel Gibson's *The Passion of the* Christ, it clearly calls attention to the greatest act of love ever performed on behalf of the human race: the sacrifice of our Lord and Savior, Jesus Christ.

plan, Jesus' Death on the cross won our salvation. It bestows on us, through the Holy Spirit, God's own abundant life. All this was accomplished when Jesus freely gave up his life for us.

As John's Gospel makes clear, Jesus' Death was a perfect sacrifice undertaken by the Lamb of God for our benefit. Early Church theology taught that this sacrifice was a "ransom" or a "redemption" that defeated the powers of evil. By substituting for each human being, Jesus took on our guilt and died a death we deserve. Why? To buy our freedom with his very person and eternal love.

Jesus Christ died for all human beings. In his unique and definitive sacrifice, Jesus took our sins to the cross and, like a new Adam, *represented* us to the Father. In his suffering and Death, Jesus' humanity became the free and perfect instrument of divine love, a self-surrendering gift of love on our behalf. It opened eternal life to us, a supreme gift that we sinners do not deserve. Anyone who reflects on Jesus' Death must be drawn to Jesus as the perfect man. He is the exemplar of love, the gracious Lord who gave all that we might live.

MEDITATING ON THE PASSION NARRATIVE

Christians for centuries have found that a great way to grow closer to Jesus is to meditate on his great act of love demonstrated on the cross. One way to do this is to read the Passion narrative while engaging in *imaginative prayer*.

The imagination is one of our most active mental faculties. It enables us to picture vividly many different scenes and enter into them. For example, you may have already spent hours trying to picture your future spouse, what kind of job you will have, where you will live, or who your children will be. Some people call this daydreaming, and it is. We can also use our imaginations in our prayer for an even higher purpose.

Praying the Gospels with our imaginations is relatively easy to do. Here's how:

- Calm yourself. Find a restful prayer position. Breathe slowly and deeply. Let the cares of the day drain from you.
- Next, enter into the presence of the Lord. Feel the warmth of his love all around you. Imagine Jesus next to you assuring you of his love.
- Now read a Gospel passage. Put yourself and Jesus into the passage. For example, make yourself a character in the story. Use all your senses—sight, smell, touch, taste, hearing. Listen carefully to the words of the passage. Pause often and let them sink in. Continue to let your imagination flow with the picture.
- Reflect on the experience. Return to the present. Ask the Lord to show you what the passage might mean for you—right now.
- Thank the Lord for your time together. Take a resolution from your prayer time and try to put it into practice.

Use this technique for imaginative prayer as you work through the Passion narrative of Mark's Gospel. Perhaps you will take the role of one of the Apostles. Perhaps in a later scene you might be a Roman guard at the trial before Pilate. Or, beneath the cross, you might simply be a curious bystander. Use all your senses. Picture Jesus looking at you. Feel his love.

Prayerfully read the Passion narrative from Mark 14:1–15:47. Check the texts and read the explanatory notes provided below.[11]

1. Conspiracy against Jesus (14:1–2). Fearing that the crowds might try to rescue Jesus, the leaders plot his death in a way that would not cause an uprising.

2. Woman anoints Jesus at Bethany (14:3–9). This anointing foreshadows the anointing of Jesus' body after his Death. Anointing a body for burial was considered of higher merit than giving money to the poor, a task that could always be done. Recall that Christ means "anointed one." This woman of simple faith recognized Jesus' true identity and mission when so many others did not. (John's Gospel identifies the woman doing the anointing as Mary, the sister of Lazarus.)

3. Judas's betrayal (14:10–11). John's Gospel says it was Judas Iscariot, Jesus' betrayer, who complained about the anointing at Bethany. John also reports that Judas kept the money purse of the Apostles and pilfered from it. This bit of information fits well with the motive Mark gives for Judas's betrayal of Jesus: *avarice* (see John 12:1–11).

4. Preparations for the Passover Supper (14:12–16). Mark hints at the impending doom, telling us that this was the day the Passover lambs were slaughtered. The man carrying the water jar would have been an unusual sight since this was normally woman's work. The disciples would have easily recognized him. Note that Jesus is planning the Passover meal, thus showing that he is in control. The sacrifice of his life for us is a free act of his will. Love is only love if it is freely given.

5. The Last Supper and the Walk to the Mount of Olives (14:17–31) (*CCC*, 610–611). Again Jesus foretells his betrayal; the Apostles still remain confused and deny that they will betray him. Jesus then celebrates a Passover meal with his Apostles. Christians see in this meal Jesus' institution of the Eucharist, a celebration of Jesus' Passover from death to new life and the gift of himself to all believers under the forms of bread and wine. Jesus' Passion, Death, and Resurrection are God's New Covenant with us, his new way of delivering his people. The Eucharist that Christ instituted at the Last Supper symbolized his offering and made it present. It is the memorial of his sacrifice. The Apostles (and their successors) will serve as his priests of the New Covenant, calling to mind what Jesus has accomplished for us and commanding us to pour ourselves out in service to others in imitation of the Lord.

After the meal, Jesus and the Apostles make their way to the Mount of Olives, where Jesus prays in great sorrow, just as King David did after his trusted son Absalom had betrayed him. On the way there, Jesus sadly predicts that the disciples will scatter when he dies. But more positively, he also tells them he will go before them to Galilee after his Resurrection, where he will once again become the shepherd who will reconstitute his flock. And sadly, over Peter's fierce denials, Jesus predicts that Peter will deny knowing him three times.

6. Gethsemane (14:32–52). Mark turns to the vivid picture of Jesus' agony. It reveals to us that Jesus, like all normal people, did not want to die. While facing the horror of his Crucifixion, Jesus was sorrowful to the point of death. From the depths of his soul, Jesus prays that the cup of impending death, which involved his battle against Satan and sin, be taken from him. But he also prays the perfect prayer that not his will, but his Father's be done.

Jesus courageously accepts his destiny and does not flee. The Apostles, on the other hand, are overcome with fear. They cannot stay awake to be Jesus' companion. Three times he tells them to stay awake and be prepared to resist the coming test, warning them that "the spirit is willing, but the flesh is weak." Their threefold failure to heed his plea foreshadows the threefold denial of Peter that is coming soon.

Cooperating with the plan of the scribes and chief priests to apprehend Jesus by stealth, an Apostle Jesus chose—Judas Iscariot—betrays him with a kiss, a sign of friendship. Note how the arrest takes place at night—the darkness that is the realm of Satan. Significantly, Jesus does nothing to encourage the use of force to defend himself after an unnamed bystander cuts off the ear of the high priest's servant. (Matthew and Luke name this defender of Jesus as one of the disciples, while John specifically says it was Peter. All three of these Gospels report that Jesus told his disciples not to use force.) Jesus rejects the expectation of many (especially the Zealots) that the Messiah would be a political Messiah.

As Jesus predicted, everyone runs away, even a naked young man who is on the outskirts of the scene. The identity of this person (only mentioned by Mark) has been given much scholarly interpretation. Was it perhaps John Mark himself, the author of the Gospel, whose mother may have owned the olive grove? Was it a new disciple who ran off when the going got tough, just as Jesus predicted, ironically leaving behind everything as he fled from Christ? Was it an angel, a symbol that Jesus is apparently abandoned by even divine helpers at his time of greatest need? We shall never know for sure. But the important point is very clear: Jesus was left alone.

7. Before the Sanhedrin (14:53–72). The so-called trial (more a legal hearing) of Jesus has stumped scholars for centuries. If you examine what is reported by all four of the Gospels, there was an interrogation before the former high priest and still influential Annas, a night trial before the high priest Caiaphas, and a session in front of the Sanhedrin. Exactly how and when each of these happened is open to debate.

Mark's Gospel simply reports a night trial before the Sanhedrin and the high priest. According to Jewish law codified in approximately the third century AD, authorities were not permitted to hold trials for capital crimes at night or on the eve of a feast day. If witnesses contradicted themselves (as in Jesus' trial), they were to undergo the penalty the accused would have suffered. Furthermore, a person was not guilty of blasphemy unless he expressly pronounced the divine name (something Jesus had not done). It is not clear, however, if any of these laws were in effect in Jesus' day. Competent scholars think there may well not have been a clear violation of any written law governing trials at the time of Jesus. However, all the Gospels do report that the high priest was insensitive to normal legal procedures.

What scholars unanimously agree on are two things: (1) The Sanhedrin had a session where they discussed Jesus, and (2) the high priest or priests interrogated him sometime soon before the Roman execution. John's account may be more accurate in showing that these may have been two separate sessions, the first some days before the meeting on the night Jesus was arrested.

Jesus does not defend himself at this legal proceeding, perhaps because he knows that it would be useless to do so against trumped-up charges. However, in Mark's Gospel he does forcefully and without hesitation acknowledge that he is the Christ, the Son of the Living God. And he predicts that the Son of Man will come in glory. This claim outrages the leaders. It reinforces the picture they had of him as one who claimed that he could speak for God. This to them was blasphemy, a crime punishable by death under Jewish Law. Thus, they accused Jesus of this crime and began to spit on, strike, and ridicule him.

In the meantime, as Jesus confesses who he is, Peter, recognized as a friend of Jesus by his Galilean accent, denies knowing Jesus. Peter, who had earlier acknowledged Jesus' true identity as Messiah, now betrays his friend and master. But he realizes what he does and bursts into tears. His repentance and sorrow should encourage any of us who have turned on Jesus. Jesus will always accept us back as his friend. Peter, the boastful leader, ends up remaining faithful to Jesus, even being crucified like him (but in an inverted position on the cross). (The Roman audience for whom Mark wrote would know Peter's destiny quite well since he was martyred shortly before Mark wrote his Gospel.)

8. Jesus and Pilate (15:1–20). Under Roman occupation, the laws in effect in Judea allowed only the

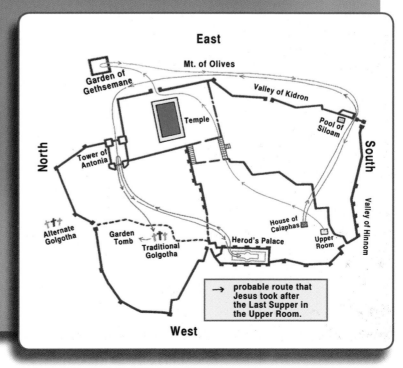

probable route that Jesus took after the Last Supper in the Upper Room.

Roman prefect the right to assign the death penalty for crimes of a non-religious nature. The Sanhedrin determined that Jesus had committed blasphemy, a capital crime, but Pilate would have scoffed at this as not worthy of death under Roman law. However, claiming to be a king in competition with Caesar (sedition) was a capital offense. So this is the charge the Jewish authorities took to Pontius Pilate, who served as the fifth prefect of Judea and Samaria from AD 26–36.

The historical record shows Pilate to be a fairly competent ruler who seemed to work well enough with Caiaphas, the high priest. However, the Jewish historian Josephus paints a rather harsh picture of him, as does the Jewish philosopher Philo. They portray Pilate as arrogant and a rogue, a picture that resembles fairly closely the portrait painted in John's Gospel. One telling report is of Pilate's unleashing his soldiers, dressed as civilians, to beat Jewish citizens who were protesting his use of the Temple treasury to build an aqueduct.

In one way or another, all the Gospels agree that Pilate knows that Jesus is innocent, that "it was out of envy that the chief priests had handed him over" (v. 10). He schemes to escape responsibility by invoking a Passover custom of freeing a prisoner of the citizens' choosing. Thinking they might ask for Jesus, Pilate miscalculated. The people, undoubtedly riled by the Jewish leaders, ask for Barabbas, a bandit (called a "killer" in Acts 3:4) who was involved in a violent civil disturbance. Caving to crowd pressure, Pilate pronounces judgment on Jesus. Ironically, he frees Barabbas, guilty of a political crime, while the Innocent One he declares guilty. Pilate then has Jesus scourged and turns him over to the soldiers for crucifixion.

Pilate also mockingly calls Jesus "King of the Jews," unwittingly speaking the truth. Jesus is indeed king of the Jews, of all people, of the universe. But Mark shows how this servant king stooped to embrace us in his love. Pilate's soldiers continue to mock Jesus, dressing him in a purple gown and crowning him with thorns. They insult him and treat him as an object—not a person—worthy only of derision. They spit on him in utter contempt.

9. The Crucifixion (15:21–47). Jesus is so weakened by his extreme beatings that he needs the help of a passerby, Simon of Cyrene, to carry the horizontal crossbeam. (The vertical beam was fixed in the ground at the site of crucifixion—Golgotha—a small elevated hill that resembled a skull.) The fact that Simon of Cyrene's sons are named hints that they may have been converts to Christianity and known to Mark's audience.

When Jesus arrives at Golgotha, he refuses the wine mixed with myrrh—a slight narcotic to ease his pain. Jesus wants to experience the full effect of his suffering for us. Crucifixion was perhaps the most cruel method of torture ever devised. Its variations included nailing or tying the extremities to the cross, stretching the arms on the crossbeam, and impaling the genitals. Crucifixion also sometimes took place in an inverted position, with the victim's head pointed to the ground. The traditional image of Jesus' wrists and feet nailed to a cross in an elongated plus sign is historically plausible. Whether his cross had a support for his feet or a little seat for his buttocks is hard to determine. The purpose of these supports was to aid breathing and thus prolong the agony. In whatever form, crucifixion resulted in a horrible death, usually by dehydration, loss of blood, shock, or respiratory arrest.

Jesus is crucified between two bandits, thus showing the indignity that has befallen the innocent Jesus. An inscription written in Hebrew, Greek, and Latin ironically advertises his crime—"King of the Jews." Passersby, priests and scribes, and the criminals torment and taunt Jesus, daring him to save himself. Imagine God's Son hanging on the cross hearing the abuse heaped on him. Once again, Jesus resists any temptation to strike his mockers dead and save himself. He is faithful to his Father to the very end.

Jesus' last words are "My God, my God, why have you forsaken me?" (This is the only time Jesus addresses his Father as "God," symbolizing his utter agony as a human being who cries out to his God.) Observers mistakenly think he is calling on Elijah for help, again displaying how the crowds continue to misunderstand him. They do not recognize that Jesus was quoting Psalm 22 ("*Eloi, Eloi, lama sabachthani?*"). Soon Jesus lets out another loud cry and dies. Mark tells us that the veil in the Temple's sanctuary is rent in two, symbolizing that the days of the Old Covenant are over. Jesus' Death begins a new age when all people can worship God directly, in truth and justice. Jesus has removed the barrier separating us from God.

Jesus' Death brings a profound profession of faith from a Roman centurion: "Truly this man was the Son of God" (v. 39). This expression is also ironic: A lone Gentile interprets Jesus correctly and recognizes his true identity.

The true disciples of Jesus are some women who remain with him to the end. Among them is Mary, his mother. Joseph of Arimathea, a member of the Sanhedrin and disciple of Jesus, asks for permission to bury the Lord. Before releasing the body, however, Pilate makes sure that Jesus is dead. Mark tells us Jesus' Death came after six hours on the cross (John 19:14 reports three hours). Due to Jesus' severe scourging and the terrible shock his body endured, he died quickly.

10. Resurrection (16:1–8, 9–20). Mark's Gospel comes to an abrupt end. On Sunday, three women go to the tomb to anoint Jesus' body. They wonder who will roll away the stone from in front of the tomb. They find, to their surprise, that the stone has already been moved aside. They meet there a young man in a white robe (an angel?) who tells them that Jesus is risen. He instructs the women to tell the disciples and Peter to meet Jesus in Galilee. The Gospel ends with Mark saying that they left in fear without telling anyone. Thus, the Gospel ends with another irony. Time and again during his public life, Jesus told people not to reveal his identity, but they do. Now that some faithful followers are asked to spread the great news of Jesus' Resurrection, they apparently fail to do so. (Scholars say that Mark's original Gospel ended at verse 8 and that later editors added verses 9–20. These other verses report some of the appearances reported by the other Gospels: to Mary Magdalene, to two disciples outside the city, to the Apostles in Jerusalem.)

Why the abrupt ending in the original Gospel? Here are two interesting theories:

- Some would hold that the Gospel concludes without any Resurrection appearances because Mark is trying to draw his audience into the narrative. The Gospel has all along been challenging us to accept Jesus as the Suffering Messiah. Peter had accepted Jesus in his glory, but had difficulty believing in Jesus the Suffering Servant. Will the readers of the Gospel be like Peter? Or will they recognize that one can only embrace Jesus if one embraces the cross? Suffering comes before glory: no cross, no crown. Ultimately, we know that the Apostles did accept Jesus. But Mark's abrupt ending challenged the original audience of the Gospel because they were under attack for their faith in Jesus. The question for them, and for us today, is, will you accept the total Christ? He is surely the Son of God, risen in all his glory. But he is the Suffering Servant as well.
- Another theory for Mark's sudden ending is to invite the readers to substitute themselves for the women at the empty tomb. The women were too frightened to spread the word. Consequently, it is up to us, the readers of Mark, to spread the Good News of Jesus' Resurrection. Unlike the women, we should do so confidently and with joy, not fear. In a sense, Mark is saying, "This Gospel has been written for you. Imitate Jesus. Go and spread his word through your actions."

FOR REVIEW

1. What is the meaning of the term *Paschal Mystery*?

2. List and discuss some things Jesus did and taught that angered the religious leaders of his day.

3. Who is responsible for Jesus' Death?

4. Why did Jesus die?

5. What does Jesus' anointing at Bethany symbolize?

6. What does Jesus do at the Last Supper?

7. Interpret the meaning of the naked young man who ran away in the Garden of Gethsemane.

8. Why did some Jewish religious leaders want Jesus crucified? Why could they not inflict capital punishment themselves?

9. Did Pilate find Jesus guilty? Why did he order execution? Identify Barabbas.

10. What is significant about the centurion's proclamation at the moment of Jesus' Death?

11. Why is it important that Jesus *really* died?

12. Suggest a reason Mark ends his Gospel the way he does.

FOR REFLECTION

*   Write Jesus' obituary in two hundred words or less.

*   Besides Jesus, which character in the Passion narrative do you most identify with? Why?

*   What does Jesus' Death mean to you?

*   Read Luke's version of the Passion and Death of Jesus (chapters 22 to 24). List in your journal at least five differences between Mark's version and Luke's.

CHAPTER SUMMARY POINTS

*   Traditionally, the author of Mark is identified as a certain John Mark, companion of Paul and Peter's interpreter. Today, most scholars believe it is impossible to determine the exact identity of the author of Mark except to say he was a Christian who came from a Jewish background.

*   A probable date for the composition of the Gospel of Mark is AD 70. Composed in either Rome or Syria, Mark was written to bolster the faith of Christians who were being persecuted. They must undergo their current suffering in imitation of their Lord and Savior.

*   The framework for Mark is the teaching, preaching, and miracle-working of Jesus in Galilee, his journey to Jerusalem, and his preaching, rejection, and Crucifixion there.

*   The basic questions addressed by Mark are: Who is Jesus? Will you follow him?

*   Jesus was an authoritative teacher. He attracted disciples, spoke with unique power and knowledge, and had the words of everlasting life.

*   Jesus claimed to have the authority to forgive sin; he backed up his word by performing miracles, thus revealing his identity.

- Jesus claimed to be Lord of the Sabbath, teaching that the Sabbath was made for man, not man for the Sabbath law.
- Jesus' seed parables involve the mystery of the Kingdom, that God will eventually bring it to fullness. What is hidden will be brought to light.
- Jesus' miracles reveal that God's power has uniquely broken into human history through his Son, Jesus, who has power over the forces of Satan, sin, the hostile forces of nature, and even death itself.
- The Gospel of Mark presents a portrait of Jesus as one who could be angry, yet compassionate and loving at the same time.
- The "messianic secret" in Mark refers to Jesus wanting his identity as Messiah to be kept hidden because people would misunderstand his true identity as the Suffering Servant.
- The title *Son of Man* refers to Jesus as a humble human being. But it also means that Jesus is God's heavenly agent who will usher in God's Kingdom in all of its power.
- The Paschal Mystery of Jesus' Passion, Death, and Resurrection is the heart of God's love for us. Baptism initiates us into this mystery of love that we celebrate in a sublime way in the Eucharist.
- Various actions and teachings of Jesus angered certain religious leaders of his day, thus leading to their plotting his death. Some of these were his forgiveness of sin, his healing on the Sabbath, his teaching with authority, his disregarding certain dietary laws, his association with tax collectors and sinners, his teaching about God's love for sinners, and his prediction about the destruction of the Temple.
- It is contrary to the teaching of Jesus to assign blame for his Death to the Jewish people as a whole. It was the Roman prefect, Pontius Pilate, who condemned Jesus to death. But, in fact, all humans are implicated in Jesus' Death.
- Key events of the Passion narrative include Judas's betrayal of Jesus; Jesus' anointing at Bethany; the celebration of a Passover meal in which Jesus gives himself to the Apostles and us in the Eucharist; Jesus' heartfelt prayer to his Father in the Garden of Gethsemane; his arrest and trial before the Jewish authorities, where Peter denies him; his trial and scourging by the Roman prefect, Pontius Pilate; his Crucifixion between two criminals; and his Death and burial in a tomb provided by Joseph of Arimathea.
- Jesus' Resurrection proves the divinity of Jesus and seals the salvation Jesus has won for all humans through his sacrifice on the cross. It is the greatest event in Salvation History.

LEARN BY DOING

1. Write a profile of St. Mark from the following references: Acts 12:12, 25; 13:5; 15:36–41; Colossians 4:10; Philemon 1:24; 1 Timothy 4:11; 1 Peter 5:13.

2. Read about Jesus' miracle of calming the storm, Mark 4:35–41. Outline the five elements of this story: (1) Introduction; (2) Faith; (3) Response; (4) Result; (5) Reaction.

    Also write responses to the following:

    - Describe the faith of the Apostles.
    - What does the miracle communicate about God's power? What does it symbolize?
    - What is the lesson of this miracle?
    - What are some signs of God's action in your life? Name any demonstrations of his power in the world.

3. The Stations of the Cross is a traditional Catholic devotion that commemorates the various scenes in the Passion of Christ. By praying and meditating on them, we make a type of pilgrimage to the chief scenes of our Blessed Lord's suffering and Death. Do one or more of the following:

   - Pray the Stations online by finding a website that leads you through them.
   - Research and report on the history of this devotion.
   - Write your own set of meditations and prayers for at least three of the Stations.
   - Construct your own visual Stations of the Cross with prayers using illustrations you download from the Internet.

4. Research and report on how crucifixion took place in the Roman world.

5. Retell the Passion story from the point of view of one of the Apostles.

6. In an artistic representation, design a crucifix that has a collage of pictures that depict the sufferings of the world that Christ redeemed by his Death on the cross. Be prepared to explain the symbolism.

7. Rewrite one of the miracles in Mark's Gospel by putting it into a modern-day setting. Be sure to follow the outline of a typical miracle story that you read about in this chapter.

8. Create a PowerPoint® presentation on Jesus in art through the ages. Begin by looking for images on the Internet. Download at least twenty images. Single out the one that best depicts who Jesus is for you and be sure to prepare an explanation for why this is so.

9. Rewrite the story of the rich young man (Mk 10:17–31) in a modern-day setting.

10. Reread Mk 13:1–37, where Jesus talks about the end times. Prepare a report on what the Catholic Church teaches about the end of the world. Compare this teaching to that of one of the evangelical Christian denominations.

11. Report on the life of Blessed Anne Emmerich.

12. Do further research on one of these aspects of Mark's Gospel:

    - Windows into the World of Jesus: Studies in Mark's Gospel: www.columbusmennonite.org/Bible/default.htm
    - Introduction to the Gospel of Mark: www.abu.nb.ca/courses/NTIntro/Mark.htm
    - Michael J. Haren, "The Naked Young Man: a Historian's Hypothesis on Mark 14, 51–52": www.bsw.org/?l=71791&a=Ani10.htm

PRAYER LESSON

In John 21:17, the resurrected Lord asked of Peter a third time:

"Simon, son of John, do you love me?" Peter answered, "Lord, you know everything; you know that I love you."

- *Reflection*: What would you answer if Jesus asked this question of you? Look in his eyes and give a heartfelt answer. What are the many ways the Lord Jesus has shown his love for you?
- *Resolution*: St. Ignatius of Loyola once asked: "What have you done for Christ? What are you doing for Christ? What will you do for Christ?" Resolve to do something special for him in the next week.

The Gospel of Matthew:
Jesus the Teacher

You are the salt of the earth. But if salt loses its taste, with what can it be seasoned? It is no longer good for anything but to be thrown out and trampled underfoot. You are the light of the world. A city set on a mountain cannot be hidden. Nor do they light a lamp and then put it under a bushel basket; it is set on a lampstand, where it gives light to all in the house. Just so, your light must shine before others, that they may see your good deeds and glorify your heavenly Father.

—Matthew 5:13–16

CHAPTER **OVERVIEW**

THE SECRET **TO GREATNESS**

Jesus unlocked the secret to happiness for both this world and the next.

BACKGROUND ON **MATTHEW'S GOSPEL**

In detailing the purpose and themes of Matthew's Gospel, teachings on judgment, messiahship, discipleship, the Church, and morality are presented in an expanded view.

JESUS **THE TEACHER**

Jesus is the Master Teacher whose five discourses—highlighted by the Beatitudes given at the Sermon on the Mount—address the particulars of Christian living.

JESUS **CHALLENGES JUDAISM**

As a follower of Jesus and a Jew, Matthew used very persuasive language in sharing the truth about Jesus and the Gospel.

The Secret **to Greatness**

Historians acknowledge Theodore Roosevelt, the twenty-sixth president of the United States, as one of the nation's greatest leaders. A multi-faceted individual, he served as a New York state assemblyman, New York governor, a deputy sheriff in the Dakota Territory, police commissioner of New York City, a US Civil Service commissioner, assistant secretary of the Navy, a colonel of the famous Rough Riders, and vice president of the United States! In addition, he helped found the National Collegiate Athletic Association (NCAA), became an accomplished historian and naturalist, raised a family of six children, and wrote over thirty-five books. With such accomplishments to his credit, it is worth listening to his inspiring words intended to encourage an active participation in society by all:

It is not the critic that counts; nor the man who points out how the strong man stumbled; nor where the doer of deeds could have done them better. The credit belongs to the man who is actually in the arena; whose face is marred by dust and sweat and blood; who strives valiantly; who errs, and comes short again and again, because there is no effort without error and shortcomings, who does actually try to do the deed; who knows the great enthusiasm, the great devotion, and spends himself in a worthy cause; . . . who, at worst, if he fails, at least fails while daring greatly. . . .

Far better it is to dare mighty things, to win glorious triumphs even though checkered with failure, than to rank among those timid souls who neither enjoy nor suffer much, because they live in the gray twilight that knows neither victory nor defeat.[12]

Teddy Roosevelt's words are truly inspirational and challenge us to rise to greatness. But even more inspired is the call of Jesus to his followers in his famous Sermon on the Mount. In this most famous of all homilies, we find Jesus teaching the **Beatitudes**, that is, "attitudes of being" to his disciples. The challenging words that we find in the Gospel of Matthew defied the conventional wisdom of Jesus' day and our day as well. They teach the way to blessed happiness—both in this life and for all eternity. But Jesus' way is often opposite of what one would expect. Happy are the spiritually poor, those who mourn, those who hunger and thirst for righteousness, those who are humble, those who forgive, those who work for peace. God's ways are not our ways. God's logic defies human logic. But God's path is the path to true greatness.

This chapter will highlight Jesus the Teacher. As covered in Chapter 4, while Mark's Gospel presents Jesus as a teacher of great authority, Mark does not give many details on exactly *what* Jesus taught. Matthew's Gospel, on the other hand, highlights many of the teachings Jesus gave his disciples—words that stress the Father's will and that are the key to happiness.

Beatitudes—The word *beatitude* means "supreme happiness." The eight Beatitudes Jesus preached in the Sermon on the Mount respond to our natural desire for happiness.

LIVING THE BEATITUDES

Note the following parallels between Jesus and Moses:

Jesus goes into exile in Egypt (Mt 2:14–15).	Moses goes into exile in Midian (Ex 2:15–17).
God tells Joseph in a dream to return to Israel because those who tried to kill Jesus have died (Mt 2:19–20).	God instructs Moses to return to Egypt because his enemies are dead (Ex 4:19).
Jesus experiences hunger after forty days and nights in the desert (Mt 4:2).	Moses remained with Yahweh for forty days and nights, fasting from food and water (Ex 34:28).

The most vivid parallel between Jesus and Moses takes place when Jesus ascends a mountain to preach his famous Sermon on the Mount. As Moses received the Ten Commandments from a mountain and delivered them to his people (Ex 19:3; 20:1–17), so Jesus gives his new law to his followers (Mt 5ff.).

The Beatitudes are the charter for Christian life. Read and memorize the Beatitudes (Mt 5:3–10). Then, in your journal, write your reflection and response to at least three of the questions that follow.

JOURNAL QUESTIONS: Choose at least three.

- When was a time you were dependent on another? How was this experience of dependence similar to being dependent on God? Different?
- Describe a time that you (or someone you love) experienced a sadness deep enough to be called mourning. How was this mourning eventually consoled?
- What do you respect about a person who is meek?
- Name an injustice that you are deeply concerned about and what you plan to do about it.
- When was a time you had difficulty forgiving another?
- Analyze your motives. Why do you want to do well in school? Please your parents? Have a good relationship with God?
- Who is someone you know who fits the profile of a peacemaker?
- How would you be treated if you expressed your faith in God more publicly and vocally by your friends? By your family members? By your enemies?

THE BEATITUDES

Blessed are the poor in spirit, for theirs is the kingdom of heaven.

Blessed are those who mourn, for they will be comforted.

Blessed are the meek, for they will inherit the earth.

Blessed are those who hunger and thirst for righteousness, for they will be satisfied.

Blessed are the merciful, for they will be shown mercy.

Blessed are the clean of heart, for they shall see God.

Blessed are the peacemakers, for they will be called children of God.

Blessed are those who are persecuted because of righteousness, for theirs is the kingdom of heaven.

Blessed are you when they insult you and persecute you and utter every kind of evil against you (falsely) because of me. Rejoice and be glad, for your reward will be great in heaven. Thus they persecuted the prophets who were before you.

FOR REFLECTION

Write some quotations that have inspired you. Why are they inspiring? Who wrote them?

Background on **Matthew's Gospel**

Matthew's Gospel is known as the "first Gospel." How so when we have already learned that the Gospel of Mark is generally agreed to be the first Gospel composed and that Matthew's Gospel draws on material from Mark?

Around AD 124, a bishop, Papias, reported that Matthew compiled Jesus' sayings in the Aramaic language. A later second-century Church writer, Irenaeus, added that Matthew composed a Gospel for the Hebrews in their own tongue. Yet another leading Church thinker, Origen, claimed that Matthew wrote the first Gospel in Aramaic for his fellow Jews and that this was the first Gospel written. The Matthew mentioned by these early Church writers is usually identified as Levi, a tax collector whom Jesus called as an Apostle (Mt 9:9).

These traditions contributed to Matthew's Gospel being known as the first Gospel. This designation came about in part because Matthew is the first book listed in the New Testament canon and the first of the four Gospels. It attained this position because early Christians believed that it had actually been composed by one of Jesus' own Apostles. Most likely, though, the Gospel of Matthew was termed the first Gospel because it is well-ordered and contains detailed teaching lessons, especially in the area of Christian ethics. And because of its emphasis on the fulfillment of Old Testament prophecy, it makes a great link between the Old and New Testaments. It became the dominant Gospel through most of history, playing a vital role in Christian instruction and worship. For example, it is Matthew's version of the Lord's Prayer, not Luke's, that we learn by heart and pray as part of our second nature.

We now know that it is unlikely that Matthew's Gospel was the first written. Also, New Testament scholars today doubt the reliability of many ancient traditions that assign authorship to Matthew, the tax collector-turned-Apostle, and the theory that it must have been the first written. Two important observations support these doubts:

1. The Gospel of Matthew contains about 80 percent of Mark's Gospel. It faithfully follows Mark's outline of Jesus' ministry in Galilee; journey to Jerusalem; and his Passion, Death, and Resurrection. In several areas, Matthew improves Mark's Greek by eliminating difficult phrases and double expressions and by writing more coherently. He also omits or changes passages from Mark that tend to paint Jesus or the Apostles in an unfavorable light (for example, he drops Mark 3:21, where Jesus' family thinks Jesus is out of his mind, and Mark 9:10, 32, which reports the Apostles do not understand the concept of the Resurrection of the dead). Matthew also writes more reverentially about Jesus and stresses the miraculous element found in Mark's Gospels. All these observations lead to the vast number of scholars concluding that the author of Matthew's Gospel borrowed heavily from Mark, which logically had to be written earlier.

2. Almost all scholars agree that the Gospel of Matthew was originally written in Greek. Thus, the traditions cited above by later Christian writers must not have been referring to the Gospel itself, but to one of Matthew's sources, which could well have been a collection of Aramaic sayings used by the Evangelist in writing his Gospel. However, if this collection ever existed, it has been lost.

As to the identity of the author, in truth, the author of the Gospel of Matthew is anonymous. Today, contemporary scholarship holds that Matthew was most likely a Jewish Christian scribe who probably knew Hebrew and perhaps even a little Aramaic. His Jewish background, theology, and thought are strongly present in this Gospel. The most we can say is that the author might have known the Apostle Matthew or used a source of sayings originally written in Aramaic.

When was Matthew's Gospel written? As noted above, the Gospel of Matthew was written sometime after the Gospel of Mark. Matthew shows knowledge of the Temple's destruction (in AD 70) and clearly reflects antagonism between early Jewish Christian communities and the Jews who survived the First Revolt. Recall that the Pharisees who revived the Jewish faith after the Roman Revolt did not look kindly on the Christians who refused to fight alongside them.

During the 80s, Christian Jews were driven out of the synagogues. This naturally resulted in strained relations with the Jews. Matthew's Gospel reflects this tension, for example, in the many sharp sayings directed against the Pharisees in Matthew 23.

The majority of scholars believe Matthew was written in Greek for a predominantly Greek-speaking Jewish Christian Church, probably in Antioch in Syria, sometime in the 80s, perhaps AD 85. Thus, the Gospel was composed by a Jewish Christian for a predominantly Jewish Christian audience. There is considerable evidence to bolster this conclusion. For example:

- The author of Matthew assumes that his audience knows Jewish customs. He uses terms like Preparation Day and talks about the ritual washing of hands before eating and the wearing of **phylacteries**. In none of these cases does he explain his terms.

The Underworld **by Francois de Nome**

- The Gospel records a manner of speaking that is Jewish, using Hebrew terms like **Gehenna** and *Beelzebul* (a Hebrew term for the devil). The author also uses "kingdom of heaven," rather than "Kingdom of God," because Jews held God's name as most sacred and would not pronounce it. Other examples include repetition, parallel expressions (for example, 7:24–27), and number symbolism. For example, the number seven appears many times: seven petitions in the Our Father, seven parables in Matthew 13, seven loaves and

phylacteries—Small leather capsules which were fastened on the forehead or on the upper left arm so that they hung at the level of the heart. They contained miniature scrolls with four passages from the Jewish Law. Jewish males would wear these all day once they reached the age of adulthood (age fourteen).

Gehenna—The Jewish term for "hell." Originally the site of human sacrifice, this Jerusalem valley was cursed by the prophet Jeremiah as a place of death and corruption. In Jesus' day it was used as a garbage dump.

seven baskets, a story about seven spirits, the question about forgiving seven times, and the question posed to Jesus about seven brothers marrying the same woman.

- Like the Gospel, Jewish writings also contained infancy narratives with genealogies.
- The author of Matthew compares Jesus to the towering Old Testament prophet and lawgiver Moses.

Why was this Gospel written, especially considering the Gospel of Mark was already recorded? There were two main issues unique to Matthew's local church that merited another written record:

1. How could the Church legitimately lay claim to Yahweh's promises to Israel?

2. How should the Church bring Gentiles into the Church?

Matthew's audience struggled with discovering how Judaism could continue now that the Temple was destroyed. Matthew makes the claim that true Judaism involves a Church gathered around the Teacher Jesus. This Church must listen to and follow his teaching. It also must acknowledge him as Lord, Son of God, and the true King of Israel.

To compose his Gospel, the author of Matthew drew on the Gospel of Mark; the sayings source known as Q, which Matthew arranges into sermon discourses; and his own unique sources (designated M). Among the unique Matthean stories are his infancy narrative (including Joseph's dream and the visit of the Magi), the dream of Pilate's wife (27:9), and Judas's suicide by hanging (27:3–10).

In writing to his Jewish Christian audience, Matthew goes to great lengths to cite Old Testament prophecies and other passages to show how Jesus' life and preaching fulfill God's promises to Israel. Over 130 passages in the Gospel of Matthew have Old Testament roots. Peculiar to Matthew is this formula: "This happened so that what had been spoken through the prophet might be fulfilled" (Mt 21:4). This theme of fulfillment is especially evident in how Matthew relates Jesus, the new lawgiver, to Moses.

Do not think that I have come to abolish the law or the prophets. I have come not to abolish but to fulfill. (Mt 5:17)

Although Matthew presents Jesus as the fulfillment of Old Testament prophecy, he strongly reminds his readers that Jesus commands his disciples to spread the Gospel to all the nations (see Mt 28:16–20). Jewish Christians, now rejected by their former co-religionists, needed to be told that they should not look too longingly to the past. Jesus is for all people everywhere. Gentiles are welcome.

Other Themes in Matthew's Gospel

Matthew's Gospel addresses several other important themes in unique ways among the four Gospels. These include the following:

- *Judgment*. Several parables deal directly with the second coming of Christ and the theme of the Last Judgment. Perhaps some of Matthew's audience was getting discouraged that the Lord had not yet returned in his full glory. The Evangelist had to remind them that we should always be ready for the Lord's return.
- *Jesus is Emmanuel*. Emmanuel means "God with us," the Messiah, who wills the salvation of Jew and Gentile alike.
- *Discipleship*. Following Jesus is hard. More than lip service, it requires humility, rejection, even suffering.
- *Church*. Matthew's is the only Gospel where the word for church (*ekklesia*) appears (Mt 16:18 and 18:17). The Church refers to the gathering of Christians at liturgy, but also the local community or the universal community of believers (*CCC*, 752).
- *Right Instruction*. Matthew's Gospel is catechetical, an instruction manual for new converts and faithful disciples alike. It teaches righteousness, prayer, and conversion.

READING THE GOSPEL OF MATTHEW

Scholars have proposed several different outlines for Matthew's Gospel. A still popular outline suggests that Matthew organized his Gospel into five major sections or blocks of material sandwiched between a prologue (the birth narratives) and an epilogue (the Passion narratives). This division reminds us of the first five books of the Old Testament (the Pentateuch), thus suggesting a comparison between Moses (who was assigned authorship of the Pentateuch) and Jesus.

This arrangement of five teachings underscores Jesus the Teacher, a major portrait of Jesus emphasized in Matthew's Gospel. In this outline, it is appropriate to think of Matthew's Gospel as a book of Christian instruction and administration.

Introduction: Birth of the Messiah (Mt 1–2)
Part 1: The Kingdom of God Proclaimed
Narrative: Jesus' Galilean ministry (3–4)
Discourse: Sermon on the Mount (5–7)
Part 2: Christian Discipleship Proclaimed in Galilee
Narrative: Ten miracles (8–9)
Discourse: Mission of the Twelve (10)
Part 3: Opposition to Jesus Grows
Narrative: Jesus and his opponents (11–12)
Discourse: Parables of the Kingdom (13)
Part 4: Jesus the Christ and His Church
Narrative: Messiah, the Shepherd of Israel (14–17)
Discourse: Advice to the Church (18)
Part 5: Journey to and Ministry in Jerusalem
Narrative: Controversies in Jerusalem (19–23)
Discourse: The Second Coming and Judgment Day (24–25)

Climax: Passion, Death, Resurrection of Jesus (26–28)
Read one of the narrative sections from the outline above. Prepare a short oral report on the section providing the following information:

- the major events in this section
- key characters

Share these reports in class before studying the major discourses in this chapter.

Comparing the Gospels of Matthew and Mark

Mark's Gospel opens with the proclamation of the "Gospel of Jesus Christ, the Son of God" and immediately launches into Jesus' public ministry. Matthew's Gospel begins with a genealogy of Jesus, tracing his ancestry to both David and Abraham. The author of Matthew clearly wants to tie Jesus into Jewish history and proclaim him the promised Messiah.

Note how the very first verse of the Gospel of Matthew is literally translated from Greek as "the book of origins." This is a direct reference to the first book of the Old Testament—the book of Genesis—that recounts God's creative acts at the beginning of time. Now, according to Matthew, Yahweh has undertaken a new creation by sending into human history the Promised One, Jesus Christ. Jesus is truly the Son of David, the Messiah, Israel's true king who rules compassionately. *Son of David* is a favorite title for Jesus in Matthew's Gospel. It is mentioned nine times in the Gospel, including in the opening verse.

Recall from Chapter 1 how Matthew's and Luke's genealogies reflected the theology of the respective authors. Matthew's genealogy presents Jesus as

Israel's Promised Savior, while Luke stresses Jesus as the Universal Messiah who has come for all people. An interesting detail in Matthew's genealogy, however, is his mentioning four women—Tamar, Rahab, Ruth, Bathsheba (the wife of Uriah)—all foreigners or Gentiles. Though writing for a Jewish Christian audience, Matthew's inclusion of these women shows that the Gospel will eventually be preached to all people, as Jesus instructed at the very end of Matthew's Gospel (Mt 28:19–20).

Next, Matthew takes up the infancy narrative of Jesus. The events of Matthew's infancy narrative are familiar:

- Joseph's dream about Jesus' virginal conception;
- Jesus' birth in Bethlehem;
- the homage of the Magi;
- the plotting of the evil King Herod;
- the warning given to Joseph in a dream;
- the flight to Egypt;
- the massacre of the infants;
- the return of the Holy Family from Egypt after the death of Herod the Great; and
- the settling of the Holy Family in Nazareth in Galilee for fear of Herod's son, Archelaus.

As you review these various story elements, though, note how Matthew portrays each of these events fulfilling a prophecy of Scripture. For example, Matthew links the Savior's conception by power of the Holy Spirit and his being given the name Jesus with a prophecy from Isaiah:

> All this took place to fulfill what the Lord had said through the prophet:
>
> "Behold, the virgin shall be with child and bear a son, and they shall name him Emmanuel," which means "God is with us." (Mt 1:22–23)

These examples from Matthew's infancy narrative help reinforce the idea that the author of Matthew was a Jewish Christian who was writing for a predominantly Jewish Christian audience. He convincingly shows Jesus to be *Emmanuel*, the promised one who fulfills the promises made to Israel.

There are other differences between Mark's Gospel and Matthew's Gospel. For example, recall that in Mark's Gospel Jesus somewhat reluctantly accepted Peter's confession of him as the Christ in the scene on the road to Caesarea Philippi (Mk 8:27–30). In contrast, in Matthew's Gospel (16:16), Peter identifies Jesus not only as the Messiah, but also as "the Son of the living God." Jesus praises Peter for this act of faith and makes a special promise to him:

> Blessed are you, Simon son of Jonah. For flesh and blood has not revealed this to you, but my heavenly Father. And so I say to you, you are Peter, and upon this rock I will build my church. (Mt 16:17–19)

Just as Peter sees that Jesus is not only the Messiah, but also the Son of God, so do the Apostles proclaim Jesus the Son of God after his walking on water (Mt 14:22–33). In contrast, Mark criticizes the Apostles for their slowness due to "hardened hearts" (Mk 6:52). In general, Matthew's Gospel presents a more flattering picture of the Apostles than the bewildered Apostles portrayed in Mark.

Finally, Mark's Gospel ends abruptly with no Resurrection appearances by Jesus. Matthew's final chapter includes two Resurrection appearances and the story about the empty tomb. Jesus first appears to Mary Magdalene and another Mary who are leaving

St. Joseph's Dream by Francesco Solimena

the garden after a dazzling vision of an angel, who instructs them to tell the Apostles to meet the Lord in Galilee. The women worship Jesus, acknowledging his true identity as the Son of God. Jesus tells them (and us) not to be afraid and repeats the angel's instructions concerning the meeting in Galilee.

Matthew then reports how the authorities concocted a story about how the Apostles stole Jesus' body. Undoubtedly, Matthew recounts this story because non-believers were circulating this rumor in the decades after the event of the Resurrection itself. Someone had to explain the empty tomb—either Jesus rose as the Apostles claimed or something else happened. Believers know the truth. Unbelievers have to deal with the fact of the missing body.

Matthew concludes the Gospel with a report of how Jesus meets the Eleven in Galilee and instructs them to preach the Gospel to all nations, baptizing them "in the name of the Father, and of the Son, and of the holy Spirit." (This baptismal formula was being used at the time Matthew's Gospel was written.) Jesus assures his abiding presence within the Church by the power of the Holy Spirit. This is a fitting bookend to the opening of the Gospel, where Matthew describes Jesus as Emmanuel. Jesus will be with us as we spread the Gospel. This is why we should not fear, as Jesus so often instructs.

Matthew's expansion of Mark's Gospel is brilliantly organized. It served as an eminently teachable source for the early Church and today's Church as well. Its greatest accomplishment, no doubt, is how its author arranged five blocks of narrative with corresponding speeches. We turn to these speeches next and look at Jesus' role as Teacher.

FOR REVIEW

1. Why is the Gospel of Matthew often called the "first Gospel"?

2. Identify the probable author of the Gospel of Matthew.

3. Offer evidence that Matthew wrote *after* Mark.

4. Give a probable date for the composition of Matthew's Gospel.

5. List two reasons why Matthew wrote his Gospel.

6. Discuss several examples of how Matthew's Gospel is the most "Jewish" of the four Gospels.

7. Read Micah 5:2. Which of the following verses quotes this passage: Mt 2:5–6; 2:14–16; 2:16–18; 2:23.

8. List at least three key themes treated in Matthew's Gospel.

9. Why may the author of Matthew have divided his Gospel into five major sections?

10. Discuss the meaning and significance of these two titles of Jesus, both found in Matthew's infancy narrative: Son of David, Emmanuel.

FOR REFLECTION

- After reading Matthew 2:1–12 (the visit of the Magi), name a gift that you could present to Jesus that would represent who you are or who you would like to become. Write a paragraph describing the symbolism of the gift.

- Which quality of Jesus is being appealed to in the following "Son of David" passages: Mt 9:27, 15:22, and 20:30?

Jesus **the Teacher**

A primary aim of Matthew's Gospel is to portray Jesus as the sole teacher worthy of our obedience. For example, Jesus instructs his disciples, "Do not be called 'Master'; you have but one master, the Messiah" (Mt 23:10). Matthew added significantly to Mark's Gospel by including many of Jesus' specific teachings collected from the source of sayings, Q, and the Evangelist's own unique traditions, **M**.

Matthew depicts Jesus as a new Moses who brings a new law to God's people. The Gospel is arranged as such, assembling Jesus' teachings into five distinct blocks of material, called discourses. Each of these, woven together deliberately with corresponding narrative sections, ends with a formula that begins with, "When Jesus finished these" and ends with either "words" (Mt 7:28; 19:1; 26:1) "commands" (11:1) or "parables" (13:53).

The topics of the discourses include love and forgiveness, standing up to ridicule, pursuing God's Kingdom with single-minded devotion, trusting God, prayer, and sharing with the needy.

Discourse One: The Sermon on the Mount (Matthew 5–7) (CCC, 1965–1970; 1983–1985)

The Sermon on the Mount is the first and most important of the five discourses in Matthew's Gospel. It summarizes the New Law of the Gospel, a law of love, grace, and freedom. As Moses delivered the Old Law from Mount Sinai, so Jesus delivers his instructions for Christian living from a mountain. Jesus teaches true righteousness because he speaks with divine authority. He far surpasses the prophets of old.

The Sermon on the Mount collects in one place Jesus' ethical teachings. It is directed to Christians, that is, to those who have accepted the Gospel. The major theme of the sermon is interior conversion that leads to putting into practice one's discipleship. In other words, one must not only talk the talk, but walk the walk:

> Not everyone who says to me, 'Lord, Lord,' will enter the kingdom of heaven, but only the one who does the will of my Father in heaven. (7:21)

In the words of the *Catechism of the Catholic Church*,

> The Lord's Sermon on the Mount, far from abolishing or devaluing the moral prescriptions of the Old Law, releases their hidden potential and has new demands arise from them: it reveals their entire divine and human truth. It does

M—The name for the approximate four hundred verses or verse fragments in the Gospel of Matthew that are not present in the Gospel of Mark or Q, which are unique to Matthew.

not add new external precepts, but proceeds to reform the heart, the root of human acts, where man chooses between the pure and the impure, where faith, hope, and charity are formed and with them the other virtues. (*CCC*, 1968)

Some of the most memorable teachings are summarized in the verses below:

- *Christians are the salt of the earth and light of the world (5:13–16).* After introducing the Beatitudes which offer blessings on unlikely people like the poor in spirit, mourners, the meek, peacemakers, and so forth, Jesus calls his followers "salt and light." Living the value of the Beatitudes will guarantee that we will significantly impact the world for the better. Note how salt flavors foods; in a similar way, faithful disciples will change the flavor of the world, making it better because they are bringing Gospel values to it. Salt is also a preservative, saving meat for future consumption. Followers of Jesus share in his mission of salvation; our presence should help make the world more loving and, consequently, livable.

Christians are also like light. They should dispel darkness, show the way, and help eliminate fear of the unknown. Our good works should serve as a beacon of light that leads other people to God the Father. The Good News is only good and newsworthy if people can see it in action.

- *Christians observe a new standard of law (5:17–48).* Jesus assures his disciples that he did not come to abolish the Law and the teachings of the prophets, but to fulfill them. He and his teachings fulfill the Old Covenant. He teaches that greatness in his Father's Kingdom depends on observance of the Law.

Jesus uses six examples from the Law to drive home the importance of a changed heart, an interior attitude of love for God and neighbor. He is an authoritative teacher who proclaims, "You have heard how it was said . . . but I say to you." The point of his teaching is that mere external observance of the Law is not enough. Interior conversion is necessary. For example,

- *We must not murder.* But we must not even be angry with others because anger leads to murder. The way to overcome anger is through reconciliation. If we cannot make peace with the neighbor we see, what is the value of worshiping the God whom we cannot see?
- *We must not commit* **adultery**. But we should also avoid lustful thoughts because they lead to disordered, sinful sexual craving that works against God's intent for sex in marriage. Jesus teaches that God intends fidelity in marriage. He forbids the divorce of lawfully married couples.
- *We must not take idle oaths or swear.* Christians are persons of integrity. They should say what they mean and mean what they say.
- *Most importantly, we must not seek revenge.* The corollary to this important teaching is that we must love

adultery—Infidelity in marriage whereby a married person has sexual intercourse with someone who is not the person's spouse.

all people, even our enemies. These teachings reinterpret for the Church the Old Testament's *lex talionis*, the law of reasonable retaliation, a system of strict justice, of "an eye for an eye and a tooth for a tooth."

For centuries the world has been struggling to put Jesus' teachings into practice. He sets high standards for us, telling us to "be perfect, just as your heavenly Father is perfect" (5:48). Is Jesus requiring us to do the impossible? On our own efforts, perhaps. But what he is calling us to do is to stretch, to be more loving, to be more forgiving, to respond to others. Why? Because God is our Father and we are his children. He loves us immeasurably. We should be like him in our loving others. What is impossible for us to achieve on our own efforts is possible when we surrender to God's love and allow God's Kingdom to rule our lives.

LIVING THE SERMON ON THE MOUNT

Evaluate how you are living some of the teachings that Jesus gave us in the Sermon on the Mount. In your journal, write a sentence or two giving an example of how you are either putting a particular teaching into practice or a specific way that you can improve in that area of your life.

- **Anger:** Do you easily and properly deal with anger by not letting it fester within?

- **Sexuality:** Do you respect your own sexuality and that of others? Do you exercise self-discipline in thought and action?

- **Oaths:** Are you a truthful person?

- **Forgiveness:** Do you forgive others when they hurt you? Do you avoid grudges?

- **Enemies:** Are you courteous to everyone, including those whom you do not particularly like?

- *Christians have a right attitude (6:1–34).* Chapter 6 of the Sermon highlights the need for a clean heart and pure intentions in living the moral life. For example, Jesus wants us to examine our motives when we perform virtuous works. Is our motive to seek the approval of others? Or is it to give glory to our loving Father? Jesus tells us that his way to holiness is the path of quiet love. For example, when we give money to the poor, we should do it in a way that does not draw attention to ourselves. When we pray, we should do so simply and sincerely. The Lord's Prayer is the model prayer for Christians. When we fast, we should do so without calling attention to ourselves. God loves us with an everlasting love and has already rewarded us. Why should we be motivated by what others think?

- Jesus tells us to trust his Father. Put first things first. God will watch out for us. If the Father takes care of the birds in the sky and the flowers of the field how much more will he watch over us, his children. Why worry? Worrying about tomorrow is empty and leads nowhere. If we make our first priority doing God's will, then he will lead us and provide what we truly need.

- *Christians do not judge others, and they pray in trust (7:1–29).* The final chapter of the Sermon on the Mount teaches that Jesus' disciples should not judge others, nor think they are morally superior to others. Just as God will forgive us as we forgive others, so he will judge us as we judge others. Thinking ourselves better than others, making them live up to our idea of what is holy, is arrogant. Jesus wants humility and gentleness in his followers. He teaches the Golden Rule, the summary of the Law of the Gospel (*CCC*, 1970):

> Do to others whatever you would have them do to you. (7:12)

Jesus instructs us to trust God always, especially when we pray. The Father knows what is good for us, and if we ask for it, he will grant it. He warns us about false prophets (perhaps a problem in the local church for whom Matthew wrote). But even today, many false prophets vie for our attention. These voices come from many directions, but Jesus says we can judge a tree by its fruits. Check out the lives of the people making promises. Are they credible? Are they loving? Do they bring joy, peace and true happiness? If not, reject them.

The Sermon concludes by encouraging us to take Jesus' words to heart and build our lives on them. It is not enough to mouth them; we must put them into action! These teachings are a solid foundation for a Christian life, a foundation that nothing can shake.

Discourse Two: Sharing the Faith with Others (Matthew 10)

In this discourse, Jesus instructs his Apostles to imitate his ministry. They should cure the sick, raise the dead, cleanse those suffering from skin diseases, and exorcise demons (10:8). This instruction follows his own intense missionary effort where he performed ten miracles and many other cures as well (see the narrative portion, Matthew 8–9). After naming the Twelve Apostles, Jesus tells them to proclaim the Gospel to the Jewish people, but to avoid contact with Gentiles. Jesus' earthly ministry was to preach the Kingdom to the Chosen People; after his Resurrection, the Church would take the message to all people.

Jesus directs the Apostles to preach the Gospel in a spirit of poverty and not burden themselves with accumulating money or carrying excess baggage. They should also receive the hospitality of anyone who offers it. Discipleship is a privilege, but it also involves the cross: "Behold I am sending you like sheep in the midst of wolves; so be shrewd as serpents and simple as doves" (10:16).

Members of the local church for whom Matthew wrote were most likely suffering the troubles described in this speech: leaders questioning and scourging them; betrayals taking place; false accusations being hurled at them; persecutions being widespread. Jesus, however, promises two things:

1. The Spirit will help the disciples stand firm and testify courageously to the Gospel truth.
2. God the Father, who has counted every hair on their heads, will watch over them with love and tenderness.

Jesus praises anyone who testifies to others about him. In turn, Jesus will stand up for believers before his heavenly Father. Jesus warns, though, that division is inevitable if we proclaim that we belong to him. We must decide without delay. The payoff? Jesus will reward us for choosing him:

> Whoever finds his life will lose it, and whoever loses his life for my sake will find it. (Mt 10:39)

Jesus uses a vivid image about bringing a sword to the earth. He is not advocating violence here. Rather, he is stating the obvious, that if we choose him as our top priority, people will turn on us. Someone who is red hot in love with the Lord will inevitably cause sparks.

This missionary discourse was meant not only for the Apostles, but also for the members of the Evangelist's local church. Moreover, it applies to us today as well. It is a great honor to proclaim Jesus in word and deed. Speaking for Jesus enables him to live in us. Being a missionary makes us Christ-for-others:

> Whoever receives you receives me, and whoever receives me receives the one who sent me. (Mt 10:40)

However, we should never forget that belonging to Jesus means that we will inevitably suffer for him.

Discourse Three: Parables about the Kingdom (Matthew 13) (CCC, 541–546; 567)

Chapter 13 of Matthew's Gospel is organized around seven parables that help reveal the nature of the Kingdom of Heaven. Recall how Jesus came to preach the advent of the Kingdom, manifested its arrival in his words and miracles, and accomplished its coming through the Paschal Mystery of his Death, Resurrection, and Glorification. He invites everyone—Jew, Gentile, rich, and poor—to gather into the family of God. His invitation comes in the form of parables:

> Through his parables he invites people to the feast of the Kingdom, but he also asks for a radical choice: to gain the Kingdom, one must give everything. Words are not enough, deeds are required. The parables are like mirrors for man: will he be hard soil or good earth for the word? What use has he made of the talents he has received? Jesus and the presence of the Kingdom in this world are secretly at the heart of the parables. One must enter the Kingdom, that is, become a disciple of Christ, in order to "know the secrets of the kingdom of heaven." For those who stay "outside," everything remains enigmatic. (*CCC*, 546)

Recall that a *parable* is simply defined as "a short story drawn from ordinary life that makes a comparison with a religious message." Typically, a parable makes one point. The key to its understanding is usually the very end of the parable. However, some parables, like that of the sower, have allegorical elements. (An allegory is a sustained comparison where many story elements correspond to some reality outside the story.)

Matthew reports that Jesus taught in parables to confound outsiders and to present truths about the Kingdom to insiders (disciples) in ways that show how God works. Unbelievers do not understand the parables because they do not have the ears and eyes of faith. They miss the truth before them. In contrast, disciples are blessed with the vision that comes from faith in Jesus Christ.

Following the Lord brings the Kingdom near and helps us to understand what it means to live in God's reign:

- *The Parable of the Mustard Seed (13:31–32)* teaches that God's Kingdom starts very small; however, in time, it will grow very large. As the birds shelter in the mustard tree, so will God's Kingdom provide refuge for people.

- *The Parable of the Yeast (13:33)* speaks of the mysterious growth of God's Kingdom. Just as the tiny mustard seed miraculously grows into a large tree, so does the dough become a leavened loaf of bread. Unseen forces cause the mysterious rise of leaven. Similarly, God's grace will bring about the miraculous growth of the Kingdom. God is at work invisibly, even if we do not see it.

- *The Parables of the Treasure in the Field and the "Pearl of Great Price" (13:44–46)* teach that the Kingdom is so precious that one should sacrifice everything for it. Discipleship demands complete and full commitment, the challenge of risking all. However, to gain entrance in the Kingdom is worth everything because it brings untold joy.

- *The Parables of the Weeds Among the Wheat (13:24–30) and the Dragnet (13:47–50)* have a similar message concerning the Kingdom and judgment. It is not always clear in this life who has chosen the Kingdom and who has not. However, at the end of time, God will separate the good from the wicked. The wicked will then be thrown into the "fiery furnace, where there will be wailing and the grinding of teeth" (v. 50).

THE PARABLE OF THE SOWER (13:1–25)

The Parable of the Sower begins chapter 13. It is one of the parables for which Jesus offers an explanation of its meaning. Let's look at two deeper interpretations of the parable:

1. In its original setting, the Kingdom is being compared to the seed and its fate. As some seed fell on bad soil and did not take root, so will the Kingdom fail to penetrate the hearts of some people. However, some seed does bear fruit, and, amazingly, its growth is far beyond what one could expect. Despite what may happen, God's Kingdom will prevail. Its growth is inevitable and beyond anything we can imagine. It will overcome all obstacles. (Incidentally, this is not a story about a bad farmer who throws seed willy-nilly. In our Lord's day, sowing came before plowing. What was bad ground before plowing may well have ended up to be good soil where seed could take root and flourish.)

2. Matthew records Jesus' allegorical interpretation of this parable, which also addressed the situation in Matthew's own local church. The allegory emphasizes the types of ground and how each does or does not provide fertile receptivity to the seeds. The ground represents those who hear the Word of God and either let it bear fruit or not bear fruit in their own lives. Matthew is trying to encourage his readers to live the Good News they have been privileged to hear. As an allegory, we can interpret the parable this way:

- The Sower is the preacher or teacher of God's Word (the seed).
- The path represents people who hear the Word of God but make no effort to understand it; the devil tempts them away from God's Word.
- The rocky ground signifies people who embrace the Word joyfully at first. However, their faith is superficial. The slightest temptation causes them to give up.
- The thorny ground symbolizes people who embrace the Word, but their love of wealth and worries about daily living strangle their commitment.
- The good soil stands for the ideal person who hears, understands, and lives the Word of God.

Jesus desires that his disciples be of this last group: hear the Word of God, understand it, and put it into practice. This is a great definition of a disciple, a fitting summary of chapter 13 of Matthew's Gospel.

Discourse Four: Jesus Founds and Instructs the Church (Matthew 18)

Matthew's Gospel is sometimes termed "the Gospel of the Church." This term is emphasized in the fourth discourse, in chapter 18. Jesus is the head of the Church, its guide, and its model. As the *Catechism of the Catholic Church* teaches, the Church "draws her life from the word and the Body of Christ and so herself becomes Christ's body" (752). Christ is present to his Church in many ways, for example, in the sacraments and in his scriptural word. But he also continues to rule, guide, teach, and sanctify it through his appointed leaders. Their leadership of service is meant to help bring others to his Father's Kingdom.

Matthew 16:18–19 clearly points out that Jesus instituted the Catholic Church when he says to Peter:

> And so I say to you, you are Peter, and upon this rock I will build my church, and the gates of the netherworld shall not prevail against it. I will give you the keys to the kingdom of heaven. Whatever you bind on earth shall be bound in heaven; and whatever you loose on earth shall be loosed in heaven.

In this important passage, Jesus not only establishes the Church, but appoints Peter as its earthly leader with the "power of the keys," that is, Christ's

hierarchical—A structure of sacred leadership; ordained leaders consisting of the pope, bishops, priests, and deacons who govern, teach, and guide the Church in holiness according to Christ's plan.

scandal—The bad example, often by religious leaders, that misleads others into sin.

own power to forgive sin and to teach authoritatively. Catholics see in this passage Christ's clear intent to found a **hierarchical** Church, one with clear lines of authority traceable to the Lord himself. Today, the Holy Father (the pope) is the successor to Peter. He is the earthly leader, the symbol of unity, who is entrusted to teach with Christ's full authority in communion with bishops around the world. The bishops succeed the Apostles and teach in unity with the Holy Father.

In Matthew 18, the kingship of God, his rule of peace and justice, is clearly present in the Church. However, Christians are also very human. They sin and need constant reminders to live as worthy members of the Kingdom. Matthew knows the intimate connection between the Church and the Kingdom, but he also knows that God's Kingdom is greater than the Church. The reign of God will come in its fullest glory only at the end of time. This teaching is made clear in Jesus' last discourse.

Until then, Christians, and in a special way, Church leaders, need reminders of how to serve the Lord. Above all else, Church leaders should not be obsessed with power or authority. Greatness lies in serving, not in being served. The task of Church leaders is to help God's Kingdom come alive in the midst of their flock. Good shepherds are even willing to suffer for their flock. Here are some more of Jesus' specific, always relevant instructions, relevant not only for Church leaders, but for all members of Christ's family:

- Be humble like children.
- Never lead others into sin. Bad example (**scandal**) is a serious sin for Church leaders. It should be avoided at all costs. We must live holy and humble lives, giving a good example to all, especially the little ones.
- Relentlessly pursue the sinner, like the shepherd who leaves ninety-nine sheep to go after one that is lost or led astray.
- Put no limits on your forgiveness (seven times seventy is a symbol for infinity).
- Imitate your heavenly Father who forgives you. If you are like the unforgiving servant, who was released from his debt, you will be dealt with harshly.
- If there are troublemakers in the local church, first confront them privately to get them to change. If that fails, then call on the testimony of other Church members to try to resolve the affair. Only if these steps fail should you report to the larger Church. If the person still fails to repent, he or she should be treated as an outsider.
- Pray together in community for your needs. Never forget Jesus' comforting words, "Where two or three are gathered together in my name, there am I in the midst of them" (Mt 16:18).

Jesus' clear statement in Matthew 16:18–19 about establishing a Church based on Peter, the rock; Jesus' missionary instructions in Matthew 10; the discourses in Matthew 18; and the great commission to preach the Good News to all people at the very end of the Gospel (Mt 28:19–20)—all these clearly show Jesus' desire to create a Church to carry on his work. Jesus is the founder of the Catholic Church.

Discourse Five: The Final Judgment (Matthew 24–25)

Matthew's last discourse is called the **eschatological** discourse from the Greek word *eschaton*, which means "end time." This is most appropriate because the theme of the discourse involves the end of the Temple, the end of the world, and the divine judgment in the last days. Daniel 7–8 provides the Old Testament background for Matthew's *apocalyptic* language used in this discourse. (Recall that apocalypse means "revelation" or "unveiling.") Apocalyptic thought appeared in Jewish and Christian writing especially during times of great persecution or trying events. It manifests itself in some strong beliefs, such as:

- God is ultimately in charge during times of trial.
- There is an ongoing war between the forces of good and the forces of evil.
- God will bring judgment upon the righteous and punish the wicked.
- Disciples should remain faithful and live upright lives—even in the face of persecution.
- Disciples should always be prepared for God's return.
- By the 80s, when Matthew was writing, the Romans had already destroyed the Temple. Thus, Jesus' predictions had come true. However, the early Church was still awaiting Christ's Second Coming. Many early Christians believed that Jesus was to return

during their lifetimes. When this did not happen, they had to reinterpret Jesus' words that gave the impression that he meant to return soon.

Using highly symbolic language to describe the coming of the Son of Man, Jesus warns that no one knows the exact day or hour. Therefore, we should always be prepared for the Lord's return. We should not be caught unaware like the contemporaries of Noah were at the time of the flood. When the Son of Man comes, of two men in the field, one will enter the Kingdom, another will be left out. "Therefore, stay awake!" (Mt 24:42).

Through another parable, Matthew also warns his readers, and especially Church leaders, not to abuse their authority.

eschatological—A term having to do with the end times or the "last things" (death, resurrection, judgment, Heaven, Hell, Purgatory, everlasting life, etc.).

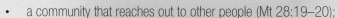

THE CHURCH

The three meanings of Church are inseparable. The Church is a liturgical assembly, a local community, and the universal community of believers. The Church is:

- a community that reaches out to other people (Mt 28:19–20);
- a community of believers (Rom 12:4–8);
- a forgiving community (Lk 19:10);
- a community founded by Christ on Peter and the Apostles (Mt 16:15–19);
- a loving community (Mt 25:31–46);
- a Eucharistic community (1 Cor 10:15–17);
- a community willing to suffer (Mt 5:10–12); and
- a community of faith as taught by the Apostles (Acts 4:1–4, 33).

Rate your own parish or school community to see if it lives up to this description of the Church and those described above. What standards should the Church have for membership? How would Jesus answer this question? How are each of the criteria listed above essential to an understanding and definition of Church?

CALLED TO SERVE

How can you serve the needy as Jesus instructed? Review the following procedure and apply it to one or more of the suggestions listed below.

Procedure

1. Study. Identify the hungry in your parish community, neighborhood, or city. What is already being done for them? What agencies are involved in helping them? How can you contact these agencies? Why are these people hungry? What keeps them this way?

2. Decide. What specific things can you do to help solve the immediate problem? What can you do to help them to work on a long-term solution?

3. Act. Assign jobs and set up a schedule. Let others know what you are doing and why. Enlist their support and help. Teens have a great way of getting others involved. Execute your plan by following through.

4. Evaluate. Judge the effectiveness of the outcome, the process, and your feelings.

Suggestions

- Serve food at a food bank or homeless center.
- Sponsor a car wash or some other event to support a hunger center.
- Sponsor a "fast day" at school to create empathy for the poor and make others aware of hunger issues.
- Sponsor a "hunger day" at school by suggesting that people give up junk food and donate the cost to a hunger-relief agency. As part of this day, hang posters with hunger facts, show films, invite guest speakers, etc.
- Celebrate a Eucharist using readings from Matthew 25. When the gifts are offered, bring to the altar food bought with your own funds or some other symbol of a commitment to help the hungry. Pray for the needy.
- Sponsor a campaign to eradicate the waste of food in the school cafeteria.

Jesus teaches that the master will return when we least expect it. He will bless the faithful servant and punish the wicked one (Mt 24:45–51). We should be like the five wise virgins who were ready for the bridegroom's return. Symbolically, their steady good works made them internally glow with love, so they were recognizable to the bridegroom. The point of the parable is clear: Always be ready.

The parable of the talents (25:14–30) teaches that we should make good use of the time the Lord has given us. God has endowed us all with two precious commodities: gifts and a life to develop them. If we do not develop and use what God has given us, then we will have wasted our lives and be cast "into the darkness outside." In relation to the Kingdom, our lives must fervently preach the Gospel. And our faith must be practiced with cleverness, boldness, and intelligence. Being lukewarm has no place in God's Kingdom.

The last discourse of Jesus (25:31–46) concludes with the famous parable of judgment at the end of time, unique to Matthew's Gospel. Jesus describes how the Son of Man will appear in the roles of shepherd (v. 32), Lord (v. 37), and king (v. 41) to separate the sheep from the goats. The good will receive their reward, the wicked their punishment.

On what basis will the Lord judge us? His criterion is this: "Whatever you did for one of these least brothers of mine, you did for me" (25:40). Jesus powerfully identifies himself with the person in need. He will recognize us as his if we see him in the faces of those around us. But it is not enough to see the Lord; we must respond to him. He makes it very clear that our eternal destiny hinges on whether we feed the hungry, give drink to the thirsty, clothe the naked, and visit the sick and imprisoned.

FOR REVIEW

1. Discuss three specific teachings from the Sermon on the Mount.

2. What is the Golden Rule? Give two examples of how you can practice it in your own life.

3. Discuss two specific teachings of Jesus in his "missionary discourse," Matthew 10.

4. Interpret the meaning of any three parables in chapter 13 of Matthew's Gospel.

5. What is a parable? What is an allegory? Why did Jesus teach in parables?

6. What advice does Jesus give Church leaders in Matthew 18?

7. How does Matthew's Gospel support the establishment of the pope as the Christ-appointed leader of the Church?

8. According to Matthew 25, on what will we be judged?

FOR REFLECTION

• What is the biggest worry you have? Why is this so? What does it mean to worry? Jesus tells us to live our lives in the present, seeking to do God's will in everything. Analyze a typical school day. Write how your life would change if you took his advice. You don't worry about anything—except loving God and other people. Would you survive the day? Would it be worth trying? Write your reflections in your journal.

• In your journal, discuss some examples of where an active Christian faith could cause (or did cause) problems in your life as a student, a participant on a sports team, and/or an employee at a part-time job.

• In light of the teaching in Matthew 18, compose some disciplinary guidelines for three serious offenses that could be committed by students at your school.

Jesus **Challenges Judaism**

The Gospel of Matthew has the most references to the Old Testament and Judaism. The Gospel is also critical of Judaism in several places. For example, in Matthew 23 Jesus harshly denounces the scribes and Pharisees. In Matthew 27:25, after Pilate condemns Jesus, Matthew reports that the "whole people" said in reply, "His blood be upon us and upon our children." Tragically, throughout history, many people have read these passages as a condemnation of Judaism. They have used them to justify anti-Semitic behavior that eventually culminated in the horror of the Holocaust in the twentieth century and many other condemnable attacks on Judaism down through the centuries.

Anti-Semitism is a form of **prejudice**. Prejudice of this type that leads to the threatening of any person's rights, or leads to physical attack or extermination, is seriously sinful and a crime against humanity. It deserves condemnation. Pope John Paul II on numerous occasions apologized for the past sins of Christians directed against the Jews. He made it very clear that to be anti-Semitic is to be anti-Christian and that it is a serious misuse of Scripture to read hate into any biblical passage attributed to Jesus.

prejudice—An unsubstantiated opinion or preformed judgment about an individual or group.

What, then, is the correct way to read Matthew 23 and its very strong language directed against Jewish leaders and teachers? First, in Matthew 23:1–12, Jesus shows tremendous respect for the authority of the Jewish leaders and the Law they were entrusted to uphold. However, he is against leaders who preach one thing and yet do another, for example, by putting religious duties on others while they themselves avoid observing them. Second, Jesus warns leaders who simply want to impress others through superficial external titles rather than trying to be humble. Jesus is not condemning calling a priest "Father," as some non-Catholic groups claim. Matthew is simply reminding his readers that religious leaders should not get arrogant or overly impressed with their office and the glitter that goes with it.

The Seven Woes

The second part of this controversial chapter—Matthew 23:13–36—contains the seven "woes" exclaimed by Jesus against the scribes and Pharisees. A woe is a prophetic form of speech, often found in the Old Testament. It shows sorrow or grief or announces a threat. Using highly colorful and even derogatory language (e.g., "brood of vipers, blind guides, hypocrites"), its purpose is to shock people into examining their behavior and reforming it.

Jesus is calling leaders to gladly announce God's Kingdom; to treat converts lovingly; to avoid foolish oaths; to follow the spirit of the Law; to be genuine, authentic, and truthful; and to be receptive and open to God's prophets. These verses should not be read simply as a condemnation of Jewish leaders, but rather as a challenge to all religious people to be sincere, compassionate, humble, respectful, merciful, just, and loving.

Understanding Matthew 23 requires reading the chapter in the historical context of the time of the writing. The Romans had destroyed the Temple and Jerusalem. The Jewish religious leaders who survived were the Pharisees. It was the Pharisaical rabbis who were charged with the task of reviving Judaism. However, their interpretation of the Law and their oral traditions conflicted with the emerging Church, which believed that the Jewish prophet Jesus was the very fulfillment of all the promises made to God's people. Jewish Christians would inevitably disagree with the meaning of the faith they shared with their fellow Jews.

Think of first-century Judaism as a complex religion made up of many "cousins" who were trying to win over the people to their own view of the faith. The author of Matthew was a Jew who accepted Jesus as the Messiah. He belonged to a group of Jewish Christians who were beginning to open their religion and faith to Gentiles. He desperately wanted his fellow Jews to accept Jesus. Most of them did not. The Pharisaical rabbis began to exclude Jewish Christians from their synagogues, considering them misguided heretics. Much of this in-fighting resulted in the strong language Matthew employed in chapter 23. He saw the new Christian movement as involved in a struggle over the future direction of Israel. To bolster his claim that God was reforming Israel through Jesus and his Church, Matthew used his vantage point of hindsight to show that the Temple was destroyed because God was fulfilling the covenant in Jesus. For Jews, this understanding required a serious change of heart, a decision, and a life-changing commitment.

Most importantly, we should not think of Matthew 23 as anti-Semitic rhetoric. It is not an attack from without, but a discussion among Jewish insiders who were trying to win over their fractured religious body to the world-changing view that Jesus of Nazareth is the Christ, the Son of God. As tremendous claims were being made, Matthew needed to use shocking language to shake others up.

◀◀ FOR REVIEW

1. Define anti-Semitism.

2. Why is it not correct to say that Matthew 23 is anti-Semitic?

FOR REFLECTION

Read Matthew 23. In your journal, list two warnings of Jesus that apply to people in all ages.

CHAPTER SUMMARY POINTS

- The author of Matthew was a Jewish Christian, perhaps a former scribe. Traditionally, the author of Matthew's Gospel is identified as Levi, the Apostle who was a tax collector.
- The Gospel is written for a predominantly Greek-speaking, Jewish-Christian audience in Syria. One of his sources may have been a collection of Aramaic sayings, perhaps compiled by an eyewitness to Jesus. The sources for the Gospel of Matthew include Mark's Gospel, Q, and M (sources unique to Matthew).
- The probable date of composition for Matthew's Gospel is sometime in the 80s when tensions were high between Jewish Christians expelled from the synagogues and Jews who survived the Roman Revolt.
- Matthew's Gospel was written to show how Christians could lay claim to Yahweh's promises made to the Chosen People, while at the same time opening up the Gospel to Gentiles.
- Matthew's Gospel was written to show how Jesus fulfills Old Testament prophecy. Judgment, discipleship, Church, and true righteousness are major themes of Matthew's Gospel.
- Matthew's Gospel is outlined in five major sections (each with a narrative and discourse) sandwiched between an infancy narrative and the Passion narrative.
- Two popular titles for Jesus in Matthew are *Son of David*, to depict him as Israel's promised Messiah, and *Emmanuel* ("God with us"), to reveal Jesus' true identity and God's love for his people.

- Matthew's Gospel ends with the famous scene of Jesus commissioning the Apostles to preach the Gospel to all people (28:19–20). Though the emphasis in Matthew is on Jesus' Judaism, the verses make it very clear here that the Son of God came for all people.
- Matthew presents Jesus as the Teacher *par excellence*, a new Moses, whose Sermon on the Mount teaches the way of Christian discipleship.
- Jesus came to fulfill, not overthrow the Law. He teaches his followers to be light and salt, to act with the purest of intentions, to pray with simplicity and childlike trust, to forgive others, to be perfect as the heavenly Father is perfect, and to abide by the Golden Rule: "Do to others whatever you would have them do to you." Jesus revised the law of retaliation by commanding us not to seek revenge and to love even our enemies.
- Jesus' missionary discourse in Matthew 10 challenges his disciples to preach the Gospel in a spirit of poverty, trusting that the Holy Spirit will enlighten and strengthen them when persecution happens.
- To teach about God's Kingdom, Jesus often taught in parables, that is, down-to-earth short stories with a religious message. Some parables have allegorical elements with many points of comparison to some other reality. For example, on one level the parable of the Sower talks about the magnificent growth of the Kingdom. Yet on the allegorical level, it describes different kinds of Christians and their level of receptivity to the Good News.

- Matthew presents Jesus as the founder of the Church. The leaders of this Church should be humble, careful to avoid scandal, forgiving, prayerful, and willing to serve even to the point of suffering.

- Catholics see in Matthew 16:18–19 not only Jesus' clear founding of the Church but also his establishment of a hierarchical leadership headed by Peter and the Apostles and their successors, the pope and the bishops.

- Jesus teaches that God will judge us based on how we treat "the least of these" (Mt 25:40).

- Jesus' strong language in Matthew 23 reflects the religious turmoil within Judaism in the AD 80s. Matthew is trying to win over his fellow Jews to the view that Jesus fulfills the promises made to Israel.

LEARN BY DOING

1. Read Mark 14:43 and Matthew 26:47. Answer the following questions: What detail did Matthew leave out in recounting the arrest of Jesus? Can you explain why he might have done so?

2. The author of Matthew quotes several Old Testament prophecies. Read the following passages from Matthew's Gospel: 1:22–23; 2:5–6; 2:15; 2:18; 2:23; 4:14–16; 8:17; 12:16–21; 13:35; 21:4–5; 21:42; 27:9. Write how Jesus fulfills each Old Testament prophecy.

3. Create a two-page newsletter (with graphics) that covers the events of the infancy narrative reported in Matthew's Gospel (Mt 1:18–2:23).

4. Create a PowerPoint® presentation that illustrates the different elements of the Lord's Prayer. Select appropriate background music.

5. Research the life of the Apostles. Write a report on any three of them.

6. Offer your own allegorical interpretation of the parable of the weeds among the wheat (Mt 13:36–43). Treat these elements:

    - Sower of the good seed
    - The field
    - The good seed
    - The weeds
    - Sower of the weeds
    - Harvest
    - Reapers

7. Compose a modern-day parable that teaches one of the themes of the parables in Matthew 13.

8. With a partner, write a script of a conflict between two teens. Illustrate how it can be resolved in a creative way employing the teachings of the Sermon on the Mount.

9. Interview at least five children under the age of ten for their beliefs and views about Jesus. Either videotape or audiotape your interviews. In your commentary, try to state what it means to be "childlike" (versus "childish") in one's faith.

10. Compose an imaginative, guided meditation from the viewpoint of someone who experienced the miracle of the loaves and fish.

11. Create a short PowerPoint® presentation that illustrates how St. Matthew has been portrayed in art. Begin your research at this website: www.textweek.com/art/matthew.htm.

12. Report on the introduction to Matthew's Gospel from the PBS Frontline program "From Jesus to Christ: The First Christians," found at: www.pbs.org/wgbh/pages/frontline/shows/religion.

13. Research the pros and cons of the death penalty. In your research, be sure to include the teaching of the *Catechism of the Catholic Church* (2263–2267). Then, in light of Jesus' teaching in the Sermon on the Mount, discuss whether or not a disciple of Jesus can actively support capital punishment.

14. Jesus gave Simon bar Jonah (Mt 16:16–19) a new name—Peter, which means "rock." Write answers to the following questions: If Jesus called you as his disciple, what nickname might he give you? Why would this be appropriate?

PRAYER LESSON (CCC, 2759–2865)

Taught in the Sermon on the Mount (Mt 6:5–15), the Lord's Prayer instructs us to pray with childlike faith and sincerity. Because the "Our Father" is so familiar, at times we may pray it without reflecting on its profound meaning. Try praying the Our Father slowly, reflecting on the questions given.

Our Father in heaven,
hallowed be your name,
- How are you like your heavenly Father?
- Calling God "Father" means others are your brothers and sisters. How do you see others as your brothers and sisters?
- How do you "hallow" God's name, that is, how do you honor our loving Creator in your actions? How do you adore and worship God?

Your Kingdom come,
your will be done,
on earth as in heaven.
- God's Kingdom is a reign of justice, love, and peace. How are you helping to work for the Kingdom by treating others with justice?
- Where can love be found in your life? How are you a person of peace?

Give us today our daily bread.
- What do you really need to live a full life—physically, emotionally, spiritually?
- What are you doing to be bread for others—especially the poor, lonely, and needy ones you meet each day?

And forgive us our debts,
as we forgive our debtors.
- How do you acknowledge that you are a sinner? How do you ask for God's forgiveness?
- Who are your enemies? How can you, with God's help, forgive them?

And do not subject us to the final test,
but deliver us from the evil one.

- How do your friends, the media, and our culture tempt you?
- How do you avoid situations and people who lead you to sin?
- How do you ask for God's help when it is needed?

Amen.

- "So be it." Do you affirm wholeheartedly what Jesus teaches in the Lord's Prayer, called the summary of the Gospel?

Reflection: Meditate on this prayer daily for the next two weeks.

Resolution: Take one of the questions above and map out a concrete plan to improve, with the Lord's help, your own loving response to God.

The Gospel of Luke and Acts of the Apostles: Jesus the Savior

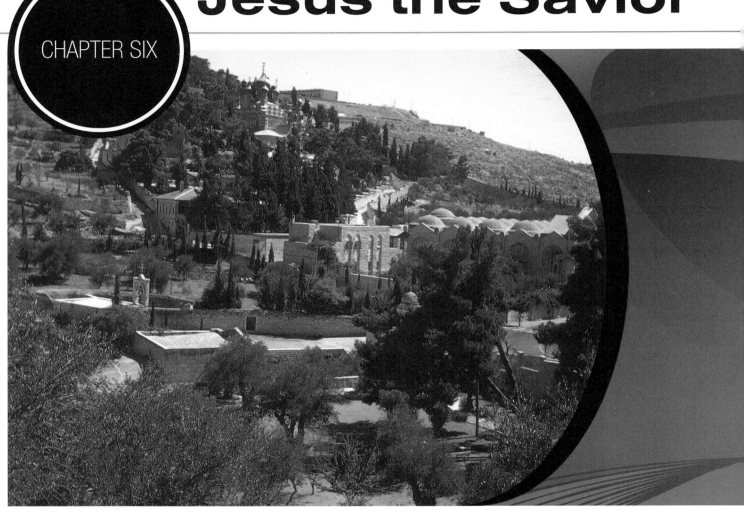

What woman having ten coins and losing one would not light a lamp and sweep the house, searching carefully until she finds it? And when she does find it, she calls together her friends and neighbors and says to them, "Rejoice with me because I have found the coin that I lost." In just the same way, I tell you, there will be rejoicing among the angels of God over one sinner who repents.

—Luke 15:8–10

CHAPTER **OVERVIEW**

LOST **AND FOUND**

In the Gospel of Luke, Jesus teaches of the immense and unending love God the Father has for us, his children.

BACKGROUND ON LUKE'S GOSPEL **AND THE ACTS OF THE APOSTLES**

St. Luke wrote his Gospel and the Acts of the Apostles for a Gentile audience, primarily for churches founded by St. Paul.

COMMON THEMES IN **LUKE AND ACTS**

Among many common themes in the Gospel and Acts, Luke addresses Jesus' role as a prophet with the Church continuing his prophetic ministry as well as the Holy Spirit's role in Christ's ministry and our lives.

JESUS: A COMPASSIONATE MESSIAH **AND UNIVERSAL SAVIOR**

Luke's Gospel emphasizes Jesus' compassion toward the poor and disadvantaged as well as his role as the Universal Savior who brings about our salvation.

OVERVIEW OF THE **ACTS OF THE APOSTLES**

The Acts of the Apostles details the coming of the Holy Spirit and the early days of the Church.

Lost **and Found**

After saving for years to take his family on a vacation to a large amusement park, he finally made the trip a reality. One evening, exhausted from standing in amusement park lines all day, and crushed by the crowds watching yet another spectacular parade, the father didn't notice when one of his children, a four-year-old, disappeared. The father, who was charged with keeping his eye out on his four children while Mom went for dinner, panicked and felt a dreadful sense of loss. After what seemed an eternity compressed into two short minutes, the father noticed his blond-haired boy with his hand in another man's hand. Being so short, the boy assumed

that the other man was his own dad and started walking away with him.

The father's joy at finding his beloved son was so overwhelming that he cried tears of joy as he picked his son up and hugged him for dear life. His anger at himself for taking his eyes off his son quickly gave way to a profound sense of relief that he had found him. He vowed never to let his son out of his sight again.

Put yourself in this father's place. Imagine his love for his son. Then realize that his love for his son pales in comparison to the love of our heavenly Father for those who stray away from him. Imagine the heavenly joy that results when one such wayward son or daughter returns to the loving embrace of God. This joy is indescribable.

The Gospel of Luke presents a Jesus who intimately knows the loving heart of his Father. The Lord Jesus comes to reveal his Father as a compassionate God who longs to save all his children. Jesus is like his Father: He is the Compassionate Savior, led by the Holy Spirit, who freely gave up his own life so that every human being—Jew and Gentile—could enter his Father's house. He embodies the forgiveness, self-surrender, love, and joy that God has for all people. The Acts of the Apostles, also written by the author of Luke, describes how the post-Resurrection Church continued to preach Jesus and his basic message of God's salvation for all people. Acts tells how the Holy Spirit led the early Church to grow and witness to Jesus. In the words of the risen Lord:

> You will receive power when the Holy Spirit comes upon you, and you will be my witnesses in Jerusalem, throughout Judea and Samaria, and to the ends of the earth. (Acts 1:8)

PARABLE THEMES AND REFLECTIONS

Recall how parables were one of Jesus' favorite forms of teaching. Parables use unparalleled, vivid word pictures that teach a truth about some aspect of God's Kingdom by using common activities and people from ordinary life, for example, fishing, farming, weddings, bread-baking, shepherding, widows, judges, farmers, vineyard owners, brothers, and housewives. Jesus' concrete images and down-to-earth people grabbed his listeners' attention, helped awaken their consciences, and moved them to action. Jesus' parables are important because:

1. They contain the heart of his message. To know them is to encounter the essence of the Gospel. They challenge us to examine our own lives in light of this Good News.

2. They represent Jesus as an outstanding teacher. The parables are highly memorable. Two of them from Luke's Gospel—the Good Samaritan and the Prodigal Son—are probably the most famous stories ever told.

3. They reveal how Jesus dealt with his opponents. He often told parables to defend his teaching. The parables not only proclaim God's Kingdom to everyone, they challenge those who resist Jesus' Gospel to challenge their own thinking.

Below are some summary statements of the key themes of Jesus' parables with a sample parable that illustrates that theme. Reflect on how you have put these themes into practice in your own life or how you might do so in the future. Write your reflections in your journal. Periodically review your progress.

1. God's Kingdom is here. Salvation is taking place. (Mustard Seed: Mk 4:30–32)
   - Describe a marvelous thing God has done for you or someone close to you.

2. God's Kingdom is a free gift. He calls everyone to enter. (Vineyard Workers: Mt 20:1–16)
   - What are three valuable gifts that you have been given for which you are most grateful to our Lord?

3. God loves sinners. We should be like God by forgiving those who have harmed us. (Unforgiving Servant: Mt 18:23–25)
   - Who requires your forgiveness? How do you plan to extend it to the person(s) in the coming weeks?

4. The Good News demands an urgent response. We should always be ready to act on it. (Hidden Treasure: Mt 13:44–46)
   - What concrete act can you do in the next twenty-four hours to show your love for others? Will you carry through?

5. God's Kingdom requires repentance. We should pray and make God our first priority in life by being faithful to him and by loving everyone we meet. (Wedding Feast: Mt 22:1–14)
   - When have you last examined your conscience? Gone to confession? Asked for God's forgiveness? If it has been a while, what would you like to do to change the situation?

6. God's Kingdom costs. It may bring suffering, but we will gain our reward. (Last Judgment: Mt 25:31–46)
   - What have you done for Christ? What are you doing for Christ? What will you do for Christ?

FOR REFLECTION

Describe the greatest joy you have ever experienced.

Background on Luke's Gospel **and the Acts of the Apostles**

Tradition identifies Luke as a Gentile Christian (who might have been attracted to Judaism) as the author of the third Gospel. This person is responsible for writing the Gospel with the most words and its sequel, the Acts of the Apostles. Together, they make up more than a quarter of the New Testament. The style, language, and organization of the Gospel of Luke and Acts are very similar. A strong proof that Luke authored them is that both works are addressed to the same person—Theophilus. Note the similarity in the outline elements of the Gospel of Luke and Acts, showing conclusively that they came from the same hand.

But do we really know the identity of the author? On the basis of certain "we passages" in Acts, Church writers, like the second-century St. Irenaeus, identify the author of Luke–Acts as St. Paul's coworker Luke, a physician who remained Paul's steadfast friend (see Acts 16:10–17, 20:5–21, 21:1–18, and 27:1–28:16). If Luke was indeed Paul's companion during some of his missionary adventures, it is likely that Luke used a travel diary to help him construct some of the history of Acts. Yet another tradition that comes from an early Prologue to the Gospel mentions that Luke was from Antioch in Syria and died in Greece.

Whoever the author was, it is certain that he did not know the historical Jesus in person. And because of mistakes Luke made about Palestinian geography, he did not come from the Holy Land. Furthermore, scholars cannot validate an ancient tradition that held that Luke was an artist who may have painted a portrait of Mary. This is probably a legend. However, one thing is clear: The author of Luke was a brilliant artist with words who wrote beautiful, polished Greek.

We can also deduce that Luke wrote for Gentile Christian churches, most likely those founded by St. Paul. The Gospel clearly appeals to a Gentile audience. One of Luke's major themes, for example, is the universality of Jesus' offer of salvation. The Gospel is intended for

GOSPEL OF LUKE

- Preface to Theophilus (1:1–4)
- Birth and Baptism of Jesus—special role of the Holy Spirit and Mary (2:1–12; 3:21–22)
- Sermons of Jesus (4:18–27; 6:20–49; 8:5–18; etc.)
- Jesus' healings (4:33–41; 7:1–17; 8:26–56; etc.)
- Jesus' mission to the Jews, openness to Gentiles (4:18–30; 24:47)
- Rejection and Passion of Jesus (22–23)

ACTS OF THE APOSTLES

- Preface to Theophilus (1:1–2)
- Birth and Baptism of the Church—special role of the Holy Spirit and Mary (1:14; 2:1–4)
- Sermons of Peter and Paul (2:14–36; 3:12–26; 13:16–41)
- Peter and Paul's healings (3:1–9; 5:12–16; 14:8–10)
- Church's mission to the Jews and full openness to Gentiles (1–9; 10–28)
- Paul's rejection and Passion (22–28)

everyone. Gentiles don't have to convert to Judaism to accept Jesus.

Another proof that Luke wrote for Gentiles is his elimination of passages that might confuse a non-Jewish audience. For example, he drops passages about the traditions of the Jews (Mk 7:1–23), the return of Elijah (Mk 9:11–13), and references to the Old Law in the Sermon on the Mount. In addition, Luke omits exclusively Jewish names; for example, he writes "master" (teacher) for rabbi and "lawyer" for scribe. He also uses the term "Savior" to explain the Jewish title Messiah (Christ). Luke also emphasizes that Jesus is the only Lord. He wants to distinguish the unique Savior from the emperors who also called themselves lords. Finally, Luke singles out Gentiles throughout his Gospel. For example, a Samaritan is the hero of a parable and another Samaritan is the only leper to return to thank Jesus for his cure.

The author of Luke used three main sources to write his Gospel:

1. Mark's Gospel (about 60 percent of it appears in the Gospel of Luke)

2. Q—the common source used by both Luke and Matthew

3. L—sources unique to Luke

Some of this special Lucan material includes early hymns, the finding of Jesus at the Temple, a genealogy, a collection of parables (including the parables of the Good Samaritan and Prodigal Son), and a group of miracle stories. Two specific passages (Lk 19:43–44 and Lk 21:20) also imply that the author was aware of Jerusalem's destruction. With these facts in mind, scholars usually date the creation of the Gospel anywhere from AD 75 to 90. The year 85 is often listed as a probable date of the composition of Luke–Acts.

The Prologue to the Gospel provides solid information on why it was written, what it is about, and how the author went about it:

The Good **Samaritan**

> Since many have undertaken to compile a narrative of the events that have been fulfilled among us, just as those who were eyewitnesses from the beginning and ministers of the word have handed them down to us, I too have decided, after investigating everything accurately anew, to write it down in an orderly sequence for you, most excellent Theophilus, so that you may realize the certainty of the teachings you have received. (Lk 1:1–4)

This passage informs us that "many" others have written a Gospel and that it is now Luke's turn to write an "orderly" account. He does so by studying his sources and organizing his materials. Thus, Luke shows a concern with historical detail and literary purpose. His interest in history helps him construct a unified work with Jerusalem as a central symbol in his presentation.

L—Specific material found in the Gospel of Luke that is unique to the Gospel; it includes five otherwise unknown miracle stories, fourteen additional parables, and many nativity and infancy details not included in the other Gospels.

Luke dedicates his Gospel to a certain Theophilus, a Greek name that means "lover of God." Whether Theophilus was a definite person, perhaps the monetary sponsor of the Gospel, or a symbol for all Christians, this name helps prove the unity of Luke's two-volume work. At the beginning of Acts, Luke writes:

> In the first book, Theophilus, I dealt with all that Jesus did and taught until the day he was taken up, after giving instructions through the holy Spirit to the Apostles whom he had chosen. (1:1–2)

If we look at Luke–Acts as a unit, we can detect Luke's master plan. It revolves around his belief in three periods of Salvation History:

1. In the first two chapters of his Gospel, Luke shows the relationship between Jesus and the history of Israel.

2. In the rest of the Gospel, Luke gives an orderly account of the life, Death, and Resurrection of the Savior, showing how Jesus is the promised Savior come for all people everywhere.

3. In Acts, Luke traces the rapid spread of the apostolic church through the Gentile world.

In his opening Gospel address to Theophilus, Luke states his major reason for writing. He wants to show Theophilus and all readers that their instruction in the Christian faith is sound. His purpose for writing the Gospel is to strengthen their faith. Gentile Christians of the first and second centuries lived in a time when Christianity was both questioned and opposed. Luke–Acts is a masterful restatement and defense of Jesus' Good News. It is also a faith-filled testimony about the continuing activity of the resurrected Lord and the Holy Spirit in history.

READING THE GOSPEL OF LUKE

Luke is an organized writer who is careful about historical detail. Luke consciously links Salvation History and ordinary history. Note how Luke situates the ministry of John the Baptist in both Roman and Jewish history. He references seven men:

> In the fifteenth year of the reign of Tiberius Caesar, when Pontius Pilate was governor of Judea, and Herod was tetrarch of Galilee, and his brother Philip tetrarch of the region of Ituraea and Trachonitis, and Lysanias was tetrarch of Abilene, during the high priesthood of Annas and Caiaphas, the word of God came to John the son of Zechariah in the desert. (Lk 3:1–2)

Luke organizes the Gospel around the symbol of Jerusalem. In Luke's infancy narrative, Jesus is taken to Jerusalem shortly after his birth. In Jerusalem, the prophecies of Simeon and Anna proclaim that Jesus is the promised Savior, the one who would deliver Israel. At age twelve, Jesus astounds the teachers in Jerusalem. He also informs Mary and Joseph that he is in Jerusalem to do his Father's work.

Although the first part of Jesus' public ministry takes place in Galilee, Luke continually reminds us of the importance of Jerusalem. Pharisees and teachers arrive from Jerusalem to criticize Jesus' teaching, and crowds of Jerusalem's citizens seek him out to hear his teaching.

The Annunciation

A pivotal verse in Luke is 9:51, where Jesus "resolutely determined to journey to Jerusalem." Jesus *must* go to the Holy City because it is there that God will fulfill all his promises. Thus begins the heart of Luke's Gospel, the long journey from Galilee to Jerusalem. Along the way, Jesus will tell his disciples that prophets must die in Jerusalem.

> Behold, we are going up to Jerusalem and everything written by the prophets about the Son of Man will be fulfilled. (Lk 18:31)

With heart and mind set on his destiny in Jerusalem, Jesus journeys there to accomplish his Father's will. Christ's Death on the Cross wins redemption for the world. The Gospel ends with Jesus telling his Apostles to preach the forgiveness of sin to all nations, "beginning from Jerusalem." But he instructs them to await the descent of the Holy Spirit:

> They did him homage and then returned to Jerusalem with great joy, and they were continually in the temple praising God. (Lk 24:52–53)

The Acts of the Apostles continues this symbol of Jerusalem. It opens with the descent of the Spirit on the Apostles on **Pentecost**. It then reports how the Gospel spreads from the holy city to the farthest reaches of the Roman Empire. Acts ends with Paul arriving in Rome, the symbolic center of the known world. The very last verse assures us that the Holy Spirit will continue his work until the whole world hears the Good News of God's salvation in Christ:

> And with complete assurance and without hindrance [Paul] proclaimed the Kingdom of God and taught about the Lord Jesus Christ. (Acts 28:31)

By means of the Jerusalem symbol, Luke points to the Christian life on the whole as a journey. Jesus resolutely had his gaze set on Jerusalem. When he arrived there, he met rejection, suffered, and died, but was raised in glory. The early Church began its journey in Jerusalem but quickly went out to share the Gospel to the ends of the earth. But the early Christian missionaries, especially Paul, also met with rejection and suffering as Jesus had.

As you read the Gospel of Luke, note how the outline of the Gospel focuses on the destination of Jerusalem.

Pentecost—The day recognized as the "birthday" of the Church when the Holy Spirit was revealed, bestowed, and communicated to the Church in fulfillment of the promises Jesus made to send another Advocate, a Comforter (Jn 14:16, 26; 15:26). The Jewish feast of Pentecost was the fiftieth day at the end of seven weeks following Passover (Easter on the Christian calendar).

Prologue: 1:1–4

I. From the Jerusalem Temple to the End of the Galilean Ministry (1:5–9:50)
 A. Infancy narratives (1:5–2:52)
 B. Preparation for the ministry (3:1–4:13)
 C. Galilean ministry (4:14–9:50)

II. Journey from Galilee to Jerusalem (9:51–19:27)

III. Events in Jerusalem (19:28–24:53)
 A. Jerusalem ministry (19:28–21:38)
 B. The Passion and Death of Jesus (chapters 22 and 23)
 C. The Resurrection (chapter 24)

FOR REVIEW

1. Identify at least three themes taught by the parables of Jesus. Name a parable that illustrates each theme.
2. Identify the author of Luke's Gospel. Offer evidence that he also wrote Acts of the Apostles.
3. When was Luke–Acts probably written?
4. What were the sources for Luke's Gospel?
5. Identify *Theophilus*.
6. Why did Luke write his Gospel?
7. How is Jerusalem a symbol in Luke's Gospel?

FOR REFLECTION

If you were writing a definitive account of the life of Jesus, what would be five essential incidents and/or themes that you would include?

Common Themes in **Luke and Acts**

There are several common themes that appear in both Luke and Acts that make these works unique. These themes enable both of Luke's works to present a common vision. Among these themes are:

- Jesus as a prophet
- the Church continues Jesus' prophetic ministry
- the role of the Holy Spirit in Salvation History
- prayer, joy, peace
- the special role of Mary and women

Jesus the Prophet (Lk 4:14–44)

> The Spirit of the Lord is upon me,
> because he has anointed me
> to bring glad tidings to the poor.
> He has sent me to proclaim liberty to captives
> And recovery of sight to the blind,
> To let the oppressed go free,
> and to proclaim a year acceptable to the Lord.
> (Lk 4:18–19)

This quotation that Jesus read at a synagogue service in his hometown of Nazareth comes from the prophet Isaiah (61:1f). Note the drama of this story. At first, Jesus' neighbors admire him, but then Jesus reveals the meaning of the text. In him, the prophecy about the Messiah is reaching fulfillment. God's Kingdom is present. What Isaiah prophesied is happening right now. In this prophecy, Jesus is detailing the main outlines of his ministry. He came to preach the Gospel, help people live freely, perform acts of mercy, work for justice, and celebrate God's presence in the world.

Jesus' explanation astonishes his fellow citizens. When his indirect claim to be the promised Messiah sinks in, they become outraged. "Who is Jesus? Isn't he the son of Joseph?" In short, how could the carpenter neighbor be the Promised One? It didn't make sense to them.

Jesus defends himself by saying no prophet ever receives honor in his own hometown. He points to the examples of Elijah and Elisha, prophets of Israel who ministered to Gentiles. Their contemporaries also rejected them. By mentioning them, Jesus strengthens his claim to be a prophet, that is, one who speaks God's will to the people. Old Testament prophets often had disturbing messages that called for change—not always popular with people.

Jesus' claims in his own hometown, and his criticism of his townsfolk, enrage them to the point that they lead him to the brow of a hill in Nazareth, fully intending to throw him off. Jesus, however, escapes. He has much work to do before he climbs the hill of Calvary in Jerusalem.

These verses in Luke's Gospel are important for many reasons. First, they reveal what Jesus thought of himself and how he conceived his mission. He is the Messiah, a Spirit-led prophet who brings good news to the poor, sets people free, and announces God's love for people. He is the Savior who has come to proclaim the Gospel and put it into action, especially for the afflicted and oppressed. Throughout the Gospel Luke reports ways Jesus fulfills Isaiah's prophecy of liberation when he:

- heals sick people from the bondage of their illnesses;
- touches and cures lepers, who were not allowed to associate with healthy people;
- ministers to the hated Samaritans and makes one the hero of one of his parables;
- treats women as equals by choosing them as disciples;
- forgives and eats meals with sinners whom the religious leaders despised;
- exorcises the demons out of those in bondage to Satan; and
- responds to a plea for help from a Roman centurion, a representative of an oppressive power.

Second, this scene at Nazareth foreshadows Jesus' public life. He meets with initial acceptance; however, people change their opinion and reject and kill the innocent prophet in Jerusalem. During the travel narrative, Jerusalem remains Jesus' destination, "for it is impossible that a prophet should die outside of Jerusalem" (Lk 13:33).

Third, the synagogue scene underscores two other themes that appear in both Luke's Gospel and Acts: the role of the Holy Spirit and the importance of prayer in the life of Jesus and the early Church. We will examine these themes in greater depth in sections that follow.

The Church Continues Jesus' Prophetic Mission (Acts 1–2)

After the dedication to Theophilus (thus linking Luke and Acts), Acts tells of the risen Lord appearing to and instructing the Apostles for forty days, during which time Jesus promised to send the Holy Spirit (Acts 1:1–5). After Jesus instructs the disciples to preach in Judea, Samaria, and to the very ends of the earth, we find a report of Jesus' **Ascension** from the Mount of Olives (1:6–12).

Acts then describes the first Church in Jerusalem, consisting of eleven Apostles: "All these devoted themselves with one accord to prayer, together with some women, and Mary the Mother of Jesus, and his brothers" (Acts 1:14). Note here the importance of prayer, the presence of women disciples, and the central role of Mary as a faithful witness to her Son and a source of strength to the Apostles and other disciples. This verse links Acts with Luke's Gospel because the Apostles could give witness to Jesus' public ministry and to the risen Lord; the women could attest to his burial and the empty tomb; and Mary, his mother, could witness to Jesus' birth and the "hidden years" of his youth.

Acts 1:15–26 reveals how prayer helped the Apostles and the initial group of Jesus' disciples (120 in number) choose Judas's successor. Since there were twelve tribes in Israel, the twelve Apostles were a symbol for a renewed Israel. Just as Christ chose the twelve Apostles, God restored the Twelve, thus preparing for the coming of the Holy Spirit and the foundation of the Church.

Chapter 2 of Acts describes the coming of the Holy Spirit to the Church. This coming of the Spirit took place on Pentecost, also known as the Feast of Weeks, a pilgrimage feast fifty days after Passover that commemorated God's giving the covenant to Israel at Sinai.

Peter's speech, a kerygmatic homily (see page 183), follows. Like prophets before him, including Jesus, Peter calls for repentance: "Repent and be baptized, every one of you, in the name of Jesus Christ for the forgiveness of your sins; and you will receive the gift of the holy Spirit" (Acts 2:38).

Three thousand converts were baptized on the first Pentecost, often called the "birthday of the Church." The Church was underway. More and more Christians were added each day:

> They devoted themselves to the teaching of the Apostles and to the communal life, to the breaking of the bread and to the prayers. Awe came upon everyone, and many

Ascension—The event in Salvation History where Jesus' humanity entered into the divine glory in Heaven forty days after his Resurrection.

wonders and signs were done through the Apostles. All who believed were together and had all things in common; they would sell their property and possessions and divide them among all according to each one's need. Every day they devoted themselves to meeting together in the temple area and to breaking bread in their homes. They ate their meals with exultation and sincerity of heart, praising God and enjoying favor with all the people. And every day the Lord added to their number those who were being saved. (Acts 2:42–47)

In these few verses, Luke depicts the characteristics of an ideal Church: Christian fellowship (in Greek, *koinonia*), prayers, breaking bread (Eucharist), and the teaching of the Apostles:

Christian fellowship or communion was brought about through the sharing of goods and love shared among all members of the Church by caring for each other's needs.

Praying for each other was a sign of Christian community then, as it is now. Acts 2:46 reports how early Christians worshiped daily in the Temple, but how they also *celebrated the Eucharist* in their homes. Sharing this sacred meal commemorated Jesus' Paschal Mystery, made Jesus present in their midst, and strengthened their identity as a community of believers who were united to their Lord.

Finally, the Church was rooted in Gospel truth as *handed on by the apostolic eyewitnesses*. This teaching included the Sacred Scriptures of the Jews, Jesus' own interpretations of the Jewish scriptures and the Law, the unique teachings that Jesus had given them, and the particular apostolic applications of Jesus' teachings to any new situations in which the early Church found itself.

The Role of the Holy Spirit in Salvation History

Luke and Acts stress the vital role of the Holy Spirit in Salvation History. Luke's use of the Isaiah quote in the Nazareth synagogue service (Lk 4:18–19) illustrates how he viewed history in three dramatic stages:

Stage 1—Age of Promise: Jesus announces that "today" God's covenant promises are being fulfilled. The Holy Spirit has singled him out to accomplish the Father's plan. John the Baptist prepared people to welcome Jesus, but he remained part of the time of preparation, "I tell you, among those born of women, no one is greater than John; yet the least in the Kingdom of God is greater than he" (Lk 7:28).

Stage 2—The Time of Jesus: Jesus is the center of history. Guided by the Spirit, Jesus begins his preaching ministry in Galilee, proclaiming a message of salvation for all. His miracles prove the power of his message. He then resolutely turns his eyes toward Jerusalem and continues his work of salvation on his journey to the sacred city. Finally, he accomplishes his Paschal Mystery of love through his Passion, Death, and Resurrection in the city that kills its prophets.

Stage 3—The Age of the Church: Acts has been termed "the Gospel of the Holy Spirit" because time and again the Spirit empowers the early Christians to continue Jesus' work until the Lord comes in glory. The disciples begin in Jerusalem, move outward to Judea and Samaria, and then eventually make it to Rome and the ends of the earth. Peter and Paul are highlighted as Spirit-inspired Apostles who continue Jesus' work of spreading the Gospel.

The Holy Spirit appears frequently in Luke and Acts. For example:

- Mary becomes the Mother of God through the power of the Holy Spirit (Lk 1:35).
- The Spirit moves the prophet Simeon to recognize the infant Jesus as the promised one (2:27).
- The Spirit descends on Jesus in the form of a dove (3:22).
- Jesus goes into the desert led by the Spirit (4:1) and emerges (4:14) to begin his public ministry preaching with power.
- Jesus prays full of power in the Spirit (10:21) and teaches us how to pray for the Holy Spirit (11:13).

These citations show how the Holy Spirit leads and directs Jesus in his own ministry. Through his Resurrection and Glorification, Jesus receives the Holy Spirit from the Father to give to the Church (Acts 2:38). Acts reports often (over seventy references) how the Holy Spirit emboldens the disciples to proclaim the message. The Spirit's presence impels the early Christians to preach the Gospel throughout the Roman Empire. The Spirit opens the hearts of hearers and thus enables preaching to fall on fertile soil. The Spirit prompts Christians in Antioch to send Barnabas and Paul out on a missionary journey. The Spirit inspires Peter and Paul in their preaching, leads Paul on his mission through Asia Minor and Greece, and comforts Paul in the face of his persecutions. The Spirit leads the Church to open up the Gospel to the Gentiles. The Spirit is given to converts when the Apostles lay hands on the newly baptized.

Whereas Jesus' public ministry begins with the Spirit leading Jesus in his work of salvation, Acts ends with St. Paul quoting another passage from Isaiah, and proclaiming that the Spirit will continue his work of converting non-Jews until the end of time:

> Let it be known to you that this salvation of God has been sent to the Gentiles; they will listen. (Acts 28:28)

QUESTIONS FROM ACTS

Answer the following questions after reading the cited passages from the Acts of the Apostles.

- Who were the candidates to replace Judas? What was the basis for choosing? How did the Apostles make their choice? (Acts 1:15–26)
- List three signs that the Holy Spirit had come. Describe the **gift of tongues** that was given on Pentecost. (2:1–12)
- What does the Spirit enable one to do? (2:17–18)
- What gesture is associated with giving the power of the Spirit? (8:17, 9:17)
- What emotional state does the Spirit often bring? (13:52)

gift of tongues—The name for the ability to communicate in words or sounds in a language unknown to the speaker, a gift afforded St. Peter at the feast of Pentecost.

Prayer

Prayer is a pervasive theme in Luke and Acts. Recall how Luke reports it was Jesus' custom to go to the synagogue to pray. The Holy Spirit and prayer were inseparable in Jesus' ministry. For example, Jesus prayed at his Baptism (3:21). He often withdrew to lonely places (like the desert) to pray (5:16). Before choosing his Apostles, he prayed for a full night on a mountainside (6:12). Before Peter proclaimed him the Christ, Jesus prayed (9:18), meditating over the various beliefs people had about him. Jesus also told Peter that he prayed for him in a special way. He also prayed at his Transfiguration. While hanging on the cross, Jesus utters the most moving prayer of all, one that reveals his profound love for all sinners:

Father, forgive them, they know not what they do. (23:34)

The message to be learned from Jesus' example is that *we* should pray often as the Master did. Prayer enables the Holy Spirit to guide us in the Christian life. Acts shows how the early Church heeded this advice well. For example, the Eleven with the Blessed Mother pray in the Upper Room awaiting the Holy Spirit (Acts 1:14). The Apostles pray for guidance to select Judas's successor (Acts

The Garden of Gethsemane

1:24). The Apostles pray regularly in the Temple (3:1), on behalf of the community (6:4), that new converts might receive the Holy Spirit (8:15), and before performing miracles in the name of Jesus (9:40). Also, the example of a Gentile, Cornelius, at prayer is praised (10:30–31). Peter has a vision while praying, a vision that welcomed Gentiles into the early Church (11:5). His fellow believers pray for him during his imprisonment (12:5,12). Paul and Barnabas pray for the Church leaders they appoint (14:23), and Paul frequently prays for his converts (20:36).

In the Gospel, Jesus offers a teaching on prayer, for example, by giving us the Lord's Prayer. He encourages his followers to pray always (21:36) and to pray in a special way for the Holy Spirit (11:13). Jesus tells us not to lose heart when we pray. We must persist in prayer, trusting that our loving Father will indeed give us what is good for us (11:9–13).

Jesus' example shows us the perfect way to pray—seeking God's will in all we do. Picture Jesus in the Garden of Gethsemane. He clearly sees that if he does not flee the city, his enemies will arrest and crucify him. He fears death. But he loves his Father even more:

> Father, if you are willing, take this cup away from me; still, not my will but yours be done. (Lk 22:42)

Every time we sincerely recite the Lord's Prayer we are, in fact, sharing in Jesus' prayer, "Your will be done." Luke teaches that praying is essential for the Christian life. We must take time to be alone, to put ourselves in the presence of God, and to ask for the

PRAYING THE "JESUS PRAYER"

But the tax collector stood off at a distance and would not even raise his eyes to heaven but beat his breast and prayed, "O God, be merciful to me a sinner" (Lk 18:13).

This passage may be the foundation of the famous Jesus Prayer, which you read about in an earlier chapter. Take the time now to pray this powerful prayer, which is recited repeatedly in harmony with one's breathing. It goes like this:

Lord Jesus Christ (*recited while breathing in*)
have mercy on me, a sinner (*recited while exhaling*).

Repeat the prayer at least twenty times, pondering each word. Let the words, and the Lord's loving goodness, calm you. Then speak to Jesus as a friend about your heartfelt concerns. Conclude your prayer time by asking him to send you the Holy Spirit to strengthen you in your life as a student, friend, and son or daughter.

Additional Prayer Reflections

Write the answer to each of the following in your journal:

- When do you usually pray and where?
- How often do you pray?
- Describe a time when prayer helped you.
- Read Luke 18:1–8. Write your own interpretation of this parable.
- Compose your own definition of prayer.
- "It is impossible to be a follower of Jesus if you don't pray." Comment.

strength of the Holy Spirit. If we do, God will draw us close to his Son and bring us what we need to live the Gospel with joy and conviction.

Joy and Peace

The themes of joy and peace are evident from the opening verses of the Gospel and are often connected with prayer. For example, John the Baptist leaps in his mother's womb when he is in the presence of the Messiah. Mary breaks into a beautiful hymn of joy (the Magnificat) when Elizabeth blesses her faith (Lk 1:44–55). The birth of the Messiah brings joy in Heaven with the angels glorifying God and announcing peace (2:13–14). On earth, frightened shepherds are the first to experience the joy and peace of Jesus as they come in from the fields to worship him (2:20).

During Jesus' public life, the crowds of his followers rejoice over Jesus' mighty works (19:37). His closest companions also experience joy working for him. For example, the seventy-two Jesus sent out to preach returned from their journey rejoicing (10:17). Zacchaeus the tax collector receives Jesus with joy into his house (Lk 19:6).

The message of several of his famous parables, especially the so-called prodigal son (see page 180), also highlights the theme of great joy over the return of lost sinners.

A key event in Jesus' life that results in joy is his entry into Jerusalem during Holy Week. There the crowds proclaim:

> Blessed is the king who comes
> in the name of the Lord.
> Peace in heaven
> and glory in the highest. (Lk 19:38)

The most joyous occasion of all, though, is Jesus' Resurrection, an event that ushers in God's peace and salvation. Jesus greets his followers with peace and urges them to rejoice at what God has accomplished for them. Their hearts were bursting with joy (24:41).

This same theme of joy is carried over to Acts. For example, the lame man Peter cures leaps for joy at what Jesus does for him (Acts 3:8). Similarly, Philip brings great joy to Samaria because of the miracles he works in Christ's name (8:8). And it seems wherever Paul traveled, he "brought great joy to all the brothers" (15:3).

The Special Role of Mary and Women

In the first-century society where Jesus lived, women were considered inferior to men, with no right to an education, possessing limited legal rights, and having no role in public life. Jesus' attitude toward women was oppositely positive and revolutionary. Luke reflects this attitude in the treatment of women in the Gospel and Acts.

For example, in the infancy narratives, Mary plays a key role; Joseph fades into the background. Mary has faith in the angel's revelation that she is to be God's Mother (1:38). Contrast this with the doubts of Zechariah (Lk 1:18) when he heard that his aged wife, Elizabeth, would conceive a child. Luke tells us of the fidelity of Elizabeth (1:24) and the patience of the prophetess Anna (2:36). The infancy narrative is replete with strong, faithful women.

In Luke's Gospel Jesus treats many other women positively: the widow of Nain, whose son Jesus raised from the dead (7:12); the repentant woman in Simon's house, whose great love for Jesus met with criticism (7:37); Mary Magdalene, out of whom he exorcised demons; Susanna and Joanna and a whole group of women who served as traveling companions and helped support Jesus' ministry

WHAT THE CHURCH BELIEVES ABOUT MARY
(CCC, 484–511; 722–726; 963; 966; 970–975)

Because of her exemplary life and her unique role in Salvation History, Catholics believe the following about Mary:

- *Immaculate Conception.* From the first moment of her conception, Mary was "full of grace" through God, preserved immune from all stain of Original Sin (see *CCC*, 491). God graced Mary with this divine favor in anticipation of Christ's Paschal Mystery. In addition, Mary lived a sinless life because of her closeness to God. This is why the angel Gabriel could address her, "Hail favored one! The Lord is with you" (Lk 1:28). American Catholics celebrate this feast as a holy day on December 8. Mary is the patron saint of the United States under the title of Our Lady of the Immaculate Conception.

- *Ever-Virgin.* Conceived by the Holy Spirit (without a human father), Jesus was born of the Virgin Mary. The Church has traditionally taught that Mary was always a virgin—before, in, and after the birth of the Lord. Our beliefs about Mary are rooted in our faith about Jesus Christ. From all eternity, God chose Mary to be the Mother of the Lord and Savior, Jesus Christ. Mary's virginity highlights the truth that God took the initiative in the Incarnation. God the Father is the only Father of our Savior!

- *Mother of God, Mother of the Church.* Jesus is one divine person, the second person of the Blessed Trinity. Thus, it is correct to say that because Mary is Christ's Mother, she is truly the Mother of God. Mary is also the Mother of the Church because on the cross Jesus gave her to us, "Behold, your mother" (Jn 19:27). Mary is the spiritual Mother of humanity (the new Eve). Her obedience to the Holy Spirit helped bring Christ into the world. Her example of faith and devotion also show us how to be true brothers and sisters to her Son. She images God's love for his people and is a model of holiness.

- *Assumption.* The doctrine of the Assumption, rooted in the ancient belief of the Church, holds that "The Immaculate Virgin, preserved free from original sin, when the course of her earthly life was finished, was taken body and soul into heavenly glory". Death's decay did not touch Mary, the first to share in her Son's Resurrection. She gives us hope that we, too, will one day be eternally united with our risen Lord. Her Assumption, celebrated on August 15 as a holy day, anticipates our own final glory.

Learn more about Mary by doing one of the following:

1. Prepare a PowerPoint® presentation on one set of Mysteries of the Rosary (Joyful, Luminous, Sorrowful, or Glorious). Search the Web for illustrations for each of the mysteries. Select an appropriate scriptural quote to accompany the mystery. Write your own short prayer of meditation on each of the mysteries. Consult these websites for ideas and other links: www.theholyrosary.org and www.scborromeo.org/prayers/rosary.htm.

2. Report on the origin and practice of a particular devotion to the Blessed Mother, for example, the Brown Scapular or Miraculous Medal or one of the approved apparitions of Mary: Guadalupe, Lourdes, Fatima. Begin your research by consulting some of the links on the Theology Library website: www.shc.edu/theolibrary/devotion.htm.

3. Prepare a report on Mary in art through the ages. Consult these websites for starters:

   - The Mary Page: http://campus.udayton.edu/mary/index.html (check out the gallery)

   - Blessed Virgin Mary: www.catholic-forum.com/saints/saintbvm.htm

(8:1–3); and "the daughters of Jerusalem," women who mourned Jesus' impending Death (23:28). Luke also shares the story of Jesus' friends Mary and Martha (10:38–42).

Jesus also includes women as the central characters in two of his parables, the lost coin (7:8–10) and the unjust judge (18:1–8). In this first parable, Jesus compares God to a woman who rejoices when she finds a coin. So, too, God rejoices over a repentant sinner. What is remarkable about this parable is that it was unheard of in Jesus' day to compare God to a woman. By doing so, Jesus broke down popular expectations about what God is like and, along the way, forced people to reexamine their attitudes toward women. The second parable praises the woman for her strong faith and persistence in pleading her case before an unscrupulous judge.

Most significantly, it is women who witness Jesus' Death on the cross (23:46–49), see the tomb in which Jesus' body is laid (23:55), and discover it empty (24:1). These women were the first to proclaim his Resurrection to the Eleven and other disciples, though undoubtedly out of prejudice, they were not believed. Why? Because they were women (Lk 24:8–9).

Women play an important role in Acts throughout. A notable example is how the homes of women, for example, of Mary, the mother of John Mark, served as centers for worship and other activity for the early Church (Acts 12:12). Also, Lydia, an early convert of Paul's in Philippi, prevailed on her whole household to become Christians and forcefully convinced Paul to make her home his center of operations (16:14–15). Acts also tells how Peter raised Tabitha (Dorcas) to life, a woman praised for her good deeds and almsgiving. Peter did so because of the mourning of the widows who were friends of this good woman (9:36-43). In fact, Acts reports how widows, who were especially powerless without the protection of their husbands in a patriarchal society, were especially cared for by the Apostles (6:1–15).

Luke gives Jesus' Mother special attention. She is the model of Christian faith. She freely responds to God's invitation to be the Mother of his Son, though she does not fully understand all that is happening to her. Mary's response, a yes to God, enables Jesus to come to humanity. Throughout her life, Mary prayerfully meditates on the meaning of her Son (2:52) and is faithful to him to the end, following him to the cross. As we have seen, she was also with the Apostles in the Upper Room, awaiting the descent of the Holy Spirit. She perfectly fulfills the criteria Jesus states for true discipleship: hearing the Word of God and putting it into action (8:21).

Mary illustrates well a major Lucan theme that we will take up next: God's preferential love for the poor. Mary was not some famous, wealthy, or glamorous person that God chose. She was a simple, humble young girl whose famous prayer, the *Magnificat*, praises God for the gift of salvation and for how God reaches out to and rescues the lonely, the hungry, and the poor. Her prayer ends by praising God, who is fulfilling all his promises made to Abraham for the salvation of humanity.

 FOR REVIEW

1. Explain the significance of Jesus' teaching in the synagogue at Nazareth.

2. How did the early Church continue Jesus' prophetic ministry?

3. What is Luke's understanding of Salvation History?

4. Give several examples of how the Holy Spirit plays a role in both the Gospel of Luke and Acts.

5. What role did prayer play in Jesus' life? in the life of the early Church?

6. Give some examples of the part women played in Luke–Acts. What does their inclusion say about Jesus and his teaching?

7. List three ways Mary has a special role in the writings of Luke.

8. Identify these Marian doctrines: *Immaculate Conception*, *Assumption*, and *Mary Ever Virgin*.

FOR REFLECTION

- Write a personal example of this saying: "No prophet is ever accepted in his own country." Describe a time when others rejected you and how you coped with it.

- In your journal, describe two of the most joyful occasions of your life. Analyze what made these occasions so joyful for you.

Jesus: A Compassionate Messiah **and** **Universal Savior**

For Luke, Jesus is a compassionate Messiah who has come to prove God's great love. This compassion makes Jesus the friend of the friendless. For example, Jesus identifies with the poor and lowly. He himself comes to us humbly. We see this at his birth when Jesus is born surrounded by farm animals. Shepherds—considered socially outcast by the pious Jews—visit him first. His parents were poor, evidenced by Mary's presenting two turtledoves, the offering of the poor, at his Presentation in the Temple.

Describing his own work to the disciples of John the Baptist, Jesus said he came to proclaim the Gospel to the poor (7:22). More than the other three Gospels, Luke reassures the poor and warns the rich. For example, compare Luke's first Beatitude to Matthew's:

**Blessed are you who are poor,
for the Kingdom of God is yours. (Lk 6:20)**

Luke adds to this blessing Jesus' warning to the rich:

> But woe to you who are rich,
> for you have received your consolation.
> But woe to you who are filled now,
> for you will be hungry.
> Woe to you who laugh now,
> for you will grieve and weep.
> Woe to you when all speak well of you,
> for their ancestors treated the false prophets
>   in this way. (Lk 6:24–26).

**Blessed are the poor in spirit,
for theirs is the kingdom of heaven. (Mt 5:3)**

Luke's Beatitudes and woes balance each other. God blesses the poor. This includes not only those who are socially disadvantaged, but also those who recognize that they are nothing without God. On the other hand, he challenges the rich to repent before it is too late. Rich people are not condemned for being wealthy but rather because they feel that they do not need God. Jesus teaches that love for the poor, manifested in concrete deeds, is a requirement for his disciples.

Compassionate to the Poor (Luke 16:19–31)

Luke's is the only Gospel that records the story of Lazarus and the rich man. The story tells of Lazarus, a poor man who suffered incredibly in his life on earth, longing for the scraps that fell from the rich man's table. But the rich man did not respond to the suffering poor man who, Jesus states simply, "died." Lazarus, a name that means "may God help," or "the one whom God helps," received his eternal reward: a life of happiness in Heaven with Abraham, the father of the Jews. The rich man "also died and was buried." He received what was due him: eternal suffering in Hell. Jesus uses an unforgettable image to describe the fate of selfishness. The rich man so thirsted that he longed for a mere drop of water from the tip of Lazarus's finger.

But Abraham denied him this small pleasure because the rich man and his brothers ignored "Moses [the Law] and the prophets." These terms remind the reader that the Sacred Scriptures tell us how to respond in justice to the needs of poor and suffering people. Finally, the story points out that if someone would come back to life, those who are selfish and have closed their eyes to human suffering will not pay attention.

Through this parable, Jesus is warning that those who have plenty in this life must share with those who have less. The heavenly Father is compassionate to the poor. His children who are blessed with material wealth must imitate God by sharing with their sisters and brothers who have less. Generous service of God and others with compassion for the poor and outcast are mandatory for the followers of Jesus.

Friend of Outcasts (Luke 19:1–10)

One rich man who heard Jesus' call was the tax collector Zacchaeus. Luke reports how Zacchaeus, a short man, scrambled up a tree to capture a glimpse of Jesus. When Jesus saw Zacchaeus, he asked to stay with him. Zacchaeus gladly accepted the invitation. In fact, he was filled with joy as he received Jesus into his home and heart.

Many people complained that Jesus would dare stay with Zacchaeus, a notorious sinner. By reaching out to Zacchaeus, Jesus was enacting a living parable of God's love for sinners. Jesus' love prompted Zacchaeus to promise that he would right his wrongs and give half of his wealth to the poor. Jesus' compassion moved this person to action. Zacchaeus was sincere and open.

Jesus' compassion also extended to outcasts like lepers, who were so reviled in Jesus' day that they had to live apart from others. One day Jesus cured ten of these feared, unclean lepers (see Luke 17:11–19). Only one, however, had the thoughtfulness to return to thank Jesus for his great mercy. He was a Samaritan, a hated enemy of the Jews. Jesus used him as an object lesson of the gratitude and faith that was lacking in those who should have known better.

Love for Enemies (Luke 10:25–37)

God's love and compassion knows no bounds, nor should ours. This is the message of the timeless parable of the Good Samaritan. The setting for this parable has a lawyer testing Jesus, asking him what is necessary to attain eternal life. Like any good teacher, Jesus asks the lawyer to recite what he already knows about the Law. The man replies,

> You shall love the Lord your God with all your heart, with all your being, with all your strength, and with all your mind, and your neighbor as yourself. (Lk 10:27)

Jesus responds affirmatively to the lawyer. The man then adds a further question: "And who is my neighbor?" All self-respecting Jews thought they knew the answer to this question, too: "My neighbor is my fellow Jew. The Law only obliges me to love my co-religionists."

Jesus, however, reveals the startling truth that our neighbor is *everyone*. We cannot say we love God unless we love our neighbor, and our neighbor even includes our bitter enemy. Rather than lecture the lawyer and make him look bad, Jesus tactfully tells a story about love-for-neighbor in action. By making a Samaritan the hero of his story, Jesus probably shocked his listeners. "How can there be a *good* Samaritan? Is this not a contradiction in terms? There is no such person." For whatever reason, the priest and the Levite, two men one would expect to come to the aid of a suffering Jew, do not risk getting involved.

They go out of their way to avoid the unfortunate victim of the bandits.

But a sworn enemy of the Jews, a Samaritan, does stop. He compassionately ministers to the victim of the robbery. He also inconveniences himself to see to proper follow-up care, even spending two silver coins, what some scholars estimate would have taken care of the victim for twenty-four days. The Samaritan also promises to return, ensuring that the helpless victim is well cared for. This Samaritan was not only good; his love was heroic.

Note how gently Jesus brings the lawyer to conclude who our neighbor is: "Which of these three, in your opinion, was neighbor to the robbers' victim?"

Unable to mention the dreaded word *Samaritan*, the lawyer responds, "The one who treated him with mercy." And Jesus answers, "Go and do likewise" (Lk 10:36–37).

Through this story, Jesus teaches that everyone, especially a person in need, is our neighbor and that God's love embraces everyone. We should break through our prejudices and imitate our loving God by embracing even our enemies.

The parable of the Good Samaritan puts in story form Jesus' own loving example. His ministry proves that his love includes everyone. He is the universal Savior, and his love embraces the lowly, Samaritans, and even Gentiles. For example, Jesus praises the faith of two Gentiles from the Old Testament era—the widow at Zarephath and Naaman the Syrian (4:24–27). Jesus also singles out the faith of the centurion whose servant Jesus cured: "I tell you, not even in Israel have I found such faith" (7:9).

Friend of Sinners (Lk 15)

Many have called Luke's chapter 15 the very heart of the entire Gospel. It contains three memorable and important parables that deal with God's great compassion and his joy over repentant sinners. The setting of these parables involves some Pharisees and scribes who criticize Jesus for welcoming and eating with sinners. Jesus tells these parables to defend his attitude and actions. In effect, Jesus was saying he was simply imitating the love of his Father.

The *parable of the lost sheep (15:4–7)* presents what appears to be a foolish shepherd who leaves ninety-nine sheep alone to go after the one that is lost. Once he finds it, he tenderly puts it on his shoulders because the sheep probably would lie down and refuse to budge. He then goes home and asks his friends to rejoice with him. God's love is like the shepherd's—seemingly foolish in human terms in its pursuit of the one who has lost his or her way.

The *parable of the lost coin (15:8–10)* compares God to a woman who goes to great lengths to find a misplaced coin. She then may even have spent more on a party celebrating its finding than the value of the coin lost. The point: God's love exceeds what the learned and "holy" ones of Jesus' day expect. His love is astonishing, excessive, and almost ridiculous compared to our standards.

The *parable of the lost or prodigal son (15:11–32)* tells even more about the boundless love of the father than of the wayward nature of the son. Note how the younger son arrogantly asks for his inheritance ahead of time. He is indeed "prodigal" (profligate, exceedingly and recklessly wasteful) when he squanders his inheritance in reckless living. When he is as

JESUS AND MONEY

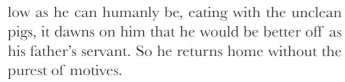

Luke's Gospel has much to say about money and possessions and what our attitude should be toward them. Write one sentence for each, explaining how you apply it to your own life.

- "Give to everyone who asks of you, and from the one who takes what is yours do not demand it back." (6:30)
- Give and gifts will be given to you; a good measure, packed together, shaken down, and overflowing, will be poured into your lap. For the measure with which you measure will in return be measured out to you. (6:38)
- Take care to guard against all greed, for though one may be rich, one's life does not consist of possessions. (12:15)
- Every one of you who does not renounce all his possessions cannot be my disciple. (14:33)
- No servant can serve two masters. He will either hate one and love the other, or be devoted to one and despise the other. You cannot serve God and mammon. (16:13)
- St. Paul quoting Jesus: "It is more blessed to give than to receive." (Acts 20:35)

Applying the Lesson

Analyze an hour's worth of TV or radio advertisements. How do the commercials appeal to pleasure, the good life, comfort, or status? Do the ads create false needs, or do they appeal to real needs? What kind of people do the commercials depict? Comment.

---

low as he can humanly be, eating with the unclean pigs, it dawns on him that he would be better off as his father's servant. So he returns home without the purest of motives.

Fully expecting harsh judgment from his father, the youth is surprised when his father receives him back unconditionally. An old man lumbering across the fields to embrace his son would have been both laughable and demeaning, yet so great was the father's love for his wayward son. Now it is his turn to be prodigal, foolishly spendthrift with his love, giving his son all the symbols of a free man (shoes) and privileges of being a member of the family (robe and ring). The son's return is an occasion of great rejoicing, and a great feast is thrown on his return.

This, however, disturbs the older brother who seemed to be faithful to his father more out of a sense of duty than of true love. He is jealous and whining, not even acknowledging that the returned youth is

his brother. Note how he calls his brother "your son" (v. 30). The father persists in his abundant love by not rebuking his older son for his insolence. Rather, he reassures him, "My son, you are here with me always; everything I have is yours. But now we must celebrate and rejoice, because your brother was dead and has come to life again; he was lost and has been found" (Lk 15:31–32).

Jesus tells these stories to defend his actions. Through them he is telling his audience—and us— "The return of sinners brings great joy in Heaven. God loves sinners." This should bring you much joy, peace, and a desire to love everyone. God's love and salvation is for all people. God is merciful to everyone, and in a special way, to the lost, the lowly, outcasts, and sinners. Our tasks are to respond in kind. Will you be like the Father in the story? Will you be like God, our Father?

The Lord's Witness (Luke 23–24)

Luke's most common title for Jesus is "Lord" (*Kyrios* in Greek). Luke, at times almost unconsciously, uses this lofty title to describe the actions of the historical Jesus. Luke is simply projecting back onto Jesus' earthly life the Easter glory of Jesus' victory over death, when his true identity is made known.

Recall how Jesus spent his time with outcasts and poor people, telling of God's mercy for sinners. His parables taught the Good News in a novel and memorable way; his miracles, like the raising of the widow's son out of pity (Lk 7:11–16), forcefully demonstrated God's compassion. At the Last Supper, Jesus explained why he came: "I am among you as the one who serves" (Lk 22:27). He hopes his disciples will imitate his example and stop bickering over who the greatest is.

The leaders, of course, do not accept Jesus or his message. Both Pilate and Herod Antipas find him innocent (23:1–12), but this does not stop the forces of evil and human weakness from condemning an innocent man.

Luke presents Jesus' Death as a witness, an example for all of how consistent, loving, faithful, and compassionate Jesus is even in his darkest hour. During his Passion and Crucifixion he continues to minister to others. He comforts the women on his way to Calvary (Lk 24:28–31); he mercifully asks his loving Abba to forgive those who condemned him (23:34); in the midst of his own agony, he promises "the good thief" that he will join him in Paradise before the day's end (23:43). (Note how a Gospel that begins with the lowly being the first to see the Promised One ends with Heaven being opened first to a condemned criminal.) Finally, Jesus dies with great dignity, expressing tremendous faith: "Father, into your hands I commend my spirit" (23:46). Another outsider, the Roman centurion, proclaims the truth about Jesus when he says, "This man was innocent beyond doubt" (23:47).

Luke concludes his Gospel with the Resurrection appearances of Jesus. The Emmaus story is especially important because it summarizes the entire Gospel. How appropriate that Luke, so fond of a journey theme, has Jesus appear to his disciples on a journey. On the day of the Resurrection, two disciples are leaving Jerusalem for the town of Emmaus seven miles away. Jesus joins them on the road, but they do not recognize him. They are greatly saddened because they believed Jesus was a mighty prophet and thought he would be the one to redeem Israel. The Lord begins to show them the meaning of the Scriptures, especially how the Scriptures prophesied that the Messiah had to die before he entered into his glory. (In Acts, Peter and Paul do the exact same thing when they preach about Jesus, relating the Good News about Jesus to Old Testament writings.) The travelers are excited and invite the stranger to stay with them for the night. It

martyr—A word that means "witness." We usually apply this term to a person who bore witness to the truth of his or her faith even unto death. Jesus died the death of a faithful martyr. St. Stephen is recognized as the first Christian martyr.

is while Jesus breaks bread with them that they recognize the risen Lord. Luke concludes:

> With that their eyes were opened and they recognized him, but he vanished from their sight. Then they said to each other, "Were not our hearts burning (within us) while he spoke to us on the way and opened the scriptures to us?" So they set out at once and returned to Jerusalem where they found gathered together the eleven and those with them who were saying, "The Lord has truly been raised and has appeared to Simon!" Then the two recounted what had taken place on the way and how he was made known to them in the breaking of the bread. (Lk 24:31–35)

As Acts shows us, the ritual of reading the Scriptures and breaking bread in Jesus' name was carried on by the earliest Christians. These are the two major elements of our own celebration of the Eucharist today. Catholics believe that we meet and can receive the living Lord today in this central sacrament of our faith, a ritual that commemorates and makes present the Paschal Mystery of divine love.

FOR REVIEW

1. Discuss several examples of how Jesus is a compassionate Savior for all people.

2. Interpret the meaning of these three parables: Lazarus and the Rich Man, the Good Samaritan, and the Prodigal Son.

3. Give several examples that show how Jesus died as he lived.

FOR REFLECTION

After reviewing what Jesus has to say about money and possessions, write a one-page reflection on what the good life is for you.

STEPHEN—FIRST MARTYR

Jesus was an innocent man put to death. Luke carries on the theme of the innocent **martyr** in the Acts of the Apostles. For example, Paul's rejection and passion (Acts 22–28) mirror that of Jesus. Another striking example is that of the first Christian martyr, Stephen. His fate is similar to Jesus'. Read Acts 6:8–8:3. List three similarities between Stephen's death and Jesus' Death.

Overview of the **Acts of the Apostles**

Jesus appeared to the disciples for forty days, instructed them about the coming of the Holy Spirit, and ascended to his heavenly Father. In the meantime, the Apostles, with Mary, prayerfully awaited the descent of the Holy Spirit and chose the successor to Judas. This part of the narrative is covered in the prologue of Acts (1:1–26).

Mission in Jerusalem (Acts 2:1–8:1a)

Chapter 2 of Acts reports the coming of the Holy Spirit, the outpouring of gifts, Peter's kerygmatic sermon, the increase of believers on Pentecost Sunday, and the ideal characteristics of the earliest Church in Jerusalem. Acts 3 tells that Peter cured a cripple and explained to the onlookers how he did this in Jesus' name. In Acts 4, Peter and John are arrested by the Sanhedrin. After being warned by the Sanhedrin not to speak in Jesus' name again, the disciples gather together for prayer. They are filled with the Holy Spirit, and they continue to proclaim Jesus boldly. Later (5:17–42), the Sanhedrin flogs some of the Apostles for their continual preaching about Jesus.

Hellenists—The name for Greek-speaking Christians (Acts 6:1; 9:29).

It is accurate to report that not all was smooth sailing in the early Church. Acts 5:1–12 tells of a husband and wife who lied to the Holy Spirit about an offering they made to the Church; their punishment was death. There was also some dissension between **Hellenists** (Greek-speaking) and Hebrew Christians, so deacons had to be appointed to make sure that the needs of the widows were taken care of. A prominent deacon chosen was Stephen, who became the first martyr.

Missions to Judea and Samaria (Acts 8:1b–12:25)

A second major section of Acts shows how Philip, one of the Greek-speaking deacons, preached the Good News to the Samaritans (8:4–8). Peter and John checked on his success. While in Samaria, they severely reprimanded Simon the Magician, who thought he could buy the gift of the Holy Spirit (8:9–25). Acts 9 recounts the conversion of Saul on the road to Damascus. This pivotal event in the history of Christianity transformed Saul into Paul, who would become the Apostle to the Gentiles. Luke recounts Paul's conversion a total of three times (9:1–19; 22:3–16; 26:2–18). Saul heard the voice of Jesus, who challenged him to stop persecuting him, that is, to stop tormenting his followers. Saul was baptized, preached in Damascus, and after a period of time, eventually visited Jerusalem.

The focus shifts to Peter, who preached in Joppa and Lydda, performed miracles, and had an important vision that instructed him to baptize a Gentile, Cornelius (10:1–23). This convinced Peter that the Lord wanted to open up the Gospel to Gentiles, a fact he had to explain patiently to the leader of the Jerusalem Church, James, a relative of the Lord (11:1–18). The early missionary activity extended to even wider circles. A prominent local church was at Antioch in Syria, where Jewish and Gentile disciples of Jesus lived together: "It was in Antioch that the disciples were first called Christians" (11:26). Barnabas, a prominent member of the Jerusalem Church, was sent to Antioch. He praised God for what he saw there and asked Paul to join him to teach the people.

In Jerusalem, King Herod began to persecute the Church and killed James the brother of John (12:1–24). He arrested Peter, who miraculously escaped from prison. Because the Jerusalem Church was under assault, the locale of missionary activity shifted to Antioch.

The conversion of Paul

Mission to the Gentiles (Acts 13:1–15:35)

Approximately AD 45, Paul and Barnabas began their first missionary journey. They preached in synagogues in places like Cyprus, Antioch in Pisidia, Iconium, and Lystra. However, when Jews rejected the Gospel, the missionaries preached to the Gentiles, many of whom responded to it positively (13:15–31). Salvation History took a new turn with the mission to the Gentiles, but this did not sit well with some Jewish Christians because Paul and Barnabas did not require Gentile converts to submit to Jewish Law before baptism. This controversy resulted in a meeting in Jerusalem (ca. AD 49), where the leaders decided the question on behalf of freedom for the Gentiles from Jewish Law. Peter reminded the assembly of his own experience of witnessing the outpouring of the Spirit on the Gentiles: The grace of the Lord Jesus saves people, not adherence to the Law. Paul and Barnabas then described in detail all the signs and wonders of God's grace working among the Gentiles to whom they preached.

James the "brother of the Lord" also spoke at this assembly and agreed that Gentile Christians should be free from most of the restrictions of the Law. The exceptions were few: avoid anything associated with the worship of false gods (**idolatry**), meat that Jewish law considered unclean, and marriages considered incestuous. These restrictions helped smooth relations with Jewish Christians who had been brought up in the Law. The decision at the Jerusalem Council opened up the future growth of Christianity to an explosion of new converts. From that time on, Church membership did not depend on a person's becoming a Jew first.

The Missions of Paul to Rome (Acts 15:36–28:31).

The last half of Acts describes two other missionary journeys of Paul spanning about fifteen years. With younger disciples like Silas (15:40), Timothy (16:1), Aristarchus (27:2) and perhaps Luke himself (16:10–17; 20:5–15; 21:1–18; 27:1–28), Paul made his way into Asia Minor, Europe, and eventually to Rome. Paul's second journey took him to many of the cities to which he subsequently wrote his famous letters: Thessalonica, Philippi, and Corinth.

Ephesus was the important city in Paul's third missionary effort, which probably began around AD 54. He spent two years in Ephesus instructing other preachers, like Apollos. He also conferred the Spirit, preached in the synagogues, performed exorcisms, and proclaimed the Gospel to the citizens. Paul was successful enough to have made a dent in the sale of miniature souvenirs of a famous pagan temple of Artemis located in Ephesus. This greatly disturbed a leading silversmith, Demetrius, who incited a riot against Paul. The mob dispersed without any significant incident, but once again Paul felt he had to move on because he was endangering the lives of his converts.

Often on these journeys, Paul found himself in conflict with the Jews who attacked, stoned, and arrested

idolatry—Giving worship to something other than the true God.

ST. PAUL AND JESUS PARALLELS

The second half of Acts has many parallels between the life of Jesus and the life of Paul. Some of these are:

- Both Jesus and Paul begin their ministries in a synagogue, where they preach about the fulfillment of the Scriptures and how the mission to the Gentiles fits in with the Old Testament (Lk 4:16–30; Acts 13:14–52).
- Both Jesus and Paul set their hearts on going to Jerusalem and are arrested there (Lk 9:51; Acts 19:21).
- Both predict their sufferings, give farewell speeches, and accept their martyrdom as part of God's will (Lk 22:21–46; Acts 20:18–38; 21:5–6, 13–14).
- And, as indicated above, the various trials before the authorities find Jesus and Paul innocent, but weak leaders go ahead and sentence them anyhow.

By means of these comparisons, it is clear that Luke is strongly showing that Jesus, the faithful witness, is the model not only for Paul, the missionary, but also for all Christians who take up the Gospel and reveal it to the world.

him. Eventually, in Jerusalem, the Romans arrested Paul because of mob violence directed against him. Sent to Caesarea because of a threat on his life discovered by Paul's nephew, Paul defended himself to the procurator Felix, who was somewhat sympathetic to Paul's cause. But Felix still refused to release Paul. Felix met frequently with Paul, in the hope that Paul would bribe his way out of the charges against him. Paul, however, would not cooperate in the selfish schemes of the procurator. As a result, Felix kept Paul under house arrest for nearly two years.

In the meantime, the Roman procurator Festus succeeded Felix and inherited the problem of Paul's confinement. In a visit to Jerusalem, Festus heard all the false charges the Sanhedrin made against Paul. To ingratiate himself to the Jewish leaders, he proposed taking Paul before the Sanhedrin. Paul, however, was no fool. He knew he would not get a fair trial in Jerusalem. Thus, Paul invoked his right as a Roman citizen—a trial in one of Caesar's courts in Rome. Festus agreed.

Before leaving Caesarea, however, Paul had the opportunity to defend his Christian conversion and missionary efforts before the visiting Jewish king, Herod Agrippa II. Agrippa and Festus concluded that Paul was innocent of the charges hurled against

him. But like Herod and Pilate in Jesus' case, the truth did not compel them to set Paul free. Rather, because Paul had demanded a hearing before Caesar, they sent him to Rome for trial.

The rest of Acts reports Paul's exciting adventure on the sea journey to Rome. Despite hardships, God's plans could not be thwarted. The Apostle to the Gentiles would reach the capital city and preach the Gospel there.

The Roman authorities put Paul under house arrest, perhaps in AD 61. Acts concludes rather abruptly:

> He remained for two full years in his lodgings. He received all who came to him, and with complete assurance and without hindrance he proclaimed the Kingdom of God and taught about the Lord Jesus Christ. (28:30–31)

This ending of Acts does not tell us about Paul's later adventures: his acquittal and further missionary trips perhaps to Spain, Asia Minor, Macedonia, and Crete. Moreover, Luke avoids telling us about Paul's second trial in Rome and his eventual condemnation to death by beheading, perhaps in the year AD 67. Luke ends his two-volume work not on a sad note of Paul's death, but hinting at a third work—the "Acts of Christians." Despite opposition, with the grace of the Holy Spirit Christians must continue to do what Paul did—proclaim the Gospel of God's compassionate love in Jesus Christ until the end of time.

Thus, Luke's ending is joyful and challenging. It is now up to us to put into action Jesus' teachings and the Apostles' preaching.

 FOR REVIEW

1. What were some gifts given to the disciples on Pentecost Sunday?

2. Who was the successor to Judas Iscariot? How was he chosen?

3. Identify Stephen.

4. What important decision was made at the Jerusalem Council in AD 49? What did it mean for the future of Christianity?

5. Who was Barnabas?

6. Where were Christians first called by that name?

7. List several ways in Acts that Jesus' life was a model for St. Paul.

8. What is the meaning of the Acts of the Apostles' ending in Rome?

FOR REFLECTION

- Read Acts 2:43–47 for a description of the early Christian community. In your journal, discuss whether you find this early Christian lifestyle attractive or not. Then reflect on how "practical" it would be in today's world.

- Read Acts 22. Summarize Paul's version of his conversion.

CHAPTER SUMMARY POINTS

- Tradition identifies Luke, a Gentile Christian, as the author of the third Gospel. He also wrote the Acts of the Apostles, which has style, language, and organization similar to the Gospel. Luke may also have been a companion of Paul on his missionary journeys. He may have originally been from Antioch in Syria.

- Luke wrote for Gentile Christian churches, most likely those founded by St. Paul. He wrote perhaps around the year AD 85, dedicating both Luke and Acts to a certain Theophilus ("beloved of God"), either the patron of his writing or a symbol for all Christians.

- Demonstrating concern for historical detail, Luke wrote to show his readers that their faith was reliable and to encourage them to continue to live it in imitation of Jesus and the early Church leaders.

- A central scene in Jesus' ministry in Galilee is his rejection as a prophet in his hometown of Nazareth. In a synagogue there Jesus showed how he was fulfilling Old Testament prophecies by proclaiming the Gospel to the poor, liberating the oppressed, and announcing God's love for all people, even the Gentiles. This last theme is a central theological issue for Luke: The Gospel is meant for everyone, not just Jews.

- Early Christians lived out Jesus' message through fellowship, praying, and breaking bread together (the Eucharist), and listening to the teaching of the Apostles.

- The Holy Spirit figures prominently in the life of Jesus and the early Church. For example, in Luke's Gospel, Mary conceives Jesus by the power of the Holy Spirit, the Spirit leads Jesus, and Jesus teaches us to pray for the Spirit. In Acts, the Holy Spirit comes in all his power on Pentecost Sunday.

- Luke views history in three stages. The first is an age of promise and ends with the coming of Jesus. The second is the time of Jesus, who is the center of history. The final period is the age of the Church, which will last until the Lord Jesus comes in glory.

- With the Holy Spirit and prayer come the fruits of joy and peace, which figure prominently in Luke–Acts.

- Luke and Acts give a key role to women, considered inferior to men in our Lord's day.

- Luke highlights the role of the Blessed Mother. She is humble, the most faithful of all disciples, a model of prayer and faith, a source of strength to Christians, and a proclaimer (through her Magnificat) of God's marvelous works of salvation.

- Because of her unique role in salvation, Catholics believe that Mary was full of grace from the first moment of her conception (Immaculate Conception); ever-virgin, thus emphasizing how God took the initiative in the Incarnation; the Mother of God and the Mother of the Church; and that when her earthly life was over, she was assumed body and soul into Heaven. Mary's Assumption gives us hope that we will also be united to the Lord one day for all eternity.

- Luke presents Jesus as a compassionate Messiah who brings good news to the poor.

- Jesus is the friend of outsiders like women, sinners, lepers, tax collectors like Zacchaeus, and Samaritans. He is the universal Savior. By means of the parable of the Good Samaritan, Jesus teaches that we must love everyone.

- Jesus preaches God's great love for, and joy over, the return of sinners. This is the heart of his Good News—God's compassionate love for sinners.

- Jesus is the martyred Lord who is the model in Acts for Church missionaries like Peter and Paul.

LEARN BY DOING

1. Summarize each of these readings from Luke: 4:14–6:49; 7:1–9:50; 9:51–12:59; 13:1–16:31; 17:1–19:27. Pay particular attention to what Jesus says and does in relationship to poor people, Gentiles, women, Samaritans, sinners and outcasts.

2. After reading Peter's kerygmatic sermon in Acts 2:14–39, create an outline for a talk you might deliver to a youth group on retreat. Emphasize the person of Jesus and what the teens should do in response to him.

3. Read the portrait of the ideal Christian community in Acts 2:43–47. Today, there are groups who are trying to live in small, "intentional" Christian communities similar to those described in Acts. Do an Internet search on one of these small Christian communities in the Catholic tradition. In your report, evaluate how practical you believe this type of Christian community to be.

4. Scholars believe that Lk 4:14–30 is a *combination* of stories about Jesus at Nazareth. The first was an initial visit where Jesus receives a favorable reception; the second visit resulted in his people turning on him. Citing particular verses, explain why this is a plausible theory. (Compare Mk 1:21f and Mk 6:1–6).

5. Review the five goals of Jesus' mission—preaching the Gospel, helping people to live freely, doing acts of mercy, working for justice, and celebrating God's presence in our midst. List authentic examples of how you can help the Lord accomplish each of them.

6. Find a graphic to illustrate several images of the Holy Spirit (examples: wind, fire, dove). Explain the imagery and select an appropriate quote from the Gospel of Luke or the Acts of the Apostles to accompany the images.

7. Read Isaiah 61:1–2. Note similarities and differences between this prophecy and Luke's quotation of it in Lk 4:18–19.

8. The parable of the Good Samaritan has been interpreted as an allegory. One famous attempt is that of St. Augustine who made these interpretations: Jerusalem = Heaven; Jericho = the world; robbers = Satan; wounded victim = Adam; priest = Torah; Levite = prophets; Samaritan = Jesus; inn = church; Samaritan's return = Jesus' Second Coming. Reread the parable of the Good Samaritan (Lk 10:29–37). Write your own version of the parable. Substitute modern elements into the story. Include an allegorical interpretation of it.

9. Do a report on foods eaten at a typical meal in the time of Jesus. Consult sources like the *HarperCollins Bible Dictionary* or a website like www.jesus-institute.org/historical-jesus/jesus-firstcenturycontext.shtml.

10. Do a report on the Jewish feast of Weeks/Pentecost. You can begin your research at the *Catholic Encyclopedia* online: www.newadvent.org/cathen/11661a.htm.

11. Acts 6:8–7:60 describes the death of the first Christian martyr, St. Stephen. Report on the life of other Christian martyrs, for example, St. Charles Lwanga and Companions, Martyrs of Uganda.

12. Read Acts 10:1–11:18. Complete the following: Who was Cornelius? Describe Peter's vision. What was the meaning of his vision?

13. Read Acts 15. Answer the following: How did the Council arrive at a decision? Who spoke at the Council? What was the decision? What was its significance for the history of Christianity?

PRAYER LESSON

Review the steps for imaginative prayer on page 127. Apply these steps to Luke 7:36–50, the scene of the woman sinner who burst into the house of Simon the Pharisee.

Imagine that you are a dinner guest. Engage all your senses.
What do you see, hear, feel, and smell?
What is Simon serving for dinner?

Turn your attention to Jesus.
What is he saying?
What does he look like?

Now see the woman run in from off the street.
What commotion does she cause?
What is she doing?
How do you feel about this?
How are the other dinner guests reacting to this scene? Listen carefully to what Jesus has to say to Simon.
Finally, savor Jesus' gentleness to the woman. Hear his reassuring words and feel their impact on you:

> So I tell you, her many sins have been forgiven; hence, she has shown great love. But the one to whom little is forgiven, loves little. . . . Your faith has saved you; go in peace. (Lk 7:47, 50)

- *Reflection*: Where does sin have control in your life? Do you believe Jesus can forgive your sins? Are you willing to take them to him and hear his message of love, forgiveness, and peace?

- *Resolution*: Examine your conscience this week on those actions and attitudes that are keeping you from being a more loving person. Resolve to celebrate the Sacrament of Penance at the earliest possible time to hear Jesus say to you, "Go in peace."

The Gospel of John:
Jesus the Word of God

I am the good shepherd, and I know mine, and mine know me, just as the Father knows me and I know the Father; and I will lay down my life for the sheep.

—John 10:14–15

CHAPTER **OVERVIEW**

NO **GREATER LOVE**

There is no greater love than God's gift of his Son so that everyone who believes in him might have eternal life.

BACKGROUND ON **THE GOSPEL OF JOHN**

Written near the turn of the second century, the theology in the Gospel of John depicts how the theology of the Christian faith had grown richer in understanding of Jesus Christ and his mission.

THE WORD **OF GOD**

The first eighteen verses of the Gospel of John serve as an overview or prologue to the Gospel.

THE BOOK **OF SIGNS**

A common theme in the seven signs recorded in this section of the Gospel is the power of Jesus' life-giving words and actions.

THE BOOK **OF GLORY**

The second part of the Gospel of John—called the Book of Glory—consists of the Last Supper discourses of Jesus and the events of his Death and Resurrection.

No **Greater Love**

There is a story told that in the French Revolution, a young man was condemned to the guillotine. Many people loved him, but one more than everyone else—his father. The father proved his love this way: When the names of the condemned were read aloud, the father, who named his son after himself, responded that he was the condemned man. The father was taken to the place of execution where the deadly guillotine severed his head. His son went free, saved by the immense love of his father.

This story is an apt image for one of the most beautiful verses in the entire Bible-composed by the author of John's Gospel: "For God so loved the word that he gave his only Son, so that everyone who believes in him might not perish but might have eternal life" (Jn 3:16).

Protestant reformer Martin Luther proclaimed this verse to be "the heart of the Bible, the Gospel in miniature." Even a child can understand the simple message it contains with Gospel truths worthy of deep reflection:

God	the greatest lover
so loved	the highest degree
the world	the greatest number
that he gave	the most generous act
his only Son	the most precious gift
so that everyone	the best invitation
who believes	the greatest simplicity
in him	the most perfect person
might not perish	the greatest deliverance
but	the biggest contrast
might have	the greatest assurance
eternal life	the most important possession

FRIENDSHIP WITH JESUS

John's Gospel expresses the great news that we, as believers, can be called friends of Jesus:

> I no longer call you slaves, because a slave does not know what his master is doing. I have called you friends, because I have told you everything I have heard from my Father. It was not you who chose me, but I who chose you and appointed you to go and bear fruit that will remain, so that whatever you ask the Father in my name he may give you. This I command you: love one another. (Jn 15:15–16)

Jesus loves each of us so much that he values our friendship. A good question, though, is what kind of friend are we to him? In a survey given to students for many years, the following qualities of friendship consistently rank as the most important ones. Judge how well each quality is evident in your relationships with a close friend and with your friend Jesus.

QUALITIES OF FRIENDSHIP

1. Trust: can *always* be counted on.
2. Honesty: truthful in relationship; holds nothing back.
3. Loyalty: devoted and faithful.
4. Common interests: likes the same things.
5. Availability: makes time for the other.
6. Caring/considerate: loving at all times.
7. Acceptance: can be oneself without having to prove anything.

- Share examples of how each of these qualities is demonstrated in your friendships.
- Name concrete ways Jesus expresses his friendship to you.
- Name three other qualities of friendship. Why are these important for you?
- Write a one-page reflection on your friendship with Jesus.

The Gospel of John, the Gospel from which this passage is quoted, contrasts sharply with the Synoptic Gospels Matthew, Mark, and Luke. Its special literary feature is long, well-developed theological discourses or monologues delivered by Jesus. In these discourses, Jesus reveals the Father, teaches profound truths about himself, and reveals that the key to being his followers is to have faith in him and his word, love others as he has loved us, and trust the Holy Spirit whom he and his Father will send.

FOR REFLECTION

Define *unconditional love.* How does your definition intersect with the love that God has for you?

Background on
the Gospel of John

The Gospel of John was written for Jewish-Christians who were expelled from synagogues after the Roman Revolt. Many Christians had fled the city and did not fight alongside their Jewish relatives. This persecution caused some of the Christians from this local church to leave Palestine and immigrate to Ephesus. Samaritan converts to Christianity (see John 4:4–42) were also in this community as well as Gentile Christians. Thus, it was a diverse group.

The Gospel was written to strengthen faith and to win converts. These goals are important because they lead to eternal life.

> Now Jesus did many other signs in the presence of (his) disciples that are not written in this book. But these are written that you may (come to) believe that Jesus is the Messiah, the Son of God, and that through this belief you may have life in his name. (Jn 20:30–31)

Unlike Mark the storyteller, Matthew the teacher, or Luke the historian, the Evangelist of John's Gospel is much more interested in theology. He stresses Jesus' identity as the revealer of God (the Word), the unique Son of the Father, and the Savior of the world.

Scholars detect two other purposes the Evangelist had in mind when writing his Gospel:

1. to combat false ideas about Jesus' full humanity or even his divinity;

2. to oppose the followers of John the Baptist, who even as late as the last decade of the first century wrongly believed he was the Messiah. Note how John's Gospel insists Jesus is superior to John the Baptist, who is reported as saying there is one coming "whose sandal strap I am not worthy to untie" (1:27).

A common understanding dates the composition of John's Gospel between AD 90 and 100. Interestingly, a small fragment from John's Gospel is the earliest section of any New

Dating from AD 125 to 160, this ancient **papyrus** fragment contains lines from John 18:31–33 on the front (recto) and lines from John 18:37–38 on the back (verso).

papyrus—A type of paper made from reed found in the delta of the Nile River and parts of Italy.

Testament book in existence. Found in Egypt, this John Rylands Greek papyrus dates from around AD 130. It shows that the Gospel of John had wide circulation throughout the Mediterranean world a mere thirty to forty years after its composition.

The author of John's Gospel may have shared common written or oral traditions with Mark's Gospel and was likely to have known certain traditions that also appear in Luke's Gospel. And it is possible that the final editor of John's Gospel had contact with of one or more of the Synoptic Gospels. However, the fourth Gospel does not directly rely heavily on any of them. Rather, its sources are independent traditions preserved in the churches from which it was created.

John differs in many ways from the Synoptic Gospels. For example, we find new characters like Nicodemus, Lazarus, a man born blind, and a Samaritan woman. Jesus attends three Passover festivals, not one, and makes several trips to Jerusalem for various festivals. There are no mentions of demon possessions. Jesus' teaching usually takes the form of long discourses, not pithy sayings or parables. He focuses on himself as God's Revelation, one who shows us the way to the Father, and he does not stress the Kingdom of God the way the Synoptics do. In addition, John's is a very poetic Gospel, thus presenting a more solemn and holy Jesus. Stylistically, it uses literary techniques like irony (where opponents often say things about Jesus that have deeper meanings than they realize), plays on words, metaphors (implied comparisons), figurative language to help clarify the many misunderstandings people have of him, and other similar techniques.

There were two major sources for the Gospel of John. The first was a collection of miracles, called a signs source. Some of the seven signs the Gospel records are found in the Synoptics, but unique to John are the changing of water into wine at Cana, the cure of a man born blind, and the raising of Lazarus. The discourses connected with these miracles were probably arranged, developed, and preached in the local church of the Evangelist.

The second major source for the Gospel was a version of the Passion and Resurrection narratives. This would have been in circulation for years before any of the Gospels were written.

As to the identity of the author, in approximately AD 180, the Church Father Irenaeus attributed the fourth Gospel to John, the "Beloved Disciple" of the Lord. Church tradition identified this John as one of the Apostles. His brother James was also an Apostle; their father was a man by the name of Zebedee. Tradition also held that John wrote his Gospel toward the end of his life at Ephesus in Asia Minor. This view of the authorship of the fourth Gospel held for centuries.

However, today scholars believe Irenaeus may have confused John the Apostle with another John, a Church elder and disciple of the Apostle John. Scholars note the complex nature of the fourth Gospel and suggest that it may have been written in several stages and edited by different people. For example, we can see how some material appears twice with only slight changes in the wording (compare 6:35–50 and 6:51–58). Chapter 21 also looks like an appendix that someone other than the original Evangelist tacked on to the end of the Gospel.

In the ancient world, authorship was attributed more to the one who inspired a particular work rather than to the one who actually wrote it. One contemporary theory is that the preaching and witness of the Apostle John is the foundation of the Gospel. A solid tradition places John in Ephesus (in present-day Turkey), where he likely gathered around him a

community of followers. These disciples took John's testimony, the story goes, meditated on his words, and later produced in stages a Gospel that addressed the concerns of their own local church. (Some scholars argue that the Gospel may have been written in Antioch of Syria or even Alexandria in Egypt.) Ultimately, though, the Evangelist claims that his testimony rests on eyewitness testimony:

It is this disciple who testifies to these things and has written them, and we know that his testimony is true. (Jn 21:24)

The "we" in this passage probably refers to the disciples of the "Beloved Disciple" who edited the final edition of the Gospel.

READING THE GOSPEL OF JOHN

Though John is a rich, complex, and theologically profound Gospel, its outline is relatively simple. After a short and important prologue, only two major sections follow this introduction. The first is called the *Book of Signs,* which treats Jesus' public ministry. Here seven signs (miracles) and accompanying speeches reveal who Jesus is. The second major division is the *Book of Glory.* Beginning with the Last Supper and extending to Jesus' Resurrection, this section of the Gospel includes theologically rooted discourses given by Jesus. An epilogue, probably added later, includes Jesus' appearances in Galilee. The outline:

Prologue: "Word made flesh" (1:1–18)

Part 1: Book of Signs (1:19–12:50)
- The wedding at Cana (2:1–11)
- The cure of the royal official's son (4:46–54)
- The cure of the paralytic (5:1–18)
- The multiplication of loaves (6:1–15)
- The walking on water (6:16–21)
- The healing of the man born blind (9:1–41)
- The raising of Lazarus (11:1–44)

Part 2: Book of Glory (13:1–20:31)
- The Last Supper (13–17)
- The Passion and Death of Jesus (18–19)
- The Resurrection (20)

Epilogue: Appearances in Galilee (21)

As you read John's Gospel, note the following theological insight that is often presented in simple, contrasting images (e.g., life and death, light and darkness, flesh and spirit, glory and eternal life) that convey profound meaning. Key themes of John's Gospel include the following:

THEME	EXPLANATION	APPLICATION
Jesus Christ, Word of God, Son of God	Jesus is the Word of God, God's total self-communication. He is the revealer and the revealed. As God's unique Son, both fully God and fully man, only he can reveal the Father fully.	Jesus is most trustworthy. Listening to Jesus puts us on the path to the "Way, Truth, and the Life."
Faith	Look to the signs Jesus performs and believe. Belief leads to eternal life.	Response to Jesus means believing in him—his life, his words, his deeds, and his Death and Resurrection.
Love	Jesus embodies God's love and shows it through service and his Paschal Mystery.	Follow the command Jesus gave to us: "This is my commandment: love one another as I love you" (Jn 15:12).
Holy Spirit	Jesus promised another **Paraclete** who would guide, comfort, and counsel Christians. Through the Spirit, the Lord will be present in believers.	The Spirit enables us to believe and understand Jesus' teaching. Allowing the Spirit to live within us helps us experience the love of the risen Lord.
Resurrection	Jesus lives! On the third day, he rose from the dead, a fact testified by the Apostles and others. It is the basic fact of Catholic faith.	Believe in Jesus! He is the Resurrection and the life. If we die united to him, we will also live forever.

Paraclete—A name for the Holy Spirit. In John 14:6, Jesus promised to send an advocate, a helper, who would continue to guide, lead, and strengthen the disciples.

Christology—The branch of theology that studies the meaning of the person of Jesus Christ.

The Word **of God** (John 1)

The first eighteen verses of John's Gospel serve as an overture or prologue to the Gospel. The prologue was likely originally an early Christian hymn that the Evangelist adopted to serve as the introduction to his Gospel. Along with the rest of the first chapter, it introduces three key theological themes of the Gospel.

Theme 1: Christology from Above

Christology is the study of Jesus Christ, that is, trying to understand who he is. All the Gospels are interested in Jesus Christ's identity, but the focus of John's Gospel stresses very strongly Jesus' heavenly origins, his fundamental identity as the Son of God, and his preexistence as the Word of God. Scholars term this emphasis in John as a "Christology from above" or "descending Christology."

In contrast to John's approach to Jesus, the Synoptic Gospels stress a "Christology from below" ("ascending Christology"). Their starting point is the concrete memories of Jesus of Nazareth and his impact on people. They then move on to develop his story as an ascent to heavenly glory through his Passion, Death, and Resurrection. Whereas the Synoptic Gospels stress a more human Jesus, the divinity of Jesus shines forth in almost every verse of John's Gospel.

The pattern of John's Gospel is that Christ the Savior comes to us first from above (1:1–13); he next reveals the Father to us and then takes us to him (1:14–18).

Note the very opening words of John's Gospel and how they begin from "above":

> In the beginning was the Word:
> and the Word was with God
> and the Word was God.
> (Jn 1:1)

Echoing the words of the book of Genesis, the Gospel of John unveils Jesus' true identity: He is the Word of God who has existed forever. This very Word of God is God himself.

By using the expression "Word of God," the Evangelist was drawing on a concept that appealed to both Jewish and Gentile Christians. In the Old Testament, "the Word of God" (*logos* in the Greek) referred to creation, the Law, God's Revelation through the prophets, and his close presence among his people. God creates through his Word. For example, when he speaks, creatures come into being. "The Word of God" also symbolized God's Wisdom, a personification of one of God's important attributes.

Word of God also meant something to Gentiles immersed in Greek philosophy. To Stoic philosophers, the Logos was the spiritual principle (or "soul") that held the world together. Gnostics, in contrast, believed that the only true realities are spiritual. Material creation is an illusion. For them, only the Word could reveal the secret knowledge (*gnosis* in the Greek) that was the key to salvation.

These rich ideas—the Word as creative, the source of true wisdom and knowledge, and God's presence among his people—blend wonderfully in John's prologue. The climax of the prologue comes in John 1:14:

> And the Word became flesh,
> and made his dwelling among us,
> and we saw his glory,
> the glory as of the Father's only Son,
> full of grace and truth.

Recall from pages 9–10 how these opening verses of John provide the strong foundation for the doctrine of the Incarnation, that God became human in the person of Jesus Christ. The Son of God, the preexisting Word of God, took on human flesh in the person of Jesus. In him, we can perceive God's glory, an Old Testament concept that refers to the visible Revelation of the power of the invisible God. In and through Jesus, God's glory—his power, radiance, and love—shines forth for us to perceive. Jesus is the revealer of God the Father; at the same time, he is the Revelation of God.

Theme 2: Major Conflicts

The prologue introduces some of the major conflicts that are developed later in the Gospel. These include:
- the light of Christ versus the darkness of the world that refuses to acknowledge Jesus;
- life-giving faith in Jesus that makes us children of God versus unbelief;
- truth versus untruth.

logos—A term that means "Word" in Greek. Jesus is the Word of God made flesh, who is both the revealer of God and God's Revelation.

Theme 3: Who Is Jesus?

After the prologue, we find out more about the identity of the Word-of-God-made-flesh. First, John the Baptist plays his proper role as one lesser than Jesus, "whose sandal strap I am not worthy to untie" (Jn 1:27). John testifies that he is not the Christ, Elijah, or "the prophet." The reader knows who really deserves these titles—Jesus. The Baptist identifies Jesus' true role: "Behold, the Lamb of God, who takes away the sin of the world" (1:29). In him the Spirit dwells. "He is the Son of God" (1:34).

In chapter 1, John the Baptist prefigures all the others who will testify for Jesus later in the Gospel. These include the Samaritan woman, the crowd at Lazarus's raising, the Twelve, and the "Beloved Disciple." Jesus, as well as the Father and the Spirit, also provides testimony for his identity as God's only Son. And, of course, Jesus' seven miracles attest to his mission and identity.

Chapter 1 tells us even more. Two disciples address Jesus as "Rabbi," the Hebrew word for "Teacher." One of them, Andrew, proclaims to his brother Simon Peter, "We have found the Messiah" (1:41). And Nathaniel, personally invited by Jesus himself to be a disciple, is astounded by Jesus' extraordinary knowledge. Nathaniel boldly proclaims, "You are the Son of God; you are King of Israel" (1:49). Jesus responds that Nathaniel has not seen anything yet: "Amen, amen, I say to you, you will see the sky opened and the angels of God ascending and descending on the Son of Man" (1:51). For John, "Son of Man" is not simply a title of a mere human being like all others. It is a title to describe a unique mediator, a go-between for Heaven and earth.

The prologue and the rest of chapter 1 use these various titles to reveal who Jesus is. Because he is God, no one designation totally describes him. We need all these titles to begin to understand Jesus' true identity and what he means for us: Word of God, Son of God, Christ, Prophet, Lamb of God, Teacher, King of Israel, Son of Man.

 FOR REVIEW

1. Who wrote the Gospel of John? Identify the Beloved Disciple.

2. When and where was it probably composed? What was the Evangelist's reason for composing it?

3. List three ways John's Gospel differs from the Synoptic Gospels.

4. Discuss three major themes in John's Gospel.

5. What does it mean to say John's Gospel has a "Christology from above"?

6. What does it mean to call Jesus the Word of God?

FOR REFLECTION

- Read the following passages from the Gospel of John about the Beloved Disciple: 13:23; 19:26; 20:2–10; and 21:7, 21–23. Answer these questions: What are some signs that Jesus favored this disciple? Describe the Beloved Disciple in relationship to Peter. What might his stepping aside to allow Peter to enter the tomb first signify?

- Like the Synoptics, John contains some rich titles for Jesus. One of these titles, "I am," is a direct connection to the name Yahweh revealed to Moses (Ex 3:14). Read the references to each of the following titles: John 6:35ff; 8:12; 10:7; 10:11; 11:25; 14:6; 15:5. Record the title in your journal, and write a reflection on its meaning.

The Book **of Signs** (John 1:19–12:50)

This portion of John's Gospel is called the Book of Signs because it is organized around seven miracles. In contrast to the Synoptic Gospels, which describe miracles as "acts of power" (*dynamis* in the Greek) that help establish the Kingdom of God, John uses either the word *ergon* (work) or *semeion* (sign) to describe Jesus' miracles. Similarly, the Old Testament referred to the *works* of God that brought Israel out of Egypt at the time of the Exodus and the *signs* of God performed through Moses.

In the Gospel of John, the miracles of Jesus reveal Jesus' identity, the purpose of his Incarnation, his heavenly glory, and his relation to his heavenly Father. In the words of Scripture scholar Fr. Raymond Brown,

> "Work" expresses the divine perspective on what is accomplished and so is a fitting description for Jesus himself to apply to his miracles. "Sign" indicates the human viewpoint wherein attention is directed not so much to the miraculous in itself (which may not lead to true faith: 2:23–24; 4:48; 12:37) but to what is revealed by the miracle to those who can see beyond.[13]

Faith also plays a key role in the understanding of signs. Typically, the Evangelist provides a long discourse after each sign to help the reader comprehend the significance of what happened. These discourses constantly remind us that faith in Jesus helps us gain eternal life.

Brief expositions of each sign and accompanying discourses follow.

EXAMINING PATTERNS IN THE BOOK OF SIGNS

The Book of Signs is organized around Jewish feasts. The pattern for John 1:19–12:50 is arranged as follows:

- 1:19–2:11: Opening weeks in Jesus' ministry
- 2–4: First Passover (including choosing the Apostles)
- 5: Sabbath "feast"
- 6: Second Passover
- 7–9: Feast of Tabernacles
- 10: Feast of Dedication
- 11–12: Prelude to the Final Passover (including the raising of Lazarus and its aftermath)

Assignment

1. Read John 1:19–2:11. Note in your journal the reactions of John the Baptist toward Jesus. Also answer: How did Jesus choose his Apostles? What role did Mary play in the first sign?

2. Choose one of the readings from the Book of Signs (see left). Answer the following:

   - What took place? What is the probable meaning of the sign given in this section?
   - Summarize the main points of any dialogues given.
   - Note how people react to Jesus.

3. Using a biblical dictionary, research some features of the "feast" (including sabbath observance) covered in your section.

4. Prepare an oral report for the rest of the class.

his heavenly mission of giving up his life so all humanity might gain eternal life (3:16).

On another level, Jesus' providing wine for the wedding represents the richness of the wisdom and revelation he brings from God, thus fulfilling Old Testament prophecies of flowing wine when the Messiah comes. Also, the sign reveals to us new life in Christ. We believe that Christ can change us as he changed ordinary water into the festive drink of fellowship. Catholics have also interpreted the water in this miracle as a symbol of baptismal waters that purify us while the wine can signify the Eucharist, which brings us spiritual life—communion with Jesus, the Lord.

Jesus' first sign helped the disciples to believe. It also demonstrated his power over nature and foreshadowed his ministry: being in touch with people and helping them by acting with authority.

Sign 1: Changing Water to Wine (John 2:1–12)

This nature miracle, performed at the beginning of Jesus' public ministry at the wedding at Cana, is the first public event where Jesus reveals his glory, leading his disciples to believe in him. By attending a wedding, a weeklong event in Jesus' time, the Lord was showing how much he participated in and enjoyed ordinary life. Weddings were festive occasions, symbols of new life in this world and a traditional symbol for the messianic banquet in God's Kingdom. Catholics hold that Jesus' attendance at this wedding blessed marriage as a sacrament of divine love.

Mary has a unique role in this miracle. Mary is a perfect model of faith. Just as Jesus heeded her request to perform this sign, we believe that she will also intercede for us when we make a request of her. In a society that greatly cherished the virtue of hospitality, it would have been a matter of great shame for the hosts of the wedding to run out of wine. Mary's compassionate concern for others, however, prompted her to intercede on their behalf. Her simple, confident, and persistent faith in her Son to save the reputation of the host family moved him to respond, even though he felt his time to manifest himself openly had not yet come. "My hour" refers to Jesus' Passion, Death, Resurrection, and Glorification when his real glory would be manifested. This sign at Cana, and the other six miracles, point to the hour of his Passion and Glorification, the climax of

JESUS AND THE SAMARITAN WOMAN

After his first sign, Jesus goes to Jerusalem for the first of three Passover celebrations reported in John's Gospel. There, he cleanses the Temple to protest its commercialization, meets a secret disciple, Nicodemus, and encounters John the Baptist again. John testifies that he is like a bridegroom whose role is to serve the groom, Jesus, the one who comes from above. In John 4:1–26, Jesus encounters the Samaritan woman at the well. Jesus satisfies the woman's thirst for true knowledge, revealing that he is the Messiah, the source of eternal life, the one who refreshes and renews and brings life.

Read about Jesus' encounter with the Samaritan woman (Jn 4:1–26), then complete the following:

- What do you imagine the woman told her fellow Samaritans about Jesus? Would this have caused them to believe in him? Why or why not? (Give evidence for your response.)
- Discuss several possible meanings for water as a basic human symbol and a Christian symbol. Explain several things Jesus could have meant by using this symbol.

Sign 2: Cure of the Official's Son (John 4:46–54)

Jesus' second sign also occurred in Cana. The power of Jesus' word is enough to heal the son of a court official from Capernaum, perhaps a Gentile. The father's faith prompts Jesus to act. This sign teaches that faith in Jesus can rescue us from spiritual death. It also teaches the power of intercessory prayer. The Lord will notice and respond to our concern for others as he did for the father who wanted health for his boy.

Sign 3: Cure of the Paralytic at the Pool (John 5:1–47)

Jesus' third sign involves healing a man on the Sabbath who was lame for thirty-eight years. The point of this third sign is that Jesus is the source of life. We must believe in him to gain eternal life. Traditionally, Jewish scholars interpreted healing a non-life-threatening illness on the Sabbath as work forbidden by the Torah. In the dialogue following the cure, Jesus explains that God does indeed work on the Sabbath: "My Father is at work until now, so I am at work" (Jn 5:17). Here Jesus is clearly claiming to be equal to God. The unique Son, like the Father, actively works on the Sabbath. Like the Father, the Son also gives life to whomever he wants. Finally, the Father gives his Son the right to judge. Jesus' claim of divine authority enrages his opponents early on in his ministry: "For this reason the Jews tried all the more to kill him because he not only broke the Sabbath, but he also called God his own father, making himself equal to God" (5:18).

Also take note how in this passage the Evangelist uses the term *Jews* in a hostile way. Several times throughout John's Gospel the antagonism between Jesus and "the Jews" is so intense that it appears anti-Semitic. Recall, though, that Jesus and all his early disciples were Jews. The Evangelist was writing for a largely Jewish Christian community that had undergone the Jewish Revolt in AD 70, was later expelled from synagogues, and met continual non-acceptance from Jewish non-believers in the places in which they lived. For the Evangelist, the term "Jews" represented those who persisted in not accepting Jesus and who were persecuting the Jewish Christians. The term "Jews" also symbolizes anyone who stubbornly refuses to accept Jesus and who engages in lifeless religious practices. In no way should we extend responsibility to all Jews of Jesus' time or Jews of different times and places for Jesus' Death.

Signs 4 and 5: The Feeding of the 5,000 and the Walking on Water (John 6:1–14, 16–24).

These signs parallel the Exodus miracles of the manna in the desert and the parting of the Red Sea. Thus, it is appropriate that the time for these signs is set close to the time of the Passover feast, just as the Old Testament miracles followed the first Passover. In the first miracle, Jesus feeds the hungry crowd that follows him, but he has to escape their attempt to make him king. John's long dialogue on the "Bread of Life" (6:25–70) explains the symbolism of this sign. Jesus has replaced the manna of the Exodus. He is the new bread God has given to them, their source of eternal life. Through him we will pass over from death to new life.

> I am the bread of life; whoever comes to me will never hunger, and whoever believes in me will never thirst. (6:35)

Jesus teaches the necessity of eating the flesh of his body and drinking his blood, a clear reference to

WOMAN CAUGHT IN ADULTERY (JOHN 7:53–8:11)

This story of the woman caught in adultery did not appear in the earliest manuscripts of the Gospel. Many scholars believe it was a separate story circulating in the tradition. Close to the theology of Luke's Gospel, a copyist inserted it into a manuscript of John's Gospel sometime in the third century. He may have thought it illustrated well a quote in John 8:15: "You judge by appearances, but I do not judge anyone."

No matter how it got into John's Gospel, it is one of the most beautiful stories in the New Testament, illustrating Jesus' message of forgiveness and non-judgment. It also shows Jesus as a brilliant teacher who was able to escape traps set by his opponents. Read and reflect on this passage by answering the following questions:

- What harm does adultery cause to marriages? families? How is adultery tolerated in our media? Give examples.
- Imagine you were in the crowd surrounding the woman. What would have been your reaction?
- What do you think Jesus wrote in the sand?
- Jesus accepted the woman, despite her sin. He told her to sin no more. Who accepts you even when you have done bad things?
- How easy or difficult is it for you to forgive yourself when you have sinned?
- What did Jesus mean when he said, "Let the one among you who is without sin be the first to throw a stone at her" (Jn 8:7)?

Feast of Tabernacles—Also called the Feast of Booths, it was originally a Canaanite celebration of the harvest. The people lived in booths to represent the small huts farmers lived in during the harvest season.

the Eucharist. The Eucharist brings about an intimate relationship between Jesus and his Church, the faithful. He abides in us and we in him. As the Father is the source of Jesus' life, so Jesus is the source of our life.

This shocking teaching about his body and blood caused many to abandon Jesus. But Peter and the Apostles put their trust in him:

> Master, to whom shall we go? You have the words of eternal life. We have come to believe and are convinced that you are the Holy One of God. (6:68–69)

Jesus' walking on the water revealed that he was indeed God's Holy One. To the knowing reader, Jesus' words "It is I. Do not be afraid" (6:21) reveal his true identity. "It is I" (*ego eimi* in the Greek) is very similar to the name God revealed to Moses—Yahweh—which means "I am." This statement of Jesus is an echo of the name Yahweh, pointing to his identity as God. His words point out that despite the storms that come our way in life, the disciples of Jesus need never fear. Jesus, God himself, is with us and will never leave us.

Transition to the Sixth Sign (John 7:1–10:21)

Before the sixth sign, the cure of a blind man, Jesus is present during the **Feast of Tabernacles** (Tents or Booths), an eight-day pilgrimage feast celebrating the autumn grape harvest and involving prayers for rain. Daily rituals connected with this feast included water and light.

While in Jerusalem, Jesus defends himself and his teaching by saying he teaches on God's behalf. He asks for just judgment. He highlights the water symbolism of the feast by proclaiming on the last day of the festival, "Let anyone who thirsts come to me and drink" (7:37–38). He brings out the light symbolism by adding, "I am the light of the world. Whoever follows me will not walk in darkness, but will have the light of life" (8:12). In various dialogues with the Pharisees, Jesus teaches about his divine authority and identity. He brings things to a boil when he says, "Before Abraham came to be, I AM"

(8:58). His opponents attempt to stone him because they believe he has blasphemed.

Sign 6: Cure of the Blind Man (John 9:1–41)

This sign contrasts a blind man who was given his sight and those who had sight yet were spiritually blind. Note how the man born blind obeyed Jesus—washed as instructed in the **Pool of Siloam**—and received his sight. As a result, he gradually began to see who Jesus really was. At first, he refers to him as "the man called Jesus" (9:11); then he calls him a prophet (9:17); next he testifies that Jesus is a man from God who was able to perform the unheard deed of giving sight to one born blind (9:33). Finally, the cured man confesses that Jesus is the Son of Man and begins to worship him (9:38). This cured man, severely challenged by the authorities, refuses to criticize Jesus, even though he is thrown out of the synagogue, a fate shared by the local church for whom the Gospel was written. This community would have learned an important lesson from the example of the blind man: remain faithful to Jesus and your faith will also deepen.

In contrast to the blind man are those who have physical sight—including some Pharisees—but who are spiritually blind. They refuse to see the source of Jesus' power or acknowledge who he is. Rather, they call him "a sinner" (9:24). This passage helps recall a theme introduced in the prologue: Jesus is the light that has come into the world. His truth dispels the darkness of ignorance. His light gives us direction and overcomes the darkness of sin. He asks for faith in him to overcome spiritual blindness. Note how the human interpretations of the meaning of the Law blinded some Pharisees. Their belief that Jesus violated the Sabbath law of rest made them unable to see God's presence in their midst. The Lord says spiritual blindness is worse than physical blindness (9:41).

Transition to the Seventh Sign (John 10:1–21, 22–42)

In John 10:1–21, as the Feast of Tabernacles section concludes, Jesus offers a beautiful speech where he calls himself the "gate for the sheep" and the "Good Shepherd" who knows his own sheep and gives his life for them.

The last feast treated is the **Feast of Dedication, or Hanukkah** (10:22–42), which commemorates the rededication of the altar and the reconstruction of the Temple under the Maccabees (164 BC) after years of desecration by profane Syrian rulers. Jesus transforms this feast by claiming to be consecrated by his Father and sent into the world (10:36). In a dialogue with his opponents, Jesus refuses to say whether he is the Messiah because they will not believe him. But he says so much more: "The Father and I are one" (10:30). Once again,

Pool of **Siloam**

Pool of Siloam—A pool of water outside of the city of Jerusalem that is a receptacle for the waters of the Gihon Spring.

Feast of Dedication, or Hanukkah—The word "Hanukkah" means "festival of lights." It marks the rededication of the Temple in the days of the Maccabees.

The Raising **of Lazarus**

Jesus is accused of blasphemy but escapes the attempts to stone and arrest him. Jesus leaves Jerusalem and returns to the area around the Jordan River near where John the Baptist ministered.

Sign 7: The Raising of Lazarus (John 11:1–44)

This most important miracle in John's Gospel prefigures Jesus' own Death and Resurrection. A message reaches Jesus that his friend is mortally ill. But he waits to go to him so his Father can glorify him through a dramatic sign.

Lazarus's grieving sister Martha misunderstands Jesus as the Lord proclaims that faith allows the believer to participate in his Paschal Mystery:

> I am the resurrection and the life; whoever believes in me, even if he dies, will live, and everyone who lives and believes in me will never die. Do you believe this? (Jn 11:25–26)

Jesus weeps for his friend Lazarus out of his love for him. He also prays to his Father, thanking him for answering his prayer. Finally, he calls Lazarus out of the grave. In a most moving scene, the dead man comes out and is freed of his burial clothes.

Lazarus's raising causes many to believe. However, some of Jesus' enemies decide to eliminate him because they dread his popularity among the people. They fear Roman reprisals. Caiaphas, the high priest, utters one of the great ironic statements in John's Gospel, not realizing the profound truth hidden in his statement: "It is better for you that one man should die instead of the people, so that the whole nation may not perish" (Jn 11:50). Jesus' Death indeed has saved the Jewish people and all nations.

This seventh sign sums up all the other signs and pulls together many theological themes in the Gospel of John:

- Jesus is the way to life.
- He is the Resurrection.
- He is God ("I Am").
- Faith is essential for us to gain eternal life with him in union with the Father and the Holy Spirit.

John 12 serves as a conclusion to the Book of Signs. Six days before Passover, Lazarus's sister, Mary, anoints Jesus at Bethany. In response to Judas Iscariot's criticism about the expense of this costly gesture, Jesus praises Mary for anticipating his coming death. The next day, Jesus rides into Jerusalem with the crowds waving palm branches and shouting "Hosanna!" Jesus prays about his coming hour of death, saying, "Whoever loves his life loses it, and whoever hates his life in this world will preserve it for eternal life" (Jn 12:25). Unlike in Mark's Gospel, where Jesus prays in the Garden of Gethsemane that the cup of suffering might pass from him if it be his Father's will, in John's Gospel, Jesus accepts his impending death. He acknowledges that it is why he came into this world and prays that it will glorify his Father.

FOR REVIEW

1. How does the author of John's Gospel understand the term *miracle*?

2. What is the symbolic meaning of Jesus' first miracle at Cana? What role did Mary play in this sign? How can we learn from her?

3. What do we learn about Jesus from his discourse with the Samaritan woman?

4. Why did so many of Jesus' followers abandon him after the sign of the bread?

5. Discuss a possible meaning of Jesus' walking on water.

6. Discuss the meaning of Jesus' raising Lazarus from the dead.

7. Identify the Feast of Tabernacles (Tents or Booths) and the Feast of Dedication (Hanukkah).

FOR REFLECTION

The Samaritans' personal encounter with Jesus highlights that *each of us must come into personal contact with him.* Write about times that you personally met Jesus. Also, reflect on what you most thirst for in your life right now. How can Jesus help quench that thirst?

The Book **of Glory** (John 13:1–20:31)

The second part of John's Gospel—the Book of Glory—consists of two major sections: The Last Supper Discourses (Jn 13–17) and Jesus' Death and Resurrection (18–20). An epilogue in chapter 21 includes Jesus' Resurrection appearances in Galilee. In the Last Supper discourses, Jesus prepares his Apostles for his hour of glory—which is his Passion—promises them the Holy Spirit, and instructs them on how to live after his Resurrection. His Passion, Death, and Resurrection reveal God's love for us and mark Jesus' triumph and the victory of salvation he has won for us.

The Last Supper Discourses (John 13–17)

John's Gospel reports that the Last Supper occurred a day earlier than reported in the Synoptics, that is, the day on which the Jews killed the lambs for the Passover meal. The Jews sacrificed lambs to recall Yahweh's releasing the Israelites from slavery in Egypt. Jesus is the Lamb of God whose sacrifice on the cross has freed all people from the slavery of sin. Every Eucharist represents the sacrifice of the cross. The *Catechism* teaches that "[the] sacrifice of Christ and the sacrifice of the Eucharist are *one single sacrifice*" (1367).

Jesus began the meal with a profound act of **humility**. He, the

humility—The virtue which reminds us that God is the author of all good. Humility tempers ambition or pride and provides the foundation for turning to God in prayer.

The Upper Room where **the Last Supper was held**

Master, washed the feet of his disciples, a task a slave was not required to perform. Peter objected, but Jesus taught that he did this as an example of the meaning of humble service and that his followers must imitate him. John is the only Gospel to record this incident.

After Judas Iscariot left the meal to go into the night (a symbol for the darkness of Satan), Jesus gives a new commandment:

> Love one another. As I have loved you, so you also should love one another. This is how all will know that you are my disciples, if you have love for one another. (Jn 13:34–35)

Jesus proved his love by dying and rising for us. He wants us, his friends, to die to our selfishness and give life to others by attending to their needs. The great twentieth-century leader Mahatma Gandhi learned this important truth taught by Jesus: "The best way to find yourself is to lose yourself in the service of others."

Chapters 14–17 of John represent the heart of Jesus' last discourse. This discourse, or testament, is like a farewell speech in which the speaker talks about the nearness of the departure, recalls his or her past life, urges the listeners to great deeds, gives them words of encouragement, promises them prayers, and so forth. For example, Jesus reassures his disciples, urging them not to be troubled. He tells us always to stay close to him because:

> I am the way and the truth and the life. No one comes to the Father except through me. . . . Whoever has seen me has seen the Father. (Jn 14:6, 9)

Once again Jesus asks for belief in him, promising that if we ask for anything in his name he will do it. Our way to the Father is through him since Jesus and the Father are one.

Jesus also promises to send the Holy Spirit, another *Paraclete*, that is, a helper, counselor, and advocate. The Spirit will open our minds and hearts, allowing us to understand and live Jesus' teaching.

Above all else, what Jesus teaches us at the Last Supper is to keep his commandments, especially his command to love. Love unites us to the Lord. Among the fruits of love are peace and joy.

Chapter 15 of John is one of the most important chapters in the entire New Testament. In it, Jesus tells of his great love for us. He is the vine, we are the branches who get our life from him. As the Father loves him, so he loves us. We must remain attached to him. We must believe in God and his Son. We must love God and one another. Loving as he loved helps us to keep Jesus' life in us.

Jesus also calls us his friends (Jn 15:13–17). He teaches us to keep his commandments and to love one another. This is the heart of the Good News. We are his friends, chosen by the Lord himself to continue his work of love. By the power of the Holy Spirit, he dwells in us. The same Spirit protects and guides us and empowers us to witness to Jesus. The Spirit enables us to love.

The Last Supper ends with a most beautiful New Testament passage, the priestly prayer of Jesus. (By definition, a **priest** is a mediator between God and people). In John 17:1–26, Jesus assumes a priestly role by interceding for us, by praying to his Father on our behalf. The Lord begins his prayer,

> Father, the hour has come. Give glory to your son, so that your son may glorify you, just as you gave him authority over all people, so that he may give eternal life to all you gave him. (Jn 17:1–2)

Jesus also prays that the Father will watch over us so we will remain united to him, our friend and Savior, and to each other. Jesus prays for unity, a oneness in community with the Father, Son, and Spirit.

Jesus asks the Father to save us from the evil one, to make us cherish the truth, and to witness to him. Jesus prays that we remain united to him so he can continue to work through us.

priest—A mediator between God and man. Jesus is the High Priest *par excellence*. As God-made-man, he bridges both Heaven and earth, bringing God to humanity and humanity to God.

FOOT WASHING

Jesus washed the feet of the Apostles at the Last Supper to teach that an important way for his disciples to show love is through service of others. Each day presents countless opportunities to serve others, often in simple ways. Put several of the following (or examples like them) into practice in the coming days.

For a Friend
- Offer a sincere compliment
- Let your friend choose the next activity you do together

For Your Family
- Help a younger brother or sister with a homework project
- Offer to babysit a younger sibling or play a game with him or her
- Ask your mom or dad if you can run an errand
- Spend some time with a grandparent

For the School Community
- Pick up trash in the lunchroom
- Hold a door open for another person
- Greet in a friendly manner someone you don't know
- Eat lunch with a lonely classmate
- Defend someone who is the object of gossip

For the Civic Community
- Collect school supplies for underprivileged children
- Participate in a canned-food drive for a hunger center
- With classmates, clean up the litter in your school's neighborhood or a nearby park or nature center
- Collect clothing, books, and useful household items to donate to the St. Vincent de Paul Society
- Write a letter of support to a pro-life politician
- Get involved in the "Make a Difference Day" service day. For ideas on how to make a difference, check this website: www.usaweekend.com/diffday/index.html

For more ideas on how to serve, view the Corporation for National and Community Service website at: http://national serviceresources.org/epicenter/practices/index.php?ep_action=view&ep_id=780

The Resurrection of Jesus (John 20–21) (CCC, 639–658)

In John's Gospel, the Resurrection is a major revelation of God the Father. All four Gospels report the fact of Jesus' Resurrection, but none of them claim that there were eyewitnesses to the event. Collectively, the Gospels give us fourteen stories that describe the Resurrection. Each emphasizes certain aspects. The Synoptics stress the empty tomb (Mark), God's power and majesty (Matthew), and Jesus alive in the Word of God and in the breaking of the bread (Luke). John's Gospel emphasizes Jesus' commissioning the leaders to continue his work of reconciliation and love.

Contextually, John's Gospel reports that Jesus appeared first to a woman, Mary Magdalene. At first she did not recognize the transformed, glorified Lord, but when he called her by name, Mary knew it was the Lord. "Rabboni!" (Teacher), she exclaimed. Personal encounter with Jesus, not an empty tomb, brings about faith. Jesus instructed Mary not to cling to him because he had yet to ascend to his Father. Rather, she was to broadcast the joyous news of his Resurrection to the disciples. The lesson of this Resurrection appearance is this: Faith and love are the keys to discipleship, not rank, wealth, position, prestige, gender, or power. Mary Magdalene, like Martha earlier (11:27), exhibited faith and love in great abundance. Perhaps this is why she is the first to see and believe in the resurrected Lord.

Imagine the shock and disbelief of the Apostles to Mary's report of Jesus' Resurrection. Peter and "the other disciple" had to run to see for themselves. The more fleet-footed disciple steps aside to allow Peter to enter the tomb first, perhaps symbolizing the leadership role of Peter.

It is not until Jesus appeared to them on the evening of the Resurrection that the disciples would know for themselves that the Lord was risen. They were frightened of their enemies and were hiding out in a room behind a bolted door. Suddenly, Jesus appeared in their midst. They "rejoiced when they saw the Lord" (20:20). He wished them peace and then commissioned them to continue his work, to be missionaries. He breathed on them, signifying the giving of the Holy Spirit, and instructed them to forgive sins in his name.

A week later, Jesus appeared to the Apostles, including Thomas, who had not been present for the risen Jesus' first appearance. By showing him his hands and side, Jesus revealed that the risen Lord is the same Jesus who lived and died. When Thomas saw Jesus, he acknowledged his divinity: "My Lord and my God" (20:28), the highest proclamation of faith in Jesus made in any of the Gospels. In answer to Thomas, Jesus blessed all of us who believe yet do not see him.

Originally, the Gospel of John ended with chapter 20. However, its final edition includes chapter 21, which reports Jesus' appearance to the Apostles in Galilee. There, Jesus helps the disciples catch fish, symbolic of their future role as fishers of people. He also prepared a breakfast for them, suggesting on a deeper level his communion with them at Eucharistic celebrations. Finally, he re-commissions Peter, who three times had denied knowing Jesus. This time the Lord elicits from Peter a threefold promise of his love.

THE SYNOPTIC GOSPELS ON THE RESURRECTION OF JESUS

Read the Resurrection narratives in the Synoptic Gospels: Mark 16:1–8, 9–20; Matthew 28:1–20; Luke 24. Answer the following questions about similarities and differences:

- Who actually witnessed the Resurrection itself?
- When does it take place?
- What was the reaction of the women in all cases?
- Where in Galilee did Jesus appear?
- Where in Jerusalem did Jesus appear?

The Resurrection Narratives Compared

When you compare the Resurrection narratives from the Synoptic Gospels and the Gospel of John, you will note how together they proclaim that the Resurrection was a real event, with historically verifiable elements. However, they differ to the point that it is impossible to blend them into one continuous narrative. The Evangelists did not even try to do so. Each Evangelist chose from the available Resurrection stories those that would be of most help and significance to his audience.

Undoubtedly, there are differences among the Resurrection stories because eyewitnesses often give dissimilar accounts of what they have seen. This is especially true when what they have witnessed is shockingly new. It should not be surprising that the four Gospels don't record the same stories. Yet, despite some minor discrepancies, the Resurrection stories do agree on essential points:

- The Resurrection took place early in the morning on the first day of the week.
- Women were present at the tomb, most certainly including Mary Magdalene.
- The stone had been rolled away and the tomb was empty. This fact did not automatically lead to the presumption that Jesus had risen. For example, in John's Gospel, Mary

Magdalene weeps because she thought someone stole Jesus' body. In Luke's account, the Apostles first think the women's report about the empty tomb is sheer nonsense. Even after they see for themselves, they are amazed, but nothing is said about what they believe. However, an empty tomb is important to the Resurrection stories. It is an essential sign of Christ's Resurrection, a first step in acknowledging God's work in bringing the Son back to life. It corroborates that something happened. The enemies of the early Christians were never able to produce Jesus' corpse, though they probably tried to do so.

- A messenger or messengers were at the tomb; they told the women to inform the disciples about what had taken place.
- Jesus appears to his disciples. Note the different disciples who are mentioned. These appearances convinced a group of frightened men and women that the crucified Jesus was alive and that he was Lord. So life-changing were these appearances that, along with the Holy Spirit's gifts of faith and fortitude, they transformed Jesus' disciples from frightened, confused, and disappointed followers into bold, courageous witnesses who willingly lived and died, proclaiming, "Jesus Christ is Lord."

THE ASCENSION OF JESUS (CCC, 659–667)

The Ascension of Jesus refers to the time when Jesus stopped appearing to the disciples in visible form and his glorified body took its rightful place in Heaven as equal to the Father. Jesus has prepared a place for us with him in Heaven and continuously intercedes for us and prays for us. In his glorified state, Jesus—true God and true man—is not limited to time and space. He lives and reigns forever. According to the *Catechism of the Catholic Church*, Jesus' body was glorified at the moment of his Resurrection, as proved by the supernatural qualities it manifested. But during his appearances to his disciples, his glory remained hidden under the appearance of ordinary humanity. "Jesus' final apparition ends with the irreversible entry of his humanity into divine glory, symbolized by the cloud and by heaven, where he is seated from that time forward at God's right hand" (CCC, 659).

- How do the Synoptic Gospels report the Ascension of Jesus? (Read Matthew 28:16–20; Luke 24:50–53; Acts 1:9; and Mark 16:19)
- Does John's Gospel have a separate Ascension scene?

Note also several other aspects of Jesus' appearances. Jesus appeared only to his disciples. Sometimes they were slow to recognize him. Why? First, they were not expecting the Lord to come back to life. And second, Jesus' resurrected body shone with the **glory of God**. They needed the Lord's own words of peace, instruction (as in Luke's account of the disciples on the road to Emmaus), and reassurance to help them to recognize him.

The Gospel accounts also insist that Jesus was not a ghost. Luke, for example, reports that the resurrected Jesus ate fish, while John adds that Jesus ate breakfast with his disciples. Furthermore, Jesus asks Thomas to touch his wounds. The resurrected Jesus is not a ghost, but neither is he a corpse that is breathing again. He is alive in a transformed, glorified body that still has an aspect of "bodiliness" to it.

The First Letter to the Corinthians (15:1–19) tells us that Jesus appeared to St. Paul. Paul also writes that Jesus made several appearances, including a significant one to over five hundred people. At the time of his writing in the early 50s, Paul assures his readers that many of these eyewitnesses are still alive. They can easily verify that the Lord rose from the dead and appeared to them.

Jesus prepares his disciples for his Ascension and the descent of the Spirit. The Gospels also share that Jesus instructs the Apostles to wait for his return (Mk 16:7) or to reflect on scriptural prophecies concerning him (Lk 24:25–27). Jesus commissions them to preach (Mt 28:18–20) and forgive sin (Jn 20:21–23). He tells them to await the Spirit, who will empower them to accomplish marvels in his name (Lk 24:49).

glory of God—The visible Revelation of the power of the invisible God.

THE TRUTH ABOUT MARY MAGDALENE, FAITHFUL DISCIPLE

With the publication of Dan Brown's controversial novel, *The Da Vinci Code* (2003), Mary Magdalene received lots of media attention. Brown's novel claims, among other things, that Jesus married Mary Magdalene and fathered a child with her whose blood line was a highly guarded secret preserved by a secret society. The novel, as well as the film based on it, claims that Leonardo Da Vinci was a member of this secret society (the Priory of Sion) that protected the secret. Further, it claims that his famous painting *The Last Supper* portrays Mary Magdalene as seated at Jesus' right side, not John the Beloved Apostle. According to Brown, Mary Magdalene is the "Holy Grail" of legend who carries on Jesus' bloodline.

Brown used his novel to attack the Catholic Church, saying it hid the real truth about Jesus—namely, that Jesus was a mere man who wished to make Mary the head of his religious movement that was supposed to restore a spirituality of the "sacred feminine." According to Brown, Peter usurped Mary's role and replaced Jesus' teaching with his own. Peter's actions forced Mary to flee to France, where she eventually died; Jesus' and her descendents survived in France's Merovingian bloodline.

Many commentators have easily dismissed the lies and errors in this popular novel. There is no evidence that scholars can muster up to support the bizarre claims found in this book. Art critics laugh at the assertion that Mary Magdalene is depicted in Leonardo's work. Historians easily debunk the claims that the Catholic Church was involved in what Brown alleges is history's greatest cover-up. Many books have been written to point out the falsehoods in *The Da Vinci Code*. Two excellent ones are Richard Abanes's *The Truth Behind the Da Vinci Code* and Amy Wellborn's *De-Coding Da Vinci: The Facts Behind the Fiction of The Da Vinci Code*.

That leaves us with the true identity of Mary Magdalene. She was, when all is said and done, one of Jesus' most important disciples. In John's Gospel, Jesus appears to Mary Magdalene first. When she first saw him in the garden, she did not recognize him. But when Jesus called her name, she cried "Rabboni" and wanted to cling to the Risen Lord. Jesus told her to stop holding on to him because he had not yet ascended to his Father. Then, he commissioned her to go and report this message to the brothers: "I am going to my Father and your Father, to my God and your God." Mary became "an Apostle to the Apostles" when she went to announce, "I have seen the Lord" (see Jn 20:11–18).

Mary came from the village of Magdala on the western shore of Lake Galilee. Luke reveals that Jesus cast out seven demons from her. In the Synoptic Gospels, Mary is the first person mentioned in the lists of Jesus' women disciples who minister to Jesus and the Apostles and "who provided for them out of their resources" (see Luke 8:2–3; Mark 15:40–41; and Matthew 27:55–56). We can deduce that Mary Magdalene was the leader of this group of women who faithfully followed Jesus from the beginning of his ministry up to the time of his Crucifixion. Significantly, all the Gospels report that she was one of the first eyewitnesses of Jesus' Resurrection.

This concludes the scriptural evidence for Mary Magdalene. In later Church traditions, some mistakenly identified her as Lazarus's sister Mary, who anointed Jesus' feet in Bethany shortly before Holy Week. Another mistaken identity is with the unnamed woman, a sinner often believed to be guilty of sexual sin, who anointed Jesus' feet at Simon the Pharisee's house (see Luke 7:36–50). Popular art through the ages often depicted Mary Magdalene as a reformed sinner, perhaps a prostitute, based on these mistaken identities. Yet another misidentification shows up in Mel Gibson's *The Passion of the Christ*, which portrays Mary Magdalene as the woman (an adulteress) whom Jesus rescued from stoning in John 8:1–11. However, most scholars today believe that Mary Magdalene, Mary of Bethany, the woman who anointed Jesus at Simon's house, and the woman caught in adultery were all separate individuals.

The Catholic Church honors Mary Magdalene as a saint whose feast day is July 22. She is honored for her faithful discipleship of Jesus.

Concerning Mary Magdalene's later life after the Resurrection, one tradition holds that she accompanied Jesus' Mother, Mary, to Ephesus and died there. Later her relics were taken to Constantinople. Yet another tradition holds that she sailed to southern France, where she lived a contemplative life for several decades before her death.

The Meaning of the Resurrection

Jesus' Resurrection is the essential fact of Salvation History, the bedrock of our faith, the heart of the Good News about Jesus. There are accompanying essential beliefs about the Resurrection, including the following:

- The Resurrection proves Jesus' claims to be God's Son. Christ's Resurrection confirms Jesus' works and teachings. It fulfills the Old Testament promises and Jesus' preaching. It proves Jesus' divinity.

- The Resurrection, following Jesus' sacrifice on the cross, accomplished our salvation. Jesus' Resurrection to a glorious body, not limited by space or time and filled with the power of the Holy Spirit, proves that he has conquered sin and death.

- While Jesus' Death frees us from sin, his Resurrection gives us new life, justifies us in God's grace, and adopts us into the divine family. As John's Gospel repeatedly insists, Jesus brings us eternal life. The Resurrection allows Jesus to live in us; thus, we already share "eternal life," the life of the Lord who abides in us.

- The Gospel promises that if we join ourselves to the risen Lord and live according to his message of love, we will also share in our own final resurrection at the end of time. Jesus' Resurrection is the promise of our eternal life with God.

The Resurrection of Jesus gives new meaning to our lives. Death does not have the last word. Eternal life with Jesus in community with the Father and the Spirit and all others who love the Lord has the last say. This central truth of our faith frees us from anxiety and brings us joy.

FOR REVIEW

1. What is the symbolic meaning of Jesus' celebration of the Last Supper one day before the Passover feast?

2. In what way did Jesus fulfill a priestly role in our salvation?

3. Describe the meaning of the Resurrection appearances of Jesus in John's Gospel.

4. Why do the four Gospels have different Resurrection stories? Does this fact make them more or less believable? Explain.

5. On what essential points about the Resurrection do all the Gospels agree?

6. Discuss three important implications of the Resurrection of Jesus.

7. What is meant by the Ascension of Jesus?

FOR REFLECTION

- "As I have loved you, so you should love one another." Write a paragraph on what this means *specifically* to you.

- In John's account of the Passion narrative, Jesus says that he "came into the world to testify to the truth. Everyone who belongs to the truth listens to my voice" (Jn 18:37). In reply to Jesus, Pilate said, "What is truth?" (Jn 18:38). How would you answer Pilate's question, especially as it relates to Jesus Christ? Write a paragraph in your journal discussing this question.

CHAPTER SUMMARY POINTS

- Written AD 90–100, John's Gospel may be based on traditions surrounding the Beloved Disciple, an unnamed follower of Jesus mentioned several times in John's Gospel.

- John's Gospel may have been written in Ephesus for a largely Jewish Christian Church that also had in it some Samaritan and Gentile believers. Its purpose was to strengthen faith and win converts.

- Themes of the fourth Gospel include Jesus as the Word of God and the Son of God; the need to believe and to love; the promise of the Holy Spirit; and the centrality of the Resurrection.

- John's Gospel presents an ascending Christology that emphasizes Jesus' divine origins and nature. Jesus is both the revealer of the Father and the Father's Revelation.

- Jesus reveals the glory of God, that is, he makes manifest, especially in his Paschal Mystery, the power, radiance, and love of the Father.

- John's concept of miracle includes God's *work* in Jesus and *signs* performed by Jesus that reveal the deeper reality of God's glory.

- The miracle in Cana symbolizes Jesus' bringing the riches of divine wisdom and Revelation. It shows Jesus' compassion, points to the hour of his Paschal Mystery, when God's glory will be fully revealed, and brings his disciples to faith. Catholics learn from Mary's role in this sign: She is a powerful intercessor on our behalf.

- In the discourse with the Samaritan woman, Jesus reveals that he is the Messiah, the living water, who teaches that we must worship God in Spirit and in truth.

- Jesus' cure of the paralytic shows that he is Lord of the Sabbath, doing his Father's work because the Father never rests.

- Jesus' multiplication of the loaves reveals him to be the Bread of Life, the source of eternal life. Catholics see a clear reference to the holy Eucharist in this miracle.

- The miracle of raising Lazarus from the dead symbolizes Jesus' own Resurrection from the dead when he will be exalted, never to die again. He asks for faith in him and the Holy Spirit, teaching us that he is the Resurrection and the life.

- At the Last Supper, Jesus teaches us to serve as he served us, to love by sacrificing for others as he loved and sacrificed for us, and to remain one in God's love by the power of the Holy Spirit.

- The Resurrection of Jesus is the bedrock truth of our faith. It proves Jesus' claims, reveals his identity, shows the love of the Father, gives us new life, justifies us in God's grace, adopts us into God's family, and gives us incredible hope for a life of eternal glory with our Triune God in the afterlife. Jesus' Passion, Death, Resurrection, and Glorification have accomplished our salvation.

- The various Gospel accounts of the Resurrection all agree on the essentials: an empty tomb, women witnesses, its taking place on Sunday, heavenly messengers giving a message, initial unbelief that is reversed when Jesus appears on various occasions to the disciples, and Jesus' giving further instructions to his disciples as they wait for his Ascension and the descent of the Holy Spirit.

LEARN BY DOING

1. Choose ten favorite quotations by Jesus from the Gospel of John. Assemble them into a prayer booklet with suitable artwork to illustrate each one.

2. Create a PowerPoint® presentation depicting several of the archaeological sites or discoveries associated with John's Gospel. For example, you might find illustrations for:

   - The "Galilee Boat"—the type of boat the Apostles might have used
   - The Garden of Gethsemane
   - Excavations at Cana
   - Sea of Galilee
   - Jacob's Well in Samaria
   - The Pool of Bethesda
   - The Pool of Siloam
   - Ossuary of Joseph Caiaphas

   View the following websites for help on the assignment:
   http://catholic-resources.org/John/Archaeology.html
   www.pohick.org/sts/archaeol.html

3. Prepare a PowerPoint® presentation on Jesus in art through the ages. Begin your research here: www.beliefnet.com/story/22/story_2283_1.html.

4. View a modern-day reading of the Resurrection (Jn 20:1–31), produced by the American Bible Association and starring the Catholic actor Jim Caviezel. Write a short review of the film. You can find the film at www.newmediabible.org/Default.htm.

5. Read John's version of the Passion narrative, John 18–19. In your journal, note at least three ways John's version differs from that of the Synoptic Gospels.

6. After reading John 2:1–11 (the wedding feast at Cana), report on how weddings took place in New Testament times.

7. Write a one-page report on Mary Magdalene. Illustrate it with an image from a famous piece of art downloaded from the Internet.

8. Create a skit that reenacts the dialogue between Jesus and the Samaritan woman at the well (Jn 4:4–42). Use a contemporary setting and colloquial language.

9. Write an eyewitness news article reporting the raising of Lazarus (Jn 11:1–44).

10. Read John 15:1–11 to see how Jesus used allegory in his teaching. Recall that an allegory has a number of points of comparison. Answer the following questions: Who is the vine? Who is the vinegrower? What does the pruning process represent? Who are the branches? What happens if the branches remain attached to the vine? What does the fruit represent?

PRAYER LESSON

Compose your own one-line prayer. When recited repeatedly, one-liners are a good way of living Jesus' injunction to "pray always without becoming weary" (Lk 18:1).

Begin by selecting three of the titles that appear in John's Gospel. You might choose from among Word of God, Son of God, Lamb of God, Rabbi (Teacher), King of Israel, Son of Man, Christ, Prophet, Bread of Life, Light of the World, Good Shepherd, the Resurrection and Life, the Way, the Truth, the Life, and True Vine. Then compose a prayer for each of your titles. Transcribe your prayers into your journal. Here are some examples:

Jesus, Light of the World, enlighten my mind to follow you.
Jesus, Way to the Father, be my path.
Jesus, Word of God, speak to my heart.

- *Reflection:* Which title of Jesus from John's Gospel speaks most powerfully to you at this stage of your life? Why?

- *Resolution:* Recite your prayer invocations several times during each day of the coming weeks. Reflect on the meaning of each word in your invocations. Remember Jesus' good news to you in Jn 15:15: "I have called you friends, because I have told you everything I have heard from my Father."

St. Paul's Letters:
Jesus the Universal Lord

CHAPTER EIGHT

For I am convinced that neither death, nor life, nor angels, nor principalities, nor present things, nor future things, nor powers, nor height, nor depth, nor any other creature will be able to separate us from the love of God in Christ Jesus our Lord.

–Romans 8:38–39

CHAPTER **OVERVIEW**

ZEALOUS **FOR CHRIST**

This section introduces St. Paul as a seemingly unlikely yet passionate disciple of Christ.

THE LIFE OF **ST. PAUL**

The life of St. Paul, including his missionary journeys described in the Acts of the Apostles, is explored in detail.

LETTERS WRITTEN **BY ST. PAUL**

Main themes of the letters traced directly to St. Paul—1 Thessalonians, Galatians, Philippians, Philemon, 1 and 2 Corinthians, and Romans—are detailed.

DEUTEROPAULINE **LETTERS**

The "Deuteropauline letters"—2 Thessalonians, Ephesians, Colossians, 1 and 2 Timothy, and Titus—refer to letters attributed to Paul but that may actually have been written by one of his disciples.

Zealous **for Christ**

Imagine you are about to meet your new parish pastor for the first time. What would you think about him initially if you knew:

- He has been considered a leader in most places that he served, but that he has never stayed in one place for more than three years, and those were in small communities at best.
- He is a good preacher but sometimes long-winded. Some in his congregations have been known to fall asleep during his sermons.
- He is fifty years old, and not entirely in robust health. But he has traveled a lot.
- He is a rather controversial figure. He has been physically forced to leave some of the places where he worked.
- Sometimes he has trouble getting along with other religious leaders.
- He's been in jail three or four times.
- He's not the best record-keeper around.

What do you think would be your initial impressions of this man? Perhaps you would be hesitant about this person's ability to pastor your parish. If so, you would be unnecessarily concerned about one of the greatest and most zealous Apostles for Jesus Christ—St. Paul.

FOR REFLECTION

Write or share your initial impressions of St. Paul based on the information in this section.

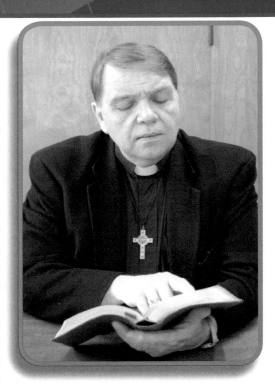

The Life **of St. Paul**

Saul of Tarsus—the future St. Paul—was an extraordinary disciple of Jesus Christ. Thirteen out of twenty-seven New Testament books are attributed to him, though scholars today agree that St. Paul probably only wrote seven of them—Romans, 1 and 2 Corinthians, 1 Thessalonians, Galatians, Philippians, and Philemon.

Six other letters—2 Thessalonians, Ephesians, Colossians, and the "pastoral letters" 1 and 2 Timothy and Titus—were likely penned by close disciples of Paul or by his admirers who wanted to keep his apostolic legacy alive. Collectively, these six letters are called ***Deuteropauline***, or secondary, Pauline letters. The teaching in these letters, however, represents the kind of thinking Paul would have used to address later problems that crept up in the various first-century local churches. The practice of using the master's name to gain support for one's own teaching was an accepted practice for disciples in the ancient world.

Who was St. Paul? Paul's own letters and the Acts of the Apostles give us a fairly detailed portrait of the man.

Saul of Tarsus of the Jewish tribe of Benjamin was born approximately AD 10 during the reign of the Emperor Augustus. Tarsus was a city in Cilicia. Like many Jews of his time living outside of Palestine, he had both a Jewish name and a Roman name. The Jewish name was that of the first king of Israel, Saul, who was also from the tribe of Benjamin; the Roman name Paul (Paulus) was a well-known family name.

Paul received an excellent Greek education in Tarsus. He also learned the trade of tentmaking there, an occupation he often used to support himself during his later missionary activity. As reported in Acts,

Paul was also a Roman citizen, an important fact that spared him a beating in Jerusalem and ultimately led him to Rome for a trial. His upbringing in Tarsus made him familiar with Gentile religions, philosophies, and customs. This knowledge would help him in later life to preach the Gospel of Christ to Gentiles.

In Acts, Luke tells us that, as a young man, Paul studied to be a rabbi in Jerusalem under the famous teacher Gamaliel. Paul was a strict Pharisee, trained in the Law, and willing to persecute anyone he thought was deviating from true Jewish practice. Thus, Paul was among the leaders who persecuted the early Christians.

After a time of persecuting Christians, around AD 36, Paul received a dramatic revelation from Christ on the road to Damascus. The glorified Lord spoke to Paul in a blinding light, identifying himself with the Christians Paul was persecuting. Paul was subsequently baptized by Ananias and then spent some time in the Arabian desert before returning to Damascus.

In AD 39, Paul took a brief trip to Jerusalem to meet Peter and James. He then returned to a city in Cilicia—possibly Tarsus—and remained there for nearly four years. In approximately AD 44 Barnabas invited Paul to help minister in Antioch, the third largest city in the Roman Empire (after Rome and Alexandria) and the future base of his missionary activity. After he had worked there for a year, the Antioch church sent Paul and Barnabas to Jerusalem to help the Christians of Judea during the time of famine.

Between 46 and 58, Paul engaged in three extensive missionary journeys, depicted on the map and described below:

Journey 1 (46–49). On the first journey, Paul and Barnabas visited the island of Cypress and the Asia Minor locales of Pamphylia, Pisidia, and Lycaonia. They established churches in Pisidian Antioch, Iconium, Lystra, and Derbe. At the end of this journey, in 49, Paul attended the famous Council of Jerusalem. There he argued for the inclusion of the Gentiles into the Church without their first converting to Judaism.

Journey 2 (50–52). Antioch was the starting point of the second journey. Accompanied by Silas, and later by Timothy and Luke, Paul revisited the churches from the first journey, then passed through Galatia, went to Macedonia, and made his way to Europe, preaching in the following cities: Philippi, Thessalonica, Berea, Athens, and Corinth. He wrote his First Letter to the Thessalonians from Corinth. He returned to Antioch by way of Ephesus and a side trip to Jerusalem.

Journey 3 (54–58). Again, this journey began in Antioch. Paul revisited the same areas as the second trip, but remained in Ephesus for three years, perhaps where he was imprisoned for a time. There he probably wrote his letters to the Philippians, Philemon, Galatians, and the First Letter to the Corinthians. In early 57, Paul left Ephesus for Troas and then went to Macedonia where he likely wrote the Second Letter to the Corinthians. He eventually made his way to Corinth, where he stayed for three months and from there wrote Romans.

Deuteropauline—Secondary Pauline writings penned by disciples, secretaries, or admirers of Paul. These letters—2 Thessalonians, Ephesians, Colossians, 1 and 2 Timothy, and Titus—have different vocabulary, style, theological themes, content, and historical context than the letters indisputably written by St. Paul.

PAUL'S FIRST MISSIONARY JOURNEY

On a return trip to Jerusalem in AD 58, Paul's enemies had him arrested. After two years' detainment in Caesarea, he finally made it to Rome around AD 61, where he was under house arrest for two more years.

The Acts of the Apostles concludes in AD 63 with Paul in Rome happily preaching the Gospel, though under house arrest. One tradition has Paul martyred under Nero in 64 about the same time Peter was killed. Another tradition claims he was released from prison, traveled to Spain, where he preached the Gospel, and returned to Rome where he was again arrested and then beheaded by Nero in the year 67.

Paul's life is an unparalleled adventure story of commitment to the Lord Jesus Christ. He eloquently describes his motivation: "I live, no longer I, but Christ lives in me; insofar as I now live in the flesh, I live by faith in the Son of God who has loved me and given himself up for me" (Gal 2:20). Paul felt this divine love so deeply that he felt compelled to preach the Good News to everyone. Because of his call to spread the Gospel, he founded countless churches, opened the Gospel to Gentiles, wrote faith-rousing letters that teach us yet today, and inspired loyal disciples to continue his work of instruction and encouragement by writing letters in his name. Paul was a model disciple of Christ, worthy of emulation for his courage alone. He wrote:

Five times at the hands of the Jews I received forty lashes minus one. Three times I was beaten with rods, once I was stoned, three times I was shipwrecked, I passed a night and a day on the deep; on frequent journeys, in dangers from rivers, dangers from robbers, dangers from my own race, dangers from Gentiles, dangers in the city, dangers in the wilderness, dangers at sea, dangers among false brothers; in toil and hardship, through many sleepless nights, through hunger and thirst, through frequent fastings, through cold and exposure. And apart from these things, there is the daily pressure upon me of my anxiety for all the churches. Who is weak, and I am not weak? Who is led to sin, and I am not indignant? (2 Cor 11:24–29)

READING THE LETTERS OF ST. PAUL

The thirteen Pauline letters have traditionally been grouped according to the following four categories. They are addressed to communities or to individuals. They are arranged in the Bible from longest to shortest.

Early Letters
1 Thessalonians (P) 50/51 (from Corinth)
2 Thessalonians (D) 51* or 90s (Asia Minor)

"Great" Letters
Galatians (P) 54/55 (Ephesus)
Philippians (P) 56 (Ephesus)
1 Corinthians (P) 56/57 (Ephesus)
2 Corinthians (P) 57 (Macedonia and Illyricum)
Romans (P) 57/58 (Corinth)

St. Paul the Apostle

"Prison" Letters

Philemon (P) 55 (Ephesus)

Colossians (D) 61–63* or 80s (Ephesus)

Ephesians (D) 61–63* or 90s (Ephesus)

P—Most scholars agree Paul probably wrote these.

D—These were probably written by a disciple of Paul.

Pastoral Letters

Titus (D) 65* or 95–100 (Asia Minor)

1 Timothy (D) 65* or 95–100 (Asia Minor)

2 Timothy (D) 64–67* or 95–100 (Asia Minor)

*This earlier date is likely correct if Paul did the writing.

Paul's letters follow the common style of letter writing in the Greco-Roman world of his day. His letters contain four sections:

1. **Opening Address.** Since the letters were not placed in envelopes, the opening salutation gives the names of the sender and the receiver and a short greeting.

2. **Thanksgiving.** A short thanksgiving sets the tone of the letter and hints at the letter's contents. Paul's thanksgivings are usually very prayerful and inspiring.

3. **Body of the letter.** The bulk of the letter has two parts to it: *doctrinal teaching* and *encouragement*. Paul elaborates key Christian truths or clarifies misunderstandings his readers are having over points of Church doctrine and applies the doctrinal teaching to Christian living. Today, we look on these sections of Paul's letters for guidance in Christian morality.

4. **Final salutations.** Paul concludes his letters by giving personal news or specific advice to individuals. His final greeting is usually a short blessing like this: "The grace of our Lord Jesus Christ be with you" (1 Thes 5:28).

You might notice while reading some of Paul's letters a conclusion like this: "This greeting is in my own hand —Paul" (1 Cor 16:21). This type of verse reveals that Paul dictated his letters to a professional scribe, a common practice in his day. Toward the end of the letter he would sign his name to assure his readers that the letter was really coming from him.

- Read the addresses of any six of Paul's letters. Record in your journal the Christian way of greeting.

- Listed below are eight summary statements that capture the essence of Paul's rich teaching. Study them carefully. Then read the italicized passages. They are among the most famous and important ones in all of Paul's writings. For each reading, jot in your journal several significant points Paul makes for that particular passage.

1) Salvation takes place through Jesus Christ, the Lord of the universe. *(Colossians 1:15–20)*
2) The Death and Resurrection of Jesus Christ is the heart of the Gospel. *(1 Corinthians 15:1–19)*
3) Christians will participate in the Resurrection of Jesus Christ. *(1 Corinthians 15:20–28)*
4) Salvation is a free gift of God that demands faith. We cannot earn it. *(Romans 5:1–11)*
5) Christians are bound together in one body, the Church, of which Jesus Christ is the head. *(1 Corinthians 12:12–30)*
6) The Holy Spirit is the life of the Church who enables us to call God "Abba." *(Galatians 4:1–7)*
7) The brothers and sisters of Jesus should treat each other with dignity. We must love. *(Ephesians 4:17–32)*
8) Following Jesus means that we must suffer for him gladly. *(Philippians 2:1–18)*

◀◀ FOR REVIEW

1. Which are the seven letters scholars agree were penned by St. Paul?
2. What does *Deuteropauline* mean? Which are the Deuteropauline letters?
3. Name at least five significant biographical details of St. Paul's life.
4. What significance did Antioch have in the ministry of St. Paul?
5. Name the parts of the four-fold outline of Pauline letters.
6. Discuss five major themes Paul addresses in his letters. Cite passages from Paul's letters to illustrate each theme.

FOR REFLECTION

Write a paragraph describing what you find most admirable in the life of St. Paul.

Letters Written **by St. Paul**

The following sections offer synopses of the letters written by St. Paul. Read the introduction to each letter in your bible to accompany the particular section. The years listed are the estimated dates of composition.

1 Thessalonians (AD 50–51)

Paul's First Letter to the Thessalonians is the earliest New Testament writing, dating from only twenty years or so after the life of Jesus. According to Acts 17:1–10, on his second missionary journey, Paul established a church in the northern Greek city of Thessalonica, an important commercial center and capital of the Roman province of Macedonia. Hostile non-believers forced him to leave. Eventually making his way to Corinth, he was joined there by his coworker Timothy, who informed Paul that the new converts were remaining firm in their faith and love despite persecution.

Paul wrote 1 Thessalonians, probably in the winter of AD 50–51, in light of Timothy's report. In it, he encourages the Thessalonians, defends his proclamation of the Gospel, shares news about his travel plans, and addresses two of the pressing issues of the time. First, Paul advises the Thessalonians to remain holy, especially by avoiding sexual immorality. Second, he assures them that Christians who have died will rise one day and live with the Lord forever. He also points out that since no one knows when the Lord will come again, those living should "stay alert and sober" (5:6), "putting on the breastplate of faith and love and the helmet that is hope for salvation" (5:8).

Galatians (AD 54–55)

Galatians is the first of Paul's "great" letters, filled with profound theological insight and timeless practical advice on Christian living. It was written from Ephesus in AD 54–55 to congregations in central Asia Minor, which Paul had founded on his second journey. It addresses some important issues that

PAUL'S SECOND MISSIONARY JOURNEY

PAUL'S THIRD MISSIONARY JOURNEY

certain Jewish-Christian evangelists had introduced into the churches he had founded. For example,

- Did Gentiles who converted to Christianity have to become Jews?
- Did they have to be circumcised and follow all the Jewish customs and food laws?
- Was Christianity merely to be another Jewish sect? Or was it open to all people who had faith in Jesus Christ?

The future of Christianity was at stake. Paul expresses anger toward the Jewish-Christian evangelists who introduced division into his Galatian churches. These "Judaizers" directly challenged Paul's authority, teaching that he was being too lenient on non-Jews who wished to follow Christ. Paul lets his anger shine through in his letter. For example, although Galatians has an address (1:1–5) and a conclusion (6:11–18), nowhere does Paul thank his readers for their spiritual condition. They had not yet proven their faith and, in fact, were showing themselves to be easily led astray by false teachers. Instead, Paul warns his readers about following a different Gospel than the one he preached (1:6–10).

The doctrinal section of Paul's letter (1:11–4:31) answers his opponents' charges. First, he defends his authentic call to be an Apostle, because Jesus had appeared to him and called him to witness to him. He reminds his readers of the Council of Jerusalem, where the leaders of the Church (Peter, James, and John) agreed with him that Gentiles did not have to be circumcised to become Christians. He even reports how he had to correct Peter for his inconsistency in Antioch for not eating with Gentile Christians who did not follow Jewish dietary laws.

Second, Paul uses a scriptural argument to defend the important truth that faith brings about a right relationship with God (known as justification). Paul's key theological point is this: Observance of the Old Law does not guarantee salvation, but only faith in the Lord Jesus Christ. Faith in Jesus teaches a person to respond to the Spirit, who guides Christians to live holy lives.

FRUITS OF THE SPIRIT

In contrast [to works of the flesh], the fruit of the Spirit is love, joy, peace, patience, kindness, generosity, faithfulness, gentleness, self-control. Against such there is no law.

—Galatians 5:22–23

In your journal: Write examples of how these "fruits of the Holy Spirit" manifest themselves in your own life.

TEACHING ON JESUS
CHRIST **IN GALATIANS:**
Jesus' Death and Resurrection
have freed us from the bondage
of the Law, the power of sin, and
the self. "For freedom Christ set
us free" (5:1).

Before the coming of Jesus, the Law served a purpose. But now the Spirit calls Christians to freedom and responsibility. The new law of love requires much more. One can never rest satisfied that he or she has kept it perfectly. Baptism incorporates us into God's family. We must act toward each other as brothers and sisters in the Lord:

> For through faith you are all children of God in Christ Jesus. For all of you who were baptized into Christ have clothed yourselves with Christ. There is neither Jew nor Greek, there is neither slave nor free person, there is not male and female; for you are all one in Christ Jesus. And if you belong to Christ, then you are Abraham's descendants, heirs according to the promise. (Gal 3:26–29)

Chapters 5 and 6 of Galatians give practical advice on Christian living. Being set free from the Law by faith in Christ does not mean license to do whatever we want to do. Christian freedom means serving Christ Jesus, boasting in his cross. Christian life does not mean becoming a slave to the flesh, but serving one another in love. Paul tells us that works of the flesh are obvious and bar entry into God's Kingdom: "immorality, impurity, licentiousness, idolatry, sorcery, hatreds, rivalry, jealousy, outbursts of fury, acts of selfishness, dissensions, factions, occasions of envy, drinking bouts, orgies, and the like" (5:19–21).

A PAULINE LETTER IN DEPTH: PHILIPPIANS (AD 56)

Acts 16:6–40 provides context for Paul's Letter to the Philippians. In Acts we learn that Paul, in AD 50–51, had a vision that he interpreted as a divine invitation to preach the Gospel in Macedonia, located in present-day northern Greece. Paul and his companions landed at the port of Neapolis and took the famous Roman road—the Egyptian Way—to the leading Macedonian city of Philippi, where a century earlier (42 BC) Mark Antony and Octavius (Augustus) defeated Cassius and Brutus, the famous assassins of Julius Caesar. In this city, Paul would establish his first local church.

A notable convert in Philippi was Lydia, a cloth merchant, who conversed with Paul near a small river, a place of prayer. Paul baptized her and her household. Lydia then invited Paul and his companions to stay with her while they were in the region. Another notable incident in Philippi recorded in Acts is Paul's exorcising an unclean spirit from a fortune-telling slave girl. When her owners could no longer profit from her fortune-telling skills, they dragged Paul and Silas before the local authorities and charged them with being troublesome Jews. They were stripped, beaten, and imprisoned.

Miraculously an earthquake jarred open their prison door, but Paul and Silas refused to escape. This so moved the jailer, who was contemplating suicide because he thought the prisoners he was responsible for had escaped, that both he and his household converted to Christ. The next day the authorities, hearing that they had abused Roman citizens without a trial, gladly asked Paul and his companions to leave the city. They did and eventually made their way to Thessalonica.

Origin of the Letter

It is clear that Paul wrote Philippians from prison. What is not as clear is from what city and when Paul wrote it, and whether or not Philippians is one unified letter or the combination of two or three short letters written over a period of time.

In Philippians, Paul hints that his martyrdom is a real possibility, leading to a share in Christ's Resurrection (3:10–11). Though he is suffering, he is joyful because he believes his trials help spread Christ's Gospel. His imprisonment leads others to preach without fear, though it seems that some were doing it out of selfish ambition, to best each other, or to outpreach the famous Paul. Paul is, of course, not happy with this way of evangelizing. He reminds the Philippians that the important thing is that Christ is preached (1:18).

With the above established, we may add two other relevant facts: Timothy was with Paul as he was writing his letter (1:1; 2:19–23), and there had been frequent contacts between Paul and the Philippians. For example, they knew Paul was in prison. They sent him gifts through a certain Epaphroditus (4:15), who became deathly ill, but whom Paul was sending (or had sent) back to them (2:25–30). And Paul hoped to send Timothy to them soon (2:19–23), and, if God willed it, he hoped to come to Philippi himself (2:24).

These bits of information help scholars date Philippians and locate its place of origin. Three possibilities emerge. The letter was written either during Paul's two-year imprisonment in Caesarea in 58–60; during Paul's house arrest in Rome, spanning the years 61–63; or during Paul's three-year stay at Ephesus from 54–56. Traditionally, scholars believed Paul penned Philippians from Rome, but today a growing number think the most likely locale was Ephesus around AD 56. A major reason for concluding this is that Ephesus is geographically closer to Philippi and could better explain the various contacts between Paul and the Philippians alluded to in the letter.

Because of a mixture of various topics in Philippians, and because verse 3:1a sounds like Paul is concluding his letter and verse 3:1b suggests that Paul had written a previous letter, some scholars conclude that Philippians may be the compilation of two or three letters written over a period of time. We cannot for sure know if this is the case. It is certainly valid to conclude that Philippians is only one letter. There is only one opening address and one concluding formula in Philippians. And the argument can be made that Paul wrote in a "stream-of-consciousness" style while in prison. He may have jumped to, and given advice on, various topics as they came to mind.

> **TEACHING ON JESUS CHRIST IN PHILIPPIANS:** Philippians is an important Pauline letter for revealing how Christians understood Christ in terms of his preexistence, Incarnation, and Paschal Mystery. Christ is the perfect model for humility and self-sacrificing love. He is the way to our own Resurrection and empowers us in all we do.

Martyrdom of Saint Paul **by Ventura Salimbeni**

OUTLINE OF PHILIPPIANS

It is best to read the letter as a unity of one, following this outline:

- Salutation and thanksgiving to the Philippians (1:1–11)
- Paul in prison and his attitude toward death (1:12–26)
- Exhortation to follow Christ's example of humility (1:27–2:16)
- Paul and the Philippians and his planned missions (2:17–3:1a)
- Warning against false teachers (3:1b–4:1)
- Instructions to live in unity, joy, and peace (4:2–9)
- Paul's current situation and Philippian generosity (4:10–20)
- Concluding formula, blessing (4:21–23)

Read the entire Letter to the Philippians. Take notes on what you perceive to be the major points of each of the sections outlined above. When finished with the entire letter, match your notes with the notes that follow.

Salutation and Thanksgiving. These follow the traditional format of a Pauline epistle. The reference to bishops ("overseers") and deacons ("ministers") in 1:1 is the earliest New Testament reference to these two offices. In his thanksgiving, Paul introduces the themes he will pursue in this letter: joy and rejoicing, spreading and upholding the Gospel, and superabundant love. Philippians shows us a joyful Paul who greatly loves his Philippian converts. Key words in the letter are "joy" or "rejoice" (used sixteen times). Others are "unity" or "oneness."

Paul in prison and his attitude toward suffering. One of Paul's most famous verses related to this theme is, "For to me life is Christ, and death is gain" (Phil 1:21). Paul wants to do God's will: If he lives, he will preach the Good News of Christ unceasingly. If he dies, he will attain the greater good of unity with Christ.

Paul's exhortation to humility. Paul encourages the Philippians to stand firm "in one spirit, with one mind struggling together for the faith of the Gospel" (1:27). This plea for humility is the heart of Paul's Epistle to the Philippians. He points to the example of Christ the Servant by quoting an early Christian hymn. The hymn praises Christ's self-emptying humility in his becoming man and his dying on the cross to be raised and exalted. These verses reveal the "high Christology" of the early Christians who clearly believed in Jesus' divinity:

> Have among yourselves the same attitude
>   that is also yours in Christ Jesus,
> Who, though he was in the form of God,
> did not regard equality with God something to be grasped.
> Rather, he emptied himself,
> taking the form of a slave,
> coming in human likeness;
> and found human in appearance,
> he humbled himself,
> becoming obedient to death,
> even death on a cross.
> Because of this, God greatly exalted him
> and bestowed on him the name
> that is above every other name,
> that at the name of Jesus
> every knee should bend,
> of those in heaven and on earth and under
>   the earth,
> and every tongue confess that
> Jesus Christ is Lord,
> to the glory of God the Father. (2:5–11)

False Teachers. After informing the Philippians that he plans to send to them Timothy, a coworker he considers almost like a son (2:22), and Epaphroditus, Paul launches into an attack of some false teachers who have infiltrated the community. He has some very strong language for them: "Beware the dogs!" (3:2). Apparently, these teachers were Jewish Christian missionaries who were trying to force the Gentile Christians to become Jews, the same issue raised in Galatians. Paul reviews his own personal history and concludes that it is faith in the Lordship of Christ Jesus and his Resurrection that brings us salvation.

Joy, Peace, and Unity. "Rejoice in the Lord always. I shall say it again: rejoice!" (4:4). These words summarize Paul's concluding chapter as he counsels two women—Euodia and Syntyche—to patch up their differences. Paul also encourages the Philippians to pray for their needs, pursue virtue, and rest in "the peace of God that surpasses all understanding" (4:7). He concludes the letter by thanking his beloved Philippians for their financial support for his ministry and blesses them with a familiar closing: "The grace of the Lord Jesus Christ be with your spirit" (4:23).

Concluding Remarks. Paul teaches in 3:10-11 of our need to conform ourselves to Christ's Death and Resurrection, that is, to live the Paschal Mystery. This is the key to a holy life and is as relevant today as it was to the Philippians as they struggled to remain one, at peace, and joyful under trying times.

Philemon (AD 55 if from Ephesus or AD 61–63 if from Rome)

Writing from prison, Paul encourages his friend, Philemon, to accept back his runaway slave as a brother. The Letter to Philemon was covered as part of the discussion on slavery (see pages 66).

1 Corinthians (late AD 56 or early 57)

Corinth, a Roman colony near Athens in Greece, was a prosperous seaport, with a reputation for permitting every known vice imaginable. The expression "To live like the Corinthians" meant that a person was very immoral. Slaves made up two-thirds of its population of 600,000. Paul spent eighteen months in Corinth during his second missionary journey (Acts 18:1–11), at which time he founded and nurtured a local church there.

When Paul was in Ephesus during his third journey, he received bad news from Corinth. The Church had broken into factions with rival groups following different leaders. In addition, many had fallen back into immoral pagan practices. So Paul wrote a letter (referred to in 1 Corinthians 5:11) to warn them away from immorality. This letter is now lost to us. When Paul received further news of division and challenges to his authority, he wrote another letter, 1 Corinthians, in approximately AD 56. It is a practical but firm letter with good advice for the people of that time and place and for people today.

The First Letter to the Corinthians has an opening formula (1:1–3) and a prayer of thanksgiving (1:4–9). The conclusion instructs his readers to take

Corinth, **near Athens**

up a collection for the needy and his usual personal greetings (16:1–24). The body of the letter takes up the following themes:

Divisions in the Corinthian Church (1:10–4:21). There were four factions that came on the scene in Corinth. Some claimed to be followers of Paul, others of the preacher Apollos, still others of Cephas. Finally, a fourth group boasted that they belonged to Christ and felt they could contact him in a direct religious experience similar to the practices of pagan religions. To all these groups, Paul has a simple answer: *Rely on the crucified Christ alone.* As he puts it:

> The message of the cross is foolishness to those who are perishing, but to us who are being saved it is the power of God. (1 Cor 1:18)

TEACHING ON JESUS CHRIST **IN** **1 CORINTHIANS:**

Jesus is the risen Christ who empowers the body of Christ and individuals to use the gifts of the Holy Spirit for the benefit of others. Jesus is the hope we all have for a future resurrected, glorified life with God.

TEACHING ON JESUS CHRIST **IN** **1 CORINTHIANS:**

Jesus is the risen Christ who empowers the body of Christ and individuals to use the gifts of the Holy Spirit for the benefit of others. Jesus is the hope we all have for a future resurrected, glorified life with God.

TEACHING ON JESUS CHRIST **IN** **2 CORINTHIANS:**

Jesus is our comfort (1:5), victory (2:14), freedom (3:17), light (4:6), judge (5:10), reconciler (5:19), gift (9:15), owner (10:7), and power (12:9).

Problems in Christian morality and living (5:1–11:1). In addressing practical issues, Paul teaches that a man living with his stepmother should be condemned for immoral behavior. He exhorts Christians to settle their own legal disputes among themselves without recourse to the judicial system. He gives advice on marriage and divorce and discusses the issue of eating food connected to pagan religious services. He condemns Christians who go to prostitutes, saying that freedom does not mean license to do whatever one wants, but freedom to serve God:

> Do you not know that your body is a temple of the holy Spirit within you, whom you have from God, and that you are not your own? For you have been purchased at a price. Therefore, glorify God in your body. (6:19–20)

Problems in Christian worship (11:2–14:40). The divisions in the Corinthian church even spilled over into the way the Eucharist was celebrated. Paul advises that women may certainly pray and prophesy in the assemblies, but must dress and look respectably.

Selfishness to the poor, drunkenness among the rich, and quarrels have no place in the Agape, the meal shared before the Eucharist. Corinthians were so divided that they did not recognize the Lord when it came time to share his body and blood. Paul tells them to eat at home before gathering and then come together to celebrate the Eucharist properly in a spirit of unity and love. Concerning the ranking of spiritual gifts given by the Holy Spirit, Paul writes movingly that love is the greatest gift of all.

The Resurrection (15:1–58). In this section, Paul clarifies proper Church teaching on the Resurrection. Christ's Resurrection is "the firstfruits of those who have fallen asleep" (15:20); we will receive the fullness of our Resurrection in Christ in the future. Paul also provides the earliest Christian creed about Jesus' Resurrection (15:3–8), an important passage for understanding this great event.

2 Corinthians (AD 57)

Between the writing of the two letters to the Corinthians, Paul returned to Corinth for a short visit to see for himself what was happening there. Neither his letter nor visit had much impact, so Paul wrote a third letter, harshly critical of Corinthian abuses. The major problem this time was false teachers who had influenced the Corinthians to adopt Jewish laws and customs against the teaching of Paul. Apparently, someone directly challenged Paul, his teaching, and his apostolic credentials. Paul responded, and this anguished letter is now lost to us, though some scholars believe that

LOVE INTO PRACTICE

For St. Paul, love is the secret to Christian life, outranking all other virtues. Read 1 Corinthians 13, Paul's great hymn to love. In your journal, add to St. Paul's list two other traits of love that you think are essential for Christian living. Then, plan a concrete strategy to put into practice one of these qualities of love during the coming week.

it was added—in chapters 10–13—to the letter we call 2 Corinthians.

Paul then left Ephesus for Macedonia. While there, he met up with Titus, who brought some good news about the Corinthians. They were beginning to respond to Paul's words and reject the false teachers. The Corinthians also asked Paul to visit them again. In response to this happy turn of events and his anticipated visit, Paul wrote 2 Corinthians from somewhere in Macedonia, perhaps in AD 57. Some scholars believe that this letter might be a composite of several others. The first nine chapters are much more cheerful and positive in tone as Paul tries to make peace with the Corinthians.

The body of 2 Corinthians deals with Paul's past relationships with the Corinthians (1:12–2:17), his ministry among them (3:1–7:4), praise for their repentance (7:5–16), an appeal for the collection for the Church in Jerusalem (8:1–9:15), and a rigorous defense of his ministry against false teachers (10:1–13:10).

There are many personal touches in 2 Corinthians that reveal the human side of St. Paul. For example, he writes of his affection for his beloved yet troublesome converts in Corinth:

> You are our letter, written on our hearts, known and read by all, shown to be a letter of Christ administered by us, written not in ink but by the Spirit of the living God, not on tablets of stone but on tablets that are hearts of flesh. (2 Cor 3:2–3)

Romans (AD 57–58)

Written from Corinth in the winter of AD 57–58, Romans is Paul's letter of introduction to the Christians living in Rome. He had not yet visited Rome, nor did he found the local church there as he did, for example, in Corinth and Thessalonica. But he was planning to stop in Rome on his way to Spain.

The Letter to the Romans is Paul's longest letter and his deepest theologically. Romans treats in more detail some themes Paul introduced in Galatians. Its central theme is that faith in Jesus Christ's Death and Resurrection reconciles us to God. Christ's sacrificial act has brought us

- justification;
- peace with God;
- the gift of the Holy Spirit;
- reconciliation with God;
- salvation from the wrath of God;
- hope of a share in God's eternal glory;
- God's superabundant love poured out on us.

Christ frees us and brings us new life. Therefore, we are not to live according to the flesh, doing whatever we want. We must live according to the Spirit of God, who raised Christ from the dead. We must live as God's children. To do this, we live in service of others.

Five key points developed in the body of Romans include:

> **TEACHING ON JESUS CHRIST IN ROMANS:**
>
> Jesus Christ is the New Adam. His righteousness before God and his death for all sinners have justified us before God. We must believe in him. The Lord's Death and Resurrection have redeemed, justified, reconciled, and saved us. One day we will share in his glory.

1. ***A description of the human condition before Christ (1:18–3:20).*** Paul shows that sin pervades human history. The Gentiles, using their human reason, should have discovered God. However, they worshiped creation instead of the Creator (1:18–2:16). The Jews should have been better off because they had the Law, but they did not keep it. Both Jews and Gentiles are under the power of sin. Apart from Christ Jesus, no one can escape God's condemnation (2:17–3:20).

2. ***Justification through faith in Christ (3:21–5:21).*** Neither Greek study nor knowledge of the Jewish Law brings salvation. Only God's gift of grace saves. Jesus' Death brings salvation to both Jew and Gentile. Christ's Death broke the dominion of sin and death. "But God proves his love for us in that while we were still sinners Christ died for us" (5:8).

   Abraham is a good example of faith; his attitude must be our attitude. Jesus is compared to Adam, the father of all humans. Because of Adam, sin and death entered human history. Because of Christ's obedience to death on the cross, grace and life and justification before God have resulted in eternal life for all. Jesus Christ is the new Adam.

3. ***Salvation and Christian freedom (6:1–8:39).*** Faith in Christ and Baptism accomplish what the Law cannot do for us: freedom from slavery to sin, freedom from the Law, and freedom from death. As the *Catechism* teaches, "By Baptism ***all sins*** are forgiven, Original Sin and all personal sins, as well as all punishment for sin" (1263). The Holy Spirit adopts us into God's family, enabling us to cry, "Abba, 'Father!'" (8:15). Our new life in Christ unites us in God's love. In one of the most beautiful passages in all of Scripture, Paul writes:

   > For I am convinced that neither death, nor life, nor angels, nor principalities, nor present things, nor future things, nor powers, nor height, nor depth, nor any other creature will be able to separate us from the love of God in Christ Jesus our Lord. (8:38–39)

4. ***God's plan for Israel (9:1–11:36).*** These chapters take up Paul's concern that God's Chosen People had rejected salvation. Paul points out that God does not contradict his promises to the Jewish people. He insists that God's apparent rejection of Israel is not final. Jewish non-acceptance of the Gospel opened the door to the Gentiles, who, like branches from a wild olive tree, were grafted onto a cultivated tree. The Gentiles are not to boast because their salvation is a pure gift of God's love. The root of the tree, God, supports them, not the reverse. Paul's deepest hope and prayer is that Israel will eventually turn to the Gospel and be regrafted onto the tree of life. God's mercy works in mysterious ways. "To him be glory forever. Amen" (11:36).

5. ***Christian behavior (12:1–15:13).*** Paul considers the way a Christian conducts himself an act of worship: "Offer your bodies as a living sacrifice, holy and pleasing to God, your spiritual worship" (12:1). This means that our faith must translate into concrete deeds of service. We must use our God-given gifts for others, not for self-glory. We must love. Paul sums up a person's responsibility: "Love does no evil to the neighbor; hence, love is the fulfillment of the law" (13:10).

FOR REVIEW

1. What is the earliest letter written by St. Paul? What is one of its key themes?

2. What is considered the first of Paul's "great" letters? What position does it take concerning Judaism and new Gentile converts?

3. What does St. Paul teach about faith and justification? What does "justification before God" mean?

4. List a couple of highlights of Paul's ministry in Philippi (Acts 16:6–40).

5. What are the likely dates of writing and city of origin for Paul's Letter to the Philippians?

6. What are some themes St. Paul discusses in Philippians?

7. What is the message of the hymn Paul quotes in Philippians 2:5–11?

8. List three problems Paul addresses in 1 Corinthians. What does he teach about each?

9. List five qualities of love that St. Paul lists in his famous hymn on love (1 Cor 13).

10. According to the Letter to the Romans, what are some benefits for us of Christ's sacrifice on the cross?

11. According to St. Paul what do faith in Christ and Baptism accomplish for us?

FOR REFLECTION

•   Reread Philippians 2:5–11, which tells of Christ's great humility. Using this passage as a guide, write your own definition of *humility*. Then write a short profile of the most humble person known to you.

•   Read Romans 12–15. In your journal, note what you consider to be the ten best rules for Christian living that St. Paul shares in these chapters.

Deuteropauline **Letters**

As covered on page 220, St. Paul likely did not write all of the letters traditionally attributed to him. A close disciple of Paul might have written six letters—2 Thessalonians, Ephesians, Colossians, 1 and 2 Timothy, and Titus. These letters were similar in content and style to Paul's other letters. These secondary letters are sometimes referred to as *Deuteropauline letters*. They definitely reflect Paul's thought, but they have different vocabulary, style, theological themes, content, and historical context than those letters attributed to Paul.

2 Thessalonians (AD 90s, or AD 51 if by Paul)

A traditional view was that Paul wrote 2 Thessalonians shortly after his First Letter to the Thessalonians to address a misunderstanding about his teaching concerning the resurrection of the dead and Christ's Second Coming, also termed the *Parousia*. (In their confusion, some of his converts thought Christ was returning any day, so they stopped working. This, of course, upset Christians who continued to work.)

Current scholarly opinion, however, favors that disciples of Paul, writing around AD 90, actually penned this letter. It is one of the six **pseudonymous** letters to be discussed in this section.

In chapter 2 of the letter, the readers are told that Jesus will not come again until certain signs take place. Patience and prayer are the weapons Christians need to prepare themselves for this return.

Chapter 3 instructs the Thessalonians what to do with non-workers. The authors point to Paul's own example—how he worked while preaching among them. The readers are instructed to go to work and earn money for their food. Those who ignore this advice should be avoided so in shame they will return to the Church (3:11–15). The purpose of shunning wrongdoers is not to punish but to encourage

pseudonymous—A work written under a name that is not the name of the person doing the actual writing. It was a common and accepted practice for disciples and admirers of great teachers to write works under their names to extend their legacies.

> TEACHING ON JESUS CHRIST **IN**
> **2 THESSALONIANS:**
> Jesus Christ is the coming Judge who will reward and punish.

TEACHING ON JESUS CHRIST IN 2 COLOSSIANS:

Jesus is the Lord of all creation, the author of reconciliation, the source of new life, the embodiment of God, the head of the Church, and the all-sufficient Savior.

repentance. Christians are brothers and sisters in the Lord, not enemies. This advice is timeless. Our motive for calling the sinner back must always be love for a brother or a sister.

Colossians (AD 80, or AD 54–56 or AD 61–63 if by Paul)

Colossians, Philippians (listed as one of the Great Letters above), Philemon, and Ephesians are sometimes referred to as the "Captivity Letters." Each reveals that its author is in prison at the time of its writing. The traditional view is that these letters were written while Paul was a prisoner, usually thought while in Rome (AD 61–63), though many believe Philippians may have been written from Ephesus (see page 227). There are few doubts that Paul wrote Philemon and Philippians; however, scholars today believe Colossians and Ephesians, closely related letters, were written by Paul's disciples after his death.

Colossae was a textile town 110 miles east of Ephesus, in modern-day Turkey. The Letter to the Colossians was written to counteract some bizarre teachings that claimed that Christ's Death and Resurrection were not enough for salvation. False teachers were spreading secret knowledge concerning astrology, the need to worship heavenly bodies and angels, and the necessity to engage in severe physical disciplines. Belief in these intermediate spirits and practices to appease them was wooing Colossian Christians away from belief in the unique saving role of Christ.

The author, who had not yet visited Colossae, addressed his letter to Epaphras, the founder of the local church there, to encourage him to combat the false teachings. The key doctrinal point of the letter is that Jesus Christ is the preeminent spiritual being; only he can save us. Christians should not engage in disciplinary practices regarding food or drink to placate false spirits. Christians now participate in Jesus' Death and Resurrection. They bring us freedom and life. Thus, Christians should live as his disciples by avoiding certain vices (3:5–11) and cultivating certain virtues (3:12–17). A true Christian turns from sin to a life of imitating Jesus in loving others.

The most important passage in Colossians comes from a famous hymn quoted to underscore the superiority of Jesus Christ:

> He is the image of the invisible God,
> the firstborn of all creation,
> For in him were created all things in heaven and on earth. . . .
> He is before all things
> and in him all things hold together.
> He is the head of the body, the Church.
> He is the beginning, the firstborn from the dead.
> (Col 1:15–18)

St. Paul **preaching**

Ephesians (AD 90s, or AD 61–63 if written by Paul)

Traditionally it was thought that Paul wrote Ephesians from a Roman prison around AD 62. Today, nearly all biblical scholars conclude that Ephesians is likely the work of a secretary or admirer of Paul writing in the 90s. The letter draws out more explicitly some of the themes touched on in Colossians. The impersonal tone of the Letter to the Ephesians suggests that it was more of an essay than a letter. Thus, many conclude that it was originally a circular letter meant to be read at many different churches in Asia Minor. Ephesians presents a developed Pauline theology on the Church imaged both as the Body of Christ (1:15–23) and his bride (5:24–33). This letter also emphasizes the unity of Gentiles and Jews in Christ.

After a short address and greeting, the body of the letter has two main divisions: the mystery of salvation related to the Church (1:3–3:21) and Paul's exhortation to Christians to live in unity (4:1–6:20). The letter ends with Paul's entrusting it to his friend Tychicus, a worthy helper who also delivered the Letter to the Colossians.

1 and 2 Timothy and Titus (AD 100)

These three letters were probably the work of the same author, a later follower of Paul. Their style and vocabulary are different from that of Paul, and they reflect a more developed Church organization than was present at the time of Paul.

These three letters have the name "pastoral letters" because they were written by one pastor (shepherd) to two other pastors, Timothy and Titus. They differ from the other Pauline and Deuteropauline letters in that they are addressed to individuals and give advice on Church leadership. Both Timothy and Titus were fellow missionaries with Paul and his faithful disciples. Each also shepherded his own local church, Timothy in Ephesus and Titus in Crete.

The First Letter to Timothy and Titus are very close in theme and content. Some of their key teachings and themes are:

- *Severe warnings against false teachings and teachers.* These false teachings involve "myths and endless genealogies" (1 Tm 1:4), wrong-headed **Asceticism** like the forbidding of marriage and the outlawing of certain foods (1 Tm 4:2–3), and "profane babbling" and "so-called knowledge." Guilty of such false teaching were the heretics known as Gnostics, who believed they received special knowledge from God that guaranteed them eternal life. **Gnosticism** distrusted material creation. On the one hand, some felt they could do whatever they wanted because their bodies would not affect the fate of their souls. On the other hand, there were Gnostics who radically disciplined their bodies to strengthen their spiritual nature. Their strict practices harmed them and, in effect, denied the goodness of God's material creation. These false teachings were counteracted in 1 Timothy. For example:

> **TEACHING ON JESUS CHRIST IN EPHESIANS:**
>
> Through his cross, Jesus Christ has broken down the wall between Jew and Gentile, reconciling both to God. He is the head of his body, the Church. His power and presence fill the church to continue his work of salvation. Christ Jesus is the source of all the gifts of the Holy Spirit that build up the Church. He is the cornerstone and the capstone of the household of God.

Asceticism—A way of living, often out of religious motivation, that is marked by self-denial, self-discipline, and austerity.

Gnosticism—A generic term for a variety of pre- and early-Christian heresies that taught that salvation rests on secret knowledge (*gnosis* in the Greek).

For everything created by God is good, and nothing is to be rejected when received with thanksgiving, for it is made holy by the invocation of God in prayer. (1 Tm 4:4–5)

- To counteract false teaching, Paul also encourages the younger Timothy to be faithful to true doctrine. "Attend to the reading, exhortation, and teaching" (1 Tm 4:13).
- *Many practical instructions for Church organization and criteria for Church leaders.* For example, the qualities of an overseer of the Church, which is the office of the bishop, are given. These include his being:

  > irreproachable, married only once, temperate, self-controlled, decent, hospitable, able to teach, not a drunkard, not aggressive, but gentle, not contentious, not a lover of money. He must manage his own household well, keeping his children under control with perfect dignity; for if a man does not know how to manage his own household, how can he take care of the church of God? He should not be a recent convert, so that he may not become conceited and thus incur the devil's punishment. He must also have a good reputation among outsiders, so that he may not fall into disgrace, the devil's trap. (1 Tm 3:2–7)

- *Instructions for Christian worship.* For example, when praying, men should lift up their hands to Heaven without being angry or arguing with others, and women should dress modestly, focusing on God and not their hairstyle, expensive jewelry, or clothing (1 Tm 2:8–10).
- *Instructions for Christian living.* Family relationships, life within the Church, and attitudes toward the government should all reflect the gentleness and love of Christ. Good Christian behavior will attract others to the Good News. A specific example that can never grow old is this advice:

  > Do not rebuke an older man, but appeal to him as a father. Treat younger men as brothers, older women as mothers, and younger women as sisters with complete purity. Honor widows who are truly widows. (1 Tm 5:1–3)

The Second Letter to Timothy is a more personal letter than 1 Timothy, taking on the tone of a last testament from the older Apostle to his younger and beloved coworker Timothy, one affectionately called "my dear child" (1:2). Paul is pictured as being in prison in Rome, alone and abandoned by his colleagues and awaiting what he believes will be his death. Toward the end of his letter, he asks Timothy to join him because his time is almost up. "I have competed well; I have finished the race; I have kept the faith" (4:7).

Timothy heads up the church in Ephesus. The letter gives much advice from his mentor on how to guard the Deposit of Faith ("this rich trust," 1:14) against some of the same false teachers criticized in 1 Timothy. Timothy is encouraged to pursue "righteousness, faith, love, and peace" (2:22). He is to be a bold pastor and:

> proclaim the word; be persistent whether it is convenient or inconvenient; convince, reprimand, encourage through all patience and teaching. For the time will come when people will not tolerate sound doctrine. . . . But you, be self-possessed in all circumstances; put up with hardship; perform the work of an evangelist; fulfill your ministry. (4:2–3, 5)

An excellent summary of the Christian faith is included in this letter:

> Remember Jesus Christ, raised from the dead. . . . If we have died with him, we shall also live with him. (2:8, 11)

Imagine Church history had the Lord not appeared to Saul of Tarsus on the road to Damascus. This startling event converted "Saul the Pharisee" into "Paul the Christian," who was the missionary to the Gentiles. Acts tells us of his courageous efforts for the Lord, whose presence he keenly felt. Paul's letters, and those of his disciples and admirers, reveal an agile, brilliant mind deeply concerned that converts not abandon the true Christ.

And who was Jesus Christ for Paul of Tarsus? None other than the crucified Lord who now reigns in glory.

Jesus is the Lord of history, the creator of the world, the firstborn from among the dead, the unique Son of the merciful Father. Jesus is also the head of his body, the Church, to which all Christians belong through the power of the Holy Spirit. Our greatest glory in this life is to allow Jesus to live in us. Paul is our model: "For to me life is Christ, and death is gain" (Phil 1:21).

> **TEACHING ON JESUS CHRIST IN THE PASTORAL EPISTLES:**
>
> Jesus is the one Mediator between God and the human race (1 Tm 2:5), the Savior of all, especially believers (1 Tm 4:10). He abolished death and brought immortality (2 Tm 1:10). He is our great God and Savior Jesus Christ (Titus 2:13).

FOR REVIEW

1. How do the pseudonymous Pauline writings differ from the letters scholars are sure St. Paul himself wrote?

2. What was the problem addressed in the Letter to the Colossians? What is the key theological teaching in this letter?

3. Which of the Pauline epistles has the most developed theology about the Church? Describe some of its theology.

4. What are the three pastoral letters, and how did they get their name? Discuss several of the qualities these letters say a Church leader should have.

FOR REFLECTION

- How should Catholics who are not fulfilling religious obligations—like not attending Mass on Sunday—be corrected? Discuss this question in light of 2 Thessalonians 3:6–15.

- List three instructions the Letter to Titus gives for people in various states of life.

- Perhaps you have heard the following saying, "Money is the root of all evil." People often mistake this as a quote from Scripture when actually the saying from 1 Timothy goes like this: "The love of money is the root of all evils" (1 Tm 6:10). Write a short reflection on the difference between these two sayings. Discuss with an example why the biblical teaching makes more sense.

CHAPTER SUMMARY POINTS

- Pivotal for the spread of Christianity was the conversion of Saul of Tarsus around AD 36, when Jesus appeared to him on the road to Damascus.

- Acts records three missionary journeys of St. Paul, spanning the years 46–49, 50–52, and 54–58. These journeys took him to Asia Minor and Europe. In AD 61, Paul was taken to Rome, where he was under house arrest for three years. He was martyred by the emperor Nero either in AD 64 or 67.

- Paul is indisputably credited with authoring at least seven letters that bear his name: 1 Thessalonians, Galatians, Philippians, 1 and 2 Corinthians, Romans, and Philemon. Typically, these letters have a common format of an opening formula, a thanksgiving, the body with a doctrinal section and words of encouragement for Christian living, and a final salutation.

- Most contemporary scholars list 2 Thessalonians, Colossians, Ephesians, Titus, and 1 and 2 Timothy as Deuteropauline writings. These letters differ in vocabulary, style, theological themes, content, and historical context from the letters indisputably written by St. Paul. They were penned by his secretaries, disciples, or admirers to apply his legacy to later situations that developed in Pauline churches. Writing pseudonymously was an accepted practice in the ancient world.

- Major themes of Pauline Epistles include salvation is a free gift of God that comes through faith in Jesus Christ and his cross and Resurrection; Christians participate in Christ's Resurrection; Christians belong to the Body of Christ—the Church—of which Jesus Christ is the head; the Holy Spirit is the life of the Church, who enables us to call God "Abba"; Christians must love in imitation of Christ and be willing to suffer for him.

- The First Letter to the Thessalonians (AD 50–51) is the first letter written by St. Paul and the earliest New Testament writing. It advises its readers to live holy lives and always be ready for the day of the Lord's return.

- The Letter to the Galatians (AD 54–55) deals with Judaizers who taught that Gentiles must submit to the Torah before becoming Christians.

- Philippians (AD 56) is a joyful letter that teaches the necessity of unity in Christ. It quotes the great self-emptying hymn of Christ's humility.

- The First Letter to the Corinthians (AD 56 or 57) teaches that we should rely on Christ alone, live an ethical life in the area of sexual morality, and worship in unity. The letter also teaches that love is the greatest spiritual gift given by the Holy Spirit and eloquently defends the Resurrection of Christ as the heart of the Gospel.

- The Second Letter to the Corinthians (AD 57) fosters reconciliation in a divisive church. Paul defends his ministry against false prophets and encourages his recipients to be generous in a collection to be taken up for Christians in Jerusalem.

- The Letter to the Romans (AD 57–58) is Paul's deepest theological letter. Written as a letter of introduction, Romans treats important Pauline themes like sin as a universal condition; our need to imitate the faith of Abraham; and faith in the Gospel of Jesus Christ as the hope of salvation for Jew and Gentile alike.

- The Second Letter to the Thessalonians (AD 90s if not written by Paul) was probably written by a disciple of Paul. It assures its readers that the day of the Lord has not come yet. In the meantime, people should not be idle but rather persist in doing right.

- The Letter to the Colossians (AD 80 if a pseudonymous writing) teaches how Christ is the preeminent spiritual being, the only source of our salvation.

- The Letter to the Ephesians (AD 90s if written by an admirer of Paul) is more an essay than a letter. It presents a developed theology of the Church as the Body of Christ with Jesus as its head.

- The first and second letters to Timothy and the Letter to Titus (AD 95–100) are the "pastoral letters." They were written for shepherds (pastors) of the Church and contain directions for good order in the Church, qualifications for Church leaders, warnings against false teachers, and instructions for good Christian behavior which will attract others to Christ.

• The Letter to Philemon (AD 55) was written from prison. It was intended to encourage Philemon to accept back his runaway slave as a brother.

LEARN BY DOING

1. After examining the following websites, create a PowerPoint® presentation of an illustrated travelogue of one of Paul's journeys.

    The Journeys of St. Paul: www.luthersem.edu/ckoester/Paul/Main.htm
    Footsteps of Paul: www.abrock.com/Greece-Turkey/FootstepsIntro.html
    Paul's Missionary Journeys: http://unbound.biola.edu/acts/index.cfm.

2. Read Galatians 3:1–29. Imitate St. Paul's fiery style by writing a letter to a group of your peers who have stopped practicing the faith. Use strong language to persuade them to renew their religious practice.

3. Philippians 2:1–11 is understood to be an early Christian hymn. Research contemporary Christian music. Pick out a favorite song, duplicate its lyrics, and write a short reflection on the Christian themes or virtues the song highlights.

4. Create a PowerPoint® prayer meditation to illustrate St. Paul's great passage on love as found in 1 Corinthians 13.

5. Prepare a short report on the Catholic Charismatic Renewal and the spiritual gifts associated with it. As background, read 1 Corinthians 14. This chapter refers to the gift of speaking in tongues (*glossolalia*), a gift that manifested itself in the early Church. This phenomenon is sometimes associated with the Catholic Charismatic Movement or Renewal, which emerged after the Second Vatican Council. See these websites for more information:

    www.holyspiritinteractive.net/features/charismaticrenewal/
    www.nsc-chariscenter.org/aboutccr.htm.

6. Learn about a foreign mission, perhaps one connected with your local diocese. Contact a person on the mission team. Write a letter asking how you and your classmates can help in the missionary activity of the Church.

7. Report on three of St. Paul's associates during his ministry. Check the following link for background information: http://catholic-resources.org/Bible/Pauline_Associates.htm.

8. Construct a one-page biography of St. Paul based on his own writings: www.paulonpaul.org.

9. Read 1 Timothy 3:1–13. In light of this reading, do one of the following: (1)Write a short report on the history of how clerical celibacy became the law for bishops and priests in the Western Church. (2) Visit the website of your diocese to research the biography of the bishop of your diocese. Prepare a short biographical sketch. (3) Interview a married permanent deacon to get his views on the qualities a deacon needs today to be an effective minister of the Gospel.

10. 1 and 2 Thessalonians deal with the Second Coming of Christ, also known as the Parousia. Prepare a short report on what the Church teaches about this future event.

11. Read Ephesians 2:11–22. Answer the following: What has Christ broken down? How? What image of the Church does the author give us in verses 19–22?
    Read Ephesians 5:21–6:24. Answer the following: How are husbands to love their wives? What is the reward for children who obey their parents? What image is used in verses 10–17 for Christians to fight the wiles of the evil ones?

PRAYER LESSON

The Pauline letters contain several prayers and blessings, including the one that follows. Prayerfully read the following passage:

> For this reason I kneel before the Father, from whom every family in heaven and on earth is named, that he may grant you in accord with the riches of his glory to be strengthened with power through his Spirit in the inner self, and that Christ may dwell in your hearts through faith; that you, rooted and grounded in love, may have strength to comprehend with all the holy ones what is the breadth and length and height and depth, and to know the love of Christ that surpasses knowledge, so that you may be filled with all the fullness of God. Now to him who is able to accomplish far more than all we ask or imagine, by the power at work within us, to him be glory in the church and in Christ Jesus to all generations, forever and ever. Amen. (Eph 3:14–21)

- *Reflection:* In your journal, list five ways God has shown "the breadth and length and height and depth" of his love for you.

- *Resolution:* Ask the Lord in prayer for an increase in the virtues of faith and love.

The Early Church:
Jesus, True God and True Man

CHAPTER NINE

Be doers of the word and not hearers only, deluding yourselves. For if anyone is a hearer of the word and not a doer, he is like a man who looks at his own face in a mirror. He sees himself, then goes off and promptly forgets what he looked like. But the one who peers into the perfect law of freedom and perseveres, and is not a hearer who forgets but a doer who acts, such a one shall be blessed in what he does.

–James 1:22–25

CHAPTER **OVERVIEW**

HIDDEN **TREASURE**

The Bible opens up the treasure that is God's Word for all who read and pray with it.

THE LETTER TO **THE HEBREWS**

The origins and theme of Hebrews—a homily that develops the theme of Christ as High Priest—is explored.

THE CATHOLIC **EPISTLES**

Christological issues are addressed in the section on the Catholic Epistles—James, 1 and 2 Peter, Jude, and 1, 2, and 3 John.

THE REVELATION **TO JOHN**

The final book of the Bible is one of the most difficult to understand. This section uncovers the meaning of Revelation and what the inspired text says about the identity of Jesus.

CHRISTOLOGY OF **THE EARLY CHURCH**

The titles the Church used for Jesus reveal much about his identity. Likewise, the Church's responses to heresies about Jesus helped to develop the expression and understanding of Jesus as True God and True Man.

Hidden **Treasure**

A true story tells how, toward the end of his life, an old man was leafing through an old family Bible. Decades earlier, his aunt died and willed it to him. Her will read, in part, "I bequeath my family Bible and all it contains . . . to my beloved nephew."

Because he was so poor, the man was rather bitter about this gift from his relative at the time of her death. He lived a life barely making ends meet. Toward the end of his life when he was about to move to his son's home, he cleaned out his attic. There tucked away in an old trunk was the family Bible he inherited. He opened it and to his amazement found banknotes totaling thousands of dollars tucked in its pages. Had he bothered to open his Bible years ago, he would have found within his grasp riches that could have helped him immensely.

The lesson of this true story is simple: We are all the poorer if we do not open and read God's Word. Who knows what treasures lie buried within its pages?

YOUR KNOWLEDGE ABOUT JESUS

This chapter will summarize some of the Church's major dogmatic statements about Jesus that developed in the early Church. (A *dogma* is a central doctrine or teaching of the Church taught with the highest authority and solemnity by the pope and bishops.) Test what you know about Jesus by answering these questions true or false.

1. There was a time when Jesus was not God.
2. As light is identical to the light from which it comes, Jesus Christ is true God.
3. The Father made the Son.
4. The Son of God shared in the creation of the world.
5. There are two "Persons" in Christ.
6. It is wrong to call Mary "the Mother of God."
7. Christ has two natures.
8. Jesus' divine nature swallows up his human nature.
9. Jesus shows us God in a human way.
10. Because he was God, Jesus did not have a human intellect.

Suffice to say that more information regarding these issues will be covered in this chapter.

FOR REFLECTION

Share the origins of a family Bible and why it is so treasured in your family.

The Letter to **the Hebrews** (AD 60s or 80s)

Though this letter shows it is associated with Paul because of a reference to Timothy (13:23), St. Paul did not write the Letter to the Hebrews. The vocabulary, style, thought development, use of the Old Testament, and theological themes differ from genuine Pauline letters. The author is anonymous. Hebrews is a written homily brilliantly developing the theme of Christ as high priest, the model of our faith. The function of a priest is to offer sacrifices. Jesus willingly offered the sacrifice of his life for us and for our sins. He is the high priest who not only offered the sacrifice on our behalf, but is also himself the sacrifice.

Hebrews was written for a local church who came to believe in Christ, had suffered in the past for their faith, but were now living at a time when their faith was becoming lifeless. This profile fits Christians in Rome in the period after their persecution under Nero in the 60s but before another wave of persecution took place under the Emperor Domitian in the 90s. The Letter to the Hebrews tries to encourage these listless Christians to persevere in their faith by pointing to Jesus Christ, the one who was tempted and suffered, yet remained faithful. Christ is the high priest, superior to the angels, greater than Moses.

Like us in everything but sin (4:15), Jesus learned obedience, though he was God's Son. Comparing Jesus' sacrifice to that of the high priest on the Day of Atonement, the Letter to the Hebrews explains how Jesus offered himself in a supreme sacrifice, one that instituted the New Covenant promised by Jeremiah. Hebrews also images the Christian vocation as a pilgrimage. Jesus is the guide who has sacrificed everything in order that we might achieve our heavenly destiny. To do so, we, too, imitate his obedience and his suffering.

> **TEACHING ON JESUS CHRIST IN HEBREWS:** Jesus is the supreme high priest who obediently suffered for us and offered the sacrifice of his Death on a cross for our sins. He is in Heaven. "So let us confidently approach the throne of grace to receive mercy and to find grace for timely help" (4:16).

READING THE LETTER TO THE HEBREWS

Focus on reading the following three passages from the Letter to the Hebrews while completing the accompanying assignments:

- Transcribe Hebrews 4:12 into your journal. Give an example of how this verse is true.

- In your journal, transcribe the description of faith from Hebrews 11:1. Also, write your own definition of faith.

- Hebrews 13 gives many instructions on Christian living, including the practice of Christian hospitality: "Do not neglect hospitality, for through it some have unknowingly entertained angels." The reference here is to the account in Genesis 18:1–8 where Abraham and Sarah welcomed strangers into their home. Read the entire chapter. Then brainstorm a list of ways you can practice the virtue of hospitality, both individually and with a group.

FOR REVIEW

1. Who wrote the Letter to the Hebrews?

2. What is the main theme of the Letter to the Hebrews?

FOR REFLECTION

A priest is a mediator between God and humans. From the Letter to the Hebrews, list one significant way Jesus is different from all other priests.

The Catholic **Epistles**

Seven New Testament documents—James; 1 and 2 Peter; 1, 2, and 3 John; and Jude—are categorized by the name Catholic Epistles. *Catholic* means "universal." The letters are called catholic for three reasons. First, they contain general advice that is helpful to all the churches. Second, they were accepted, even if only gradually, by all the Eastern and Western churches. And third, these letters help us understand better how the catholic, that is, universal or worldwide, Church developed.

Like the secondary Pauline letters, the catholic letters were written by pseudonymous writers, presenting what the named Apostle might well have said in dealing with the situations that developed in the various churches at the end of the first century.

James (most likely AD *80s or 90s)*

This letter bears the name of "the brother of the Lord," that is, the pillar of the Jerusalem church who was martyred in AD 62. However, the actual author is unknown. The letter is written in polished Greek and addressed to Jewish Christians outside of the Holy Land. Writing in the tradition of Old Testament wisdom literature, James resembles a sermon more than a letter. It gives much practical, Christ-inspired advice and encouragement on themes of Christian living, for example, how to handle temptation, how to control the tongue, love of neighbor, the power of prayer, and the anointing of the sick.

The Church has drawn on the letter for its social teaching. One of the letter's key themes is God's preferential love for the poor (2:5) and the need for rich people to care for the poor. As the letter states, the measure of true religion is "to care for orphans and widows in their affliction and to keep oneself unstained by the world" (2:17).

This quotation highlights another important theme, namely, the requirement of good works in addition to faith. The author of James probably emphasized this point because some Christians may have misunderstood St. Paul's teaching about the necessity of faith in Jesus alone—and not performing the works of the Old Law—as the way to share in Christ's Paschal Mystery. Paul himself, however, taught that faith must express itself in good works, the "fruits of the Spirit" (Gal 5:22–23).

READING THE LETTER OF JAMES

Focus on reading the following passages from the Letter of James while completing the accompanying assignments:

- Read James 1:26 and James 3. In light of what the author says about the power of speech and the use of the tongue in these verses, reflect on the following questions in your journal:
  1. Name three items to which the author compares the tongue.
  2. Write of a time when your speech got you into trouble.
  3. In the recent past, who has been on the receiving end of your hurtful words or gossip?
- Write a resolution to rectify any harm you might have caused with your speech in the past month or so, perhaps by verbalizing an apology to a person or paying a compliment to someone you may have slighted. Then follow through.

Reflection: Do your words reveal who you are or do they hide the true you? Are your words bitter or uplifting?

1 Peter (AD 70–90, or AD 60–63 if written by Peter)

Today's scholarship classifies the First Letter of Peter as pseudonymous, written by a disciple of Peter in Rome to some communities in northern Asia Minor, perhaps sometime between AD 70 and 90. The purpose of the letter is to bolster the spirit of Gentile Christian converts to bear witness to Christ in a largely pagan world that does not understand Christ and his Gospel.

The letter resembles a sermon, exhorting its readers to remain firm in their faith. It points to Jesus as the Suffering Servant, the model in whose footsteps the suffering should walk (2:21). The First Letter of Peter also gives the New Testament's clearest teaching on suffering, especially the suffering of innocents. It teaches that Christians should not return evil for evil; rather they should return abuse with blessing. Christians should keep doing good despite the attacks of others; their good example will eventually help people recognize the truth and put detractors to shame. Finally, Christians should look on their sufferings as a test of their faith and see them as a share in Christ's own sufferings.

The First Letter of Peter also includes many references to baptism, reinforcing the belief that it was written for new converts. The themes of the dignity of the Christian vocation and suffering for Christ are also brought out in this quote:

> But rejoice to the extent that you share in the sufferings of Christ, so that when his glory is revealed you may also rejoice exultantly. If you are insulted for the name of Christ, blessed are you, for the Spirit of glory and of God rests upon you. (4:13–14)

TEACHING ON JESUS CHRIST **IN 1 PETER:**

Christ is the Suffering Servant who gave his life for us. We should join his Paschal Mystery by suffering for his sake, thus witnessing to the Gospel.

READING THE FIRST LETTER OF PETER

Focus on reading the following passages from the Letter of Peter while completing the accompanying assignments:

- Read 1 Peter 3:8–18. What advice is given on suffering? How do we suffer today "for bearing Christ's name"?

- Read 1 Peter 4:8. Discuss some specific examples of what this passage might mean.

Jude (AD 90–100) and 2 Peter (ca. AD 130)

These two letters—Jude and the Second Letter of Peter—are treated together because 2 Peter borrows heavily from Jude 1:4–16.

Jude is another pseudonymous work. A good hypothesis is that Jude was likely written from Palestine to Christians influenced by false teachers who have led some to errors of faith. The Letter of Jude denounces certain outsiders who have come into the Church. They are upsetting faithful Christians by deviating from apostolic faith and engaging in various acts of immorality, probably sexual in nature. Jude is a hard-hitting letter

Parousia—The Second Coming of Christ, which will usher in the full establishment of God's Kingdom on earth as it is in Heaven.

warning these outsiders that they will be punished severely, just as certain Old Testament figures received punishment for their infidelities. Jude shows why remaining true to the faith of the Apostles is important so as to have an objective standard for Christian faith and Christian living, both of which go hand-in-hand. The verses most representative of Jude's major theme also refer to the Blessed Trinity:

> But you, beloved, build yourselves up in your most holy faith; pray in the holy Spirit. Keep yourselves in the love of God and wait for the mercy of our Lord Jesus Christ that leads to eternal life. (1:20-21)

The Second Letter of Peter is also a pseudonymous work, penned to a general audience, perhaps from Rome to Christians in Asia Minor. Since it incorporates almost all of Jude, most scholars believe that the Second Letter of Peter is the last New Testament work written, dated as late as AD 130. Like Jude, the Second Letter of Peter also concerns Christians who were beginning to distort the true teaching that they received. The author—writing as Peter—tells how he heard God's voice

Transfiguration of **Jesus**

at Jesus' Transfiguration. Thus, he speaks with authority against the false prophets infiltrating the communities to which the letter is addressed. He assures his readers that God will punish these false teachers.

The major theological contribution of the Second Letter of Peter concerns Christ's Second Coming (the **Parousia**). Written approximately 80 to 100 years after Jesus' public life, the letter had to deal with some teachers who were denying that Christ would ever come back again. This led to some of them falling back into old habits of an immoral lifestyle, forgetting that Christ will eventually judge us for our deeds.

Despite the scoffing at the idea of Christ's return, the Second Letter of Peter proclaims that the Lord keeps his word and that he will indeed come again. The apparent delay is merely from our perspective: "With the Lord one day is like a thousand years" (3:8). Christ is giving people time to repent of their sins, but rest assured, "The day of the Lord will come like a thief" (3:10). We should always be ready for his return.

The Second Letter of Peter reveals that toward the end of the New Testament period, Christian faith in Jesus included a set of dogmas or formal beliefs about him. These dogmas needed to be defended and explained by authoritative teachers who were in a line of apostolic authority that went back to the eyewitnesses who knew Jesus. The author of the Second Letter of Peter was one such teacher. He appealed to the authority of St. Peter to correct other Christian teachers who were distorting traditional beliefs about Jesus, most notably in their denying that Christ would return again.

This letter encourages its readers to remain faithful to true teaching and continue to live the Christian life.

READING THE LETTER OF JUDE AND THE SECOND LETTER OF PETER

Focus on reading the following passages from the Letter of Jude and the Second Letter of Peter while completing the accompanying assignments:

- Read the entire Letter of Jude. Note how the letter points to the following themes: (1) being careful of false teachers who seek to destroy the faith and (2) perseverance in leading a Christian life.

- Read 2 Peter 3:1–18. Answer these questions in your journal: How does the author explain the apparent delay of the Lord? How should we live until the day the Lord comes?

1, 2, 3 John (all around AD 100)

The similarity in style and teaching in these three letters reveals an intimate connection to John's Gospel. All letters were written sometime after the Gospel of John, perhaps in the late 90s or around the year 100.

Both the Second Letter of John and the Third Letter of John identify the author as "the Elder," that is, a disciple in the community that produced the writings associated with the Gospel. Each of these letters is very short. The Second Letter of John is addressed to "the Lady," that is, to a particular local church. It reminds Christians there to love one another and warns against anyone who denies the doctrine of the Incarnation, calling such a person the Antichrist.

The Third Letter of John is addressed to Gaius, a faithful disciple of John the Elder. The letter condemns a certain Diotrephes who was challenging the teaching authority of John the Elder and refusing to receive his emissaries. Both the second and third letters of John reveal that the author had considerable influence in certain local churches. They also show that the early Church had its problems to work out, just as our current Church does.

The most important of the three letters is the First Letter of John. A circular letter in the form of a treatise, it was written to bolster the Johannine Church threatened by a schism (split) caused by false teachers. The opening mirrors the prologue of John's Gospel:

> What was from the beginning,
> what we have heard,
> what we have seen with our eyes,
> what we looked upon,
> and touched with our own hands
> concerns the Word of life. (1 Jn 1:1)

The letter takes up the theme of Jesus—who he truly is and what he requires of us. The focus on Jesus' identity arose because some teachers in the Church were denying the true humanity of Jesus, claiming that he never took on human flesh. They taught that Jesus only "seemed" to be man. The heresy in question was an early form of *Docetism* (from the Greek word *dokein*, meaning "to seem"). Those teaching it boasted of special knowledge (in the Greek, *gnosis*) about Jesus and the Christian life, knowledge they claimed they received from mystical experiences with Christ. Holding that the physical world was evil, these teachers falsely taught that Jesus was only a spiritual being, a "light-bearer," who came to teach a select few the secrets of eternal life.

Docetists could not imagine how the almighty God—pure Spirit—could become human in the person of his Son, Jesus. Thus, they denied the Incarnation of Jesus Christ. What follows from this false teaching is that Jesus was not really man. Thus, he did not really die for us, nor did he rise from the dead. If

> **TEACHING ON JESUS CHRIST IN 1 JOHN:**
> Jesus Christ is Light, Love, the Son of God, the Messiah, our Savior, true God and true man. He came to us in the flesh.

this were true, then Jesus could not really be the Savior of the world.

The First Letter of John relentlessly attacks these Docetist views throughout the letter. Christians must have true belief in Jesus Christ, the Son of God and Messiah whose blood cleanses us from sin. If we wish to be children of the light, then we must turn from sin and live upright lives:

> This is how you can know the Spirit of God: every spirit that acknowledges Jesus Christ come in the flesh belongs to God, and every spirit that does not acknowledge Jesus does not belong to God. This is the spirit of the antichrist that, as you heard, is to come, but in fact is already in the world. (4:2–3)

Moreover, true belief in Jesus must show forth in concrete acts of love, imitating the love of Christ. Those holding false beliefs considered themselves superior to others. The First Letter of John would have none of that. It emphasized that a person cannot call himself or herself a Christian unless he or she abides in the love of Christ.

READING THE FIRST, SECOND, AND THIRD LETTERS OF JOHN

Read all three of the Letters of John, focusing on how they are similar in style and teaching to the Gospel of John. Focus particularly on 1 John 3:11–4:21. Answer the following questions in your journal:

- How must we love (3:16–18)?
- How do we know that we have the Spirit of God in us (4:1–3)?
- Why should we love (4:7)?
- How do we know that God lives in us (4:12)?

 ## FOR REVIEW

1. What are the seven Catholic Epistles, and how did they get their name?
2. What are the two ways the Letter of James serves as a foundation for the Church's social teaching?
3. Why did the author of the Letter of James emphasize good works in addition to faith?
4. What does the First Letter of Peter say about the role of suffering in the life of Christians?
5. What is the relationship between the Letter of Jude and the Second Letter of Peter?
6. How does the Second Letter of Peter deal with the delayed return of the Lord?
7. According to the Second Letter of John, who is the Antichrist?
8. Identify the term *Docetism*.
9. What does the First Letter of John say about love?

FOR REFLECTION

In speaking of God as light, the author of the First Letter of John writes, "If we say that we have no sin, we deceive ourselves, and the truth is not in us" (1 Jn 1:8). Write a reflection on why this statement is true for all people. Give an example of where it might be true in your own life.

The Revelation **to John** (AD 92–96)

The Revelation to John (also known as the Apocalypse) is the last book of the Bible. Because of its symbolic and highly imaginative language, for many Revelation is the least read and understood book in the New Testament. It is easy to see why. What are we to make of many-headed dragons and beasts, a Christ-figure with seven horns and seven eyes, and trumpets blasting out plagues on humanity to mention just three of its images? An ancient scholar said that studying the book of Revelation either finds us crazy or makes us crazy. St. Jerome commented that it contains as many secrets as it does words.

Some Christians, however, elevate Revelation to a place of supreme importance among all the New Testament books. They believe the book has hidden meaning about God's ultimate plans for us, even down to the very day when our present world will end. Preachers fill the airwaves telling us what to look for as we approach the great cosmic clash which, in their judgment, is just around the corner.

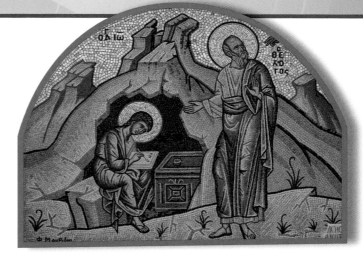

The Context of the Revelation to John

Picture yourself as a Christian living in Ephesus, the capital of the Roman province of Asia Minor and one of the early centers of Christianity. The year is AD 95 and the reigning emperor is Domitian (AD 81–96). His father, Vespasian (emperor from 69–79), had waged war against the Jews during the Great Revolt; his brother, Titus (emperor from 79–81), had overseen the leveling of Jerusalem. In order to bring about unity in his vast Empire, Domitian had himself proclaimed god, hoping that the cult of emperor worship would bring unity to the various peoples living in the province.

Domitian took for himself the title *Dominus et Deus Noster*—"Our Lord and Our God." Domitian ordered all Romans who were not exempt by ancient law to burn incense before his statue, thus proclaiming his divinity. Worship of the emperor and state was to be part of one's civic duty. Penalties for not doing so involved the prohibition of being able to carry on commerce within the empire and even death, depending on the local governors and how strongly they tried to enforce the cult.

If you were a faithful Christian at that time, you would never worship a false god like the emperor. To do so would be to deny your faith in the unique divinity of God's own Son, Jesus Christ. Thus, many lost their livelihood and even their lives witnessing (*martyr* means "witness") to Jesus Christ and by refusing to participate in the civic cult. They were believers first and citizens second. However, with the threat of death, some other Christians gave up their faith, and many others were wavering in their faith.

The author of Revelation, a prophet named John, knew firsthand the danger of being a Christian under Domitian. He was exiled to the island of Patmos because he publicly preached the Gospel. The author was probably an Aramaic-speaking Jewish Christian who had a great command of Old Testament writings, especially apocalyptic writings. He alludes to Old Testament writings between two hundred and five hundred times, most notably to the books of Daniel, Ezekiel, Isaiah, and Zechariah. His Greek is the poorest in the New Testament and, at times, ungrammatical. One theory claims John of Patmos left Palestine at the time of the Jewish Revolt in the late 60s and may have settled in Ephesus. His contact with the Ephesus Church may have given him some familiarity with the Gospel of John and the Johannine writings.

Major Themes in the Revelation to John

The Revelation to John is a "revelation," or "apocalypse" in the Greek, literally an "unveiling" of the risen Lord Jesus Christ. The prophet John claims that the Lord Jesus sent him visions to unveil what is going to take place in the future—the ultimate victory of God. This unveiling allows us to see things from the heavenly perspective. This message was to be read aloud, most probably in the Sunday liturgies, to reassure those who were suffering that the Lamb of God has triumphed! Victory is ours! Persevere: "I am coming soon" (22:20). The first verses of the book introduce this theme:

> The revelation of Jesus Christ, which God gave to him, to show his servants what must happen soon. He made it known by sending his angel to his servant John, who gives witness to the word of God and to the testimony of Jesus Christ by reporting what he saw. Blessed is the one who reads aloud and blessed are those who listen to this prophetic message and heed what is written in it, for the appointed time is near. (1:1–3)

John of Patmos wrote the book of Revelation to wavering Christians to encourage them to *remain faithful* during these times of persecution, false teaching, and complacency. Revelation's second theme for Christians is to *remain hopeful*: Christ will ultimately vanquish the powers of this world that are persecuting Christians. He has already rescued us from sin and death by his Death and Resurrection. In the coming battle he will conquer for all time the forces of evil: the unholy trinity of Satan (the dragon) and his two minions—the beast of the sea (the emperor) and the beast of the land (the local authority). Rome will fall. Satan will be sent to hell for all time. And the heavenly city, Jerusalem, will be established for eternity.

Apocalyptic Literature

The book of Revelation contains several types of biblical literature. It has dramatic elements where groups and individuals speak in direct dialogue. It also has the qualities of an Epistle or letter. In fact, chapters 2 and 3 contain letters written to seven churches. (The number seven is symbolic of perfection—the sum of three, which represents Heaven, and four, which represents earth. When writing to "seven" churches, the author is actually writing to the universal Church.) In addition, the opening verses tell us right off that the book has many prophetic elements. But overriding all of these writing styles is the dominant literary form of *apocalypse*.

What is apocalyptic writing? Apocalyptic writing was very popular in Jewish circles around 200 BC to AD 200. The book of Daniel (especially Daniel 7–12) is an excellent example of apocalyptic writing from the Old Testament. The book of Revelation borrows heavily from it and other Jewish apocalyptic literature.

Apocalyptic writing has many common elements: visions given to a human being, usually by a heavenly being who takes him to a heavenly vantage point; symbolic words, images, and numbers; and pessimism about a world in the grip of the devil, but optimism about God's final triumph. Apocalypses were written in times of crisis to bolster the faith of believers and to help give them hope about the future, a time when God will establish his heavenly Kingdom on earth.

The basic message of apocalyptic writing is that God controls history and the outcome of events, not

the present evil rulers or the forces of evil. God will usher in a New Age, a golden age of peace and justice. The glorious outcome is God's pure gift; nothing we do can bring it about. In the meantime, we should patiently endure the sufferings and live a Christian life.

The theme of apocalyptic literature, therefore, was pretty simple to understand: faithfully endure present difficulties until the Lord comes in his glory. The symbolism is what increases the confusion. We must assume that Revelation's original audience knew the meaning of most of the references, many of which came from the Old Testament books of Ezekiel and Daniel. With a little study, we can also figure out many of the symbols. A plausible reason the prophet disguised his message in symbols was so he could write about his enemies without them knowing it. In this time of persecution everything connected with Christianity was suspect. John of Patmos prudently referred to Rome and the evil emperors symbolically in case the book would fall into their hands. For example, he called Rome by the name of Babylon, Israel's ancient oppressor.

Understanding the Symbols in the Revelation to John

Revelation includes several symbols, including numbers and colors. Careful study has revealed their meaning. For example, as mentioned previously, the number seven refers to wholeness or perfection. John sends out seven letters to certain churches in Asia Minor, churches that he both praises and criticizes. After a glorious vision of God's heavenly throne, Christ the Lamb opens seven seals and angels blow on seven trumpets and pour out seven bowls of wrath. These three sets of seven detail punishments that will be meted out to those who rebel against God with the intention of getting them to repent.

The number six, one short of seven, is associated with imperfection. The number 666 is ultimate imperfection, incompleteness, meaninglessness. This was the symbol of the beast, the emperor. Many scholars calculate that it corresponds to the emperor Nero, the terrible persecutor of Christians in the 60s. They calculate that when the name Nero(n) Caesar is written in Hebrew letters, its numerical equivalent is 666. The formula goes like this: NRWN QSR = 50+200+6+50+100+60+200 = 666.

The number 12 signifies Israel, the twelve Apostles, or God's people today—the Church. The number 1000 symbolizes an incalculable amount or eternity. Also, 12 x 12 x 1000 equals 144,000, a symbol of the new Israel that embraces every nation, race, people, and language. (Contrary to some so-called Christian sects who claim otherwise, the number 144,000 represents all God's people and not just a certain number.)

Of the symbolic colors, black represents suffering; red means war, violence, killing, and the blood of martyrs; white symbolizes victory; pallor stands for death and decay; and purple represents royalty.

Finally, there are several other symbols in the Revelation to John:

- *Babylon*, an ancient city that persecuted the Jews, stands for the modern persecutor of the Christians, Rome. She is a *harlot* (prostitute), and anyone who worships the emperor is a *fornicator* or adulterer. Nero and Domitian, both of whom persecuted Christians, are *beasts*. Satan, the *dragon*, is their master.
- A *dragon* is the personification of evil, Satan. Defeated in heaven, he wreaks havoc on earth. But Christ the Lamb will defeat him here, as well.
- The *four horses* of the Apocalypse are symbolic in this way: the white horse symbolizes conquering power; the red horse signifies bloody war; the black horse means famine; and the green horse represents death.
- A *horn* symbolizes power, while *eyes* symbolize knowledge. Describing Jesus as having seven eyes and seven horns is a symbolic way of saying he is all-powerful and all-knowing.

Jesus' Identity in the Revelation to John

In Revelation, Jesus is the risen Lord exalted by God the Father in eternal glory. Jesus is God, the Alpha, the First Letter of the Greek alphabet, and the Omega, the last letter of the Greek alphabet (1:8; 22:13). He is the beginning and the end. Jesus is also *Pantokrator* ("Ruler of All"), a title used nine times in Revelation to highlight him as a majestic, powerful ruler. He is also described as the Root of David, the Lion of Judah, that is, the Messiah, the Christ. Paradoxically, and most importantly, the Lion is also the Lamb of God whose suffering, Death, Resurrection, and Glorification have won eternal life for the saints. He has conquered death, sin, and Satan. (The bride of the Slain Lamb is the Church.) Jesus is the Victor, the Word of God (19:13), the King of kings and Lord of lords (19:16). He will come again. He is the judge of the living and the dead, punishing the wicked and rewarding the faithful. He alone is the one we should worship.

Interpreting Revelation Today

What do the symbols and messages of the book of Revelation tell us today? For example, does knowledge of their meaning give us the ability to know when the world is going to end? The Catholic position on these questions is that the author of the book of Revelation wrote the way he did primarily to encourage the people living in his time. Our first task is to try to understand what the author was trying to say to them.

Yet, the basic message of Revelation has universal application. In our own day, we need hopeful reminders of the Lord's control of history, that good will triumph over evil. This is even more necessary in a world where terrorism is a threat to our basic freedoms and sense of security. In addition, we also need encouragement to remain faithful to Jesus in times of crisis, temptation, and suffering. We also must put our trust in, and worship exclusively, the one true God and not the gods of power, possessions, prestige, and prettiness—all sold to us by our secular society as the keys to happiness.

Revelation was not written so we can look to the latest earthquake, dictator, war, or terrorist attack as the definitive sign of Christ's Second Coming. People who speculate too much on the exact time of the world's end are ignoring Jesus' teaching (Mk 13:32) to leave the timing of the end of the world in God's hands. We should worry more about living each day in a committed, loving, serving way. No one knows when the exact end is coming; anyone who claims he or she does is a fraud. In the words of Fr. Raymond Brown, "The author of Revelation did not know how or when the world will end, and neither does anyone else."[14]

Christians look to the future with hope. But we also believe we can meet the Lord in the Eucharist, in the Scripture, in the depths of our own hearts, and in all the people he sends into our lives, including, in a special way, the suffering and outcast. When we pray, "Come, Lord Jesus" (Rev 22:20), we also know that he is already here.

READING THE REVELATION TO JOHN

Perhaps the best way to read The Revelation to John is to do so straight through without worrying about the meaning of specific verses or images. Try to get a feeling for what is being described. Don't worry about understanding everything. Many brilliant scholars still have not figured it out, even after many years of study.

In fact, scholars even disagree on an outline for Revelation. Some think the letters in chapters 2 and 3 were tacked on when the basic apocalypse was written. Others think the main body of the work—chapters 4–22—reflects one or two editings by the author because there are many parallel passages and repetitions. The following outline is generally accepted, and it reflects the symbolic number seven as an organizing principle of the work:

1. Prologue (1:1–3).

2. Letters to the churches in Asia (1:4–3:22).
In a voice sounding like a trumpet, the Alpha and Omega (the risen Lord) instructed the prophet John to write on a scroll what he witnessed and send it to the various churches. The theme of the letters is encouragement to remain faithful in the midst of persecution. Seven represents the universal Church. Most of the letters have the same format: a description of the risen Christ; blame and/or praise for the Church; a threat and/or warning; encouragement; and a promise.

3. John's vision of God (4:1–5:14).
John's second vision transports him to Heaven where he has a profound and beautiful vision of God. Around God's throne are four creatures that represent the noblest (lion), strongest (bull), wisest (human), and swiftest (eagle) creatures in creation. There are twenty-four smaller thrones on which sit the elders. God holds a papyrus with seven seals. Only Christ can open it.

4. Visions of the day of the Lord (chapters 6–16).
Borrowing heavily from the story of the plagues in Exodus, these chapters of Revelation show how God deals with evil that opposes good. But his judgment is a prelude to the new creation, when evil will be no more. These chapters are organized around:

- Seven seals (chapters 6–7): disasters
- Seven trumpets (chapters 8–11): terror
- Serpent (chapters 12–14): Satan's beasts war on the earth

- Seven bowls (chapters 15–16): plagues

5. The Destruction of Babylon and the Defeat of Pagan Nations (17–20).
These chapters read like an adventure story, but on a cosmic scale. Revelation assures its readers that the Roman Empire that is persecuting Christians will fall. The Word of God on a white horse will bring about Rome's end. The heavens will rejoice at the establishment of God's reign. The just are raised from the dead and will rule with Christ for a thousand years, after which time Satan will lead the forces of Gog and Magog (pagan nations) against the Christians. But this time, Satan will meet lasting defeat as Heaven will cast him into the eternal fires. All people will receive judgment according to their deeds; those whose names are not found in the book of life will be "hurled into the burning lake" (20:15).

6. New Jerusalem (chapters 21–22).
These last chapters describe the heavenly city that awaits all Christians who endure suffering in this life by worshiping the one true God. Their constant prayer, "Come, Lord Jesus," is answered now and will be answered always.

After you have finished reading The Revelation to John all the way through in one sitting, go back and reread the following passages and complete the assignments that follow:

1) Read Revelation 1–3. Answer the following questions: (1) Describe the risen Lord, described in 1:12–16. Using the footnotes in your Bible or a commentary, interpret the meaning of the various symbols connected with Christ's appearance. (2) Using the fourfold division of the seven letters, outline the contents of one letter.

2) Read Revelation 4–5. Complete the following: (1) Who might the twenty-four elders represent? (2) Since the second century, the four creatures in Revelation 4 have been used as symbols of the four Evangelists. Match each creature with the correct Gospel. (3) List two titles given to Christ in chapter 5. Discuss the significance of these titles.

3) Read Revelation 12:1–13:18. Complete the following: (1) One interpretation of the woman is that she represents Israel, God's people. Explain how this might be the case. (2) Another traditional interpretation is that the woman symbolizes Mary, the Mother of both Jesus and the Church. Explain how this might be so. (3) Who is the person in 12:17? Who is the offspring of the woman? (4) What does the reign of forty-two months signify (13:5)? (5) Many people thought Nero would come back to life to terrorize his subjects. At the time of Revelation's composition, who might the 666 (13:18) refer to?

4) Read Revelation 21–22. Complete the following: (1) Why is there no need for a Temple in the new city? (2) What is your own image of heaven? Compare it to Revelation's poetic image.

FOR REVIEW

1. Why shouldn't we look to The Revelation to John for answers about the end of the world?

2. Who wrote Revelation and why? Why does the book contain so much symbolism?

3. What is apocalyptic writing? What purpose does it serve?

4. What is the theme of The Revelation to John? What are some of its views of Jesus?

5. Discuss the meaning of any five symbols in Revelation. Identify the meaning of 666.

FOR REFLECTION

When you pray the words "Come, Lord Jesus" what images come to mind?

Christology of the **Early Church** (CCC, 465–467)

Christology deals with who the person of Jesus Christ is. The New Testament demonstrates time and again, through many and various titles, exactly who Jesus is. He is the:

Christ, the Messiah	unique Son of God
Lord	Savior of humanity
Son of Man	Suffering Servant
Word of God (*Logos*)	Resurrection
Bread of Life	Living Water
Way, Truth, and Life	Almighty
Lamb of God	Judge
Good Shepherd	Vine
Light of the World	

All these titles reveal something profound about the identity of this unique person Jesus Christ. But, even in New Testament times, some people questioning these beliefs. For example, the Docetists could not accept both the divinity and the humanity of Christ. They held that God could not become truly man and yet remain God. So they taught that Jesus only *appeared* to be man. This view was firmly condemned by John the Elder, the author of 1 John. A prominent early Church writer, St. Ignatius of Antioch (d. AD 111), also wrote vigorously against Docetists. His influence was clearly felt with the addition of the phrase "born of the Virgin Mary" to the Apostles' Creed to safeguard the humanity of Jesus.

As the Church moved into the Gentile world with its Greek philosophy, she met many more questions about Jesus' identity:

- Who was Jesus really?
- Did he always exist?

- Is he equal to the Father?
- If he is God, yet man, how can God be one?
- How can he be both God and man at the same time?

Mistakes were inevitably made while wrestling with the scriptural assertions about Jesus. At times, people would teach something about Jesus that was incompatible with the testimony of the Apostles. They were guilty of *heresy*, that is, false teaching about some major point of Church doctrine.

The Church of the first five centuries or so refined its understanding of Jesus through the writings of the Church Fathers and the teachings of the **ecumenical councils**. *Church Fathers* were a group of bishops, theologians, teachers, and scholars whose writings have greatly contributed to Church doctrine and practice. They lived roughly from the second through the eighth centuries and represented both parts of the Empire— East and West—and are classified by their different eras. The *Apostolic Fathers* personally knew the Apostles or their disciples. Two examples were St. Clement of Rome (d. 101?) and St. Ignatius of Antioch. Church Fathers from the second and third centuries are often known as the **apologists**. Two prominent apologists were St. Justin Martyr (ca. 100–165) and St. Irenaeus (ca. 130–202), the first theologian to arrange Church teachings in a comprehensive order.

In his major work, *Against Heresies*, Irenaeus attacked Gnosticism, which denied the true humanity of Jesus, his Resurrection, the validity of Scriptures, and the authority of the bishops to rule the Church. In his defense of orthodox (true) teaching, Irenaeus affirmed the importance of Christian tradition and the need for Christians to look to bishops for guidance. He taught that because the Roman Church traces herself to Peter, the Christ-appointed leader of the Church, she is the true source of right teaching and belief.

Two other key fathers of this era were Tertullian (ca. 160–230), a North African and the first major Church writer to use Latin, and Origen (ca. 185–254), the prolific author of over six hundred books.

The *Golden Age of the Church Fathers* spanned the fourth and fifth centuries. It produced some of Christianity's most fertile minds. In the East were Sts. Basil, Gregory of Nyssa, and Gregory of Nazianzen. The East also produced the most brilliant orator of the day, St. John Chrysostom, and a vigorous defender of orthodoxy, St. Athanasius.

St. Athanasius (ca. 297–373), bishop of Alexandria in Egypt, engaged in the bitter debates over the serious heresy of *Arianism*, begun by a popular preacher of Alexandria, the priest Arius. Arius could not fathom how God could become man; thus, he taught that Jesus was God's greatest creature, an adopted son, but not God. This dangerous teaching, which denied Christ's divinity, split Christianity down the middle. The emperor Constantine convoked the first worldwide (ecumenical) council at Nicea in AD 325 to counteract Arianism. The council issued the famous Nicene

ecumenical council—A worldwide, official assembly of the bishops under the direction of the pope. There have been twenty-one ecumenical councils, the most recent being the Second Vatican Council (1962–1965).

apologist—A defender of Christianity and the Church who tries to show the reasonableness of the faith.

St. **Athanasius**

theotokos—an important title bestowed on Mary at the Council of Ephesus (431), meaning "God-bearer." This title asserts that Jesus is one divine person and that Mary is truly the "Mother of God."

Fathers of the Church—An honorary title given to outstanding early Church theologians whose teaching has had lasting significance for the Church.

Vulgate—St. Jerome's fifth-century AD Latin translation of the Bible into the common language of the people of his day.

Creed, later confirmed at the Council of Constantinople in 381, which taught that Jesus is of the same substance (*homoousios*) as God. Thus, Jesus is divine.

Arianism should have died at this council, but later emperors tolerated Arians. Thus, the heresy spread, especially in the Eastern Empire, where Arian missionaries converted many of the barbarians. At great personal risk and despite being exiled five times, St. Athanasius valiantly defended the Nicene teaching. He taught, "Christ was made man that we may be made divine." He correctly held that if Christ is not divine, then he could not be our Savior. Only God can restore people to communion with himself. Nicknamed "Father of Orthodoxy," St. Athanasius and his teaching prevailed at the Council of Constantinople.

St. Cyril of Alexandria (d. 376–444) carried on Athanasius's work by defending orthodox Church belief against *Nestorianism*. This heresy began when the patriarch of Constantinople, Nestorius, taught there were two persons in Jesus—one divine, the other only human. Nestorius refused to call Mary the Mother of God, claiming that she only gave birth to the human Jesus. St. Cyril, on the other hand, defended the title **theotokos** as a legitimate way to talk about Mary as truly the Mother of God. He also taught that Jesus was one person, a divine person, the Second Person of the Blessed Trinity. The Council of Ephesus (AD 431) upheld Cyril's view and condemned Nestorianism.

Another heretic, Eutyches, claimed that Jesus' divine nature absorbs his human nature ("like a drop of honey into the water of the sea"). This teaching, known as *Monophysitism* (meaning "one nature"), in effect, denied the true humanity of Jesus. Pope St. Leo the Great (ca. 400–461) combated it in his *Tome*. So did the important Council of Chalcedon (AD 451), which taught this famous faith formula: "Jesus is one divine person with two natures—a divine nature and a human nature." This teaching was reaffirmed at the Third Council of Constantinople (AD 681).

Other prominent **Fathers of the Church** from the West included the following:

- St. Ambrose (340–397), the bishop of Milan, who helped stamp out Arianism in the Western church. His preaching aided in the conversion of St. Augustine.
- St. Jerome (ca. 343–420), who became the secretary of Pope Damasus, who commissioned Jerome to translate the Bible into Latin. Jerome's famous **Vulgate** translation became the authorized Bible that the Catholic Church used until modern times.
- St. Augustine of Hippo (354–430), the most famous of all the Church Fathers. After his conversion, he became a strong defender of the Catholic faith against heresies like

Donatism, Pelagianism, and Manicheism. He also authored some of Christianity's most influential theological works, most notably his *Confessions* and *On the Trinity*, a brilliant theological treatise on the Blessed Trinity still studied today. Another famous work is *The City of God*, which he wrote in the wake of the Visigoth sack of Rome in 410.

Key Dogmatic Teachings about Jesus *(CCC, 464–483)*

The important ecumenical councils that defined the nature of Jesus Christ include Nicea (325), Constantinople I (381), Ephesus (431), Chalcedon (451), Constantinople II (553), and Constantinople III (680–681). The main teachings of these councils about Jesus Christ are stated below.

- *Jesus is the only Son of God.* Although Christ had a natural human mother, Mary, he had no natural *human* father. Jesus' father is the first Person of the Trinity, God the Father. All humans are the adopted children of God; only Jesus is the natural son. Jesus shares in the very nature of God.
- *Jesus Christ is true God.* He was born of the Father and is of one substance with the Father. There was never a time when he was not God.
- *Jesus Christ is true God, God from God, Light from Light.* Like the Father, the Son has a divine nature. The Son proceeding from the Father is of one substance with the Father. Jesus Christ is true God, just as light is identical to the light from which it comes.
- *Jesus is "begotten, not made, one in Being with the Father."* The always-existing Son "proceeds" from the Father—he always proceeded and always will proceed. The Father did not generate the Son the way human fathers generate their sons. Christian faith holds that the Son is not made by the Father because the Son is not a created being. Rather, the Father *begets* the Son, who is one in being with the Father.

  The Council of Nicea distinguished between *begotten* and *created*. The Father begets his Son and creates the world. The Son always existed in relationship to the Father from whom he proceeds. If Jesus is truly the only Son of God, then he

The Holy Trinity by Hendrick van Balen

must always have been so. As John's Gospel so eloquently states:

> In the beginning was the Word [the Son]:
> and the Word was with God
> and the Word was God. (Jn 1:1)

- *All things were made through the Son.* Since the Son is one in being with the Father, he also shares in the creation of the world. "All things came to be through him" (Jn 1:3).
- *There is only one person in Christ, the divine person.* Christ is the Word of God, the second Person of the Blessed Trinity. Thus, everything in Christ's human nature is to be attributed to his divine person, for example, his miracles and even his suffering and Death.
- *Mary, by conceiving God's Son, is truly the Mother of God.* As Jesus was divine from the very moment of his conception, Mary is proclaimed as *Theotokos*, "bearer of God."
- *There are two distinct natures in the one person of Christ.* Jesus has a divine nature and a human nature. He is perfect in divinity and perfect in humanity. Jesus Christ is true God and true man. The union of the human and divine natures in the one person of Jesus is so perfect it is said that in Jesus God truly shared humanity, truly suffered, truly experienced death, and truly rose victorious over death.
- As a true human being, body and soul, *Jesus embodies the divine ways of God in a human way.*

- As true God and man, *Jesus has a human intellect and a human will*. Both are perfectly attuned and subject to his divine intellect and will, which he has in common with the Father and the Holy Spirit.

- *Jesus, God-made-man, is our Savior.* By uniting ourselves to his Death and Resurrection through faith, we will share in the eternal life he has promised.

- *The mission of Jesus Christ and the Holy Spirit are distinct but inseparable.* Whenever the Father sends his Son, he always sends his Spirit.

FOR REVIEW

1. What is Christology? List at least three titles of Jesus that reflect a New Testament Christology.

2. Define *Church Fathers*. List four important Church Fathers who defended orthodox belief in Jesus.

3. What did each of the following heresies teach: Arianism, Nestorianism, and Monophysitism?

4. List and explain four principal teachings of the Church about Jesus Christ.

5. What is the Chalcedon formula?

FOR REFLECTION

Review the statements of the Nicene Creed. Rate how strongly your own beliefs are on these major statements of Christian teaching. Choose two statements. Write one paragraph for each that explains your response.

- I believe in God the Father, Creator of all that is seen and unseen.
- I believe that Jesus Christ is God and man.
- I believe that Jesus died and rose again.
- I believe Jesus is my friend.
- I believe in the power of the Holy Spirit.
- I believe in the Ten Commandments.
- I believe that each person is God's child and my brother or sister.
- I believe that I must love everyone, especially "the least of these" in our midst.
- I believe in the power of the sacraments, especially the Eucharist and Reconciliation.
- I believe that the pope is the successor to Peter, the vicar of Christ.
- I believe in the Trinity, three Persons in one God.
- I believe in the power of prayer.
- I believe that the Lord will judge me at the end of time.
- I believe that I must love God above everything and my neighbor as myself.
- I believe in the Catholic Church.
- I believe that I am destined for an eternal life of glory with the Lord.

CHAPTER SUMMARY POINTS

- The anonymous author of the Letter to the Hebrews, writing perhaps in the 80s, developed the theme of Jesus the high priest, the one who offered himself as the supreme sacrifice on our behalf.

- The letters of James, 1 and 2 Peter, 1–3 John, and Jude are called the Catholic Epistles because they contain general advice for Christians, were accepted by the universal Church, and show how the worldwide Church developed.

- James, written perhaps in the 80s or 90s, is more a sermon than a letter. One of its key themes is God's preferential love for the poor; another is the need to translate our faith into action. Faith without works is dead.

- Generally acknowledged to be pseudonymous, the First Letter of Peter, written between 70 and 90, encourages Gentile Christian converts to witness to Christ in a hostile, pagan world.

- The Second Letter of Peter is the latest New Testament book, written perhaps in 130. It incorporates most of Jude (90–100). Both works were written to warn against false teachers who were deviating from apostolic teachings.

- The three letters of John are similar in style and teaching to John's Gospel. All were written around the year 100. The First Letter of John is the most important of the three. In the form of a treatise, it defends Jesus' true humanity against the Docetists, who claimed Jesus only *seemed* to be a man.

- John of Patmos wrote the book of Revelation between 92 and 96, during the reign of the emperor Domitian, who had ordered the citizens of the Empire to worship him as a god. The Revelation to John was written to encourage Christians to worship the one true God alone and to assure them that Christ would conquer evil once and for all.

- *Revelation* comes from the Greek word *apocalypse*, meaning "unveiling." Apocalyptic writing was popular in Judaism between 200 BC and AD 200.

- A major reason for the use of symbols in apocalyptic writing was so that enemies could be pointed out without actually naming them. This would help protect the persecuted group should its writings fall into the hands of the rulers.

- Jesus, as depicted in the Revelation to John, is God the Almighty, the Alpha and the Omega, the Messiah, and the Lamb of God whose suffering, Death, Resurrection, and Glorification have conquered sin, death, and Satan for all time.

- Catholics believe the book of Revelation is not a code book to be read for interpreting how or when the world is to end.

- Christology deals with the study of who Jesus Christ is. Titles like *Lord*, *Christ*, *Word of God*, *Suffering Servant*, *Son of God*, and *Son of Man* all reflect the Christology of the New Testament writers.

- The Fathers of the Church and ecumenical (worldwide) councils developed the Christology of Jesus in response to heretical teachings about him, including Arianism, Nestorianism, and Monophysitism.

- The key teachings about Jesus that came from the early ecumenical councils of Nicea (325), Constantinople I (381), Ephesus (431), Chalcedon (451), Constantinople II (553), and Constantinople III (680–681) include:

  ➤ Jesus is the only Son of God, true God, Light from Light, begotten not made, one in being with the Father.

  ➤ All things were made through the Son.

  ➤ There is only one person in Christ, the divine person, the Word of God, the second Person of the Blessed Trinity.

  ➤ Mary, by conceiving God's Son, is truly the Mother of God.

  ➤ There are two distinct natures in the one person of Christ. Jesus has a divine nature and a human nature.

- ▶ Jesus embodies the divine ways of God in a human way.
- ▶ As true God and man, Jesus has a human intellect and a human will. In Jesus, God truly shared humanity, truly suffered, truly experienced death, and truly rose victorious over death.

- ▶ Jesus, God-made-man, is our Savior. By uniting ourselves to his Death and Resurrection through faith, we will share in the eternal life he has promised.

LEARN BY DOING

1. Visit the following website to take a virtual tour of a refugee camp: www.refugeecamp.org/home Then prepare a one-page report on one of the topics you learned about after following the links at that site. Connect the topics to the virtue of hospitality as detailed in the Letter to the Hebrews.

2. Read 1 Peter 3:10–16. Write your own version of how the day of the Lord will come about. Then, list what you would do the day before the Lord's arrival if you knew in advance he was coming.

3. The Letter of James underscores the dignity of all human beings. It speaks about the need for an active faith, one that looks out for the needs of the poor. Forming our consciences in light of Church teaching on issues that affect human dignity is an important feature of an active Catholic faith. Do one of the following:

   - Visit the Justice for Immigrants website. Report on some facts and figures that underlie the current debate: www.justiceforimmigrants.org.
   - After checking the following website, report on some aspect of world hunger: www.churchworldservice.org/decisions/index.htm.
   - Check out some of the following websites and report on a social justice initiative—either national or international—in which the Church is actively involved.
     - ▶ Social Development and World Peace: www.usccb.org/sdwp
     - ▶ Poverty USA: www.usccb.org/cchd/povertyusa/edcenter/index.htm
     - ▶ Catholic Relief Services: www.crs.org
     - ▶ CRS Fair Trade Program: www.crsfairtrade.org

4. Responsible living is a theme of the New Testament letters (e.g., 1 John 4:7–21). Responsible living requires us to care for the environment, not only for those who are alive today, but for future generations as well. Consult the EarthTrends Environmental Information website and report on a current environmental issue in the news that requires urgent action: http://earthtrends.wri.org.

5. Select a difficult passage from the book of Revelation. Check three biblical commentaries to find out what it might mean. Report your findings.

6. If you have an artistic bent, try creating an illustration of one of the beasts described in the book of Revelation.

7. Do a study of the symbolism in the book of Revelation. Use illustrations downloaded from the Internet.

8. Construct a twenty-five question and answer Catechism on beliefs about Jesus. Your target reader is a fourth-grader. Present it as a booklet with images and symbols downloaded from the Internet.

9. Create a collage of symbols of Jesus. Incorporate several from the book of Revelation.

10. Do a short report on one of the following:

    *   an early Christological heresy
    *   an early ecumenical council
    *   an important Church Father

PRAYER LESSON

One of the great mystics of the Church was St. Teresa of Avila. The following prayer was found in her breviary after her death. She captured well the theme of Revelation, and indeed, of the New Testament itself. Pray this prayer often to remind you of who is really important in your life.

Let nothing disturb you,
Let nothing frighten you,
All things pass away:
God never changes.
Patience obtains all things.
He who has God
Finds he lacks nothing;
God alone suffices.

*   *Reflection*: Name something disturbing you in your life right now.

*   *Resolution*: Turn over your concerns to the Lord. He alone is enough for you.

The Living Jesus Today:
Constant Friend and Companion

CHAPTER TEN

For where two or three are gathered together in my name,
there am I in the midst of them.

—Matthew 18:20

CHAPTER **OVERVIEW**

ARE *YOU* **JESUS?**

One of the ways that Jesus is present in the world is through the words and actions of his followers.

JESUS IS PRESENT **IN THE CHURCH**

The Church was founded by Christ in order to continue his saving mission.

JESUS IS PRESENT IN OTHERS, **ESPECIALLY THE POOR AND SUFFERING**

Jesus identified with the poor, the lowly, the outcast, and all those not accepted by the well-established, and we must also.

JESUS MEETS US **IN THE SACRAMENTS**

Jesus is present in all of the sacraments and preeminently in the Sacrament of Eucharist.

JESUS MEETS **US IN SCRIPTURE**

The Scriptures are God's Word, a powerful sign of the Lord's presence and love.

JESUS MEETS **US IN PRAYER**

Prayer helps us to establish a lasting relationship and deeper friendship with Jesus Christ.

JESUS AND **CONTEMPORARY CINEMA**

While no film captures who or what Jesus was really like, some films do adequately present the basic facts about his life.

Are *You* **Jesus?**

A true story tells of a group of salesmen running through an airport late to catch their flight. One of them inadvertently kicked over a table holding a basket of apples. No one stopped except one man with a compassionate heart. He waved goodbye to his companions knowing that he would miss his flight, but he felt compelled to help the little ten-year-old girl whose table was upturned. He was glad he did, because she was blind.

The salesman restored the table to its original state. He noticed that he and his friends had bruised some of the fruit the girl was selling. So the man opened his wallet and put $20 into the girl's hand. He said, "Sorry for the accident. Please take this for the damage. I hope you have a good day."

As the man began to walk away to schedule a new flight, the girl gently asked him, "Are you Jesus?"

The man suddenly stopped and grew very quiet. And he wondered.[15]

This story also gets us to stop and think. Where, in fact, can we find the risen Jesus in our world today? Where can we meet him?

We must never forget that one of the ways Jesus is present in today's world is through his presence in each of us. This mystery is part of the ongoing Good News of the Gospel. We are so precious and valuable in the eyes of the Father that his Son Jesus, our risen Lord, has chosen us to be his ambassadors, to be his presence in the world for others. Read Jesus' words:

> I am the true vine, and my Father is the vine grower. . . . I am the vine, you are the branches. Whoever remains in me and I in him will bear much fruit. (Jn 15:1, 4–5)

Our Baptism incorporates us into the Church, making us members of Christ's body, attaching us to the vine, and making us temples of the Holy Spirit. The Holy Spirit works in many ways to build up the Church in love; not only in Baptism, but by the other sacraments, by the "grace of the Apostles, the virtues, and by many special graces called charisms" (*CCC*, 798). Through the conjoined mission of Christ and the Holy Spirit acting in the Church, we receive tremendous dignity, value, and worth. Christ reaches out to today's world through us. Christ lives in us. In the words of St. Paul:

> I have been crucified with Christ; yet I live, no longer I, but Christ lives in me; insofar as I now live in the flesh, I live by faith in the Son of God who has loved me and given himself up for me. (Gal 2:19–20)

Faith is the God-given virtue that enables us to see the reality of who Christ is. It enables us to believe in the Gospel. It helps us respond to Jesus' invitation to love.

St. Teresa of Avila observed that if we are looking for where the Lord is in today's world, we should look in the mirror. We are the hands of Christ to heal those who are hurting, the feet of Christ to walk to those in need, the eyes of Christ to search out the suffering, the voice of Christ to proclaim the Good News.

Recall how Jesus called his disciples the "light of the world" and "salt of the earth" in the Sermon on the Mount (5:13–16). These are apt images for the Christian life. Jesus is the source of light; he is the sun. But he has made us moons that reflect his love, glory, and Gospel. We are to draw others to the source of the light, to the Good News of the Gospel, to Jesus himself.

St. Teresa of **Avila**

We are also the salt of the earth. Salt flavors and preserves food. We can bring a certain flavor to this world and help the Lord in his work of salvation by entering into his Paschal Mystery. We do this at least weekly when we celebrate the Eucharist.

But we also enter into the Paschal Mystery when we pick up the crosses that come into our lives and join them to the sufferings of Christ. At times, this may mean that we have to stand up to the falsehoods in our contemporary world and take abuse for being true to Jesus and his message. It might mean denying ourselves for the greater good. It might be letting go of our own desire and following in the footsteps of Jesus by loving others, no matter how difficult. But just as Jesus' Passion and Death led to his Resurrection and Glorification, our acts of sacrifice will help us experience freedom in our own lives and a taste of the new life of the Resurrection. They will transform us from self-centered persons into loving servants who will attract others to the Gospel. Living the Paschal Mystery—imitating Christ—will bring a different flavor to the world and will help the Lord continue his work of salvation for persons who so desperately need to experience it.

A person once asked, "Why doesn't someone do something about all the poverty and suffering in the world?" Then the questioner observed, "Suddenly, I realized I am someone!"

The New Testament repeatedly teaches us that we have the responsibility to be Christ for others. With Christ living in us, each of us is a *someone*. We are given the power to continue his goodness in the world. We are never alone because the Lord is with us. Reflect on his words at the Last Supper:

> I pray not only for them, but also for those who will believe in me through their word, so that they may all be one, as you, Father, are in me and I in you, that they also may be in us, that the world may believe that you sent me. (Jn 17:20–21)

RECOGNIZING CHRIST

As a review, name some of the people from the New Testament who met and recognized Jesus. Check the references to see how many you got right.

1. This person said, "Come see a man who told me everything I have done. Could he possibly be the Messiah?" (Jn 4:29)

2. This man said, "Who are you, sir?" After Jesus revealed himself to the man, he found out that he was blinded. (Acts 9:5–9)

3. They traveled with Jesus for seven miles without knowing who he was, but came to realize who he was when they had dinner with him. (Lk 24:13–31)

4. He said, "You are the Messiah, the Son of the living God." (Mt 16:16)

5. This man thought Jesus was the Son of God because Jesus told him, "I saw you under the fig tree." (Jn 1:48–50)

6. They recognized Jesus as a king when they gave him gifts of gold, frankincense, and myrrh. (Mt 2:1–11)

7. Some thought this man was the Messiah, but he said, "One mightier than I is coming. I am not worthy to loosen the thongs of his sandals." (Lk 3:16)

8. This person said, "My Lord and my God!" Jesus answered him, "Blessed are those who have not seen and have believed." (Jn 20:28–29)

9. When he saw Jesus, he cried out and fell down before him; in a loud voice he shouted, "What have you to do with me, Jesus, son of the Most High God? I beg you, do not torment me!" (Lk 8:28–30)

10. Jesus refused to perform miracles for this person. In talking with him, Jesus quoted some passages from the Old Testament including, "You shall not put the Lord, your God, to the test." (Mt 4:1–11)

11. You. What would you say to Jesus? Write what you would say in your journal.

FOR REFLECTION

Tell about an occasion when you encountered Christ in another. Tell about a time when you were Christ's presence in the world.

Jesus Is Present **in the Church**

(*CCC*, 737–747; 774–776; 779)

Jesus set up the Church to continue his saving mission. During his earthly ministry, he formed his disciples and showed them how he was the Way, the Truth, and the Life. Before his Ascension into heaven, Jesus instructed his disciples to go into the world to continue his work—to preach, teach, forgive sin, heal, drive out demons, announce the coming of the Kingdom, and serve others as he had served them. Jesus' call can be summarized by his charge to us to love—especially the poorest and neediest persons.

Jesus expects the Church to be missionaries, ambassadors for him and his Father. However, he did not abandon us to work alone and unaided. "And behold, I am with you always, until the end of the age" (Mt 28:20). Earlier he had assured his disciples of his ongoing presence: "For where two or three are gathered together in my name, there am I in the midst of them" (Mt 18:20).

On Pentecost Sunday, the risen Lord Jesus and his heavenly Father sent the Holy Spirit to us to empower his followers to continue his work. By the power of the Holy Spirit, Christ continues his work of redemption in the Church. Christ pours out the gift of the Holy Spirit, who gives us the life and power to continue the Lord's work. The Second Vatican Council teaches us how Christ is present in the Church:

> Christ, having been lifted up from the earth, is drawing all men to Himself (Jn 12:32). Rising from the dead (cf. Rm 6:9), He sent His life-giving Spirit upon His disciples and through this Spirit has established His body, the Church, as the universal sacrament of salvation. Sitting at the right hand of the Father, he is continually active in the world, leading men to the Church, and through her joining them more closely

> to Himself and making them partakers of His glorious life by nourishing them with His own body and blood. (*Dogmatic Constitution on the Church*, No. 48)

The Church is the *Body of Christ*. Jesus is the head; we are the members. Baptism incorporates us into the Body. Each of us must use our talents to build up the Body and continue Jesus' work of salvation and sanctification in the world. But again, as individual members we are not alone when we gather together as the Church.

The Church is also a *sacrament*, that is, a visible sign and instrument of the hidden mystery and reality of salvation in Jesus Christ. Blessed Mother Teresa of Calcutta used to say that she was like a pencil in God's hand, an instrument that Christ used to serve the poor and dying. In a similar way the Church is an instrument in Christ's hand which points to the unity between mankind and God accomplished by Jesus' sacrifice. Christ continuously uses Christians to bring about the unity of the human race by giving us the

Holy Spirit to help us continue his work. We become a sign and an instrument of Christ's continuing work of salvation when we:

- *proclaim* his message of love and forgiveness;
- *build community* among our fellow believers;
- *serve others*, especially those who most need our words and deeds of compassion; and
- *worship* God in truth and love.

MORE ON THE CHURCH

Locate a copy of the Second Vatican Council's *Dogmatic Constitution on the Church* (**Lumen Gentium**). You can find it online at the Vatican website: www.vatican.va. Read the first chapter and identify in your journal any three images or metaphors of the Church described there. Then write a paragraph discussing which image most appeals to you. Explain why.

Lumen Gentium—The name of one of the principal documents of the Second Vatican Council. It was promulgated by Pope Paul VI November 21, 1964. The Latin term means "Light of the Nations."

FOR REVIEW

1. In what way is the Church the Body of Christ?

2. What does it mean to call the Church the Sacrament of Christ?

3. Name four activities that help carry on the work of Christ's saving acts.

FOR REFLECTION

Name at least three concrete ways Catholic teens can be a sign and instrument of Christ.

Jesus Is Present in Others, **Especially the Poor and Suffering**

You are the presence of the Lord in today's world, but so is each person you meet. With the eyes of faith, the Holy Spirit enables us to recognize our true identity as God's adopted children, brothers and sisters to our Savior, Jesus Christ, and, in him, brothers and sisters of one another. As we have seen, Jesus emphatically taught that love of God and love of neighbor are inseparable:

> You shall love the Lord your God with all your heart, with all your soul, with all your mind, and with all your strength. . . . You shall love your neighbor as yourself. (Mk 12:30–31)

RESPONDING TO CHRIST IN OTHERS

Mohandas K. Gandhi once said, "There are so many hungry people in the world that God cannot appear to them except in the form of bread." Discuss what this means for Catholics who derive nourishment from Holy Eucharist. Next, read the parable of the Good Samaritan (Lk 10:29–37). Identify victims of society's neglect in the neighborhood of your school. Devise a short service project to respond to these people, other Christs in your midst. Work with others to enact your plans.

To love Jesus means simply that we must love everyone he loves. The message of the parable of the Good Samaritan is that everyone, even our enemy, is our neighbor. Each person has tremendous dignity and is worthy of our love and respect. Jesus says we cannot love the invisible God if we fail to love the person we can see.

In a special way, Jesus identified himself with the lowly, the outcast, and those who were not accepted by the well-established. He taught that we will be judged by how we welcome the stranger, feed the hungry, give drink to the thirsty, and visit the sick and the imprisoned:

> Amen, I say to you, what you did not do for one of these least ones, you did not do for me. (Mt 25:45)

Our Christian faith requires us to find Christ in others. Active love for others is the measure of our commitment to the Lord. The opportunities to love are countless. We can begin with those who are closest to us, sometimes so familiar that we fail to see Christ in them—members of our family, our friends and classmates, and our coworkers. The lonely, the misunderstood, and the mistreated all need us to pay attention to them. The poor, the handicapped, the mentally ill, and the aged are waiting for our care. Victims of prejudice are all around us and need our love. Christ wants us to see him in all these people and to go out of our way to love them, to meet their needs, to give them our friendship.

 ## FOR REVIEW

1. What is the message of the parable of the Good Samaritan?

2. Why should Christians have a preferential love for the poor, lonely, and suffering?

FOR REFLECTION

Reflect on and list your five greatest strengths. Then, discuss some personal examples of how you might use them to lead others to Christ, that is, to be "light of the world" and "salt of the earth."

Jesus Meets Us **in the Sacraments**
(*CCC*, 1113–1134)

Jesus is present to us in the sacraments, visible signs of his care and love for us. The Lord knows that being human means having a body, our way of contacting and relating to the material world. When the Word became flesh, God made the human body and all created reality holy.

Jesus expressed God's love bodily when he ate with people, walked with them, laughed at their jokes, and cried when his friends died. He showed his love by touching the sick, holding children in his lap, and most perfectly by suffering in his Passion and Death. We know love when we experience it through gestures, embraces, symbols, and words. We need signs because we are human.

Jesus instituted the sacraments so we can "stay in touch" with him. They are material symbols that use words, actions, and concrete signs to express the love, concern, forgiveness, and real presence of the Lord. Through and in them Jesus meets us and touches our hearts. By the power of the Holy Spirit, the sacraments guarantee an encounter with Jesus that helps us to grow in grace and friendship with him. When we celebrate the sacraments attentively we can experience the peace and joy Jesus has in store for us in his heavenly Kingdom. The sacraments sanctify us (make us holy), build up Christ's body, and help us to worship God. They presuppose faith, but "they also nourish, strengthen, and express it" (*CCC*, 1123).

The sacraments confer the grace they signify. They are *efficacious* signs, that is, they bring about what they point to. Christ is always present in and works through the Seven Sacraments. For example:

- In *Baptism*, Christ forgives Original Sin and all personal sin. Baptism joins us to Christ's Body, the Church, giving us a new birth into his life and making us adopted children of his Father, temples of the Holy Spirit, and sharers in Christ's own priesthood (*CCC*, 1279). Through the presence and concern of other Christians, in Baptism, the Lord supports us on our life's journey to the Father.

- *Confirmation* strengthens our faith commitment by giving us the Holy Spirit. The Spirit roots us more deeply into God's family, strengthens our commitment to Christ and his Church, associates us more closely with his mission, and empowers us to bear witness to our Catholic faith in both words and deeds (*CCC*, 1316).

- In the *Sacrament of Matrimony*, the Lord brings about a communion of love between a man and woman, a symbol of the union between Christ and his Church. This sacrament gives the spouses the capacity to love with a Christlike love. It is a union that is open to the transmission of human life and the sharing of love (*CCC*, 1660–1661; 1664). Jesus promises to be with a husband and wife in their lovemaking, in their struggles to be faithful, and in the daily trials of ordinary life.

- Through *Holy Orders*, Christ calls men to serve the Church in his name and person by teaching, leading us in worship, and governing as a good shepherd willing to sacrifice his life for his flock. Since the beginning, the sacrament is conferred in three degrees: bishop, presbyter (priest), and deacon. (*CCC*, 1592, 1593).

- In the *Sacrament of the Anointing of the Sick,* Jesus sustains us spiritually and sometimes heals us physically. This sacrament unites the sick person to Christ's Passion for his or her own good and that of the whole Church. It also gives strength to endure sufferings because of old age or grave illness; forgives sin if the sick person could not receive forgiveness through the Sacrament of Penance; restores health, if this will benefit the salvation of the person's soul; and prepares one for death (*CCC,* 1527; 1532).

Note how in the each of these sacraments, Jesus meets us in many of the key events of our life. He meets us at birth. He meets us when we need strength and the help of the Holy Spirit to live out his command to love and witness to our faith. He meets us when we choose a state in life either as a married person or a Christ-called servant of God's people. He also meets us during the trying times of old age. Some of these sacraments we may receive only once—Baptism, Confirmation, and Holy Orders—because they confer a special sacramental *character,* that is, an indelible spiritual mark that permanently configures a person to Christ and gives him or her a special standing in the Church. Others may be received more than once, for example, Anointing of the Sick and remarriage after the death of a spouse.

Two sacraments that may be received as often as we want are the Sacrament of Penance and the Holy Eucharist.

The *Sacrament of Penance* (*CCC,* 1486–1487; 1496)—also known as the Sacrament of Conversion, Confession, and Reconciliation—is an important way to meet Jesus and receive his healing touch of forgiveness for sins committed after Baptism.

When we sin, we wound God's honor and love, harm our own dignity as a child of God, and upset the spiritual well-being of God's people. The first action of the sinner—**contrition,** or sorrow—is the most important. When the contrition is motivated by love it is called "perfect" contrition. Perfect contrition remits venial sins; it also obtains forgiveness for mortal sins if the promise is made to receive sacramental confession as soon as possible. Contrition called "imperfect" refers to contrition that arises from awareness of the sin's ugliness and possible penalties for the sin. This process, too, is the start of interior conversion, which can be brought to completion in the Sacrament of Penance, with the help of God's grace.

Especially when we have sinned seriously, we need to ask for God's pardon in the Sacrament of Penance. It is through this sacrament—exercised through bishops and priests—that a person's sins are forgiven. We need to repent and sorrowfully confess our sins with the firm intention to repair any harm we have caused in Christ's body. In turn, the Lord—through the ministry of the priest—reassures us of his love and forgiveness. Many Catholics find a caring, loving,

contrition—Heartfelt sorrow and aversion for sins committed along with the intention of sinning no more. Contrition is the most important act of penitents, necessary for receiving the Sacrament of Penance.

sensitive Jesus in this sacrament. They find a Jesus who accepts them in their weakness and gives them the strength to try again to live the vocation of love he has bestowed on them. The graces of this sacrament are many:

- reconciliation with the Church;
- remission of the eternal punishment incurred by mortal sins;
- remission, at least in part, of the temporal punishments resulting from sin;
- peace of conscience; and
- spiritual strength to live the Christian life (*CCC*, 1496).

The Eucharist *(CCC, 1406–1407; 1409; 1413; 1415–1416)*

Jesus is present to us in many ways, but a preeminent way he meets us is in the Sacrament of Love, the Eucharist (*CCC*, 1406–1407; 1409; 1413; 1415–1416). The Second Vatican Council teaches:

> Christ is always present in His Church, especially in her liturgical celebrations. He is present in the sacrifice of the Mass, not only in the person of His minister, "the same one now offering, through the ministry of priests, who formerly offered himself on the cross," but especially under the Eucharistic species. By His power He is present in the sacraments, so that when a man baptizes it is really Christ Himself who baptizes. He is present in His word, since it is He Himself who speaks when the holy Scriptures are read in the church. He is present, finally, when the Church prays and sings, for He promised: "Where two or three are gathered together for my sake, there am I in the midst of them" (Mt 18:20). (*The Constitution on the Sacred Liturgy*, No. 7)

The Eucharist (a word that means "thanksgiving") is the central sacrament. It both celebrates and creates Church. It represents the sacrifice of the cross—that is, God's incredible love for us in Jesus. It reminds us to be Christ for others, to be "bread for the world."

Catholics believe that Jesus is truly present, Body and Blood, in the bread and wine consecrated by a validly ordained priest in the Eucharistic liturgy (the Mass). The *Catechism of the Catholic Church* states clearly what Catholics believe:

> Under the consecrated species of bread and wine Christ himself, living and glorious, is present in a true, real, and substantial manner: his Body and his Blood, with his soul and his divinity. (1413)

We receive the Lord himself in Holy Communion. The Eucharist is our greatest source of strength and nourishment as Christians. Worthy reception of the Eucharist unites us more closely with Jesus, forgives our venial sins, keeps us from mortal sin, and strengthens our unity with other members of Christ's body, the Church.

When we receive the Lord in Holy Communion, he transforms us, living in us as we meet and serve people in our daily life. The concluding words of the

Mass tell us to go into the world to love and serve God and each other. These words remind us to receive Jesus and not to keep him to ourselves, but to let him shine through us as we become "light of the world" and "salt of the earth."

EUCHARISTIC REVERENCE

Blessed Mother Teresa of Calcutta once told her sisters that they must not only reverence Jesus in the Blessed Sacrament, but also in others. When they go out to minister to lice-infested, diseased, foul-smelling, and dying persons, they must treat these persons as other Christs.

- How should we show reverence to the Lord in the Blessed Sacrament? How do *you* show reverence to him?

- What are some ways "irreverence" is shown to others in your school, in your neighborhood, in your local community? What are some ways *you* can show reverence to these people who are often the victims of societal callousness?

Identify one person that you can "reverence." Speak a kind word to or do a random act of kindness for this person the coming week. (For ideas on "random acts of kindness," check out this website: www.actsofkindness.org.)

FOR REVIEW

1. Why did Christ institute the sacraments?

2. Define *sacramental character.* Which sacraments convey a sacramental character?

3. List several effects of meeting Christ in the Sacrament of Penance.

4. What does the word *Eucharist* mean? What are some of the effects of receiving the Lord in Holy Communion?

FOR REFLECTION

Write about your participation at Mass. Tell why you go to Mass if you do. Or, tell why you do not go to Sunday Mass if you don't. Also, answer: What does it mean to participate at Mass?

Jesus Meets **Us in Scripture** (CCC, 101–104)

The Scriptures are the Word of God. They hand on the truth of God's Revelation. The central object of the New Testament is Jesus Christ, "God's incarnate son: his acts, teachings, Passion and Glorification, and his Church's beginnings under the Spirit's guidance" (*CCC*, 124). Reading the Word of God touches and transforms us. The Scriptures are a powerful sign of the Lord's presence and love.

Faithful followers of Jesus will read Scripture quietly, slowly, and reflectively. Convinced that the risen Lord meets us in his holy Word, we cannot remain the same if we read the Bible regularly. An anonymous author wisely observed, "The best thing we can do with God's holy word is to *know* it in our heads, *stow* it in our hearts, *sow* it in the world, and *show* it in life." A Bible that is read and lived opens the doors to Heaven.

As this course on Jesus and the New Testament concludes, challenge yourself to commit to one of the following:

- Read the New Testament for ten minutes a day. Use one of the following techniques for prayer and study:

  1. Study an individual book using a good commentary. The *Collegeville Bible Commentaries* are outstanding because they are simple and clear and include the text of the New American Bible. *The New Jerome Biblical Commentary* is also excellent. Additionally, the New American Bible offers commentary notes within the pages of the New Testament.

  2. Study a particular New Testament theme by reading all the various passages that treat it. A concordance will help you locate all the places where the theme occurs. Some examples of major New Testament themes include Kingdom of God, faith, love, friendship, salvation, forgiveness, conversion, and witness.

  3. Choose New Testament passages at random. Refer to biblical commentaries and dictionaries to get further background on what you have chosen for the day.

- Pray for ten minutes each day using the New Testament. Select a favorite passage, for example, the parables or the miracles or the Sermon on the Mount. After calming down and putting yourself in the Lord's presence, read the passage as though the Lord is speaking directly to you. Engage all your senses in the scene of the passage. Imagine that these verses are written specifically for you. Listen to what they are saying. Reflect on them as if the Lord is sitting next to you.

- Form a Scripture study group with some friends in school or in your parish. Meet on a weekly or bi-weekly basis. Study an entire book of the Bible together. Ask an interested teacher, parent, youth minister, or priest to guide you.

FOR REVIEW

1. Why is Jesus the central object of the New Testament?

2. How are we called to read the Scriptures?

FOR REFLECTION

How can you develop and enact a regular schedule for reading and praying the Bible?

Jesus Meets Us in Prayer (CCC, 2565; 2607–2615; 2620–2621)

Prayer is the secret ingredient to grow in a friendship with Jesus. All friendships are built on communication and availability. Friends are open to each other and try to get to know one another.

The *Catechism of the Catholic Church* defines prayer as: "the living relationship of the children of God with their Father who is good beyond measure, with his Son Jesus Christ and with the Holy Spirit" (2565).

Prayer is the way to talk with and listen to Jesus Christ. It helps us to spend time with him, to become aware of his presence, and to allow him to contact us and come into our lives. Simply talking and listening to Jesus can be the best prayer of all.

Jesus himself prayed frequently in his public life. He taught us to pray with forgiving hearts, childlike confidence, simplicity, faith, persistence, watchfulness, and in his name. He also taught us the perfect prayer—the Gospel in miniature—the Lord's Prayer, the Our Father (see page 306).

Four traditional prayer forms include *vocal prayer*, expressed in either your own words or those of another; *meditation*, which is thinking about some aspect of God and his meaning for you; *affective prayer*, which involves your feelings and imagination; and *contemplation*, which is resting in the Lord's presence, not thinking about anything in particular but simply enjoying God's company.

Jesus is involved in your life. When you reflect on the people you have met and the events that have happened to you during the course of a day, you might be able to see the Lord working through them. At night before going to sleep, try examining your day in the presence of Jesus. Ask him to show you the good you have done. Thank him for all those things. Also examine how you did not do as well, including any occasions of sin. Ask Christ's forgiveness and resolve to improve the next day.

We can pray anytime and anywhere. However, it is wise to have a special time and place (for example, in the morning in the family room) for conversing with the Lord.

Prayer demands commitment. Distractions will inevitably come your way. But merely attempting to pray is itself a prayer.

Remember the old adage, "Seven days without prayer makes one weak." And seven days without meeting your friend Jesus in prayer, or receiving him in the holy Eucharist, makes one spiritually dead.

No one who prays is left unchanged. The Lord will meet you if you pray. He will become your best friend, one who loves you beyond what you can imagine, one who will change you for the better. He will give you the power and courage to love others as he loves you. Any effort you make to meet your friend Jesus in prayer is well worth the effort.

FOR REVIEW

1. Define *prayer*.
2. List four types of prayer.

FOR REFLECTION

- Interview two people whom you consider to be close to Jesus. Learn how and why they pray. Write a report naming and explaining their strategies.

- Compose a prayer of thanksgiving to the Blessed Trinity.

Jesus and Contemporary Cinema

Sad to say, many people do not read the New Testament, or at least read it as much as they should. They do not take the time to meet the Word of God revealed within its pages. Too often their only concept of Jesus is what documentaries or feature films might present about him. How accurate are these productions? Do they present the real Jesus?

Documentaries. Though many of these productions have interesting and accurate background information about New Testament customs, places, and beliefs, too often they are pushing a particular view of Jesus at odds with traditional belief. They often draw on a group of scholars who like to downplay belief in Jesus' divinity, the New Testament as inspired writing, and the Church as an authentic interpreter of Jesus Christ.

A beginning student of the New Testament must be wary of accepting at face value all their claims. It is fine to watch these special programs on Jesus, but take the next step and discuss what you viewed with knowledgeable teachers, priests, and scholars who can help you separate the wheat of truth from the chaff of the political agendas of the producers.

Jesus Christ is also a popular subject for feature films. But again, the Jesus portrayed in them is often the creation of the filmmaker and may be more or less accurate as measured by the biblical record. Liberties are often taken in the script, for example, by adding fictitious characters and subplots to advance the dramatic story. Key details and sayings of Jesus are often left out; others are disproportionately stressed. Some films only try to portray Jesus as described in a particular Gospel, while others try to "harmonize" or combine features from all the Gospels. The actor chosen to play Jesus typically reflects what might be pleasing to the audience. Physically or temperamentally, he may have little resemblance to the Jewish Jesus of two thousand years ago.

Keeping these points in mind, realize that no film can possibly capture who Jesus is or what he was *really* like in his earthly ministry. Particular films can more or less do an adequate job of presenting the basic facts about Jesus. In general, the major strength of Jesus films is that they get people thinking about who Jesus is and what his message is all about. They can provide some stunning visuals to help recreate the environment of the New Testament world. This can be very helpful when we use our imaginations to meditate on New Testament passages. These Jesus films can send you back to the authentic record—the Gospels—to see what the Evangelists recorded about Jesus' words and actions.

After studying the Gospels, *you* are wonderfully positioned to critique almost any film made about Jesus. For example, you should be able to:

- judge whether certain characters or events depicted in these films appear in the Gospel record or not;
- recognize whether Jesus said or did something the film claims he did;
- evaluate the validity of the actor's portrayal of Jesus against the Jesus you met in the Gospels;
- discover the agenda of the producer—for example, a Jesus who preaches political violence.

Without a doubt, many of these films are worth viewing and discussing. They will send you back to the Gospels and get you to consider not who is the "reel" Jesus, but who is the "real" Jesus.

Following are short synopses of some feature-length films you often see on television, shown typically around Christmas or Easter.

King of Kings (1961). Jesus was played by the blue-eyed, blond teen idol Jeffrey Hunter, who was, at times, moody and confused and, at other times, compassionate and self-possessed. The story highlights Judas and Barabbas as political revolutionaries who use Jesus as a pawn in their game. The Jesus in this film is strong, self-controlled, and gentle. There is little passion in this portrayal of Jesus. Critics panned Hunter's portrayal when they retitled the film "I Was a Teenage Jesus."

From *King of Kings*

The Gospel According to St. Matthew (1964). This film was a low-budget, black-and-white production dedicated to Pope John XXIII by its director, the Italian Marxist-atheist Pier Pasolini. The cinematography has a "you-are-there" documentary style to it as it captured the poor villages of rural southern Italy and the cast of extras, all of whom were non-actors. The Jesus of this film was portrayed by a Spanish student, Enrique Irazoqui, who had a narrow face, high forehead, stubbly beard, sad expression, and piercing black eyes. Limited to depicting only Matthew's Gospel, the film presents an angry Christ who tries to whip up the populace into some kind of revolutionary frenzy. This Jesus has emotion, but he definitely reflects the politics of the director.

Greatest Story Ever Told (1965). A commercial failure, this grand Hollywood production, filmed against the stunning background of the red-cliff mesas of Utah, starred the distinguished Swedish actor Max von Sydow. Light imagery is used to great effect in this film. The portrayal of Lazarus's raising from the dead, against the backdrop of Handel's *Messiah*, is stunning. Distracting, though, are the cameo appearances of Hollywood stars who appear frequently as bit players. John Wayne as the Roman soldier who pronounced, "Truly, this was the Son of God" toward the end of the film evokes laughter from today's viewers. Von Sydow's impeccable appearance, mesmerizing Swedish accent, and piercing blue eyes present an unearthly, controlled, mystical Christ who is easy to admire but hard to warm up to. Jesus' divinity is clearly stressed in this film.

Jesus Christ Superstar (1973). Based on Webber and Rice's rock opera, the film version stars Ted Neeley as an energetic, almost hyperactive Jesus who cries, craves companionship, and is typically harsh and angry. The rock lyrics of the early 1970s are anguished and fit the blaring musical score well. Many critics found the film anti-Semitic in its harsh portrayal of the Jewish leaders and were turned off by a hippie, flower-child Jesus, who, with wispy beard and flowing white gown, sings in a falsetto voice. A glaring omission in the film is the lack of a clear reference

From *Jesus Christ Superstar*

to Jesus' Resurrection. Though popular with teens in the 1970s, today's students often find this film dated and silly.

Jesus of Nazareth (1977). This six-and-a-half-hour made-for-TV movie was directed by Franco Zeffirelli. Many critics and viewers consider it to be the most reverential, accurate, and inspiring portrayal of Jesus ever filmed. Starring the British actor Robert Powell, Jesus is dignified, idealistic, in control, polished, and visionary. The film does a good job showing Jesus as one divine person with two natures. It overemphasizes neither his divine nature nor his human nature, as films have a tendency to do. The miracles are handled tastefully, showing how the Father worked through his Son. The film did garner some negative criticism, however, for its depiction of an otherworldly Jesus whose message seems untouched by his earthly context. Some commentators found the blue-eyed, fair-skinned Powell to be a contradiction in a film that strove for historical accuracy. However, this film is well worth watching. It takes the time to depict the Gospel scenes accurately.

Jesus (1979). Based on the Gospel of Luke and promoted by evangelical Christians, this film does a fine job presenting the Gospel and Jesus (played by Brian Deacon), who laughs, dances at wedding parties, and enjoys being with his disciples. The film shows a human side of Jesus, yet one who is still divine and sure of his mission. The most marketed of any film made about Jesus, it has been used for mission outreach throughout the world and dubbed in over six hundred languages. It has its own website, where you can watch the movie online: www.jesusfilm.org.

Jesus (1999). A CBS made-for-TV movie, *Jesus* stars Jeremy Sisto, who presents a human, attractive Jesus who loves, laughs, enjoys children, gets angry at the death of Joseph, and shows fear in the face of his Passion. However, his mother knows more about his identity than he does. Further, he shows too much reluctance about embracing his ministry. Today's youth find this portrayal interesting, believable, and easy to discuss in light of the Gospels.

The Visual Bible: The Gospel of John (2003). This three-hour feature film is a remarkable effort to translate John's Gospel word-for-word to film using the American Bible Society's *Good News Bible* translation. The British actor Henry Ian Cusick portrays Jesus in a gentle, compassionate, friendly, and authoritative manner. The actor has human warmth about him, but the film (as does the Gospel) clearly identifies Jesus as the Word, the unique Son of God. It also highlights Jesus' central message of love. The distinguished Canadian actor Christopher Plummer serves as the narrator of the Gospel text. Great care was taken to use authentic costumes and settings and to assemble a talented supporting cast and thousands

DIRECTING THE GOSPEL

Choose and complete one or more of the following assignments:

- View one or more of the films cited in the text. Critique the portrayal of Jesus in light of the Jesus you discovered in the Gospels. Write up your own capsule comments about the portrayal of Jesus.

- List the scenes you would include in a film about Jesus. What essential sayings, miracles, and characters would you absolutely want to include?

- Write a brief description of the kind of person you would want to play Jesus Christ in a film about him. What would he look like? What would his age be? Perhaps if you have artistic ability, you may want to sketch his portrait.

of extras. The film also has a beautiful soundtrack that uses replicas of musical instruments played in Jesus' day. Viewing this film—one of the very best of the Jesus films—is a wonderful way to appreciate anew one of the most beloved of all Gospels. (You can learn more about this film at its website: www.gospelofjohnthefilm.com.)

The Passion of the Christ (2004). Reviewed in chapter 4 of this text (page 126).

The Nativity (2006). This is a moving retelling of the Christmas story, drawing on the infancy narratives of both Luke and Matthew's Gospels. The portrayal of Joseph as a strong man of faith is especially well acted and effective. The dialogue between the characters is believable, the setting quite realistic, and the quotations from Scripture, for example, the recitation of Mary's Magnificat, well integrated into the story. The film also has a light touch in the interactions among the Magi, whose back-and-forth dialogue elicits smiles. Overall, a beautiful, uplifting, happy account of the events and people surrounding the Savior's birth.

Other notable Jesus films are:

- *Godspell* (1973), which presents Jesus as a counter-cultural clown;
- country singer Johnny Cash's low-budget *The Gospel Road* (1973), which shows a hippie, always smiling Jesus;
- the controversial Martin Scorsese film *The Last Temptation of Christ* (1988), which offends many Christians with its depiction of a tortured, weak, doubting Jesus who is tempted to have a sexual relationship with Mary Magdalene;
- *Jesus of Montreal* (1989), a French Canadian allegory about an acting troupe that puts on a Passion play and begins to take on the stories of the characters they play;
- South African director Reghardt Van den Bergh's *The Gospel According to St. Matthew* (1996), which uses the *New International Version of the Bible* as if it were a film script and presents such a joyous Jesus that he seems unreal;

- *The Miracle Maker* (2000), a highly rated animated version of the life of Jesus, using the voices of some of Britain's finest actors, including Ralph Fiennes as a brooding, yet humble Jesus.

This journey of studying Jesus and the New Testament began with Jesus' ever-important question, "Who do you say that I am?" How do you answer his question now?

Remember that reading the Bible and studying about Jesus are important to grow in our faith, but it is more important for you to *know* Jesus Christ *personally*. To know Jesus as your best friend is life's greatest joy and most important task. Jesus is the source of true happiness. May he walk with you all the days of your life! God bless you.

 FOR REVIEW

1. Write a brief synopsis of one important feature film about Jesus.

2. Discuss at least two methods for watching Jesus films in an intelligent, critical way.

FOR REFLECTION

Write your opinion of your favorite film about Jesus. Explain why it is your favorite.

CHAPTER SUMMARY POINTS

- Baptism incorporates us into Christ's body, the Church, and makes us temples of the Holy Spirit.
- As Christ's disciples and presence in the world, we must live the Paschal Mystery daily, thus helping the Lord continue his work of salvation.
- The risen Lord has chosen to be present to us through his Body, the Church.

- The Church is also the Sacrament of Christ, a visible sign and instrument of the hidden mystery and reality of salvation in Jesus Christ.
- We become instruments in Christ's hands to continue his work when we proclaim the Gospel, build community, serve others, and worship God.
- Love of God and love of neighbor are inseparable. Christ especially identifies with poor, suffering,

and lonely people. By loving and serving them, we love and serve our Lord.

- The Lord comes to us in the sacraments, sacred signs of his love. They sanctify us, build up Christ's body, and give worship to God.

- The sacraments confer the graces they signify. Baptism incorporates us into the Church, makes us adopted children of God, and forgives sin. Confirmation strengthens our faith and gives us the gift of the Holy Spirit to live a Christian life. Matrimony gives a husband and wife the capacity to love in a Christlike way that is open to the transmission of human life. Holy Orders ordains men to serve the Church through the ministries of teaching, worship, and pastoral governance. Anointing of the Sick strengthens people in times of sickness and old age, giving them spiritual healing and sometimes physical healing.

- Baptism, Confirmation, and Holy Orders confer a sacramental character, an indelible spiritual mark that permanently configures a person to Christ, giving him or her a special standing in the Church.

- The Sacrament of Penance—also known as the Sacrament of Conversion, Confession, or Reconciliation—gives us the healing touch of Christ's forgiveness after we have sinned.

- The Eucharist is a supreme sign of Jesus' love. It both celebrates and creates the Church as it commemorates the Paschal Mystery of Christ's loving sacrifice. Jesus himself comes to us under the forms of bread and wine and challenges us to take him into the world.

- Prayer and reading the Bible are ways to experience Jesus' love and presence. We must make time for them if we wish to grow in holiness.

- In evaluating various documentaries and feature films made about Jesus, we must be aware that the producers often have viewpoints that are not exactly in harmony with the New Testament portrait of Jesus or Christian beliefs about him. We must view these works critically, though they can often be helpful in depicting the biblical world of Jesus' times.

LEARN BY DOING

1. Create a fifteen-minute audiotape of Jesus in music through the ages.

2. Interview five practicing Catholics and ask for their definition or description of the Church. Record your interview either on audio or videotape.

3. Obtain brochures on the service organizations sponsored by your parish or a local parish. Interview the person in charge of one of them to discover how that particular organization helps build Christian community.

4. Compose your own prayer of thanksgiving after Holy Communion.

5. Read a current issue of a Catholic periodical or newspaper to see how modern-day Catholics are engaged in bringing Christ to the world. Report on one of the articles you read. Here are some periodicals to investigate: *Catholic Digest, Liguorian, St. Anthony Messenger, U.S. Catholic, America, Commonweal, Our Sunday Visitor, Columbia Magazine, National Catholic Reporter.*

6. Research and report on one of these Catholic organizations dedicated to helping the poor:

   - Saint Vincent de Paul Society: www.svdpusa.org

   - Catholic Relief Services: www.catholicrelief.org

7. Attend a Byzantine, Melkite, or Maronite rite Mass that might be celebrated somewhere in your diocese. Report on some differences in the liturgical celebration compared to the Roman rite with which you are familiar.

8. Locate the readings from one of next month's Sunday's liturgies at www.nccbuscc.org/nab. Focus on what the readings might say about Jesus and his message. Prepare a two-minute presentation on their meaning for daily living. Your target audience should be your classmates.

9. Research and report on a religious community of men or women whose mission is to comfort the sick, elderly, or dying. If possible, personally interview a member of such a community.

10. The Church continues to preach of Jesus the Divine Physician and teaches that we should practice the corporal works of mercy, including "visiting the sick." To put this work into practice, identify someone who is ill, either at home or in the hospital. List several needs for this person, and then devise and implement a plan to meet those needs.

11. Assemble a booklet of three or four favorite prayers to Jesus. Illustrate it with images downloaded from the Internet. Investigate websites like the following to find some good Jesus prayers while also composing your own Jesus prayers: www.prayingeachday.org/prayersites.html; www.catholic.org (look under "Prayers"); www.yenra.net/catholic/prayers; www.ourcatholicfaith.org/prayer/p-tojesus.html.

12. Report on the work of The Christopher Organization. Its creed is stated simply as, "It is better to light one candle than to curse the darkness." Visit the Christopher website at www.christophers.org and do one or more of the following:

    - Read about their variety of works.
    - Sign up to receive their excellent free News Notes.
    - Consider entering their art contest for high-school students.
    - Watch and report on one of their Closeup video clips.

PRAYER LESSON

Put yourself in the presence of the Lord. Thank him for helping you complete another semester. Now picture Jesus sitting next to you. He is asking you some questions. How would you answer them?

- Do you accept me as God's Son, your Savior, and your friend who loves you beyond what you can imagine?

- Will you spend some time talking to me in prayer, listening to my word in Scripture, and simply enjoying the love I have for you?

- Will you express your sorrow to me when you sin and ask for my abundant forgiveness?

- Will you receive me in the Eucharist each week?

- Will you recognize me in your fellow Christians and look to me for guidance through my Church and the leaders I have appointed to instruct you?

- Will you try to imitate me, especially by trying to serve others? Will you make an effort to help those who are especially close to me—the poor, the handicapped, the sick, the victims of injustice, and the like?

  ▶ *Reflection*: What do you think about this, my precious child? I love you! My Father loves you. And our Holy Spirit is our gift to you so that you may love, too. We bless you!

  ▶ *Resolution*: What will you do for Christ?

Notes

1. Cornelius Tacitus, *The Annals of Imperial Rome*, trans. with an introduction by Michael Grant, rev. ed., with new bibliography (Harmondsworth, England; New York, NY: Penguin Books, 1971), p. 365, as cited in Phillip J. Cunningham, C.S.P., *A Believer's Search for the Jesus of History* (New York: Paulist Press, 1999), p. 10.

2. Suetonius, *Claudius* 25.4, as cited by F. F. Bruce in *Jesus and Christian Origins Outside the New Testament* (Grand Rapids, MI: William B. Eerdmans Publishing Company, 1974), p. 21.

3. *Josephus, Jewish Antiquities*, Vol. 18, as cited by Nahum N. Glazer in *Jerusalem and Rome: The Writings of Josephus* (New York, NY: Meridian Books, Inc., 1960), p. 145.

4. New York: Doubleday, 1997.

5. Anthony de Mello, S.J., *The Song of the Bird* (Garden City, NY: Image Books, 1984), p. 112.

6. Josephus, *Antiquities* 18:12, 15, found at the "Into His Own: Perspectives on the World of Jesus" website: <http://virtualreligion.net/iho/pharisee.html#principles> (5 September 2008).

7. Bible.org, "Sermon illustrations,=http:dev.bible.org/netbible/illustration.php?topic=835

8. The Light of the World, found at <http://www.williamholmanhunt.com/explorer/main.htm>.

9. *The Parables of the Kingdom*, New York: Charles Scribner's Sons, 1961.

10. Both stories are adapted from Anthony Castle, *A Treasury of Quips, Quotes and Andecdotes for Preachers and Teachers* (Mystic, CT: Twenty-Third Publications, 1998), pp. 164 and 208.

11. Some of these reflections come from the two-volume study by Raymond Brown, S. S., *The Death of the Messiah* (New York: Doubleday, 1994).

12. Quoted in Matthew Kelly, *The Rhythm of Life: Living Every Day with Passion & Purpose* (New York: Fireside Book, Simon & Schuster, 2004), p. 288.

13. Raymond E. Brown, S. S., *An Introduction to the New Testament* (New York: Doubleday, 1997), p. 340.

14. *Ibid*, p. 810.

15. An adapted story originally told by Brennan Manning and reported in Brian Cavanaugh, T.O.R., *More Sower's Seeds: Second Planting* (New York: Paulist Press, 1992), p. 14.

Catholic Handbook
for Faith

A. Beliefs

From the beginning, the Church expressed and handed on its faith in brief formulas accessible to all. These professions of faith are called "creeds" because their first word in Latin, "credo," means "I believe." The following creeds have special importance in the Church. The Apostles' Creed is a summary of the Apostles' faith. The Nicene Creed developed from the Councils of Nicaea and Constantinople and remains in common use between the Churches of both the East and West.

Apostles' Creed

I believe in God, the Father almighty,
Creator of heaven and earth.
I believe in Jesus Christ, his only son, our Lord.
He was conceived by the power of the Holy Spirit,
and born of the Virgin Mary.
He suffered under Pontius Pilate,
was crucified, died, and was buried.
He descended into hell.
On the third day he rose again.
He ascended into heaven,
and is seated at the right hand of the Father.
He will come again to judge the living and the dead.
I believe in the Holy Spirit,
the holy catholic Church,
the communion of saints,
the forgiveness of sins,
the resurrection of the body,
and the life everlasting. Amen.

Nicene Creed

We believe in one God,
  the Father, the Almighty,
  maker of heaven and earth,
  of all that is seen and unseen.
We believe in one Lord, Jesus Christ,
  the only Son of God,
  eternally begotten of the Father,
  God from God, Light from Light,
true God from true God,
  begotten, not made, one in Being with the Father.
  Through him all things were made.
  For us men and for our salvation
  he came down from heaven:
by the power of the Holy Spirit
  he was born of the Virgin Mary, and became man.
For our sake he was crucified under Pontius Pilate;
  he suffered, died, and was buried.
    On the third day he rose again in fulfillment of the
      Scriptures;
  he ascended into heaven and is seated at the right hand of
      the Father.
He will come again in glory to judge the living and the dead,
  and his kingdom will have no end.
We believe in the Holy Spirit, the Lord, the giver of life,
  who proceeds from the Father and the Son.
With the Father and the Son he is worshiped and glorified.
He has spoken through the Prophets.
We believe in one holy catholic and apostolic Church.
We acknowledge one baptism for the forgiveness of sins.
We look for the resurrection of the dead,
  and the life of the world to come. Amen.

Gifts of the Holy Spirit

1. Wisdom
2. Understanding
3. Counsel
4. Fortitude
5. Knowledge
6. Piety
7. Fear of the Lord

Fruits of the Holy Spirit

1. Charity
2. Joy
3. Peace
4. Patience
5. Kindness
6. Goodness
7. Generosity
8. Gentleness
9. Faithfulness
10. Modesty
11. Self-control
12. Chastity

The Symbol of Chalcedon

Following therefore the holy Fathers, we unanimously teach to confess one and the same Son, our Lord Jesus Christ, the same perfect in divinity and perfect in humanity, the same truly God and truly man composed of rational soul and body, the same one in being (*homoousios*) with the Father as to the divinity and one in being with us as to the humanity, like unto us in all things but sin (cf. Heb 4:15). The same was begotten from the Father before the ages as to the divinity and in the later days for us and our salvation was born as to his humanity from Mary the Virgin Mother of God.

We confess that one and the same Lord Jesus Christ, the only-begotten Son, must be acknowledged in two natures, without confusion or change, without division or separation. The distinction between the natures was never abolished by their union but rather the character proper to each of the two natures was preserved as they came together in one person (*prosôpon*) and one hypostasis. He is not split or divided into two persons, but he is one and the same only-begotten, God the Word, the Lord Jesus Christ, as formerly the prophets and later Jesus Christ himself have taught us about him and as has been handed down to us by the Symbol of the Fathers.

—From the General Council of Chalcedon (AD 451)

B. Faith in God: Father, Son, and Holy Spirit

Our profession of faith begins with God, for God is the First and the Last, the beginning and end of everything.

Attributes of God

St. Thomas Aquinas named nine attributes that seem to tell us some things about God's nature. They are:

1. *God is eternal.* He has no beginning and no end. Or, to put it another way, God always was, always is, and always will be.

2. *God is unique.* There is no God like Yahweh (see Isisah 45:18). God is the designer of a one-and-only world. Even the people he creates are one of a kind.

3. *God is infinite and omniscient.* This reminds us of a lesson we learned early in life: God sees everything. There are no limits to God. Omnipotence is a word that refers to God's supreme power and authority over all of creation.

4. *God is omnipresent.* God is not limited to space. He is everywhere. You can never be away from God.

5. *God contains all things.* All of creation is under God's care and jurisdiction.

6. *God is immutable.* God does not evolve. God does not change. God is the same God now as he always was and always will be.

7. *God is pure spirit.* Though God has been described with human attributes, God is not a material creation. God's image cannot be made. God is a pure spirit who cannot be divided into parts. God is simple, but complex.

8. *God is alive.* We believe in a living God, a God who acts in the lives of people. Most concretely, he came to this world in the incarnate form of Jesus Christ.

9. *God is holy.* God is pure goodness. God is pure love.

The Holy Trinity

The Trinity is the mystery of one God in three Persons—Father, Son, and Holy Spirit. Viewed in the light of faith, some of the Church dogmas, or beliefs, can help our understanding of this mystery:

- *The Trinity is One.* There are not three Gods, but one God in three Persons. Each one of them—Father, Son, and Holy Spirit—is God whole and entire.

- *The three Persons are distinct from one another.* The three Persons of the Trinity are distinct in how they relate to one another. "It is the Father who generates, the Son who is begotten, and the Holy Spirit who proceeds" (Lateran Council IV quoted in *CCC*, 254). The Father is not the Son, nor is the Son the Holy Spirit.

- *The three divine Persons of the Blessed Trinity are related to one another.* While the three Persons are truly distinct in light of their relations, we believe in one God. The three Persons do not divide the divine unity. The Council of Florence taught: "Because of that unity the Father is wholly in the Son and wholly in the Holy Spirit; the Son is wholly in the Father and wholly in the Holy Spirit; the Holy Spirit is wholly in the Father and wholly in the Son" (quoted in *CCC*, 255).

St. John Damascus used two analogies to describe the doctrine of the Blessed Trinity.

Think of the Father as a root,
of the Son as a branch,
and of the Spirit as a fruit,
for the substance of these is one.

The Father is a sun
with the Son as rays
and the Holy Spirit as heat.

Read the *Catechism of the Catholic Church* (232–260) on the Holy Trinity.

Faith in One God

There are several implications for those who love God and believe in him with their entire heart and soul (see *CCC* 222–227):
- It means knowing God's greatness and majesty.
- It means living in thanksgiving.
- It means knowing the unity and dignity of all people.
- It means making good use of created things.
- It means trusting God in every circumstance.

C. Deposit of Faith

"Deposit of Faith" refers to both Sacred Scripture and Sacred Tradition handed on from the time of the Apostles, from which the Church draws all that she proposes is revealed by God.

Canon of the Bible

There are seventy-three books in the canon of the Bible, that is, the official list of books the Church accepts as divinely inspired writings: forty-six Old Testament books and twenty-seven New Testament books. Protestant Bibles do not include seven Old Testament books in their list (1 and 2 Maccabees, Judith, Tobit, Baruch, Sirach, and the Wisdom of Solomon). Why the difference? Catholics rely on the version of the Bible that the earliest Christians used, the *Septuagint.* This was the first Greek translation of the Hebrew Scriptures begun in the third century BC. Protestants, on the other hand, rely on an official list of Hebrew Scriptures compiled in the Holy Land by Jewish scholars at the end of the first century AD. Today, some Protestant Bibles print the disputed books in a separate section at the back of the Bible, called the *Apocrypha.*

The twenty-seven books of the New Testament are detailed in Chapter 2. The New Testament is central to our knowledge of Jesus Christ.

There are forty-six books in the Old Testament canon. The Old Testament is the foundation for God's self-revelation in Christ. Christians honor the Old Testament as God's Word. It contains the writings of prophets and other inspired authors who recorded God's teaching to the Chosen People and his interaction in their history. For example, the Old Testament recounts how God delivered the Jews from Egypt (the Exodus), led them to the Promised Land, formed them into a nation under his care, and taught them in knowledge and worship.

The stories, prayers, sacred histories, and other writings of the Old Testament reveal what God is like and tell much about human nature, too. In brief, the Chosen People sinned repeatedly by turning their backs on their loving God; they were weak and easily tempted away from God. Yahweh, on the other hand, *always* remained faithful. He promised to send a Messiah to humanity.

Listed below are the categories and books of the Old and New Testament:

The Old Testament

The Pentateuch

Genesis	Gn
Exodus	Ex
Leviticus	Lv
Numbers	Nm
Deuteronomy	Dt

The Historical Books

Joshua	Jos
Judges	Jgs
Ruth	Ru
1 Samuel	1 Sm
2 Samuel	2 Sm
1 Kings	1 Kgs
2 Kings	2 Kgs
1 Chronicles	1 Chr
2 Chronicles	2 Chr
Ezra	Ezr
Nehemiah	Neh
Tobit	Tb
Judith	Jdt
Esther	Est
1 Maccabees	1 Mc
2 Maccabees	2 Mc

The Wisdom Books

Job	Jb
Psalms	Ps(s)
Proverbs	Prv
Ecclesiastes	Eccl
Song of Songs	Sg
Wisdom	Wis
Sirach	Sir

The Prophetic Books

Isaiah	Is
Jeremiah	Jer
Lamentations	Lam
Baruch	Bar
Ezekiel	Ez
Daniel	Dn
Hosea	Hos
Joel	Jl
Amos	Am
Obadiah	Ob
Jonah	Jon
Micah	Mi
Nahum	Na
Habakkuk	Hb
Zephaniah	Zep
Haggai	Hg
Zechariah	Zec
Malachi	Mal

The New Testament

The Gospels

Matthew	Mt
Mark	Mk
Luke	Lk
John	Jn
Acts of the Apostles	Acts

The New Testament Letters

Romans	Rom
1 Corinthians	1 Cor
2 Corinthians	2 Cor
Galatians	Gal
Ephesians	Eph
Philippians	Phil
Colossians	Col
1 Thessalonians	1 Thes
2 Thessalonians	2 Thes
1 Timothy	1 Tm
2 Timothy	2 Tm
Titus	Ti
Philemon	Phlm
Hebrews	Heb

The Catholic Letters

James	Jas
1 Peter	1 Pt
2 Peter	2 Pt
1 John	1 Jn
2 John	2 Jn
3 John	3 Jn
Jude	Jude
Revelation	Rv

How to Locate a Scripture Passage

Example: 2 Tm 3:16–17

1. Determine the name of the book.

    The abbreviation "2 Tm" stands for the book of Second Timothy.

2. Determine whether the book is in the Old Testament or New Testament.

    The book of Second Timothy is one of the catholic letters in the New Testament.

3. Locate the chapter where the passage occurs.

    The first number before the colon—"3"— indicates the chapter. Chapters in the Bible are set off by the larger numbers that divide a book.

4. Locate the verses of the passage.

    The numbers after the colon indicate the verses referred to. In this case, verses 16 and 17 of chapter 3.

5. Read the passage.

    For example: "All Scripture is inspired by God and is useful for teaching, for refutation, for correction, and for training in righteousness, so that one who belongs to God may be competent, equipped for every good work."

Relationship Between Scripture and Tradition

The Church does not derive the revealed truths of God from the holy Scriptures alone. The Sacred Tradition hands on God's word, first given to the Apostles by the Lord and the Holy Spirit, to the successors of the Apostles (the bishops and the pope). Enlightened by the Holy Spirit, these successors faithfully preserve, explain, and spread it to the ends of the earth. The Second Vatican Council fathers explained the relationship between Sacred Scripture and Sacred Tradition:

> It is clear therefore that, in the supremely wise arrangement of God, Sacred Tradition, Sacred Scripture, and the Magisterium of the Church are so connected and associated that one of them cannot stand without the others. Working together, each in its own way, under the action of the one Holy Spirit, they all contribute effectively to the salvation of souls. (*Dei Verbum* 10)

Relevant Church Teaching on Reading and Studying Scripture

If one carefully reads the Scriptures, he will find there the word on the subject of Christ and the prefiguration of the new calling. He is indeed the hidden treasure in the field—the field in fact is the world—but in truth, the hidden treasure in the Scriptures is Christ. Because he is designed by types and words that humanly are not possible to understand before the accomplishment of all things, that is, Christ's second coming.

—St. Irenaeus (second century AD)

[Christ's words] are not only those which he spoke when he became a man and tabernacled in the flesh; for before that time, Christ, the Word of God, was in Moses and the prophets . . . [their words] were filled with the Spirit of Christ.

—Origen (third century AD)

You recall that one and the same Word of God extends throughout Scripture, that it is one and the same Utterance that resounds in the mouths of all the sacred writers, since he who was in the beginning God with God has no need of separate syllables; for he is not subject to time.

The Scriptures are in fact, in any passage you care to choose, singing of Christ, provided we have ears that are capable of picking out the tune. The Lord opened the minds of the Apostles so that they understood the Scriptures. That he will open our minds too is our prayer.

—St. Augustine of Hippo (fifth century AD)

My dear young friends, I urge you to become familiar with the Bible, and to have it at hand so that it can be your compass pointing out the road to follow. By reading it, you will learn to know Christ. Note what St. Jerome said in this regard: "Ignorance of the Scriptures is ignorance of Christ" (PL 24,17; cf *Dei Verbum*, 25). A time-honoured way to study and savour the Word of God is *lectio divina* which constitutes a real and veritable spiritual journey marked out in stages. After the *lectio*, which consists of reading and rereading a passage from Sacred Scripture and taking in the main elements, we proceed to *meditatio*. This is a moment of interior reflection in which the soul turns to God and tries to understand what his Word is saying to us today. Then comes *oratio* in which we linger to talk with God directly. Finally we come to *contemplatio*. This helps us to keep our hearts attentive to the presence of Christ whose Word is "a lamp shining in a dark place, until the day dawns and the morning star rises in your hearts" (2 Pet 1:19). Reading, study and meditation of the Word should then flow into a life of consistent fidelity to Christ and his teachings.

St. James tells us: "Be doers of the word, and not merely hearers who deceive themselves. For if any are hearers of the word and not doers, they are like those who look at themselves in a mirror; for they look at themselves and, on going away, immediately forget what they were like. But those who look into the perfect law, the law of liberty, and persevere, being not hearers who forget but doers who act— they will be blessed in their doing" (1:22–25). Those who listen to the Word of God and refer to it always, are constructing their existence on solid foundations. "Everyone then who hears these words of mine and acts on them," Jesus said, "will be like a wise man who built his house on rock" (Mt 7:24). It will not collapse when bad weather comes.

To build your life on Christ, to accept the Word with joy and put its teachings into practice: this, young people of the third millennium, should be your programme! There is an urgent need for the emergence of a new generation of Apostles anchored firmly in the Word of Christ, capable of responding to the challenges of our times and prepared to spread the Gospel far and wide. It is this that the Lord asks of you, it is to this that the Church invites you, and it is this that the world—even though it may not be aware of it—expects of you! If Jesus calls you, do not be afraid to respond to him with generosity, especially when he asks you to follow him in the consecrated life or in the priesthood. Do not be afraid; trust in him and you will not be disappointed.

—Pope Benedict XVI (twenty-first century AD)

D. Church

The Church is the Body of Christ, that is, the community of God's people who profess faith in the risen Lord Jesus and love and serve others under the guidance of the Holy Spirit. The Roman Catholic Church is guided by the pope and his bishops.

Marks of the Church

1. *The Church is one.* The Church remains one because of its source: The unity in the Trinity of the Father, Son, and Spirit in one God. The Church's unity can never be broken and lost because this foundation is itself unbreakable.

2. *The Church is holy.* The Church is holy because Jesus, the founder of the Church, is holy, and he joined the Church to himself as his body and gave the Church the gift of the Holy Spirit. Together, Christ and the Church make up the "whole Christ" (*Christus totus* in Latin).

3. *The Church is catholic.* The Church is catholic ("universal" or "for everyone") in two ways. First, she is catholic because Christ is present in the Church in the fullness of his body, with the fullness of the means of salvation, the fullness of faith, sacraments, and the ordained ministry that comes from the Apostles. The Church is also catholic because she takes its message of salvation to all people.

4. *The Church is apostolic.* The Church's apostolic mission comes from Jesus: "Go, therefore, and make disciples of all nations" (Mt 28:19). The Church remains apostolic because she still teaches the same things the Apostles taught. Also, the Church is led by leaders who are successors to the Apostles and who help to guide us until Jesus returns.

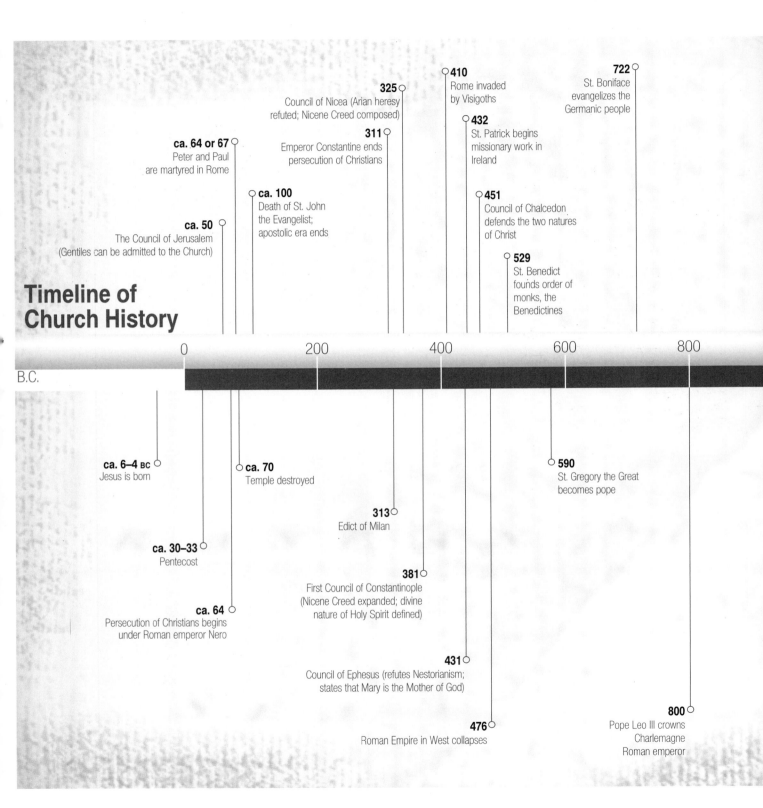

Timeline of Church History

722
St. Boniface evangelizes the Germanic people

410
Rome invaded by Visigoths

325
Council of Nicea (Arian heresy refuted; Nicene Creed composed)

432
St. Patrick begins missionary work in Ireland

ca. 64 or 67
Peter and Paul are martyred in Rome

311
Emperor Constantine ends persecution of Christians

451
Council of Chalcedon defends the two natures of Christ

ca. 100
Death of St. John the Evangelist; apostolic era ends

529
St. Benedict founds order of monks, the Benedictines

ca. 50
The Council of Jerusalem (Gentiles can be admitted to the Church)

0   200   400   600   800

B.C.

ca. 6–4 BC
Jesus is born

ca. 70
Temple destroyed

590
St. Gregory the Great becomes pope

ca. 30–33
Pentecost

313
Edict of Milan

381
First Council of Constantinople (Nicene Creed expanded; divine nature of Holy Spirit defined)

ca. 64
Persecution of Christians begins under Roman emperor Nero

431
Council of Ephesus (refutes Nestorianism; states that Mary is the Mother of God)

476
Roman Empire in West collapses

800
Pope Leo III crowns Charlemagne Roman emperor

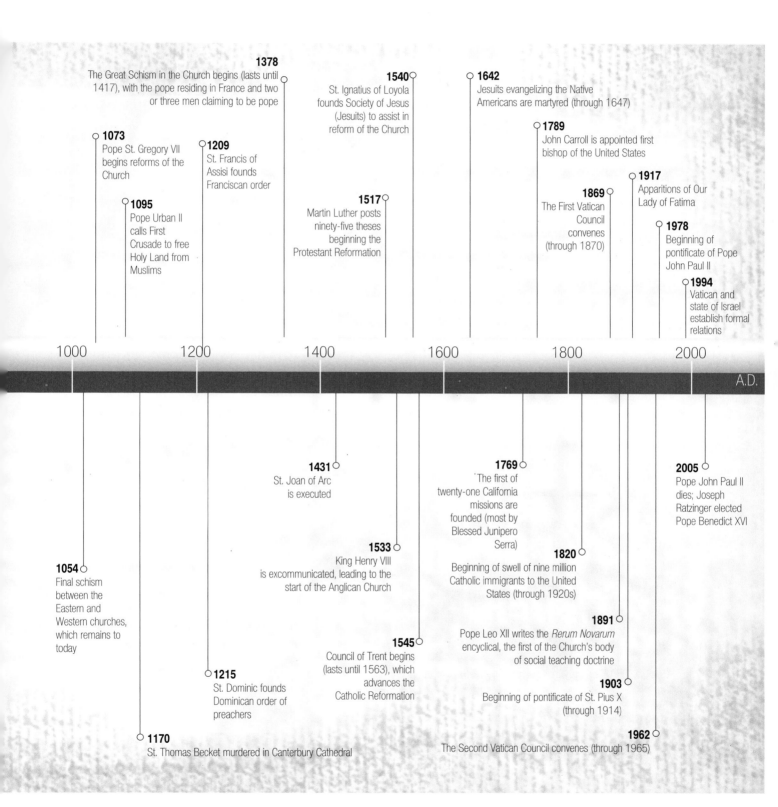

1378
The Great Schism in the Church begins (lasts until 1417), with the pope residing in France and two or three men claiming to be pope

1540
St. Ignatius of Loyola founds Society of Jesus (Jesuits) to assist in reform of the Church

1642
Jesuits evangelizing the Native Americans are martyred (through 1647)

1073
Pope St. Gregory VII begins reforms of the Church

1209
St. Francis of Assisi founds Franciscan order

1789
John Carroll is appointed first bishop of the United States

1917
Apparitions of Our Lady of Fatima

1095
Pope Urban II calls First Crusade to free Holy Land from Muslims

1517
Martin Luther posts ninety-five theses beginning the Protestant Reformation

1869
The First Vatican Council convenes (through 1870)

1978
Beginning of pontificate of Pope John Paul II

1994
Vatican and state of Israel establish formal relations

1000   1200   1400   1600   1800   2000

A.D.

1431
St. Joan of Arc is executed

1769
The first of twenty-one California missions are founded (most by Blessed Junipero Serra)

2005
Pope John Paul II dies; Joseph Ratzinger elected Pope Benedict XVI

1054
Final schism between the Eastern and Western churches, which remains to today

1533
King Henry VIII is excommunicated, leading to the start of the Anglican Church

1820
Beginning of swell of nine million Catholic immigrants to the United States (through 1920s)

1891
Pope Leo XII writes the *Rerum Novarum* encyclical, the first of the Church's body of social teaching doctrine

1215
St. Dominic founds Dominican order of preachers

1545
Council of Trent begins (lasts until 1563), which advances the Catholic Reformation

1903
Beginning of pontificate of St. Pius X (through 1914)

1170
St. Thomas Becket murdered in Canterbury Cathedral

1962
The Second Vatican Council convenes (through 1965)

The Apostles and **Their Emblems**

St. Andrew
Tradition holds that Andrew was crucified on a X-shaped cross, called a *saltire*.

St. Bartholomew
Bartholomew was flayed alive before being crucified. He was then beheaded.

St. James the Greater
James the Greater, the brother of John, was beheaded by Herod Agrippa. It is the only death of an Apostle mentioned in Scripture (Acts 12:2). The shell indicates James's missionary work by sea in Spain. The sword is of martyrdom.

St. James the Less
James the Less is traditionally known as the first bishop of Jerusalem. The saw for his emblem is connected with the tradition of his body being sawed into pieces after he was pushed from the pinnacle of the Temple.

St. John the Evangelist
John was the first bishop of Ephesus. He is the only Apostle believed to have died a natural death, in spite of many attempts to murder him by his enemies. One attempt included his miraculous survival after drinking a poisoned drink.

St. Jude
Some traditions have Sts. Jude and Peter martyred together. It is thought that he traveled throughout the Roman Empire with Peter.

St. Matthew
Matthew's shield depicts three purses, reflecting his original occupation as tax collector.

St. Matthias
Matthias was the Apostle chosen by lot to replace Judas. Tradition holds that Matthias was stoned to death and then beheaded with an ax.

St. Peter
Simon Peter was the brother of Andrew. The first bishop of Rome, Peter was crucified under Nero, asking to be hung upside down because he felt unworthy to die as Jesus did. The keys represent Jesus' giving Peter the keys to the Kingdom of Heaven.

St. Philip
Philip may have been bound to a cross and stoned to death. The two loaves of bread at the side of the cross refer to Philip's comment to Jesus about the possibility of feeding the multitudes of people (Jn 6:7).

St. Simon
The book with fish depicts Simon as a "fisher of men" who preached the Gospel. He was also known as Simon the Zealot.

St. Thomas
Thomas is thought to have been a missionary in India, where he is thought to have built a church. Hence, the carpenter's square. He may have died by arrows and stones. It is then thought that he had a lance run through his body.

The Pope

The bishop of Rome has carried the title "pope" since the ninth century. Pope means "papa" or "father." St. Peter was the first bishop of Rome and, hence, the first pope. He was commissioned directly by Jesus:

> And so I say to you, you are Peter, and upon this rock I will build my church, and the gates of the netherworld shall not prevail against it. I will give you the keys to the kingdom of heaven. Whatever you bind on earth shall be bound in heaven; and whatever you loose on earth shall be loosed in heaven. (Mt 16:18–19)

Because Peter was the first bishop of Rome, the succeeding bishops of Rome have had primacy in the Church. The entire succession of popes since St. Peter can be traced directly to the Apostle.

The pope is in communion with the bishops of the world as part of the Magisterium, which is the Church's teaching authority. The pope can also define doctrine in faith or morals for the Church. When he does so, he is infallible and cannot be in error.

The pope is elected by the College of Cardinals by a two-thirds plus one majority vote in secret balloting. Cardinals under the age of eighty are eligible to vote. If the necessary majority is not achieved, the ballots are burned in a small stove inside the council chambers along with straw that makes dark smoke. The sign of dark smoke announces to the crowds waiting outside St. Peter's Basilica that a new pope has not been chosen. When a new pope has been voted in with the necessary majority, the ballots are burned without the straw, producing white smoke and signifying the election of a pope.

Recent Popes

Since 1900 and through the pontificate of Pope Benedict XVI, there were ten popes. Pope John Paul II was the first non-Italian pope since Dutchman Pope Adrian VI (1522–1523). The following is a list of the most recent popes with their original names, place of origin, and years as pope:

- Pope Leo XIII (Giocchino Pecci): Carpineto, Italy, February 20, 1878–July 20, 1903.
- Pope St. Pius X (Giuseppe Sarto): Riese, Italy, August 4, 1903–August 20, 1914.
- Pope Benedict XV (Giacomo della Chiesa): Genoa, Italy, September 3, 1914–January 22, 1922.
- Pope Pius XI (Achille Ratti): Desio, Italy, February 6, 1922–February 10, 1939.
- Pope Pius XII (Eugenio Pacelli): Rome, Italy, March 2, 1939–October 9, 1958.
- Pope John XXIII (Angelo Giuseppe Roncalli), Sotto il Monte, Italy, October 28, 1958–June 3, 1963.
- Pope Paul VI (Giovanni Battista Montini): Concessio, Italy, June 21, 1963–August 6, 1978.

Pope **Benedict XVI**

- Pope John Paul I (Albino Luciani): Forno di Canale, Italy, August 26, 1978–September 28, 1978.
- Pope John Paul II (Karol Wojtyla): Wadowice, Poland, October 16, 1978–April 2, 2005.
- Pope Benedict XVI (Joseph Ratzinger): Marktlam Inn, Germany, April 19, 2005–present

Fathers of the Church

Church Fathers, or Fathers of the Church, is a traditional title that was given to theologians of the first eight centuries whose teachings made a lasting mark on the Church. The Church Fathers developed a significant amount of doctrine that has great authority in the Church. The Church Fathers are named as either Latin Fathers (West) or Greek Fathers (East). Among the greatest Fathers of the Church are:

Latin Fathers	Greek Fathers
St. Ambrose	St. John Chrysostom
St. Augustine	St. Basil the Great
St. Jerome	St. Gregory of Nazianzen
St. Gregory the Great	St. Athanasius

Doctors of the Church

The Doctors of the Church are men and women honored by the Church for their writings, preaching, and holiness. Originally the Doctors of the Church were considered to be Church Fathers Augustine, Ambrose, Jerome, and Gregory the Great, but others were added over the centuries. St. Teresa of Avila was the first woman Doctor (1970). St. Catherine of Siena was named a Doctor of the Church the same year. The list of Doctors of the Church is on the following page.

Name	Life Span	Designation
St. Athanasius	296–373	1568 by Pius V
St. Ephraem the Syrian	306–373	1920 by Benedict XV
St. Hilary of Poitiers	315–367	1851 by Pius IX
St. Cyril of Jerusalem	315–386	1882 by Leo XIII
St. Gregory of Nazianzus	325–389	1568 by Pius V
St. Basil the Great	329–379	1568 by Pius V
St. Ambrose	339–397	1295 by Boniface VIII
St. John Chrysostom	347–407	1568 by Pius V
St. Jerome	347–419	1295 by Boniface XIII
St. Augustine	354–430	1295 by Boniface XIII
St. Cyril of Alexandria	376–444	1882 by Leo XIII
St. Peter Chrysologous	400–450	1729 by Benedict XIII
St. Leo the Great	400–461	1754 by Benedict XIV
St. Gregory the Great	540–604	1295 by Boniface XIII
St. Isidore of Seville	560–636	1722 by Innocent XIII
St. John of Damascus	645–749	1890 by Leo XIII
St. Bede the Venerable	672–735	1899 by Leo XIII
St. Peter Damian	1007–1072	1828 by Leo XII
St. Anselm	1033–1109	1720 by Clement XI
St. Bernard of Clairvaux	1090–1153	1830 by Pius VIII
St. Anthony of Padua	1195–1231	1946 by Pius XII
St. Albert the Great	1206–1280	1931 by Pius XI
St. Bonaventure	1221–1274	1588 by Sixtus V
St. Thomas Aquinas	1226–1274	1567 by Pius V
St. Catherine of Siena	1347–1380	1970 by Paul VI
St. Teresa of Avila	1515–1582	1970 by Paul VI
St. Peter Canisius	1521–1597	1925 by Pius XI
St. John of the Cross	1542–1591	1926 by Pius XI
St. Robert Bellarmine	1542–1621	1931 by Pius XI
St. Lawrence of Brindisi	1559–1619	1959 by John XXIII
St. Francis de Sales	1567–1622	1871 by Pius IX
St. Alphonsus Liguori	1696–1787	1871 by Pius IX
St. Thérèse of Lisieux	1873–1897	1997 by John Paul II

Ecumenical Councils

An ecumenical council is a worldwide assembly of bishops under direction of the pope. There have been twenty-one ecumenical councils, the most recent being the Second Vatican Council (1962–1965). A complete list of the Church's ecumenical councils with the years each met:

Nicea I	325
Constantinople I	381
Ephesus	431
Chalcedon	451
Constantinople II	553
Constantinople III	680
Nicea II	787
Constantinople IV	869–870
Lateran I	1123
Lateran II	1139
Lateran III	1179
Lateran IV	1215
Lyons I	1245
Lyons II	1274
Vienne	1311–1312
Constance	1414–1418
Florence	1431–1445
Lateran V	1512–1517
Trent	1545–1563
Vatican Council I	1869–1870
Vatican Council II	1962–1965

E. Morality

Morality refers to the goodness or evil of human actions. Listed below are several helps the Church offers for making good and moral decisions.

The Ten Commandments

The Ten Commandments are a main source for Christian morality. The Ten Commandments were revealed by God to Moses. Jesus himself acknowledged them. He told the rich young man, "If you wish to enter into life, keep the commandments" (Mt 19:17). Since the time of St. Augustine (fourth century), the Ten Commandments have been used as a source for teaching baptismal candidates.

I.	I, the Lord am your God: you shall not have other gods besides me.
II.	You shall not take the name of the Lord, your God, in vain.
III.	Remember to keep holy the sabbath day.
IV.	Honor your father and your mother.
V.	You shall not kill.
VI.	You shall not commit adultery.
VII.	You shall not steal.
VIII.	You shall not bear false witness against your neighbor.
IX.	You shall not covet your neighbor's wife.
X.	You shall not covet your neighbor's goods.

The Beatitudes

The word *beatitude* means "happiness." Jesus preached the Beatitudes in his Sermon on the Mount. They are:

Blessed are the poor in spirit, for theirs is the kingdom of God.

Blessed are they who mourn, for they will be comforted.

Blessed are the meek, for they will inherit the land.

Blessed are they who hunger and thirst for righteousness, for they will be satisfied.

Blessed are the merciful, for they will be shown mercy.

Blessed are the clean of heart, for they will see God.

Blessed are the peacemakers, for they will be called children of God.

Blessed are they who are persecuted for the sake of righteousness, for theirs is the kingdom of heaven.

Cardinal Virtues

Virtues—habits that help in leading a moral life—that are acquired by human effort are known as moral or human virtues. Four of these are the cardinal virtues, as they form the hinge that connects all the others. They are:

Prudence   Fortitude
Justice   Temperance

Theological Virtues

The theological virtues are the foundation for moral life. They are gifts infused into our souls by God.

- Faith   • Hope   • Love

Corporal (Bodily) Works of Mercy

1. Feed the hungry.
2. Give drink to the thirsty.
3. Clothe the naked.
4. Visit the imprisoned.
5. Shelter the homeless.
6. Visit the sick.
7. Bury the dead.

Spiritual Works of Mercy

1. Counsel the doubtful.
2. Instruct the ignorant.
3. Admonish sinners.
4. Comfort the afflicted.
5. Forgive offenses.
6. Bear wrongs patiently.
7. Pray for the living and the dead.

Precepts of the Church

1. You shall attend Mass on Sundays and on holy days of obligation and rest from servile labor.
2. You shall confess your sins at least once a year.
3. You shall receive the Sacrament of Eucharist at least during the Easter season.
4. You shall observe the days of fasting and abstinence established by the Church.
5. You shall help to provide for the needs of the Church.

Catholic Social Teaching: Major Themes

The 1998 document Sharing Catholic Social Teaching: Challenges and Directions—Reflections of the U.S. Catholic Bishops—highlighted seven principles of the Church's social teaching. They are:

1. Life and dignity of the human person
2. Call to family, community, and participation
3. Rights and responsibilities
4. Preferential option for the poor and vulnerable
5. The dignity of work and the rights of workers
6. Solidarity
7. Care for God's creation

Sin

Sin is an offense against God.

Mortal sin is the most serious kind of sin. Mortal sin destroys or kills a person's relationship with God. To be a mortal sin, three conditions must exist:

- The moral object must be of grave or serious matter. Grave matter is specified in the Ten Commandments (e.g., do not kill, do not commit adultery, do not steal, etc.).
- The person must have full knowledge of the gravity of the sinful action.
- The person must completely consent to the action. It must be a personal choice.

Venial sin is less serious sin. Examples of venial sins are petty jealousy, disobedience, "borrowing" a small amount of money from a parent without the intention of repaying it. Venial sins, when not repented, can lead a person to commit mortal sins.

Vices are bad habits linked to sins. Vices come from particular sins, especially the seven capital sins: pride, avarice, envy, wrath, lust, gluttony, and sloth.

F. Liturgy and Sacraments

The sacraments and the Divine Office constitute the Church's liturgy. The Mass is the most important liturgical celebration.

Church Year

The cycle of seasons and feasts that Catholics celebrate is called the Church Year or Liturgical Year. The Church Year is divided into five main parts: Advent, Christmas, Lent, Easter, and Ordinary Time.

Holy Days of Obligation in the United States

1. Immaculate Conception of Mary, December 8
2. Christmas, December 25
3. Solemnity of Mary, Mother of God, January 1
4. Ascension of the Lord, Forty days after Easter
5. Assumption of Mary, August 15
6. All Saints Day, November 1

The Seven Sacraments

1. Baptism
2. Confirmation
3. Eucharist
4. Penance and Reconciliation
5. Anointing of the Sick
6. Holy Orders
7. Matrimony

How to Go to Confession

1. Spend some time examining your conscience. Consider your actions and attitudes in each area of your life (e.g., faith, family, school/work, social life, relationships). Ask yourself, Is this area of my life pleasing to God? What needs to be reconciled with God? with others? with myself?

2. Sincerely tell God that you are sorry for your sins. Ask God for forgiveness and for the grace you will need to change what needs changing in your life. Promise God that you will try to live according to his will for you.

3. Approach the area for confession. Wait an appropriate distance until it is your turn.

4. Make the Sign of the Cross with the priest. He may say: "May God, who has enlightened every heart, help you to know your sins and trust his mercy." You reply: "Amen."

5. Confess your sins to the priest. Simply and directly talk to him about the areas of sinfulness in your life that need God's healing touch.

6. The priest will ask you to pray an Act of Contrition. Pray an Act of Contrition you have committed to memory or say something in your own words, like: "Dear God, I am sorry for my sins. I ask for your forgiveness, and I promise to do better in the future."

7. The priest will talk to you about your life, encourage you to be more faithful to God in the future, and help you decide what to do to make up for your sins—your penance.

8. The priest will then extend his hands over your head and pray the Church's official prayer of absolution:

> God, the Father of mercies, through the Death and Resurrection of his Son, has reconciled the world to himself and sent the Holy Spirit among us for the forgiveness of sins; through the ministry of the Church may God give you pardon and peace, and I absolve you from your sins in the name of the Father, and of the Son, and of the Holy Spirit.
> You respond: "Amen."

9. The priest will wish you peace. Thank him and leave.

10. Go to a quiet place in church and pray your prayer of penance. Then spend some time quietly thanking God for the gift of forgiveness.

Order of Mass

There are two main parts of the Mass, the Liturgy of the Word and the Liturgy of the Eucharist. The complete order of Mass:

The Introductory Rites

> The Entrance
> Greeting of the Altar and of the People Gathered
> The Act of Penitence
> The *Kyrie Eleison*
> The *Gloria*
> The Collect (Opening Prayer)

The Liturgy of the Word

> Silence
> The Biblical Readings (the reading of the Gospel is the high point of the Liturgy of the Word)
> The Responsorial Psalm
> The Homily
> The Profession of Faith (Creed)
> The Prayer of the Faithful

The Liturgy of the Eucharist

> The Preparation of the Gifts
> > The Prayer over the Offerings
> > The Eucharistic Prayer
> > > Thanksgiving
> > > Acclamation
> > > Epiclesis
> > > Institution Narrative and Consecration
> > > Anamnesis
> > > Offering
> > > Intercessions
> > > Final Doxology
> > The Communion Rite
> > > The Lord's Prayer
> > > The Rite of Peace
> > > The Fraction (Breaking of the Bread)
> > > Communion
> > > Prayer after Communion

The Concluding Rites

Communion Regulations

To receive Holy Communion properly, a person must be in the state of grace (free from mortal sin), have the right intention (only for the purpose of pleasing God), and observe the Communion fast.

The fast means that a person may not eat anything or drink any liquid (other than water) one hour before the reception of Communion. There are exceptions made to this fast only for the sick and aged.

Three Degrees of the Sacrament of Orders

There are three degrees of the Sacrament of Holy Orders: the ministries of bishop, priest, and deacon.

The bishop receives the fullness of the Sacrament of Orders. He is the successor to the Apostles. When he celebrates the sacraments, the bishop is given the grace to act in the person of Christ, who is the head of the body of the Church.

Priests are ordained as coworkers of the bishop. They, too, are configured to Christ so that they may act in his person during the Sacraments of Eucharist, Baptism, and the Anointing of the Sick. They may bless marriages in the name of Christ and, under the authority of the bishop, share in Christ's ministry of forgiveness in the Sacrament of Penance and Reconciliation.

Deacons are ordained for service and are configured to Christ the servant. Deacons are ordained to help and serve the priests and bishops in their work. While bishops and priests are configured to Christ to act as the head of Christ's body, deacons are configured to Christ in order to serve as he served. Deacons may baptize, preach the Gospel and homily, and bless marriages.

G. Mary and the Saints

The doctrine of the communion of saints flows from our belief that we Christians are closely united as one family in the Spirit of Jesus Christ. Mary is the Queen of the Saints. Her role in the Church flows from an inseparable union with her son.

Mother of God

Mary, the Mother of Jesus, is the closest human to cooperate with her Son's work of redemption. For this reason, the Church holds her in a special place. Of her many titles, the most significant is that she is the Mother of God.

The Church teaches several truths about Mary.

First, she was conceived immaculately. This means from the very first moment of her existence she was without sin and "full of grace." This belief is called the Immaculate Conception. The feast of the Immaculate Conception is celebrated on December 8.

Second, Mary was ever-virgin. She was a virgin before, in, and after the birth of Jesus. As his Mother, she cared for him in infancy and raised him to adulthood with the help of her husband, Joseph. She witnessed Jesus' preaching and ministry, was at the foot of his cross at his crucifixion, and was present with the Apostles as they awaited the coming of the Holy Spirit at Pentecost.

Third, at the time of her death, Mary was assumed body and soul into Heaven. This dogma was

proclaimed as a matter of faith by Pope Pius XII in 1950. The feast of the Assumption is celebrated on August 15.

The Church has always been devoted to the Blessed Virgin. This devotion is different from that given to God—Father, Son, and Holy Spirit. Rather, the Church is devoted to Mary as the first disciple, the Queen of all Saints, and her own Mother. Quoting the fathers of the Second Vatican Council:

> In the meantime the Mother of Jesus, in the glory which she possesses in body and soul in heaven, is the image and the beginning of the Church as it is to be perfected in the world to come. Likewise she shines forth on earth, until the day of the Lord shall come, a sign of certain hope and comfort to the pilgrim People of God. (*Lumen Gentium*, 68)

Marian Feasts Throughout the Year

January 1	Solemnity of Mary, Mother of God
March 25	Annunciation of the Lord
May 31	Visitation
August 15	Assumption
August 22	Queenship of Mary
September 8	Birth of Mary
September 15	Our Lady of Sorrows
October 7	Our Lady of the Rosary
November 21	Presentation of Mary
December 8	Immaculate Conception
December 12	Our Lady of Guadalupe

Canonization of Saints

Saints are those who are in glory with God in Heaven. *Canonization* refers to a solemn declaration by the pope that a person who either died a martyr or who lived an exemplary Christian life is in Heaven and may be honored and imitated by all Christians. The canonization process first involves a process of beatification that includes a thorough investigation of the person's life and certification of miracles that can be attributed to the candidate's intercession.

The first official canonization of the universal Church on record is St. Ulrich of Augsburg by Pope John XV in 993.

Some non-Catholics criticize Catholics for "praying to saints." Catholics *honor* saints for their holy lives, but we do not pray to them as if they were God. We ask the saints to pray with us and for us as part of the Church in glory. We can ask them to do this because we know that their lives have been spent in close communion with God. We also ask the saints for their friendship so that we can follow the example they have left for us.

Patron Saints

A patron is a saint who is designated for places (nations, regions, dioceses) or organizations. Many saints have also become patrons of jobs, professional groups, and intercessors for special needs. Listed below are patron saints for several nations and some special patrons:

Patrons of Places

Americas	Our Lady of Guadalupe, St. Rose of Lima
Argentina	Our Lady of Lujan
Australia	Our Lady Help of Christians
Canada	St. Joseph, St. Anne
China	St. Joseph
England	St. George
Finland	St. Henry
France	Our Lady of the Assumption, St. Joan of Arc, St. Thérèse of Lisieux
Germany	St. Boniface
India	Our Lady of the Assumption
Ireland	St. Patrick, St. Brigid, St. Columba
Italy	St. Francis of Assisi, St. Catherine of Siena
Japan	St. Peter
Mexico	Our Lady of Guadalupe
New Zealand	Our Lady of Help Christians
Poland	St. Casmir, St. Stanislaus, Our Lady of Czestochowa
Russia	St. Andrew, St. Nicholas of Myra, St. Thérèse of Lisieux
Scotland	St. Andrew, St. Columba
Spain	St. James, St. Teresa of Ávila
United States	Immaculate Conception

Special Patrons

Accountants	St. Matthew
Actors	St. Genesius
Animals	St. Francis of Assisi
Athletes	St. Sebastian
Beggars	St. Martin of Tours
Boy Scouts	St. George
Dentists	St. Apollonia
Farmers	St. Isidore
Grocers	St. Michael
Journalists	St. Francis de Sales
Maids	St. Zita
Motorcyclists	Our Lady of Grace
Painters	St. Luke
Pawnbrokers	St. Nicholas
Police Officers	St. Michael
Priests	St. John Vianney
Scientists	St. Albert
Tailors	St. Homobonus
Teachers	St. Gregory the Great, St. John Baptist de la Salle
Wine Merchants	St. Amand

H. Devotions

Catholics have also expressed their piety around the Church's sacramental life through practices like the veneration of relics, visits to churches, pilgrimages, processions, the Stations of the Cross, religious dances, the rosary, medals, and many more. This section lists some popular Catholic devotions.

The Mysteries of the Rosary

Joyful Mysteries

1. The Annunciation
2. The Visitation
3. The Nativity
4. The Presentation in the Temple
5. The Finding of Jesus in the Temple

Mysteries of Light

1. Jesus' Baptism in the Jordan River
2. Jesus Self-manifestation at the Wedding of Cana
3. The Proclamation of the Kingdom of God and Jesus' Call to Conversion
4. The Transfiguration
5. The Institution of the Eucharist at the Last Supper

Sorrowful Mysteries

1. The Agony in the Garden
2. The Scourging at the Pillar
3. The Crowning with Thorns
4. The Carrying of the Cross
5. The Crucifixion

Glorious Mysteries

1. The Resurrection
2. The Ascension
3. The Descent of the Holy Spirit
4. The Assumption of Mary
5. The Crowning of Mary as the Queen of Heaven and Earth

How to Pray the Rosary

Opening

1. Begin on the crucifix and pray the Apostles' Creed.
2. On the first bead, pray the Our Father.
3. On the next three beads, pray the Hail Mary. (Some people meditate on the virtues of faith, hope, and charity on these beads.)
4. On the fifth bead, pray the Glory Be.

The Body

Each decade (set of ten beads) is organized as follows:

1. On the larger bead that comes before each set of ten, announce the mystery to be prayed (see above) and pray one Our Father.
2. On each of the ten smaller beads, pray one Hail Mary while meditating on the mystery.
3. Pray one Glory Be at the end of the decade. (There is no bead for the Glory Be.)

Conclusion

Pray the following prayer at the end of the Rosary:

Hail, Holy Queen

Hail, holy Queen, Mother of Mercy,
our life, our sweetness, and our hope.
To thee do we cry,
poor banished children of Eve.
To thee do we send up our sighs,
mourning and weeping in this valley of tears.
Turn then, most gracious advocate,
thine eyes of mercy toward us;
and after this our exile,
show unto us the blessed fruit of thy womb, Jesus.
O clement, O loving, O sweet Virgin Mary.
Pray for us, O holy Mother of God,
that we may be made worthy of the promises of Christ.
Amen.

Stations of the Cross

The Stations of the Cross is a devotion and also a sacramental. (A sacramental is a sacred object, blessing, or devotion.) The Stations of the Cross are individual pictures or symbols hung on the interior walls of most Catholic churches depicting fourteen steps along Jesus' way of the cross. Praying the stations means meditating on each of the following scenes:

1. Jesus is condemned to death.
2. Jesus takes up his cross.
3. Jesus falls the first time.
4. Jesus meets his Mother.
5. Simon of Cyrene helps Jesus carry his cross.
6. Veronica wipes the face of Jesus.
7. Jesus falls the second time.
8. Jesus consoles the women of Jerusalem.
9. Jesus falls the third time.
10. Jesus is stripped of his garments.
11. Jesus is nailed to the cross.
12. Jesus dies on the cross.
13. Jesus is taken down from the cross.
14. Jesus is laid in the tomb.

Some churches also include a fifteenth station, the Resurrection of the Lord.

Novenas

The novena consists of the recitation of certain prayers over a period of nine days. The symbolism of nine days refers to the time Mary and the Apostles spent in prayer between Jesus' Ascension into Heaven and Pentecost.

Many novenas are dedicated to Mary or to a saint with the faith and hope that she or he will intercede for the one making the novena. Novenas to St. Jude, St. Anthony, Our Lady of Perpetual Help, and Our Lady of Lourdes remain popular in the Church today.

Liturgy of the Hours

The Liturgy of the Hours is part of the official, public prayer of the Church. Along with the celebration of the sacraments, the recitation of the Liturgy of the Hours, or Divine Office (office means "duty" or "obligation"), allows for constant praise and thanksgiving to God throughout the day and night.

The Liturgy of Hours consists of five major divisions:

1. An hour of readings
2. Morning praises
3. Midday prayers
4. Vespers (evening prayers)
5. Compline (a short night prayer)

Scriptural prayer, especially the Psalms, is at the heart of the Liturgy of the Hours. Each day follows a separate pattern of prayer with themes closely tied in with the liturgical year and feasts of the saints.

The Divine Praises

These praises are traditionally recited after the benediction of the Blessed Sacrament.

Blessed be God.
Blessed be his holy name.
Blessed be Jesus Christ, true God and true man.
Blessed be the name of Jesus.
Blessed be his most Sacred Heart.
Blessed be his most Precious Blood.
Blessed be Jesus in the most holy sacrament of the altar.
Blessed be the Holy Spirit, the Paraclete.
Blessed be the great Mother of God, Mary most holy.
Blessed be her holy and Immaculate Conception.
Blessed be her glorious Assumption.
Blessed be the name of Mary, Virgin and Mother.
Blessed be St. Joseph, her most chaste spouse.
Blessed be God in his angels and his saints.

I. Prayers

Some common Catholic prayers are listed below. The Latin translation for three of the prayers is included. Latin is the official language of the Church. There are several occasions when you may pray in Latin; for example, at a World Youth Day when you are with young people who speak many different languages.

Sign of the Cross

In the name of the Father,
and of the Son,
and of the Holy Spirit.
Amen.

In nómine Patris,
et Filii,
et Spíritus Sancti.
Amen.

Our Father

Our Father
who art in heaven,
hallowed be thy name.
Thy kingdom come;
thy will be done on earth as it is in heaven.
Give us this day our daily bread
and forgive us our trespasses
as we forgive those who trespass against us.
And lead us not into temptation,
but deliver us from evil.
Amen.

Pater Noster qui es in celis:
sanctificétur Nomen Tuum;
advéniat Regnum Tuum;
fiat volúntas Tua,
sicut in caelo, et in terra.
Panem nostrum
cuotidiánum da nobis hódie;
et dimítte nobis débita nostra,
sicut et nos
dimíttimus debitóribus nostris;
Et ne nos inducas in tentatiónem,
sed libera nos a Malo.
Amen.

Glory Be

Glory be to the Father
and to the Son
and to the Holy Spirit,
as it was in the beginning,
is now,
and ever shall be,
world without end.
Amen.

Glória Patri
et Filio
et Spiritui Sancto.
Sicut erat in princípio,
et nunc et semper,
et in sae'cula saeculórum.
Amen.

Hail Mary

Hail Mary, full of grace,
the Lord is with thee.
Blessed art thou among women
and blessed is the fruit of thy womb, Jesus.
Holy Mary, Mother of God,
pray for us sinners now
and at the hour of our death.
Amen.

Ave, María, grátia plena,
Dóminus tecum.
Benedicta tu in muliéribus,
et benedíctus fructus ventris
tui, Iesus.
Sancta María, Mater Dei,
ora pro nobis peccatoribus
nunc et in hora mortis nostrae.
Amen.

Memorare

Remember, O most gracious Virgin Mary,
that never was it known
that anyone who fled to your protection,
implored your help,
or sought your intercession was left unaided.
Inspired by this confidence,
I fly unto you,
O virgin of virgins, my Mother,
To you I come, before you I stand,
sinful and sorrowful.
O Mother of the word incarnate,
despise not my petitions,
but in your mercy hear and answer me. Amen.

Hail, Holy Queen

Hail, holy Queen, Mother of Mercy,
our life, our sweetness and our hope!
To you do we cry,
poor banished children of Eve;
to you do we send up our sighs,
mourning and weeping in this valley of tears.
Turn then, O most gracious advocate,
your eyes of mercy toward us,
and after this exile,
show us the blessed fruit of your womb, Jesus.
O clement, O loving, O sweet Virgin Mary.
V.   Pray for us, O holy Mother of God.
R.   That we may be made worthy of the promises of Christ. Amen.

The Angelus

V.   The angel spoke God's message to Mary.
R.   And she conceived by the Holy Spirit.
     Hail Mary . . .
V.   Behold the handmaid of the Lord.
R.   May it be done unto me according to your word.
     Hail Mary . . .
V.   And the Word was made flesh.
R.   And dwelled among us.
     Hail Mary . . .
V.   Pray for us, O holy Mother of God.
R.   That we may be made worthy of the promises of Christ.
     Let us pray: We beseech you, O Lord, to pour out your grace into our hearts. By the message of an angel we have learned of the Incarnation of Christ, your son; lead us by his Passion and cross, to the glory of the Resurrection. Through the same Christ our Lord. Amen.

Regina Caeli

Queen of heaven, rejoice, alleluia.
The Son you merited to bear, alleluia,
has risen as he said, alleluia.
Pray to God for us, alleluia.
V.   Rejoice and be glad, O Virgin Mary, alleluia.
R.   For the Lord has truly risen, alleluia.
     Let us pray.

God of life, you have given joy to the world by the Resurrection of your son, our Lord Jesus Christ. Through the prayers of his Mother, the Virgin Mary, bring us to the happiness of eternal life. We ask this through Christ our Lord. Amen.

Grace at Meals

Before Meals

Bless us, O Lord,
and these your gifts,
which we are about to receive from your bounty,
through Christ our Lord. Amen.

After Meals

We give you thanks, almighty God,
for these and all the gifts
which we have received
from your goodness
through Christ our Lord. Amen.

Guardian Angel Prayer

Angel of God, my guardian dear, to whom God's love entrusts
me here, ever this day be at my side, to light and guard, to rule
and guide. Amen.

Prayer for the Faithful Departed

Eternal rest grant unto them, O Lord.

R: And let perpetual light shine upon them.
May their souls and the souls of all faithful departed,
through the mercy of God, rest in peace.

R: Amen.

Morning Offering

O Jesus, through the Immaculate Heart of Mary, I offer you my
prayers, works, joys, and sufferings of this day in union with the
holy sacrifice of the Mass throughout the world. I offer them for
all the intentions of your Sacred Heart: the salvation of souls,
reparation for sin, the reunion of all Christians. I offer them for
the intentions of our bishops and all members of the apostleship
of prayer and in particular for those recommended by our Holy
Father this month. Amen.

Act of Faith

O God,
I firmly believe all the truths that you have revealed
and that you teach us through your Church,
for you are truth itself
and can neither deceive nor be deceived.
Amen.

Act of Hope

O God,
I hope with complete trust that you will give me,
through the merits of Jesus Christ, all necessary grace in this
world
and everlasting life in the world to come,
for this is what you have promised
and you always keep your promises.
Amen.

Act of Love

O my God, I love you above all things, with my whole heart
and soul, because you are all good and worthy of all my love. I
love my neighbor as myself for the love of you. I forgive all who
have injured me, and I ask pardon of all whom I have injured.
Amen.

Prayer for Peace (St. Francis of Assisi)

Lord, make me an instrument of your peace.
Where there is hatred, let me sow love;
where there is injury, pardon;
where there is doubt, faith;
where there is despair, hope;
where there is darkness, light;
where there is sadness, joy.
O Divine Master,
grant that I may not seek so much to be consoled as to
console;
to be understood, as to understand,
to be loved, as to love.
For it is in giving that we receive,
it is in pardoning that we are pardoned,
and it is in dying that we are born to eternal life.

Glossary

Abba—An Aramaic term of endearment meaning "daddy." Jesus used this word to teach that God is a loving Father.

adultery—Infidelity in marriage whereby a married person has sexual intercourse with someone who is not the person's spouse.

allegory—A story involving a sustained comparison in which people, things, and events symbolically represent something else.

angels—God's messengers; angels are created beings that possess free will and intelligence but who are pure spirits, without bodies.

apocalypse—A word meaning "revelation" or "unveiling." Apocalyptic writings, usually written in times of crisis, use highly symbolic language to bolster faith by reassuring believers that the current age, subject to the forces of evil, will end when God intervenes and establishes a divine rule of goodness and peace.

apologist—A defender of Christianity and the Church who tries to show the reasonableness of the faith.

Ark of the Covenant—The portable shrine built to hold the tablets on which Moses wrote the Law. It was the sign of God's presence to the Israelites. King Solomon built the Temple in Jerusalem to house the Ark.

Ascension—The event in Salvation History where Jesus' humanity entered into the divine glory in Heaven forty days after his Resurrection.

asceticism—A way of living, often out of religious motivation, that is marked by self-denial, self-discipline, and austerity.

Beatitudes—The word *beatitude* means "supreme happiness." The eight Beatitudes Jesus preached in the Sermon on the Mount respond to our natural desire for happiness.

blasphemy—Any thought, word, or act that expresses hatred or contempt for God, Christ, the Church, saints, or holy things.

canon—The official list of the inspired books of the Bible. Catholics list forty-six Old Testament books and twenty-seven New Testament books in the canon.

catechesis—The process of religious instruction and formation in the major elements of the Catholic faith.

Christ—A title given for Jesus that means "anointed one." It translates the Hebrew word for Messiah.

Christology—The branch of theology that studies the meaning of the person of Jesus Christ.

contrition—Heartfelt sorrow and aversion for sins committed along with the intention of sinning no more. Contrition is the most important act of penitents, necessary for receiving the Sacrament of Penance.

Dead Sea Scrolls—Ancient scrolls containing the oldest known manuscripts of the books of the Old Testament in Hebrew. They were discovered near Qumran on the Dead Sea between 1947 and 1953.

Deuteropauline—Secondary Pauline writings penned by disciples, secretaries, or admirers of Paul. These letters—2 Thessalonians, Ephesians, Colossians, 1 and 2 Timothy, and Titus—have different vocabulary, style, theological themes, content, and historical context than the letters indisputably written by St. Paul.

disciple—A follower of Jesus. The word means "learner."

Divine Revelation—God's self-communication whereby he makes known the mystery of his divine plan. God most fully revealed himself when he sent us his own divine Son, Jesus Christ.

dogma—A central truth of Revelation that Catholics are obliged to believe.

ecumenical council—A worldwide, official assembly of the bishops under the direction of the pope. There have been twenty-one ecumenical councils, the most recent being the Second Vatican Council (1962–1965).

Epiphany—The term to describe the mystery of Christ's manifestation as Savior of the world.

eschatological—A term having to do with the end times or the "last things" (death, resurrection, judgment, Heaven, Hell, Purgatory, everlasting life, etc.).

Evangelist—A person who proclaims the Good News of Jesus Christ. "The four Evangelists" refers to the authors of the four Gospels: Matthew, Mark, Luke, and John.

exorcism—The public and authoritative act of the Church to protect or liberate a person or object from the power of the devil in the name of Christ (CCC, 1237).

Fathers of the Church—An honorary title given to outstanding early Church theologians whose teaching has had lasting significance for the Church.

Feast of Dedication, or Hanukkah—The word "Hanukkah" means "festival of lights." It marks the rededication of the Temple in the days of the Maccabees.

Feast of Tabernacles—Also called the Feast of Booths, it was originally a Canaanite celebration of the harvest. The people lived in booths to represent the small huts farmers lived in during the harvest season.

Gehenna—The Jewish term for "hell." Originally the site of human sacrifice, this Jerusalem valley was cursed by the prophet Jeremiah as a place of death and corruption. In Jesus' day it was used as a garbage dump.

Gentiles—A term for non-Jews.

gift of tongues—The name for the ability to communicate in words or sounds in a language unknown to the speaker, a gift afforded St. Peter at the feast of Pentecost.

glory of God—The visible Revelation of the power of the invisible God.

Gnosticism—A generic term for a variety of pre- and early-Christian heresies that taught that salvation rests on secret knowledge (*gnosis* in the Greek).

Gospel—Literally, "Good News." Gospel refers to (1) the Good News preached by Jesus; (2) the Good News of salvation won for us in the person of Jesus Christ (he is the Good News proclaimed by the Church); (3) the four written records of the Good News—the Gospels of Matthew, Mark, Luke, and John.

Hasmonean Dynasty—Descendants of the Maccabees who ruled in Judea after the ousting of the last of the Syrians in 141 BC until the establishment of the Roman authority in 63 BC. John Hyrcanus was the first ruler in this dynasty and ruled until 128 BC.

Hellenists—The name for Greek-speaking Christians (Acts 6:1; 9:29).

hierarchical—A structure of sacred leadership; ordained leaders consisting of the pope, bishops, priests, and deacons who govern, teach, and guide the Church in holiness according to Christ's plan.

humility—The virtue which reminds us that God is the author of all good. Humility tempers ambition or pride and provides the foundation for turning to God in prayer.

idolatry—Giving worship to something other than the true God.

Incarnation—A core Catholic teaching that the Son of God took on human flesh in the person of Jesus Christ.

inspiration—The guidance given to the human authors of Sacred Scripture so they wrote what God wanted written for our benefit.

kerygma—The core teaching about Jesus Christ as Savior and Lord.

Kingdom (Reign) of God—The proclamation by Jesus that inaugurated his life, Death, and Resurrection. It is the process of God's reconciling and renewing all things through his Son, to the point where his will is being done on earth as it is in Heaven. The process has begun with Jesus and will be perfectly completed at the end of time.

L—Specific material found in the Gospel of Luke that is unique to the Gospel; it includes five otherwise unknown miracle stories, fourteen additional parables, and many nativity and infancy details not included in the other Gospels.

logos—A term that means "Word" in Greek. Jesus is the Word of God made flesh, who is both the revealer of God and God's Revelation.

Lord—A title for Jesus which translates the Greek word *Kurios*, which rendered the Hebrew word for God. To call Jesus "Lord" is to call him God.

Lumen Gentium—The name of one of the principal documents of the Second Vatican Council. It was promulgated by Pope Paul VI November 21, 1964. The Latin term means "Light of the Nations."

M—The name for the approximate four hundred verses or verse fragments in the Gospel of Matthew that are not present in the Gospel of Mark or Q, which are unique to Matthew.

Magisterium—The official teaching authority of the Church that resides in the pope (the successor of Peter) and the bishops in communion with him.

martyr—A word that means "witness." We usually apply this term to a person who bore witness to the truth of his or her faith even unto death. Jesus died the death of a faithful martyr. St. Stephen is recognized as the first Christian martyr.

Messianic Secret—A phrase that refers to certain passages in the Gospels where Jesus tells his disciples not to reveal his true identity.

midrash—A literary form that relates past scriptural events to help explain and interpret present events.

miracle—A powerful sign of God's Kingdom worked by Jesus.

Mystery—A term referring to God's infinite incomprehensibility, his plan of salvation and redemption, and the events of Jesus' life that show and accomplish this plan.

New Covenant—The climax of Salvation History, the coming of Jesus Christ, the fullness of God's Revelation.

papyrus—A type of paper made from reed found in the delta of the Nile River and parts of Italy.

parable—A typical teaching device Jesus used. It is a vivid picture story drawn from ordinary life that conveys religious truth, usually related to some aspect of God's Kingdom. It teases the listener to think and make a choice about accepting the Good News of God's reign.

Paraclete—A name for the Holy Spirit. In John 14:6, Jesus promised to send an advocate, a helper, who would continue to guide, lead, and strengthen the disciples.

Parousia—The Second Coming of Christ, which will usher in the full establishment of God's Kingdom on earth as it is in Heaven.

Paschal Mystery—God's love and salvation revealed to us through the life, Passion, Death, and Resurrection and Glorification of his Son Jesus Christ. The sacraments, especially the Eucharist, celebrate the Paschal Mystery and enable us to live it in our own lives.

Pentateuch—The name for the first five books of the Old Testament: Genesis, Exodus, Leviticus, Numbers, and Deuteronomy. It contains the Law (Torah).

Pentecost—The day recognized as the "birthday" of the Church when the Holy Spirit was revealed, bestowed, and communicated to the Church in fulfillment of the promises Jesus made to send another Advocate, a Comforter (Jn 14:16, 26; 15:26). The Jewish feast of Pentecost was the "fiftieth" day at the end of the seven weeks following Passover (Easter on the Christian calendar).

phylacteries—Small leather capsules which were fastened on the forehead or on the upper left arm so that they hung at the level of the heart. They contained miniature scrolls with four passages from the Jewish Law. Jewish males would wear these all day once they reached the age of adulthood (age fourteen).

Pool of Siloam—A pool of water outside of the city of Jerusalem that is a receptacle for the waters of the Gihon Spring.

prejudice—An unsubstantiated opinion or preformed judgment about an individual or group.

priest—A mediator between God and man. Jesus is the High Priest *par excellence*. As God-made-man, he bridges both Heaven and earth, bringing God to humanity and humanity to God.

pseudonymous—A work written under a name that is not the name of the person doing the actual writing. It was a common and accepted practice for disciples and admirers of great teachers to write works under their names to extend their legacies.

Q—An abbreviation for *Quelle* (German for "source"), a common source of sayings of Jesus used by the Evangelists Matthew and Luke in the composition of their Gospels.

Qumran—An ancient Essene monastery on the northwestern shore of the Dead Sea. Near it were found the ancient Dead Sea Scrolls.

Sacred Tradition—The living transmission of the message of the Gospel in the Church.

Salvation History—The story of God's saving activity in human history.

Sanhedrin—The seventy-one-member supreme legislative and judicial body of the Jewish people. Many of its members were Sadducees.

scandal—The bad example, often by religious leaders, that misleads others into sin.

Septuagint—A second-century BC Greek translation of the Hebrew Bible made at Alexandria, Egypt.

Son of Man—A title Jesus used to refer to himself. It emphasizes both Jesus' humanity and divinity. Its origins are in Daniel 7:13: "I saw . . . one like a son of man coming on the clouds of heaven."

Synoptic Gospels—The Gospels of Matthew, Mark, and Luke, which, because of their similarities, can be "seen together" in parallel columns and mutually compared.

Testament—A word meaning "covenant," the open-ended contract of love between God and human beings. Jesus' Death and Resurrection sealed God's New Covenant of love for all time.

theotokos—an important title bestowed on Mary at the Council of Ephesus (431), meaning "God-bearer." This title asserts that Jesus is one divine person and that Mary is truly the "Mother of God."

Torah—The Law or divine teaching revealed to Judaism. It is the foundation of the Jewish religion and is found in the Pentateuch.

Transfiguration—The mystery from Christ's life in which God's glory shone through and transformed Jesus' physical appearance while he was in the company of the Old Testament prophets Moses and Elijah. Peter, James, and John witnessed this event.

Vulgate—St. Jerome's fifth-century AD Latin translation of the Bible into the common language of the people of his day.

Index

Scripture Index

Mark

Luke

Acts

Catechism of the
Catholic Church Index

Photo **Credits**

AgnusImages
page 5, 112, 166, 248, 251, 254,

ArtResource
page 89 - Scala/Art Resource, NY
page 183 - Finsiel/Alinari/ Art Resource, NY

AssociatedPress
page 40, 65, 264

CorbisImages
page 4 (a,b,c,d), 7, 9, 22, 25 (a,b), 26, 39, 41, 44, 47, 52, 55,
57, 64, 73, 74, 75, 76, 87, 88, 89, 99, 111, 113,
117, 124, 126, 140, 144, 146, 151, 153, 154, 156,
167, 178, 181, 192, 202, 209, 211, 213, 227, 246,
249, 258, 268, 270, 272, 274, 278 (a,b), 295

TheCrosiers
page 3, 19, 33, 267

GettyImages
page 82

istock
page 10, 11, 12, 14, 15, 24, 28, 95, 115, 130, 220

JupiterImages
page 231

ChristopherPennock
page 1, 143, 200, 256

Veer
page 246, 271, 275